First World War
and Army of Occupation
War Diary
France, Belgium and Germany

32 DIVISION
Divisional Troops
219 Field Company Royal Engineers
20 November 1915 - 27 October 1919

WO95/2384/1

The Naval & Military Press Ltd
www.nmarchive.com
Published in association with The National Archives

Published by

The Naval & Military Press Ltd

Unit 10 Ridgewood Industrial Park,

Uckfield, East Sussex,

TN22 5QE England

Tel: +44 (0) 1825 749494

www.naval-military-press.com

www.nmarchive.com

This diary has been reprinted in facsimile from the original. Any imperfections are inevitably reproduced and the quality may fall short of modern type and cartographic standards.

© **Crown Copyright**
Images reproduced by permission of The National Archives, London, England, 2015.

Contents

Document type	Place/Title	Date From	Date To
Heading	WO95/2384 Nov 15-Oct 19 Div Signal Company		
Heading	32nd Division Divl Engineers 32nd Divl Signal Coy R.E. Nov. 1915-1919 Oct.		
Heading	32nd Div. Signal Coy Vol 1 121/7928		
War Diary		20/11/1915	31/12/1915
Heading	32nd Divisional Engineers 32nd Divisional Signal Company R.E. January 1916		
Heading	32nd Signal Vol 2		
War Diary		01/01/1916	31/01/1916
Heading	32nd Divisional Engineers 32nd Divisional Signal Company R.E. February 1916		
Heading	32nd Signal Vol 3		
War Diary		01/02/1916	29/02/1916
Heading	32nd Divisional Engineers 32nd Divisional Signal Company R.E. March 1916		
Heading	War Diary 32nd Divisional Signal Coy R.E. March 1st 1916-31st March 1916		
War Diary		01/03/1916	31/03/1916
Heading	32nd Divisional Engineers 32nd Divisional Signal Company R.E. April 1916		
Heading	War Diary Of 32nd Divisional Signal Coy R.E. April 1st-April 30th 1916		
War Diary		01/04/1916	30/04/1916
Heading	32nd Divisional Engineers 32nd Divisional Signal Company R.E. May 1916		
Heading	War Diary Of 32nd Signal Company R.E. From 1st May-31st May 1916		
War Diary		01/05/1916	31/05/1916
Heading	32nd Divisional Engineers 32nd Divisional Signal Company R.E. June 1916		
Heading	War Diary 1st June To 31st June 1916		
War Diary		01/06/1916	30/06/1916
Heading	32nd Divisional Engineers 32nd Divisional Signal Company R.E. July 1916		
Heading	War Diary Of 32nd Divl Signal Coy R.E. From 1st July 1916 To 31st July 1916		
War Diary		01/07/1916	31/07/1916
Miscellaneous Diagram etc	For Operation Order		
Miscellaneous			
Heading	32nd Divisional Engineers 32nd Divisional Signal Company R.E. August 1916		
Heading	War Diary Of 32nd Division Signal Coy R.E. From 1st Aug 1916 to 31st Aug 1916		
War Diary		01/08/1916	31/08/1916
Heading	32nd Divisional Engineers 32nd Divisional Signal Company R.E. September 1916		
Heading	War Diary of 32nd Div Signal Coy R.E. From 1st September 1916 to 30th September 1916		
War Diary		01/09/1916	30/09/1916

Heading	32nd Divisional Engineers 32nd Divisional Signal Company R.E. October 1916		
Heading	War Diary of 32nd Div Signal Coy From 1st October 1916 to 31st October 1916		
War Diary		01/10/1916	31/10/1916
Heading	32nd Divisional Engineers 32nd Divisional Signal Company R.E. November 1916		
Heading	War Diary of 32nd Divl. Signal Coy. R.E. from 1st November 1916 to 30th November 1916		
War Diary		01/11/1916	30/11/1916
Heading	32nd Divisional Engineers 32nd Divisional Signal Company R.E. December 1916		
Heading	War Diary of 32nd Divl. Signal Coy. R.E. from 1st December 1916 to 31st December 1916		
War Diary		01/12/1916	31/12/1916
Heading	War Diary of 32nd Divl. Signal Coy. R.E. from 1st July 1917 to 31st January 1917		
War Diary		01/01/1917	31/01/1917
Heading	War Diary of 32nd Divl. Signal Coy. R.E. from 1st February 1917 to 28th February 1917		
War Diary		01/02/1917	28/02/1917
Miscellaneous	14 Bde H.Q		
Miscellaneous	Div. Train		
Heading	War Diary of 32nd Divl. Signal Coy. R.E. for 1st March 1917 to 31st March 1917		
War Diary		01/03/1917	31/03/1917
Heading	War Diary of 32nd Divl. Signal Coy. R.E. From 1st April 1917 to 30th April 1917		
War Diary		01/04/1917	30/04/1917
Heading	War Diary of 32nd Divl. Signal Coy. R.E. From 1st May 1917 to 31st May 1917		
War Diary		01/05/1917	31/05/1917
Diagram etc			
Heading	War Diary of 32nd Divl. Signal Coy. R.E. from 1st June 1917 to 30th June 1917		
War Diary		01/06/1917	30/06/1917
Heading	War Diary of 32nd Divl. Signal Coy. R.E. from 1st July 1917 to 31st July 1917		
Miscellaneous			
War Diary		01/07/1917	31/07/1917
Miscellaneous			
Heading	War Diary of 32nd Divl. Signal Coy. R.E. from 1st August 1917 to 31st August 1917		
War Diary		01/08/1917	31/08/1917
Diagram etc	Diagram of Communications 32nd Division		
Diagram etc			
War Diary		01/09/1917	18/09/1917
War Diary	Field	19/09/1917	30/09/1917
Diagram etc	September Traffic Chart		
Miscellaneous	War Diary Lt trench R.E. 32Div Signal		
War Diary	Field	01/10/1917	31/10/1917
Diagram etc	Traffic Chart		
War Diary	Field	01/11/1916	30/11/1916
War Diary		17/12/1916	31/12/1916
War Diary		01/12/1917	03/12/1917
Diagram etc	Traffic Chart-October 1917		

Type	Description	From	To
Miscellaneous	Company Office		
Diagram etc	Traffic Chart Dec 1917		
Miscellaneous	D.A.A.G.H.Q. 325 Division		
War Diary	Field	01/01/1918	30/01/1918
Diagram etc	Traffic Chart		
Diagram etc			
War Diary	Field	01/02/1918	28/02/1918
Heading	32nd Divisional Engineers 32nd Divisional Signal Company R.E. March 1918		
War Diary	Field	01/03/1918	31/03/1918
Miscellaneous	March 1918		
Heading	War Diary 32nd Divisional Signal Company R.E. April 1918		
War Diary	Field	01/04/1918	30/04/1918
Miscellaneous	Traffic Section For April 1918		
War Diary		01/05/1918	31/05/1918
Miscellaneous	Traffic Return For May 1918		
Heading	32nd Division Herewith War Diary of this Coy for June 1918 2nd July 1918		
War Diary		01/06/1918	30/06/1918
Miscellaneous	Traffic Return June 1918		
War Diary	Field	01/07/1918	31/07/1918
Miscellaneous	Traffic Return for July 1918		
War Diary		09/08/1918	31/08/1918
War Diary	Field	01/08/1918	31/08/1918
Heading	Lancashire Division (Late 32nd Divn) Divl Signal Coy R.E. Jan-Oct 1919		
War Diary	Field	01/01/1919	31/01/1919
War Diary	Bonn	01/02/1919	28/02/1919
War Diary	Bonn Germany	04/04/1919	31/08/1919
Miscellaneous	Xth. Corps. "A" Reference C.R.O. 4206. d/-2/9/19	01/10/1919	01/10/1919
War Diary		01/09/1919	27/10/1919

WO 95/2384
Nov 15 – Oct 19
Div Signal Company

32ND DIVISION
DIVL ENGINEERS

32ND DIVL SIGNAL COY R.E.

NOV 1915 - ~~DEC 1918~~
1917. OCT

3d W Afri. Sigal Co
Vol I

1/51
7938

Army Form C. 2118.

WAR DIARY
of
INTELLIGENCE SUMMARY.
(Erase heading not required.)

Instructions regarding War Diaries and Intelligence Summaries are contained in F. S. Regs., Part II, and the Staff Manual respectively. Title pages will be prepared in manuscript.

Hour, Date, Place.	Summary of Events and Information.	Remarks and references to Appendices.
SAT. NOV. 20th 1915	Left CODFORD at 1.20 P.M. with H.Q. Section and No.1 Section – Arrived at SOUTHAMPTON 3.45 P.M. – Embarked at once on S.S. MAIDAN – Sixty men and 83 horses on S.S. MAIDAN – The remainder on S.S. MONAS QUEEN – Left SOUTHAMPTON at 5.30 P.M.	
SUN. NOV. 21st 1915	Arrived HAVRE at 10 A.M. – Unloaded ship all day marching to No 5 rest camp at 4.30 P.M. Left rest camp at 8.0 P.M. and entrained at GARE DES MARCHANDISES – Left HAVRE midnight.	
MON. NOV. 22nd 1915	Arrived PONT REMY at 11.0 A.M. detrained and marched to AILLY-LE-HAUT-CLOCHER, which is divisional headquarters.	
TUES NOV 23rd 1915	Laid out cable lines at 4.45 A.M. to 95th Bde at LE REQUIER – 96th Bde at LE PLOUY – C.R.A at FRANCIERES – R.T.O at PONT REMY. A line from C.R.R. already in the office.	
WED NOV 24th 1915.	Made an extension on the line to 96th Bde, leaving in at GORENFLAS for the 97th Bde who arrive tonight. Visited 95th and 96th Bdes Signal offices, lines working in 95th Bde Office, but not laid at 96th Bde Office.	
THURS. NOV 25th 1915.	Motored over to 36th Divn. Donart. to arrange about handing over wires – O.C. 36th Divn Signals arrived in the afternoon – Agreed to hand over all wires receiving eight drums in exchange, thirty iron pegs and twelve poles.	

Army Form C. 2118.

WAR DIARY
of
INTELLIGENCE SUMMARY.
(Erase heading not required.)

Instructions regarding War Diaries and Intelligence Summaries are contained in F. S. Regs., Part II, and the Staff Manual respectively. Title pages will be prepared in manuscript.

Hour, Date, Place.	Summary of Events and Information.	Remarks and references to Appendices.
FRIDAY NOV 26 1915.	Motored over to FLESSELS to arrange about taking over lines from 30th Divn – Car broken down left at FLESSELS. 96th and 97th Bde line dis‡ to ¾ hours 6.30 P.M. to 4.15 P.M.	
SATURDAY NOV 27th	95th – 96th – 97th Brigades moved to: VILLE-LE-MARCELET; FLIXECOURT, and BELLOY respectively. Communication was maintained to these Brigades by D.R.L.S. – Seven columns moved off during the morning and a D.R. was attached to each with orders in relation to Divl. Hq. at 5.0 P.M. The 36th Divn. Signals sent over 8 drums D5 to replace our lines taken away by them.	
SUNDAY NOV 28th	The Divl HQ moved to FLESSELS – L' Ronen and a party were sent over at 8 a.m. to take over the OFFICE of the 30th Divn – 3½ lines taken over being "a comie air" line to "MOLLIENS" and a D6 line to VAUX – A permanent line belonging to XIII Corps to VIGNACOURT. The remainder of the section marched with Divl HQ under W. Farr. arriving off at 9.30 a.m. The 96th Bde moved to RAINNEVILLE, 97th to MOLLIENS, 95th to VIGNACOURT. CRA to OLLINCOURT. On 96th return to OLLINCOURT was laid by a hassen party in the afternoon, and an extension was made from where the comic air lines crosses the PIERREGOT – RAINNEVILLE ROAD to RAINNEVILLE for the 96th BDE. LINES laid as follows. (a) To 3rd Army worked by operator from 3rd Army (b) Buzzer line to VIGNACOURT 95th BDE. (c) Buzzer line to RAINNEVILLE and MOLLIENS line stations on our line (a) Buzzer line to VAUX (iii) G and Q branches into CHATEAU Divl HQ	
MONDAY NOV 29th	The following lines were laid today (a) A metallic return D5 to OLLINCOURT to C.R.A and placed into exchange (b) A metallic return D5 to VIGNACOURT for the 95th BDE and placed into exchange (c) A metallic return D6 to RAINNEVILLE and MOLLIENS for 96th and 97th BDES respectively and placed on the exchange	

Army Form C. 2118.

WAR DIARY
or
INTELLIGENCE SUMMARY.
(Erase heading not required.)

Instructions regarding War Diaries and Intelligence Summaries are contained in F. S. Regs., Part II, and the Staff Manual respectively. Title pages will be prepared in manuscript.

Hour, Date, Place.	Summary of Events and Information.	Remarks and references to Appendices.
MONDAY NOV 29th 1915.	Went over to 10th Corps QUERRIEUX to meet O.C. Signals 5th Divn to which late HQ and No.1 Section are to go for training. Office being used by some men of 10th Corps.	
TUESDAY NOV 30th	An early return. D5 laid to VIGNACOURT to 95th BDE. Office being worked by men from 10th Corps. Lines now as follows completed (a) To 3rd Army - a line on double current key and a line on telephone exchange. (b) To CRA - a line on Vibrator and a line on exchange (c) To 95th Bde - a line on vibrator and a line on exchange (d) 96th Bde a line on exchange (e) 97th Bde - a line on vibrator and a line on exchange on telephone exchange (f) S.S.O. a line on exchange (g) To G.O.C. 32nd Divn a line on exchange (h) To G branch a line on exchange (i) To Q branch a line on exchange (j) To Signal master a line on exchange.	
WEDNESDAY DEC 1st	Nothing to report - DR's wasting time getting away from the Office after being handed despatches - line to 97th Brigade metallic circuit giving trouble, the fault not in the house but in the ringing telephone to other end.	
THURSDAY DEC 2nd	Nothing to report - lines working satisfactorily. The line to 97th Brigade clear again.	
FRIDAY DEC 3rd	To the 5th Division at ETINGHEM to see their system of office work and laying of lines - Called up Revee in the evening who reports everything	

Gulab Singh & Sons, Calcutta—No. 22 Army C.—5/8/14—1,07,000.

Army Form C. 2118.

WAR DIARY
or
INTELLIGENCE SUMMARY.
(*Erase heading not required.*)

Instructions regarding War Diaries and Intelligence
Summaries are contained in F. S. Regs., Part II,
and the Staff Manual respectively. Title pages
will be prepared in manuscript.

Hour, Date, Place.	Summary of Events and Information.	Remarks and references to Appendices.
FRIDAY DEC 3rd 1915	Is to be working satisfactorily, in 32nd Divisional Signal Office.	
SATURDAY DEC 4th	Went round the Brigade section Offices – Two brigades at BRAY and one with Chateau at SUSZANNE. In the afternoon through the workshops and stables and along the Divisional line and Cattle line – Rose reports everything satisfactory, in 32nd Divisional Signal Office.	
SUNDAY DEC 5th	Rode out to Brigade report centre to see the system of lines. Back to FLESSELS in the afternoon. Mapped map have been repaired and runs complete. Party of 4 N.C.O's and 9 operators and 9 linesmen sent to 5th Division for ten days, to learn air line and to see the working of the Signal Company.	
MONDAY DEC 6th	Rode out to VAUX EN AMIENOIS to see a D5 earth circuit which is surplus this will be tested up tomorrow – Rode up the D5 metallic circuit from "B" truss which is surplus. Exercise party parade daily at 9:30 AM under a Sergt for one hours road work – All dismounted men of the Company parade at that hour outside the Company office, this parade does not include the men on duty. Ten miles of comic wire and 100 mandrillos arrived from D.A.D.O.S. – Requisitioned for 200 hp poles No 4 Sqn from C.R.E. – Sent two motor bicycles to Supply Columns for Exchange.	
TUESDAY DEC 7th	Inspected lines to MOLLIENS AU BOIS and RAINNEVILLE – D5 earth	

Army Form C. 2118.

WAR DIARY

or

INTELLIGENCE SUMMARY.

(Erase heading not required.)

Instructions regarding War Diaries and Intelligence Summaries are contained in F. S. Regs., Part II, and the Staff Manual respectively. Title pages will be prepared in manuscript.

Hour, Date, Place.	Summary of Events and Information.	Remarks and references to Appendices.
TUESDAY 7th DEC'15	Circuit to VAUX reeled up.	
WEDNESDAY DEC 8th	Went over to 51st Divn at SENLIS - Went over the Signals of the right Brigade in the line at AVELUY also divisional lines - Reported all correct from 32nd Divisional Signals	
THURSDAY DEC 9th	Reported all correct from 32nd Division Signals	
FRIDAY DEC 10th	Went over Signals of the left Brigade with line at MARTINSART, also divisional lines - Reported all correct from 32nd Division Signals.	
SATURDAY DEC 11th	Returned to FLESSELLES - line laid to D.A.D.O.S. circuit tied into metallic circuit running to C.R.A. Two single current sets arrived. Wired to ask if wires to VIGNACOURT can be reeled up. A.M. cable section cutting poles locally for Comic Coy line.	
SUNDAY DEC 12th	Poles for air line being insulated.	
MONDAY DEC 13th	A.M. cable section start air line instruction - laying a line to VIGNACOURT. Ruling up earth circuit and metallic circuit D's from VIGNACOURT. Sent Singer Car to Divl. Amln. Sub Park to be exchanged for touring Car. Inspection of horses by A.D.V.S. Visit from O.C. Signals K.C.O.	

Army Form C. 2118.

WAR DIARY
or
INTELLIGENCE SUMMARY.
(Erase heading not required.)

Instructions regarding War Diaries and Intelligence Summaries are contained in F. S. Regs., Part II, and the Staff Manual respectively. Title pages will be prepared in manuscript.

Hour, Date, Place.	Summary of Events and Information.	Remarks and references to Appendices.
TUESDAY 14th Dec 1915	Connic Air line to VIGNACOURT completed - Branch line to C.R.A. OLLINCOURT completed and working - D5 earth circuit to OLLINCOURT needs up - Visited 97th Bde Section at MOLLIENS, 96th BDE section at ALBERT and 95th BDE section at SAILLY LORETTE. - Trial standard erected outside office for leading in wires. Carpenters making test boxes and table trestles. G.O.C. Signals visited headquarters. A 88, B 11, C 100, SP² 297.	
WEDNESDAY DEC 15th	Bought oil stoves for mens billets - Also equipment for drawing diagrams of lines. Carpenters making test boxes. A 104, B, 24 C, 94 SP² 290	
THURSDAY DEC 16th	Making connic air line poles for metallic circuit. Finishing the new trestle terminating post for leading into the office - A 106, B. 20, C 90, SP² 277	
FRIDAY DEC 17th	Laid connic air line metallic circuit to OLLINCOURT - First party came back from 5th Division - from training - Second party went out to 5th Divn for training. A. 86, B. 29, C. 105, SP² 350 = 570.	
SATURDAY DEC 18th	Laid metallic circuit air line to within one mile of MOLLIENS. Line to C.R.A. short circuited from 8.30 AM - 9.15 A.M. Party running wire on drums. A 116, B, 18, C. 102, SP² 294 = 527	

Army Form C. 2118.

WAR DIARY
or
INTELLIGENCE SUMMARY.
(Erase heading not required.)

Instructions regarding War Diaries and Intelligence Summaries are contained in F. S. Regs., Part II, and the Staff Manual respectively. Title pages will be prepared in manuscript.

Hour, Date, Place.	Summary of Events and Information.	Remarks and references to Appendices.
SUNDAY DEC 19th 1915	One party cutting saplings for our line - a party under H/Cpl Enoch rewiring and mending wire D.S. Visited C.R.A and 97th Bde Signals. Sent the N.C.O's for transfer to 95th - 96th - 97th Bdes. Despatched one Drum D.S cable to 96th Bde Section.	
Monday DEC. 20th	2/LT Rowe, four linesmen and two D.R's sent to the Signals 51st Divn to become familiar with the Communications and hands. Lt Osmaston and Lt Churchill with the linesmen each attached to a Brigade Section of the 51st Divn at MARTINSART to learn the Communications. One fifteen way exchange arrived from the Base. Two new Triumphs arrived from Supply Column. An Iron metallic circuit to MOLLIENS complete. A 82, B 26, C 99, SPs 284. = 491	
TUESDAY DEC. 21st	Major Robertson from 51st Divn Signals arrived to see Ritleton - Conference at 3rd Army about trench lines. Rewiring and mending cable. A 102, B 24, C 100, SPs 316. = 542	
WEDNESDAY DEC 22nd	Ruling up metallic circuit DS to MOLLIENS - A.M. cable section reeling up DS earth circuit from MOLLIENS to CONTAY. Kent went to 51st Divn and Rowe returned. A 105, B 26, C 121, SPs 277 = 529	
THURSDAY DEC 23rd	A.M. Cable Section returned to 13th Corps.- A.L. Cable section ordered to report here. Four drums of DS given to A.M. Section to make them up to establishment. Rewinding and mending cable. A 109, B 42, C 65, SPs 270 = 506.	

Army Form C. 2118.

WAR DIARY
INTELLIGENCE SUMMARY.
(Erase heading not required.)

Instructions regarding War Diaries and Intelligence Summaries are contained in F.S. Regs., Part II, and the Staff Manual respectively. Title pages will be prepared in manuscript.

Hour, Date, Place.	Summary of Events and Information.	Remarks and references to Appendices.
FRIDAY DEC 24TH. 1915.	A.L. Cable section reported from to 13th Corps - Kent came back from SENLIS - A.L. operators taken over the Army line. Farrier Corporal Chandler returned to the ranks for inefficiency - S.G. Judson made a/Farrier Corporal. - L/Cpl Renouf's party mending D5 cable. Metallic circuit comm. own line reported to MOLLIENS reported to be in need of repairs. A 121, B 58, C 90, SP5 315 = 584.	
SATURDAY DEC. 25TH.	Nothing to report. A 96, B 4, C 101, SP5 257 = 458.	
SUNDAY. DEC 26TH.	Party sent out to repair air line to MOLLIENS. - D.A.D.O.S. moved up to SENLIS. Party mending D5 cable. A 121, B 27, C 115, SP5 280 = 543.	
MONDAY DEC 27TH.	Rouse and a party gone to SENLIS with Company stores to get signal office ready. - A.L. Cable Section moves to X Corps. Lorry returns from SENLIS with stores of 51st Signal Company. 53rd Division Artillery have left the division A 156, B 16, C 122, SP5 258 = 552.	
TUESDAY DEC 28TH.	Lorry load went up to SENLIS - Party mending wire - Two motor bicycles from Supply Column, C.R.A of 31st Divisional Artillery which is relieving 32nd Divisional Artillery established headquarters at ARGOEUVRES. A 106, B 22, C 93, SP5 299 = 520.	

Gulab Singh & Sons, Calcutta—No. 22 Army C.—5-8-14—1,07,000.

Army Form C. 2118.

WAR DIARY
or
INTELLIGENCE SUMMARY.
(Erase heading not required.)

Instructions regarding War Diaries and Intelligence Summaries are contained in F. S. Regs., Part II, and the Staff Manual respectively. Title pages will be prepared in manuscript.

Hour, Date, Place.	Summary of Events and Information.	Remarks and references to Appendices.
WEDNESDAY 29th 1915.	Line from St SAUVEUR prolonged to the Chateau at ARGOEUVRES to C.R.A. 32nd Divisional artillery. 32nd Divisional artillery arrive tomorrow. C.R.E 5th Divn moved to OLLINCOURT CHATEAU and using metallic circuit to own exchange. 153rd BDE laid in D5 line into OLLINCOURT-VAUX - ST SAUVEUR - ARGOEUVRES). A 111, B 23, C 103, SP's 339 - 576. Line at VAUX.	
THURSDAY 30th DEC.	Visited 10th Corps Signals to show plans for a buried system within new area. Visited 96th Infantry Brigade at HENENCOURT - handed over to 96th Brigade Signals their Portable D³ telephones and our eight way terminals board. Visited 51st Division Signals to see how work was progressing with new Office. Both our 15 way and 10 way exchanges up in position and working. Two trestle erected outside office for leading in wires. A party of the 32nd Divisional Artillery arrived at ST SAUVEUR, moving to ARGOEUVRES tomorrow morning.	
FRIDAY 31st DEC.	Mending and rewinding cable. III rd Army brought in a line outs exchange from 96th Field Coy R.E. at NAOURS.	

C.H.Walsh
Captain,
O.C. 32nd Divisional Signal Coy, R.E.

32nd Divisional Engineers

32nd DIVISIONAL SIGNAL COMPANY R. E.

JANUARY 1 9 1 6

32nd Serials
Vol: 2

WAR DIARY
of
INTELLIGENCE SUMMARY.
(Erase heading not required.)

Hour, Date, Place.	Summary of Events and Information.	Remarks and references to Appendices.
SATURDAY. JAN'y 1st 1916	Sergt Foster and his instrument room party left for SENLIS, and an instrument room party arrived at FLESSELLES to take over his instrument room. Took 12 telephones up to SENLIS at 11.0 PM - brought back two telephones from 51st Divn for G and Q branches A 64, B 75, C 77, SP's 276 = 492.	
SUNDAY. JAN'y 2nd	Signal Company left FLESSELS at 8.0 AM marching to SENLIS arriving (less at 1.30 PM. Handed over signals to 51st Divn in FLESSELS and took over 51st DIVNL SIGNALS in SENLIS at 10.0 AM. 96th BDE left HENENCOURT and relieved 152nd BDE. WILTS. (Wheelers at MARTINSART. COMMUNICATIONS as follows. (i) Permanent line to 4th DIVISION at ACHEUX, Division omnes left (ii) Comne own line from exchange to its Heavy Artillery at MARTINSART and MESNIL (iii) Sounder, Comne own line to Infantry Brigade headquarters at MARTINSART. (iv) Comne own line from exchange to its R.F.A Brigade at MARTINSART (v) Comne own line from exchange to its Infantry Brigade headquarters at AVELUY (vi) Comne own line from exchange to Infantry Brigade headquarters at Pionier Bataillon at BOUZINCOURT (viii) Permanent line from exchange to B.G.R.A. at BOUZINCOURT (ix) Permanent line to Howitzer Brigade at ALBERT (x) Permanent line to R.F.A. Brigade at Albert (xi) Sounder, Comne own line to Infantry Brigade at AVELUY (xii) Comne own line (dual) to MOULINS DE VIVIERE (xiii) Permanent line from exchange to Infantry Brigade at HENENCOURT at HENENCOURT (xiv) Sounder permanent line to X Corps test troops on ALBERT-AMIENS ROAD (xv) Pair from exchange - permanent line from exchange to wagon lines at BRESLE	

Army Form C. 2118.

WAR DIARY
of
INTELLIGENCE SUMMARY.

(Erase heading not required.)

Instructions regarding War Diaries and Intelligence
Summaries are contained in F. S. Regs., Part II,
and the Staff Manual respectively. Title pages
will be prepared in manuscript.

Hour, Date, Place.	Summary of Events and Information.	Remarks and references to Appendices.
SUNDAY JAN'Y 2nd (Continued)	(XVII) A [main] comic air line to E Corps from exchange (XVIII) Comic air line, double current, to E Corps at QUERRIEUX (XIX) Comic air line from exchange to Hospital at WARLOY. (XX) Comic air line from exchange to Transport at VADENCOURT and TRAIN at CONTAY. A 134, B 69, C 126, SPs 293 = 622.	
MONDAY, JAN'Y 3rd	95th Brigade moved into HENENCOURT from SAILLY LORETTE. 91st Brigade headquarters moved to BOUZINCOURT from AVELUY. Terminated its sounder and telephone comic air lines North and South of BOUZINCOURT and laid lines into BOUZINCOURT to its 94th Bde headquarters. Took away its telephone from the Pioneer Battalion in BOUZINCOURT and laid its line into the Brigade headquarters as an emergency unit. A 158, B 45, C 132, SPs 363 = 698	
TUESDAY JAN'Y 4th	Visited 96th, 94th Brigade sections in the morning - 96th Brigade section sounder out of order - temporary repairs made by instrument repairer. Two miles of G.P. twin cable given to 96th and 94th Bde sections for use between the battalion headquarters and company headquarters. X Corps brought up another sounder. Visited 94th and 95th Bde sections in the afternoon. - A 186, B 45, C 139, SPs 333 = 701 Reconnoitered ground for burying cable from AVELUY CHARTEPU to Divisional report centre. Visited 94th Bde headquarters. New telephone taken down to 2nd Highland R.F.A Bde at Montincourt. Fresh telephone placed in C.R.A's office. Line to Supply Column at FRANVILLERS completed and No 15 on exchange board. A 113, B 62, C 125, SPs 320 = 608.	
WEDNESDAY Jan'y 5th		

Army Form C. 2118.

WAR DIARY
or
INTELLIGENCE SUMMARY.
(Erase heading not required.)

Instructions regarding War Diaries and Intelligence Summaries are contained in F. S. Regs., Part II, and the Staff Manual respectively. Title pages will be prepared in manuscript.

Hour, Date, Place.	Summary of Events and Information.	Remarks and references to Appendices.
TUESDAY JAN" 11th 1916.	Works party completed 350 yds of horse lines. 2/Lt Ormanby and 10th Corps detachment straightening the wires of the MARTINSART BDE. Works party left for burying line at 4.0 P.M. A 146, B 90, C 189, SP 220 = 645.	
WEDNESDAY JAN"Y 12th	Works party completed 320 yds of horse lines. 10th Corps detachment out at MARTINSART. 2/Lt RAINSFORD clearing dead wires out of the village and labelling local circuits. Works party left for burying line at 4.0 P.M. A 110, B 73, C 112, SPs 324 = 619	
THURSDAY JAN" 13th	Went out to left Bde section to see positions of Bde Report Centres. Started line from SENLIS to BOUZINCOURT dug dugway — X Corps party working on left Brigade section lines. A 133, B 66, C 112, SPs 218, =629.	
FRIDAY JAN"Y 14th	Continuing trench towards BOUZINCOURT to hold wire lines — a party at BOUZINCOURT making test dug out—. A 132, B 65, C 116, SPs 380 = 695	
SATURDAY JAN"Y 15th	Preparing trench for burying cable and moving forward with the trench. Party continuing test dug out. A 145, B 49, C 118, SPs 268 = 680.	
SUNDAY JAN"Y 16th	Visited left section of the line to see position of Bde Report Centre. Party continuing test dug out. Laid wire lines shadow cables and from 'S' SubStn Centre in the trench for a distance of 300 yards. A 119, B 39, C 108, SPs 404 = 670	

Army Form C. 2118.

WAR DIARY
INTELLIGENCE SUMMARY.
(Erase heading not required.)

Instructions regarding War Diaries and Intelligence Summaries are contained in F. S. Regs., Part II, and the Staff Manual respectively. Title pages will be prepared in manuscript.

Hour, Date, Place.	Summary of Events and Information.	Remarks and references to Appendices.
MONDAY JAN'Y 17TH	Party continuing trench towards BOUZINCOURT - Straightening and carrying in the seven wires laid yesterday. A party under 2/Lt ROOSE continuing telephone line from DIVL. TRANSPORT at CONTAY to DIVL. AMTN. COLUMN at BAVILINCOURT. The extension being carried over line from permanent line at EBART FARM. A 96, B 59, C 110, SP 296 = 562	
TUESDAY JAN'Y 18TH	Party of Cyclist company continuing trench towards BOUZINCOURT, slow working anything heart struck chalk - Party filling in trench in which the wires have been laid. Party carrying on with test dug out - One wire party put up aeronic line on poles from CONTAY to EBART FARM, this line has to be dismantled by orders of 10th Corps Signals. A 135, B 46, C 110, SP 316 = 607.	
WEDNESDAY JAN'Y 19TH	Party under 2/Lt ROOSE laying comic air line from CONTAY to EBART FARM. Cyclist party continuing trench - X Corps party filling in line already laid. Cpl Clark's party working at Test dug out. A 122, B 38, C 110, SP 300 = 565.	
THURSDAY JAN'Y 20TH	Fixing up 168" R.F.A Bde and 11th How. Bde both at WARLOY on to a switch at the Telephone office WARLOY HOSPITAL - Laid wires in trench for another two hundred yards. One reserve mile test dug out completed. A 135, B 32, C 113, SP 415 = 695	
FRIDAY JAN'Y 21ST	Line to D.A.C. BAVELINCOURT and 164" & 168" Bdes WARLOY. working. Laid wires in trench for one hundred yards. Trouble on the line to the 27th Siege battery MESNIL. Finish dug out, also parties filling in and burying the wire, also party working on test dug out. continuing the trench. A 118, B 35, C 115, SP 320 = 588.	

Army Form C. 2118.

WAR DIARY
or
INTELLIGENCE SUMMARY.
(Erase heading not required.)

Instructions regarding War Diaries and Intelligence Summaries are contained in F. S. Regs., Part II, and the Staff Manual respectively. Title pages will be prepared in manuscript.

Hour, Date, Place.	Summary of Events and Information.	Remarks and references to Appendices.
SATURDAY JAN'Y 22nd 16	Party out relaying line from West Redoubt Battery MARTINSART WOOD to 27th Siege Battery MESNIL. Digging cable Trench across ALBERT – HÉDAUVILLE ROAD. Party on that dug out – completing second room. A 112, B 57, C 104, SP 381 = 634	
SUNDAY JAN'Y 23rd	A party of 80 men from 2nd Manchester Regt and 90 men from 19th Lancashire Fusiliers on the cable Trench. Cyclists trimming the trench – Signal party laying and filling in Trench. A dis: in one of the two shuttered cellars which was mended and a sleeve put on. Party finishing laying wire to MESNIL. A 116, B 32, C 116, SP 362 = 626.	
MONDAY. JAN'Y 24th	A party of 100 men from 11 Borders and 100 men from 16th H.L.I on the Trench – Cyclists trimming the Trench. – Signal party filling in Trench. Visited 96th Bde at MARTINSAT and 97th Bde at BOUZINCOURT. A 65, B 29, C 109, SP 323 = 606	
TUESDAY. JAN'Y 25th	Party of 16 H.L.I. cleaning out the Trench – Party on test dug out – Party on filling in the Trench. A 123, B 56, C 128, SP 246 = 553.	
WEDNESDAY JAN 26th	No working party to-day owing to Brigades relieving in G sector – on party cutting out the ditch or filling in the Trench. A 142, B 43, C 133, SP 355 = 673.	
THURSDAY JAN 27	Party of Cyclist Company cleaning up the Trench – Our own party filling in the Trench. 2/Lieut ORMANDY left for leave. A 155, B 52, C 143, SP 280, = 630	

Army Form C. 2118.

WAR DIARY
OF
INTELLIGENCE SUMMARY.
(*Erase heading not required.*)

Instructions regarding War Diaries and Intelligence Summaries are contained in F. S. Regs., Part II, and the Staff Manual respectively. Title pages will be prepared in manuscript.

Hour, Date, Place.	Summary of Events and Information.	Remarks and references to Appendices.
FRIDAY JAN. 28th 1916.	Signal party laying cable. Fatigue party digging trench up to Test Dug out. Evening fatigue party filling in to trench. A 149, B 39, C 152, SP 335 = 675.	
SATURDAY JAN 29th	Signal party laying cable and trenching towards IC roads. Fatigue party filling in trench. A 127, B 48, C 116, SP 309 = 600	
SUNDAY JAN. 30th	Finished digging main trench, length 3000 yards, to Test Dug Out. Signal party laying wire. Started on trench to BOUZINCOURT. Evening fatigue party filling in trench. A 127, B 48, C 116, SP 309 = 600	
MONDAY JAN. 31st	Laying cable which is nearly up to Test dug out, except two S. Substitute. Trench will be finished tomorrow. A 131, B 46, C 127, SP 350 = 654.	

C. H. Walshcroft
Lt.
O/C Signals 32nd Division

32nd Divisional Engineers

32nd DIVISIONAL SIGNAL COMPANY R. E.

FEBRUARY 1 9 1 6

32mo Signals
Vol: 3

Army Form C. 2118.

WAR DIARY

INTELLIGENCE SUMMARY.

(Erase heading not required.)

Instructions regarding War Diaries and Intelligence Summaries are contained in F. S. Regs., Part II, and the Staff Manual respectively. Title pages will be prepared in manuscript.

Hour, Date, Place.	Summary of Events and Information.	Remarks and references to Appendices.
FEBUARY 1st 1916.	Main trench to Test dug out completed and wires laid in onto terminal board. A 129, B 57, C 123, SP's 375 = 684.	
FEBUARY 2nd	Reconnoitred ground for new buried system and permanent wires to HENENCOURT from ALBERT and BOUZINCOURT. Party placing rails round test boxes. 15 miles of "S" Subsystem from Corps. A 126, B 41, C 107, SP's 294 = 568	
FEBUARY 3rd	Sent lorry to BETHENCOURT for saplings. Went over to HENENCOURT to look for a signal office in the Chateau. Party dismantling Corvée air line (not used) from SENLIS to MOULIN DE VIVIER. Party digging trench from new office HENENCOURT. A 121, B 57, C 107, SP's 288 = 528.	
FEBUARY 4th	Two parties erecting Corvée air line from MILLENCOURT to HENENCOURT. Remainder digging cable trench. A 128, B 66, C 132, SP's 341 = 677	
FEBUARY 5th	Parties shortening Corvée lais yestiean - Also laying buried telephone line in HENENCOURT. Line (permanent) to ALBERT repaired - Trench cable being continued. A 96, B 44, C 108, SP's 372 = 620	

WAR DIARY

INTELLIGENCE SUMMARY.

(Erase heading not required.)

Instructions regarding War Diaries and Intelligence Summaries are contained in F. S. Regs., Part II, and the Staff Manual respectively. Title pages will be prepared in manuscript.

Hour, Date, Place.	Summary of Events and Information.	Remarks and references to Appendices.
FEBRUARY 6th 1916.	Bringing cable trench - Erected triangular gallows for "lowering in" to officers' line from HENENCOURT to MILLENCOURT laid. A 129, B 444, C 117, SP5 235 = 623.	
FEBRUARY 7th	Bringing cable trench - Filling up offices in HENENCOURT - Transferring Company stores A 121, B 33, C 129, SP5 318 = 601	
FEBRUARY 8th	Line to MILLENCOURT erected - Party digging trench. Transferring Company stores to HENENCOURT. A 148, B 36, C 146, SP5 378 = 708	
FEBRUARY 9th	Comid. party laid to MONTIGNY from HENENCOURT for use of 11th Bde. Laying line in ALBERT for 17th Northumberland Fusiliers (pioneers ?) and to 97th Bde. living offices. A 201, B 41, C 161, SP5 326 = 739	
FEBRUARY 10th	Completing lines in ALBERT for 97th Infantry Bde. and 7th Fusiliers. Laying and filling in trench line. Line to MONTIGNY completed. A 174, B 51, C 155, SP5 385 = 765.	
FEBRUARY 11th	Line laying had into MILLENCOURT for 96th Brigade. Through to 17th Fusiliers in ALBERT on new line at 11.0 A.M. Through to 97th Infantry Bde. on horse and telephone lines at 12.0 noon. 10th Corps out party laying in Corps line. A 149, B 57, C 144, SP5 287 = 637	

WAR DIARY
INTELLIGENCE SUMMARY.
(Erase heading not required.)

Instructions regarding War Diaries and Intelligence Summaries are contained in F. S. Regs., Part II, and the Staff Manual respectively. Title pages will be prepared in manuscript.

Hour, Date, Place.	Summary of Events and Information.	Remarks and references to Appendices.
February 12th 1916.	Moving the company over to HENENCOURT. The 49th Division Signal Company came into SENLIS. Wiring the exchange at HENENCOURT and strengthening lines already laid. A 171, B 73, C 134, SPs 385 = 410	
February 13th	Laid "a-conic" line to 92nd Field Ambulance at BAIZEUX. Took over the Signal office at HENENCOURT at 12.0 noon. Lines as follows Exchange board. (a) Two pairs to 10th Corps Test House (b) a direct pair to 10th Corps (c) Pair to 49th Division at SENLIS (d) Earth circuit to 161st Bde R.F.A at ALBERT (e) Earth circuit to 96th Bde MILLENCOURT (f) Earth circuits to 97th Bde at ALBERT (g) Earth circuit to 17th Pioneer Battn at ALBERT (h) Earth circuits to 23rd Bde R.G.A at BOUZINCOURT (i) Earth circuit to 92nd Field Ambulance at BAIZIEUX (k) Telephone to 114th Bde at MONTIGNY with a tee off to Divisional Train at BEHENCOURT. Local lines on exchange (A) "G" Staff. (B) "Q" Staff (C) Company Office Signals (D) D.A.D.O.S (E) A.D.M.S (F) C.R.A. (G) C.R.E. Morse Lines (a) To 10th Corps (b) To 97th Bde at ALBERT (c) To 96th Bde at MILLENCOURT (d) To 114th Bde at MONTIGNY. Putting up electric light wires. A 132, B 82, C 119, SPs 247 = 580.	

WAR DIARY

or

INTELLIGENCE SUMMARY.

(Erase heading not required.)

Instructions regarding War Diaries and Intelligence Summaries are contained in F. S. Regs., Part II, and the Staff Manual respectively. Title pages will be prepared in manuscript.

Hour, Date, Place.	Summary of Events and Information.	Remarks and references to Appendices.
February 14th 1916	Linesmen out on new lines finding out faults. Fixing up electric light wiring. A 150, B 26, C 115, SPs 246 = 537	
February 15th	Digging Trench, 600 yards done by 100 men 2'6" deep, labelling lines on units outside office. A 151, B 23, C 109, SPs 269 = 552.	
February 16th	Extension built from the telephone line HENENCOURT-MONTIGNY to 1st Divisional Horse at ASHEN COURT. A party digging the cable trench. A 139, B 23, C 116, SPs 303 = 581	
February 17th	Laying cable in trench and burying. Weather bad, trench full of water, fire at HENENCOURT CHATEAU, no lines damaged. A 111, B 29, C 103, SPs 271 = 514.	
February 18th	Laying cable and digging trench. A 128, B 36, C 146, SPs 371 = 681	
February 19th	Laying cable and digging trench. Night parties digging & burying cable. One party of 50 men built AVELUY-DIVISIONAL REPORT CENTRE line. 150 men built DIVL-REPORT CENTRE - HENENCOURT line. Signal Company dug out also struth at expot centre. A 128, B 36, C 146, SPs 371 = 681	

WAR DIARY
or
INTELLIGENCE SUMMARY.
(Erase heading not required.)

Instructions regarding War Diaries and Intelligence Summaries are contained in F. S. Regs., Part II, and the Staff Manual respectively. Title pages will be prepared in manuscript.

Hour, Date, Place.	Summary of Events and Information.	Remarks and references to Appendices.
February 20th 1916.	Digging trench & laying cable also covering in same. Night parties carried on with the advance wires from AVELUY - DIVISIONAL REPORT CENTRE. Party also continued on Dug out. A 94. B.14. C.112. SP: 376 = 496.	
February 21st	Continuation of trench from HENENCOURT to MILLENCOURT & laying cable in same. Night parties made further progress with their burrow within 3 Dug out. Commenced building stabling for 20 horses at present jackshed out. A.84. B.25. C.95. SP: 307 = 511.	
February 22nd	14th BDE moved from MONTIGNY to ST GRATIEN. Ruled the wires from MONTIGNY to BEHENCOURT & from BEHENCOURT carried on with the field cable to ST GRATIEN. Covered in cable trench. Night parties continued digging trench, laying cable & covering in same. Dug out party also carried on. Party continued building stables. A.112. B.23. C.118. SP: 331 = 573.	
February 23rd	Continued digging trench to MILLENCOURT. Trade further progress with stables. Night parties dug trench from DIVISIONAL REPORT CENTRE down ALBERT ROAD & completed the wires from AVELUY. Dug out party carried on. Weather bad frozen & cold. A.114. B.36. C.104. SP: 335 = 589.	
February 24th	Cable trenches continued both by day & night parties. Cable laid & covered in. Stables & Dug out continued. A.163. B.29. C.138. SP: 298 = 618.	
February 25th	Trench dug to within 80yds of Bde Hdqrs MILLENCOURT & cable laid in same. Night parties cancelled owing to snowstorm. A.127. B.32. C.131. SP: 303 = 393.	
February 26th	Trench completed to MILLENCOURT BDE HDQRS & communication through Signals opened. Night party continued on ALBERT road. A.147. B.37. C.134. SP: 204 = 522.	

WAR DIARY
or
INTELLIGENCE SUMMARY

(Erase heading not required.)

Instructions regarding War Diaries and Intelligence Summaries are contained in F. S. Regs., Part II, and the Staff Manual respectively. Title pages will be prepared in manuscript.

Hour, Date, Place.	Summary of Events and Information.	Remarks and references to Appendices.
February 27th.	Morning working party continued cable trench from HILLENCOURT dos towards DIVISIONAL REPORT CENTRE & also carried the remainder of trench to the rear. Night party continued towards ALBERT. Dug out also progressed with. A 140. B 34. C. 130 SP 306 = 610	
February 28th.	Morning working party continued trench forward. Night party continued ALBERT trench & finished a finished all work necessary to be done by night. Dug out party carried on. A 167. B.47. C.121. SP. 358 = 693.	
February 29th.	Working party of 50 men continued trench for DIVISIONAL lines towards REPORT CENTRE. Another party of 100 men worked back on same trench from DUG OUT towards HENENCOURT. Party of 50 men worked on ALBERT trench. 14th BDE took over from 93rd BDE, laid two comic lines from HILLENCOURT to ALBERT to connect up new BDE HDQRS. Two limbers picked 100 saplings from BEHENCOURT. A. 136 B 81 C. 153 SP. 265 = 635	

WM Lanefird Lt. Col. for Captain,
O.C. 32nd Divisional Signal Coy., R.E.

32nd Divisional Engineers

32nd DIVISIONAL SIGNAL COMPANY R. E.

MARCH 1 9 1 6

32 Div Signals Vol 1

CONFIDENTIAL

WAR DIARY

32nd Divisional Signal Coy RE

March 1st 1916 – 31st March 1916

WAR DIARY
INTELLIGENCE SUMMARY.
(Erase heading not required.)

Army Form C. 2118.

Instructions regarding War Diaries and Intelligence Summaries are contained in F. S. Regs., Part II, and the Staff Manual respectively. Title pages will be prepared in manuscript.

Hour, Date, Place.	Summary of Events and Information.	Remarks and references to Appendices.
March 1st 1916.	Working party of 150 men continued cable trench towards REPORT CENTRE. Party of 9 men completed two comic lines from HENENCOURT to BDE HDQRS ALBERT; noises + telephone signals both good. Party of 11 men laid comic line from HENENCOURT to 93rd BDE R.F.A. ALBERT. A.173 B.102 C.159 SPs 325 = 759	
March 2nd.	Working party of 150 men continued digging cable trench forward REPORT CENTRE. Party of six men laid direct cable for French. Three men repaired roads where lines crossed. Comic air line party commenced noises + telephone circuit to 97th Bde at MOULIN DE VIVIER. Dug out party worked on DUG OUT. A.181. B.141 C.130 SPs 288 = 590	
March 3rd.	Comic air line party completed WIA'S to MOULIN DE VIVIER. Reeled up lines of telephone circuit to 158 BDE R.F.A. at MEAULTE line which formerly ran to 161 BDE. R.F.A. ALBERT via BOUZINCOURT was led into 98 BDE office at BOUZINCOURT. 161 BDE R.F.A. connected up direct on the old 96 BDE telephone circuit. Dug out party worked at night. A.124. B.96 C.143 SPs 388 = 761.	
March 4th.	A party of 50 cyclists under Mr Rainsford working outer buzz line. Connected up the 92nd Field Ambulance and Divisional Ammunition Columns who are both at WARLOY onto RD 18 which is a line belonging to 49th Division. We now get line units through to 49th Divisional Exchange. The telephone comic lines to the 96th Brigade and 19th Northumberland Fusiliers repaired, broken by some and wind. The lines to 97th Bde MOULIN DE VIVIER retained, broken by bad weather. A.156, B.95, C.146, SPs 365 = 741	

Army Form C. 2118.

WAR DIARY
OF
INTELLIGENCE SUMMARY.

(Erase heading not required.)

Instructions regarding War Diaries and Intelligence Summaries are contained in F. S. Regs., Part II, and the Staff Manual respectively. Title pages will be prepared in manuscript.

Hour, Date, Place.	Summary of Events and Information.	Remarks and references to Appendices.
March 5th 1916	Party of 50 cyclists filling in buried line - Sergt Maude setting up MONTIGNY pair of comics. Party laying comic line to ALBERT-AMIENS road. A second line put through to C.R.A's office. A 203, B 35, C 185, SP° 352 = 775	
March 6th 1916	Party of 50 cyclists filling in buried line - Party laying a pair of comics to WARLOY and VADENCOURT - The 92nd Field Ambulance, and the Divisional ammunition Column being on one line, and the Divisional Supply Column and Divisional train on the other. A 136, B 46, C 157, SP° 398 = 737.	
March 7th 1916	Party out strengthening WARLOY and VADENCOURT comics - Party out setting up remainder of MONTIGNY comic. 50 Cyclists and remainder of workers party digging French and hungar cable. A 179, B 49, C 143, SP° 330 = 701.	
March 8th 1916.	Digging French and burying cable - Completing no stables for 40 horses - Cleaning waggons + cable carts. A 158, B 47, C 158, SP° 368 = 731	
March 9th 1916.	Fixing up lines to Hd Quarters at Martinsart and thence filling up road crossing into BOUZINCOURT - HEDAUVILLE ROAD - Connecting up road line from BOUZINCOURT to ALBERT by means of Ringdon. A 163, B 40, C 151, SP° 362 = 716	

Gulab Singh & Sons, Calcutta—No. 22 Army C.—5-8-14—1,07,000.

WAR DIARY

Instructions regarding War Diaries and Intelligence Summaries are contained in F. S. Regs., Part II, and the Staff Manual respectively. Title pages will be prepared in manuscript.

INTELLIGENCE SUMMARY.

(Erase heading not required.)

Hour, Date, Place.	Summary of Events and Information.	Remarks and references to Appendices.
March 10th 1916.	Party on the burid line to the report centre – lateral lines being fixed up between 111th Infantry Bde ALBERT and the 97th Infantry Bde Moulin de Vivier – line already being laid out and simplified. A 155, B 41, C 159, SP 375 = 730.	
March 11th 1916.	Report centre being changed – Party taken off buried line to present report centre and put onto line from Survey post to the Test dug out BOUZINCOURT which will be dug tonight – Six line buried in Tara trench. A 180, B 57, C 147, SP 426 = 810.	
March 12th 1916.	Party dug 180 yards of trench 1ft wide, 4' deep, laid six cables and filled in trench. Party under 2/Lt Meade connecting up the two ends of buried line between HENENCOURT and old report centre by air line about 1500 yards. A 180, B 42, C 152, SP 332 = 112.	
March 13th 1916.	Party under 2Lt Kitchingman last night completed two yards of buried line. Crossing the BOUZINCOURT – AVELUY ROAD. Two hundred men of 2nd Manchesters digging cable trench between HENENCOURT and Dirt report centre. Capt Williams and Sapper Richens wiring 168" R.F.A. Bde Signal Office. A 155, B 32, C 167, SP 258 = 452.	
March 14th 1916.	Party under 2Lt Kitchingman completed 100 yards of buried cable. 2/5 Rivers and Ormesby with a working party of 200 men completed 600 yds of the HENENCOURT – REPORT CENTRE buried line. Inspected buried line of 97th 15de. A 147, B 50, C 147, SP 371 = 715.	

WAR DIARY

INTELLIGENCE SUMMARY.

(Erase heading not required.)

Instructions regarding War Diaries and Intelligence Summaries are contained in F. S. Regs., Part II, and the Staff Manual respectively. Title pages will be prepared in manuscript.

Hour, Date, Place.	Summary of Events and Information.	Remarks and references to Appendices.
March 15th 1916.	No working party today - 2/Lieut Kent returned from Corning - 2" Kitchinerwear party completed 160 yards of burial line last night. A 153, B 22, C 165, SP's 407 = 747.	
March 16th 1916.	Working party of 100 men on the HENENCOURT – REPORT CENTRE line which is now complete except for sixty yards. Night party under Lieut Kitchingman completed 140 yards of burial line last night. A 106, B 29, C 143, SP's 409 = 909.	
March 17th 1916.	Finished the HENENCOURT – REPORT CENTRE LINE which has now been litted and is complete. Night-digging party completed 170 yards of burial lines. A 158, B 29, C 155 SP's 388 = 730.	
March 18th 1916.	Night party completed 160 yards of burial line - establishing a straightening the burial line to MILLENCOURT and the REPORT CENTRE. A 113, B 29, C 135, SP's 431 = 718.	
March 19th 1916.	Night party completed 160 yards of burial line - Party out putting up barbed wire fences round tash boxes and sandbagging them. Lt Churchill returned from leave. A 131, B 20, C 189, SP's 362 = 651	
March 20th 1916.	Night party completed trenches up to left dug out - Moved the 16th "Stratforshire Btn from the 161st R.T.A. Coln line and put them on the 15th 14th Northumberland Fusiliers line. A 161, B 30, C 159 SP's 335 = 685. 2/Lt ROUSE 2/Lt Churchill died of wounds received in ALBERT	

Instructions regarding War Diaries and Intelligence Summaries are contained in F. S. Regs., Part II, and the Staff Manual respectively. Title pages will be prepared in manuscript.

INTELLIGENCE SUMMARY.

(*Erase heading not required.*)

Hour, Date, Place.	Summary of Events and Information.	Remarks and references to Appendices.
March 21st 1916.	No working party last night – Repairing and strengthening trench lines. Cleaning cable waggons and light Springs. A = 138, B 30, C 150, SPS 336 = 654. 2Lt Ronae burried at MILLENCOURT CEMETERY.	
March 22nd 1916.	Buried line party commencing a few line trench from its left dug out to BOUZINCOURT. Inspecting area for dead cable, which is very abundant. Sergt Maude and five men are forming a Salvage party in the BOUZINCOURT area. Up to date have collected 1½ miles D⁵, 5 miles D¹, A 133, B 31, C 164, SP⁵ 235 = 663.	
March 23rd 1916.	Trench was completed up to 440 yards towards BOUZINCOURT. Sergt Maude's party collected 3½ miles D³, 1½ D¹. A 111, B 42, C 128, SP⁵ 443 = 724.	
March 24th 1916.	No working party to-day – Line Sunny Franks owing to heavy snow – Party in Q.M.S Stores, another party strengthening trench lines. A 126, B 34, C 164, SP⁵ 330 = 654.	
March 25th 1916.	Digging party onto BOUZINCOURT LINE. Heavy snow during the night which broke line wires – working parties were sent out to strengthen these lines – Snowing most of to-day, lot of earth on its lines.	

INTELLIGENCE SUMMARY.
(Erase heading not required.)

Instructions regarding War Diaries and Intelligence Summaries are contained in F. S. Regs., Part II. and the Staff Manual respectively. Title pages will be prepared in manuscript.

Place	Date	Hour	Summary of Events and Information	Remarks and references to Appendices
March	26th	1916	Working party on the BOUZINCOURT buried line - A 131, B 125, C 153, SPS 243 = 652.	
March	27th	1916	Working party on the buried line now in BOUZINCOURT - line should be finished by Thursday 30th. Commenced Visual Signal training - The dug out party have now dug a French hasty foot long and 5 feet deep, and battens up its sides with corrugated iron and 9×3 timber. A 133, B 29, C 160, SPS 380 = 702.	
March	28th	1916.	No working parties today owing to cyclist training. Night dug out party working as usual. A 169, B 29, C 174, SPS 368 = 738.	
March	29th		Buried cable party working through BOUZINCOURT now within 160 yards of Brigade Headquarters - Night dug out party working. A 142, B 52, C 156, SPS 334 = 658	
March	30th		Buried cable to BOUZINCOURT finished and terminates in Brigade Signal Office - Night dug out party commenced to tunnel in having reached a depth of twelve feet. A 137, B 46, C 159, SPS 328 = 670	
March	31st		Line being altered preparatory to move, fresh lines being laid out 92nd Field Ambulance office to connect up to the 92nd Field Ambulance & the Divisional Ammunition Column - a line also laid in to Divisional Supply Column to connect up with Divisional Supply Column and Divisional train. A 152, B 75, C 189, SPS 125 = 521.	

C. Milward
Capt 15th
OC 32 Div Sig Coy.

32nd Divisional Engineers

32nd DIVISIONAL SIGNAL COMPANY R. E.

APRIL 1916

Army Form C2118
82 Sig Coy
Vol 5

WAR DIARY
or
INTELLIGENCE SUMMARY.
(Erase heading not required.)

CONFIDENTIAL

WAR DIARY
OF
82 DIVISIONAL SIGNAL COY RE

APRIL 1st — APRIL 30th 1916

Army Form C. 2118.

WAR DIARY
INTELLIGENCE SUMMARY.
(Erase heading not required.)

Instructions regarding War Diaries and Intelligence Summaries are contained in F. S. Regs., Part II. and the Staff Manual respectively. Title pages will be prepared in manuscript.

Place	Date	Hour	Summary of Events and Information	Remarks and references to Appendices
April	1st	1916.	Offices at SENLIS having wired. Lines brought in to CORBIE for 96th Brigade who are moving into lines brought into WARLOY for 97th Brigade. Permanent lines being traced over for 161 RFA Brigade and 164th Howitzer Bde at ALBERT. A 140, B 81, C 155, SP ^{c} 368 = 744.	
April	2nd		Preparing lines for moving over to SENLIS. Night party continuing its dug out. A 167, B 69, C 162, SP ^{c} 345 = 743.	
April	3rd		Moved to SENLIS at 12.0 noon—lines in as follows. Local circuits (a) G. Staff (b) Q Staff (c) Company Office (d) C.R.E. (e) C.R.A. (f) DADOS (g) A.D.M.S. all these lines are metallic. Trunk circuits (a) Down to 9th Division HENENCOURT (b) pair to 36th Division HARPONVILLE (c) Pair to 10th Corps TOUTENCOURT. (d) Circt to H.A.G (HEDAUVILLE) (e) Circt to 27th Siege Battery MESNIL (f) Circt to Infantry Bde BOUZINCOURT (g) Circt to 27th Siege Bde BOUZINCOURT (h) Circt to 17th (Pioneer) (Newfoundland) Battalion (h) through to 9th Division to 11th Division Bde, 155th R.T.A Bde, 97th Infantry Bde, 108th 90th Field Ambulance. R.T.A. Pale. (k) Circt to 161st R.F.A Bde (l) Circt to 161st Bde Intelligence (M) Circt to 92nd Field Ambulance and Divisional Ammunition Column WARLOY (N) Divisional Supply Column and Divnl train WARLOY and VADENCOURT. Summer circuits. (2) To Kite Corps (b) 14th Infantry Bde. (c) 97th Infantry Bde. (d) 97th Infantry Bde A, 181, B 99, C 152, SP ^{c} 327 = 759.	

Army Form C. 2118.

WAR DIARY
~~INTELLIGENCE~~ SUMMARY.
(Erase heading not required.)

Instructions regarding War Diaries and Intelligence Summaries are contained in F.S. Regs., Part II. and the Staff Manual respectively. Title pages will be prepared in manuscript.

Place	Date	Hour	Summary of Events and Information	Remarks and references to Appendices
April	4th		Lt Clery posted to 32nd Signal Coy RE. from the 36th Company. — Night party not working tonight owing to reliefs. A 116, B 74, C 162, SP's 361 = 760	
April	5th		Lt Armytage digging MARTINSART - AUTHUILLE buried line. Night party continuing dug outs. A 193, B 92, C 174, SP's 374 = 828	
April	6th		Party under Lt Armytage digging MARTINSART - AUTHUILLE buried line - Night party digging dug outs. A 168, B 66, C 119, SP's 351 = 702	
April	7th		Party out under Lt Armytage digging to MARTINSART - AUTHUILLE line - Night party digging dug outs - One dug out 9'in. and the other 6'. Lt Rainsford returned to Headquarters Section. Lt Osmaston having returned from leave. A 150, B 90, C 130, SP's 379 = 749	
April	8th		Lt Armytage out to MARTINSART - AUTHUILLE buried line. Night dug out party at its repair contd. A 145, B 73, C 138, SP's 371 = 727	

T2134. Wt. W708—776. 500000. 4/15. Sir J. C. & S.

Army Form C. 2118.

WAR DIARY
INTELLIGENCE SUMMARY.
(Erase heading not required.)

Instructions regarding War Diaries and Intelligence Summaries are contained in F. S. Regs., Part II. and the Staff Manual respectively. Title pages will be prepared in manuscript.

Place	Date	Hour	Summary of Events and Information	Remarks and references to Appendices
April	9th		L. Cumflage's parties have now turned as farmers the BOIS D'AVELUY. Night party continuing the Report Centre dug outs. Chose a place for visual dug out which will be at W 16 a m 2. A 167, B 55, C 132. SP 368 = 752.	
April	10th		L. Cumflage with his party continuing the buried line towards AUTHUILLE. L. Ramsford starting with a party from Report Centre to Centre Brigade Report Centre — two lines which attends one running to H.A.G. exchange with "DOGS LEG" — the remaining four teams going up to the dug outs East of AUTHUILLE. Night party on the Divisional Report Centre Dug Outs continuing. A 157, B 66, C 134, SP 293 = 650	
April	11th		L. Cumflage's party on the buried line which will branch off W of AUTHUILLE towards & up to JOHNSON'S POST which will be the Left Brigade Report Centre. L. Ramsford party on one at the "DOGS LEG". DUG OUT party under Corporal Clerke continuing on the DIVISIONAL REPORT CENTRE DUG OUTS. A 149, B 66, C 119, SP 352 = 686.	
April	12th		No working parties today owing to relief of of the 14th Brigade by the 97th Bde. Instrument Room Stables, & works' Parties changing over. Remaining men engaged in two-wheeled carts with six light springs to ambulance f/w Staples. A 128, B 84, C 1114, SP 373 = 699	

Army Form C. 2118.

WAR DIARY
or
INTELLIGENCE SUMMARY.
(Erase heading not required.)

Instructions regarding War Diaries and Intelligence Summaries are contained in F. S. Regs., Part II. and the Staff Manual respectively. Title pages will be prepared in manuscript.

Place	Date	Hour	Summary of Events and Information	Remarks and references to Appendices
April	13th		Digging party under Lt Armytage carrying on towards JOHNSONS POST - Digging party under Lt Clay working at night towards AUTHUILLE - Dug out party finishing dug outs. A 200, B 88, C 132, SPs 362 = 782	
April	14th		Nothing to report - Same working parties as April 13th. A 207, B 168, C 138, SPs 391 = 844	
April	15th		Nothing to report - Same working parties as April 15th. A 148, B 64, C 139, SPs A15 = 766	
April	16th		Working out the loops of the overhearing instrument. Working parties as usual.	
April	17th		Working parties under Lt Armytage and Lt Rainsford as usual - Dug out party continues at night. A 154, B 64, C 139, SPs 357 = 714	
April	18th		Nothing to report - Working parties as usual. A 195, B 115, C 149, SPs 451 = 910	
April	19th		Nothing to report. Working parties as usual. A 160 B 92, C 128, SPs 475 = 855	
April	20th		Visual Station arranged for at JOHNSON POST to Central Visual Station - Working parties as usual - Report cable dug outs are now not going to be used - but all going to be finished - A 163, B 102, C 192, SPs 327, 720.	
April	21st		Working parties as usual - A 164, B 104, C 127, SPs 327 911. 327. 719	
April	22nd		No working parties. Artillery trying to obstruct Wirls - Wireless tested during raid onto German Trenches - Prisoners cover its taken from front to rear, but not forward from Divisional Rallt. Station to its trenches trying to the concearmin of the artks moving to crystal, Directly the bombardment	

Army Form C. 2118.

WAR DIARY
of
INTELLIGENCE SUMMARY.
(Erase heading not required.)

Instructions regarding War Diaries and Intelligence Summaries are contained in F.S. Regs., Part II. and the Staff Manual respectively. Title pages will be prepared in manuscript.

Place	Date	Hour	Summary of Events and Information	Remarks and references to Appendices
April	22nd		Ceased messages were easily received both ways. the wires held up to Battalion Headquarters but beyond that were mostly cut. A 193, B 105, C 144, SP's 442 = 860.	
April	23rd		Two working parties busy to repair wires — One to the 27th Siege Battery, other one to headquarters moved last night. A 172, B 123, C 128, SP's 299 = 722	
April	24th		Working parties at night - One party under Lt Cunningtine working to post Q 36 c 7.5. Another working party at post W to d S.S. working towards lower heroes under Lt Ransford. Cpl Clarke's party continuing to dig out by day. A 158, B 114, C 157, SP's 349 = 782.	
April	25th		Working parties same as 24.4.16. A 137, B 166, C 109 SP's 204 = 706.	
April	26th		Divisional report centre dug out finished today. Other working parties as usual A 158, B 78, C 132, SP's 287 = 655.	
April	27th		Working parties as usual. Cpl Clarke's party starting Visual Central Station tonight. A 120, B 101, C 121 SP's 273 = 621. Received a supersonic machine from 10th Corps, which has been working all day. Strong breakers to take down Rain line 11.0 A.M. AS - V - KB - U three letter cipher. Rain 3.0 PM broke. German stations at 6 and 9.0 PM. B letter cipher. British Reuters Wireless all day. Rain time 11:00 PM - Rain Press 11:45 PM.	
April	28th		Working parties as usual. Commenced to mount dug out with Cpl Clarke's party. A 167, B 123, C 118 SP's 303 = 711	
April	29th		Working parties as usual. A 155, B 111, C 145 SP's 300 = 711	
April	30th		L Cunninghams party have been working by day other two working parties as usual. A 148, B 97 C 132, SP's 360 = 757.	

C. H. Worth Capt.
O/C Signals 32nd Division.
30/4/16

32nd Divisional Engineers

32nd DIVISIONAL SIGNAL COMPANY R. E.

M A Y   1 9 1 6

Army Form C. 2118.

32: Signal Coy
Vol 6

WAR DIARY
or
INTELLIGENCE SUMMARY.
(Erase heading not required.)

CONFIDENTIAL

WAR DIARY.

OF

32nd Signal Company R.E.

From 1st May — 31st May 1916.

Vaz [illegible]
for Captain,
O.C. 32nd Divisional Signal Coy., R.E.

Army Form C. 2118.

WAR DIARY
INTELLIGENCE SUMMARY.
(Erase heading not required.)

Instructions regarding War Diaries and Intelligence Summaries are contained in F.S. Regs., Part II. and the Staff Manual respectively. Title pages will be prepared in manuscript.

Place	Date	Hour	Summary of Events and Information	Remarks and references to Appendices
May	1st		Lt Armitage party on day work - buried cables to the BLUFF - Lt Rawnsfords party night work burying cables to Right Prineade - Cpl Clarkes party on visual dug out. A 135, B 89, C 114, SPs 300 = 638	
MAY	2nd		Same working parties as 1st - Nothing to report. A 153, B 94, C 133, SPs 322 = 752	
MAY	3rd		Lt Armitages party on day work - Lt Rawnsfords party on night work - Cpt Clarkes party on visual dug out. A 186, B 130, C 130, SPs 328 = 694.	
MAY	4th		Lt Rawnsfords party on day work. Taste with Aeroplane lamp signaling by day - Results reported by R.F.C. to have been satisfactory. L'Armytages party day work into BLUFF LINE. A 149, B 132, C 130, SPs 333 = 743	
MAY	5th		No working parties today coming to relief - Lt Rawnsford and his sappers assisting L'Armytage with the working party from the 36th Division onto BLUFF LINE. A 140, B 150, C 131 SPs 294 = 715.	
MAY	6th		No working parties owing to Brigade relieving - Colonel Clarkes party onto visual dug out. A 136, B 108, C 135, SPs 321 = 700	
MAY	7th		Working party Lt Rawnsford only 11 men instead of 100 - working party from 36th Brion inunder Lt Armitage working on the BLUFF LINE. Cpt Clarkes party onto visual dug out. A 166, B 61, C 147, SPs 339 = 750	
MAY	8th		Working parties correct again - fifty men under L'Armytage - Sixty on new union Lt Rawnsford. Work as before - A 142, B 93, C 116, SPs 351 = 672.	

T2134. Wt. W708—776. 500000. 4/15. Sir J. C. & B.

WAR DIARY

INTELLIGENCE SUMMARY.
(Erase heading not required.)

Instructions regarding War Diaries and Intelligence Summaries are contained in F.S. Regs., Part II. and the Staff Manual respectively. Title pages will be prepared in manuscript.

Place	Date	Hour	Summary of Events and Information	Remarks and references to Appendices
MAY	9th		Nothing to report. Messages for the day. A 133, B 76, C 126, SP^s 317 = 652.	
MAY	10th		Working parties as usual – Nothing to report. A 165, B 74, C 146, SP^s 371 = 756.	
MAY	11th		Very slow work on the buried line from MARTINSART to the Sandbagged 2^d Ramparts party commencing to take trench from AVELUY CHATEAU to A/V 21, B 62, C 103. SP^s 362 = 656.	Divisional R.E. park Centre.
MAY	12th		Nothing to report. A 156, B 59, C 122, SP^s 358 = 695.	
MAY	13th		Working parties on buried lines – nothing to report – A 148, B 82, C 112, SP^s 361 = 709.	
MAY	14th		Nothing to report – A 183, B 95, C 123, SP^s 406 = 767.	
MAY	15th		Contact aeroplane test with 2^d K.O.Y.L.I. postponed in the morning owing to bad weather – Same test with the 11th Border Regt. postponed into afternoon – weather unsuitable – Buried cable parties as usual – LtReid inspecting R.A. aerial trenches. A 159, B 61, C 111, SP^s 391 = 311.	
MAY	16th		Working parties as usual. Contact aeroplane tests with the 16th H.L.I. and 17th H.L.I. Found satisfactory. A 146, B 73, C 119, SP^s 350 = 688.	
MAY	17th		No working parties after 10 pm today owing to relief. Cadence aeroplane test with 16th Northumberland Fusiliers and 15th Northumberland Fusiliers.	
MAY	18th		60 cyclists added to Buried cable working parties – No infantry working parties today owing to relief. Contact aeroplane tests with Humbling Fusiliers and 16th Lancashire Fusiliers. A 175, B 81, C 133, SP^s 336 = 725.	

INTELLIGENCE SUMMARY.

(Erase heading not required.)

Instructions regarding War Diaries and Intelligence Summaries are contained in F.S. Regs., Part II. and the Staff Manual respectively. Title pages will be prepared in manuscript.

Place	Date	Hour	Summary of Events and Information	Remarks and references to Appendices
MAY	19th		Lt Rainsford working on the report centre - AVELUY LINE - Lt Armitage laying line 5 + C.C. cables from BOUZINCOURT to the 15th dug out, with afternoon. Oxford Clarkes party onto new visual dug out. Lt Armitage laying two 2 C.C. cables from Report Centre towards the 9th Divn report centre. Change over of the Inskinnings Reserve Stables, and works parties. A 181, B 91, C 137, SP⁵ 396 = 710	
MAY	20th		97th Infantry Brigade Scheme with Contract aeroplane from 3.0 AM – 5.45 AM. Working parties as yesterday. 19th (Amentine Trailer) party did not report at AVELUY CHATEAU. A 148, B 66, C 119, SP⁵ 345 = 678	
MAY	21st		Lt Rainsford on leave - Captain Clery returned from leave - Lt Ramsden's Gutters - Lt Armitage with ?? working on the BLUFF LINE. Lt Kent with 40 men working on the RED HOUSE LINE. Night working party under Capt. Clarke working onto visual dug out. A 163, B 57, C 144, SP⁵ 348 = 712	
MAY	22nd		Visited Lt Armitage's party on the BLUFF line - party had him men knocked ask go. Sent back Lt Kent's party who was working in full view of an observation Balloon - Lt Kent's party returned to work in the evening. Maj'd out new line for Lt Kent to dig to the Reserve and Centre Peroples. Visited the night working party who have started turneling. A 1113, B 19, C 36, SP⁵ C = 757	
May	23rd		Working parties as usual. 19th Bomb'r 48 men + 19th Lancashire Fusiliers 48 men. Cyclists 40 men and Motorists 20 men	
May	24th		Line to the BLUFF Completed - Line from Divisional Report Centre to AVELUY CHATEAU completed. A 159, B 61, C 105, SP⁵ 386 = 710. A 166, B 94, C 114, SP⁵ 413 = 787	

Instructions regarding War Diaries and Intelligence
Summaries are contained in F. S. Regs., Part II.
and the Staff Manual respectively. Title pages
will be prepared in manuscript.

INTELLIGENCE—SUMMARY.
(Erase heading not required.)

Place	Date	Hour	Summary of Events and Information	Remarks and references to Appendices
MAY	25th		Lt Reed working cable line from AVELUY CHATEAU to reserve and right brigades, to Amiens layer lines from Bouzincourt, repair Cavilier and Bombardment lines. Test dug out. A 73, B 66, C 112, SP² 207 = 713	
MAY	26th		Working parties as usual. A 114, B 73, C 124, SP² 383 = 693.	
MAY	27th		Working parties as usual. A 194, B 82, C 124, SP² 388 = 768	
MAY	28th		Started to lay artillery line into BOIS D'AVELUY, working parties as usual. A 185, B 91, C 140, SP² 407 = 803.	
MAY	29th		Indian Cavalry party arrived in Bois D'AVELUY to work on cable lines. Laid artillery and infantry cable lines through AUTHUILLE WOOD. A 112, B 140, C 135, SP² 440 = 827.	
MAY	30th		Indian Cavalry of 200 men working on Artillery cable line. Party of 4th ROYAL (200 men) arrived to work on Cable lines. 96 Bde relieved 97 Bde into line. A 159, B 99, C 189, SP² 317 = 774	
MAY	31st		Indian Cavalry party 200 men working on Artillery Cable Trenches. Party of 4th ROYAL digging along HAMEL – AVELUY railway on artillery cable trenches, and from AUTHUILLE to JOHNSTON'S POST on Infantry Bde Cable Trenches. A 146, B 73, C 127, SP 417 = 757.	V.A.C. Copy. Capt R.E. for Capt.

T2134. Wt. W708—776. 500000. 4/15. Sir J. C. & S.

O.C. 32nd Divisional Signal Coy., R.E.

32nd Divisional Engineers

32nd. DIVISIONAL SIGNAL COMPANY R. E.

JUNE 1916::

32nd Div Signals
Vol 7

Army Form C. 2118.

WAR DIARY
or
INTELLIGENCE SUMMARY.
(Erase heading not required.)

Confidential.
WAR DIARY.
1st June to 31st June 1916

Army Form C. 2118.

WAR DIARY
or
INTELLIGENCE SUMMARY.
(Erase heading not required.)

Instructions regarding War Diaries and Intelligence Summaries are contained in F. S. Regs., Part II. and the Staff Manual respectively. Title pages will be prepared in manuscript.

Place	Date	Hour	Summary of Events and Information	Remarks and references to Appendices
JUNE	1st.		Contact Patrol Scheme. Visual signalling by Venetian Blind pattern of ground panels used from Bde to Aeroplanes — latter answering with lamp. This was found very satisfactory by Bde. Digging Parties as usual. A.136 B.81 C.120 S.P.390 = 727.	
JUNE	2nd.		Aeroplane Squadron report Venetian Blind Signalling was a great success yesterday. Cartilling Digging Parties as usual. 2nd Lt Armytage examined and reported on progress of 17th Siege Bty cable lunging parties. Captain Cleary interviewed representatives of signals of 8th Divn, 36th Divn, 3rd Corps, 10th Corps to arrange putting wires into Trenches outside our area. A.169 B.81 C.119 S.P.400 = 709.	
June	3rd.		Wires laid by 2nd Lt Kent with armoured cable from W.17.A.10.7 to W.17.B.8.9. Wires laid by 2nd Lt Armytage from W.12.A.6.5 — W.11.B.4.1. (12 drums twisted D.5 used) and by 2nd Lt Rawnsford from W.9.B.7.5 to W.10.B.9.2. (13 drums twisted D.6 used). A.143 B.83 C.126 S.P.375 = 727.	
June	4th.		2nd Lts Rawnsford and Armytage proceeded with the labelling and testing of the wires on previous day. 2nd Lt Rawnsford also laid wires to Battery Postn from W.9.B.3.10 to W.9.A.7.7. 2nd Lt Armytage from W.11.B.6.1 down to the river, and 2nd Lt Kent from W.9.D.8.3 to W.9.D.8.6.. 20 drums cable twisted during the day by Cpl Clarke's and Gunner Baker A.137 B.78 C.117 D.336 = 678	
June	5th.		2nd Lt Rawnsford preparing trenches for putting in Kemmeyard. 2nd Lt Kent employed his infantry deepening trench from W.17.B.9.6 to W.17.D.9.7 and his N.1.H. filling in 30x of trench near guns in W.9.D. 2nd Lt Armytage laid wires (9 pairs) 6:6 from W.35.c.3.9.10 W.36.c.10.7 in Artillery Trench. A.116 B.68 C.117 S.P.363 = 673	

T2134. Wt. W708—776. 500000. 4/15. Sir J. C. & S.

WAR DIARY or INTELLIGENCE SUMMARY

Army Form C. 2118.

Place	Date	Hour	Summary of Events and Information	Remarks and references to Appendices
June	6th		2nd Lts Armytage and Kent laid June to Corps and 7 Fr Artillery in trench from W11B.3.1 to W11D.7.4. Captain Cleary decided, in view of extra wires now available, to dig two new trenches from W11D.7.4 to W11D.9.4 and W11C.2.D to W9D.6.4, starting tomorrow. 2nd Lt Ravensford initialling lines etc. Very wet day, which considerably hampered work. A140 B65 C118 SP308 = 631	
June	7th		2nd Lt Armytage laid 2 wires for Heavy Battery in ALBERT, from rendezvous at W22D.9.8 to W16D.9.2 (In III Corps Trench). Work not completed owing to large number of other wires in trench. 2nd Lt Ravensford laid 6 wires for junctions and 1 for 8th Divn. from W11A.3.0 to W17C.1.9. 2nd Lt Kent continued work carrying up trenches Y13 and Y10 by short trenches. Cavalry dugout new trench from W9D 9.6 to W11C.3.0. A165 B101 C138 SP327 = 731	
June	8th		2nd Lt Armytage completed wires for Heavy Bty in ALBERT from W16D.9.2 to W22D.9.8. 2nd Lt Ravensford completed junction trench from Y15 to Y10, and prepared poles for wiring from W11A.3.0 to W17C.1.9. 2nd Lt Kent completed wiring from W17D.9.8 to W17B.9.8 for wiring tomorrow. Cavalry furnished trench from W17D.8.6 to W17C.2.7. A122 B88 C129 SP358 = 697	
June	9th		2nd Lt Armytage laid wires from Q.33 D7.0 to W3D.4.5. 2nd Lt Rainsford from W3D.4.5 to W9D.8.6. Cavalry digging party loaned to Lt Primrose for carrying our lines to the MESNIL O.P.s. 2nd Lt Kent laid wires from W17D.9.8 to W17B.9.8 and wired the junction trench from Y13 to Y10. A114 B117 C167 SP304 = 722.	

Army Form C. 2118.

WAR DIARY
INTELLIGENCE SUMMARY
(Erase heading not required.)

Place	Date	Hour	Summary of Events and Information	Remarks and references to Appendices
	June 10th		Lt Kent carrying on with lines to Rifle and Cattle Redt headquarters – Lt Fealty arrive to assist in laying Artillery wires – Lt Armytage laying artillery wires E of MARTINSART – Lt Rainsford laying Artillery wire across to march. A 172. B 121. C 152. SP^s 330 = 775	
	June 11th		Capt Clery; Lt Fealty, Lt Rainsford digging trench & laying wire for Lt O.P.'s in Pendel Hill. Shoot – Lt Kent making trunk lines. Wires dug out and were made over the top of Kew W of BOIS D'HEDZUT. Lt Armytage carrying on with artillery trench E of MARTINSART. A 197. B 149. C 138 SP^s 369 and the unregistered = 773	
	June 12th		Working parties as yesterday a 162. B 195. C 145 SP^s 387 and 107 unregistered = 996	
	June 13th		Lt Armytage finishing Battery positions N°s 11 & 12 East of Martinsart. Lt Kent finishing battery positions 3, 4, 5 South of Crucifix Corner. Lt Gates & Rainsford carrying on with O.P.'s in Pendel Hill Shoot. Capt. Clery finishing trench up to PENDEL HILL O.P's. Lt Lomax carrying on with trench positions N.E. of BOIS D'AVELUY. A 240 B 208 C 194 SP^s 409 & 150 unregistered = 1192.	
	June 14th		Lt Armytage & Lt Kent laying Artillery wires from Crucifix Corner towards the Right and Reserve Group headquarters. Lt Rainsford wiring O.P's PENDEL HILL. Lt LOMAX finishing positions 14.15.16. Capt Clery wiring up to PENDEL HILL O.P. Capt Walsh wiring Report Centre Office. a 169, B 145, C 161 SP^s 358 = 833.	

Army Form C. 2118.

WAR DIARY
or
INTELLIGENCE SUMMARY.
(Erase heading not required.)

Instructions regarding War Diaries and Intelligence Summaries are contained in F. S. Regs., Part II. and the Staff Manual respectively. Title pages will be prepared in manuscript.

Place	Date	Hour	Summary of Events and Information	Remarks and references to Appendices
	June 15th		Artillery and Infantry wires being completed. A 221, B 146, C 175, SP 355 = 908.	
	June 16th		Artillery wires and Infantry wires being finished – A 222, B 79, C 199, DRLS 371 = 971.	
	June 17th		Artillery wires being finished – Capt Renouf bringing in wires N° 26–30 to Bouzincourt Signal Office – Capt Usad fitting up electric fittings for Bouzincourt – Billets in Bouzincourt allotted. A 216, B 173, C 119, DRLS 372 = 907	
	June 18th		Right Group Artillery wires better, and so left front wire better. Capt Renouf laying wires N° 31–35 from kit box to Fst Dug Out. Dirt wire to Right Group HQrs Completed. A 220, B 204, C 77, SP 404 = 1005.	
	June 19th		Artillery wires having finishing touches put to them – Kilometrage laying some aerial wire to the R.A.M.C. Buried Cable trenches being filled in. Luminous paint letting buried wires. A 207, B 154, C 175, DRLS 476 = 1527	
	June 20th		Artillery wires being finished off. Wires being laid to Offices in BOUZINCOURT from SIGNAL OFFICE. Wireless sets complete being sent out to 96th & 97th Bdes. A 143, B 142, C 148, SP 351 = 784.	
	June 21st		Artillery trenches trails completed. Shelter light wiring in Bouzincourt – taught direct telephone wires to Bouzincourt to C.R.E. C.R.A. (1) G. Staff office (2) Signal office. A 178, B 148, C 161, DRLS 328 = 815	
	June 22nd		Artillery trenches wiring filled in, wires being led down into the caves at Bouzincourt.	

Army Form C. 2118.

WAR DIARY
or
INTELLIGENCE SUMMARY.
(Erase heading not required.)

Instructions regarding War Diaries and Intelligence Summaries are contained in F. S. Regs., Part II. and the Staff Manual respectively. Title pages will be prepared in manuscript.

Place	Date	Hour	Summary of Events and Information	Remarks and references to Appendices
	June 22nd		from the Signal Office. Roads B.1148, C.181, D.R.L.S. 437 = 982	
	June 23rd		14th Bde got back to the WARLOY - 96th and 97th Brigades moved into Bouzincourt. Test dug out exchange station sent up at 4.0 pm - Line from RDQ taken through to 162nd Bde Headquarters. The Right Gp/s Artillery line brought back to T.O.O. A 216, B.1148, C.181 D.R.L.S. 437 = 982	
	June 24th		A 261, B 154, C 216, 2nd SP 438 unregistered 75 = 1194	
	June 25th		Artillery lines being tested and finally put straight under Captain Clery. A 277, B 122, C 235, SP5 trunk and iro unregistered = 1178	
	June 26th		Baron Festies sent out to Brigades. Backing up preparatory to moving. McCamylage his G.O.C's line from MEULTE to BOUZINCOURT Test dug out. A 319, B 138, C 281, SP5 395 and 65 unregistered = 1198.	
	June 27th		Brigades moved up to their battle stations - Division "G" moved to BOUZINCOURT and Corps moved to SENLIS. G few lines giving trouble into evening. i.e. 14th Bde scrounger faults due to 14th Bde not putting on their earth. 10th Corps direct phones to "G" Staff. look on the Test Dug Out exchange very heavy. L/Cpl Rainford and McCamylage on duty on the Signal Office. L/ Kent in charge of the visual. Lines running to Left Gp/s O.P's cut meanded after four hours - lines in Pendel Hill OP's cut	

T2134. Wt. W708—776. 500000. 4/15. Sir J. C. & S.

Army Form C. 2118.

WAR DIARY
~~INTELLIGENCE~~ SUMMARY.
(Erase heading not required.)

Instructions regarding War Diaries and Intelligence Summaries are contained in F. S. Regs., Part II. and the Staff Manual respectively. Title pages will be prepared in manuscript.

Place	Date	Hour	Summary of Events and Information	Remarks and references to Appendices
	June 27"		Traded, Corporal Few sent up to PENDEL HILL STREET to remain there and look after lines.	
	June 28"		A 235, B 67, C 187, SOS Rejections 313, investigation 150 = 973. 9th Phone faulty — not able to ring. Shows a full earth. Sgt. Tolin sent out to Adjutant's post MESNIL with a ringing telephone. 9th Bde moved back to BOUZINCOURT in the evening, lent them a telephone pair and am sending them urgent messages to AUTHUILLE VALLEY for them until somewhere. 14th Bde moved back into SERLIS. Traffic being disposed of to them through X Corps Report Centre. 96th Bde remaining at the BLUFF. New line laid to CRA. so that he has his own exchange and one to H.A.G. line a bit weak at night.	
	June 29"		All lines reported good except lateral to 8th Divn. Divn who ought to do their own maintenance, however being that the Southern and northern end maintains to the northern businessmen out making wet joints onto buried lines. Trouble due exchange in SERLIS being handed over to 1st C.Q.M.S. for cleaning.	
	June 30"		Lines to left Bde and left Artillery Group broken by shell fire. All other lines good — Lines to left Bde working again 8.0 P.M. — Vibrators working through to left Bde all the time.	

C. Worsley Capt.
O.C. Signals 32nd Divn.

32nd Divisional Engineers

32nd DIVISIONAL SIGNAL COMPANY R. E.

JULY 1916.

Army Form C. 2118.

32 July
Div Signal
Vol 8

WAR DIARY
or
INTELLIGENCE SUMMARY.
(Erase heading not required.)

CONFIDENTIAL

War Diary
of
32nd Divl Signal Coy R.E.

From 1st July 1916 to 31st July 1916

Army Form C. 2118.

WAR DIARY ~~of~~ INTELLIGENCE SUMMARY.
(Erase heading not required.)

Instructions regarding War Diaries and Intelligence Summaries are contained in F. S. Regs., Part II. and the Staff Manual respectively. Title pages will be prepared in manuscript.

Reference MAP FRANCE EDITION I. Sheet 57 D

Place	Date	Hour	Summary of Events and Information	Remarks and references to Appendices
	July 1st		The lines laid for the offensive were as follows. (a) From the Corps — a telephone pair onto the 32nd Divisional Exchange in the "Test Dug out" and a Sounder earth return line were both brought to depth. A telephone pair laid by the Corps which were taken straight into the "G" Staff Office and rung onto the Corps exchange. A pair from the Corps which were taken straight into the C.R.A's Office and which rung onto the Corps exchange. (b) A pair to the 36th Division report centre at Q.32.a.0/1 which was on the 32nd Division exchange in the "Test dug out" which was situated at W.5.a.4/4@ to the Left Brigade which had its head quarters in the "BLUFF" at Q.36.c.6/7. The following lines were laid — a telephone line for the use of the Left Group Artillery which was on the Exchange board in the "Test Dug Out", a telephone line for the use of the Left Infantry Brigade, onto the Exchange board at the "Test dug out", a Sounder line for the Left Infantry Pole which was stopped level with test dug out and cause into the 32nd Division Signal Office in BOUZINCOURT. These lines were buried 4' deep, where they crossed over the MARSH the working party were 1st Anzac's could only dig 2' deep owing to the nature of the ground, in order to strengthen this portion of the line which was about 500 yds long time is for lack of sandbags were utilised to make a traverse to track. Lines to the Right Brigade consisted of a telephone line to the Right Group Artillery onto the Exchange board in the Test Dug Out, a telephone line to the Right Infantry Brigade	

WAR DIARY or INTELLIGENCE SUMMARY.

(Erase heading not required.)

Army Form C. 2118.

Place	Date	Hour	Summary of Events and Information	Remarks and references to Appendices
	July 1st		onto the 32nd Divisional Exchange, and a sounder line which was strapped through into "Test Dug Out" to the 32nd Signal Office. The Reserve Infantry Brigade who were holding outs at W12.a b/8 and next door to the Right Infantry Brigade, has a telephone line onto the Divisional Exchange board and a sounder line which was strapped through into "Test Dug Out" and came into the 32nd Division Officer. The 41st Siege Battery has a line onto its Exchange board, as they came under the 32nd Division, R.A. The latter unit [1 ??] 8th Division who were on our right at W.27.c.2/8 was lead into its Exchange boards. The local Officers in Bouzincourt has lines as follows (1) G. Staff Officer, a telephone pair onto Divisional exchange — a telephone pair straight through onto the X Corps Exchange. (2) C.R.A. a telephone pair to the Heavy Artillery Groups exchange in Bouzincourt. Two telephone pairs onto the divisional exchange. A telephone pair to the X Corps Exchange. An air line to the Waggon Lines in Senlis. (3) C.R.E. a telephone pair to the Divisional Exchange (4) Signal Officer and Signal Master a telephone pair onto the Divisional Exchange. A complete set of air lines was [?] Bouzincourt to the "CAB RANK" at W10.c.5/5 where the Motor Ambulances were parked. Canvas lines from the "CAB RANK" to the Advanced dressing Station at BLACK HORSEBRIDGE, and an air line from the "CAB RANK" to the Advanced dressing	

WAR DIARY or INTELLIGENCE SUMMARY

Army Form C. 2118.

Place	Date	Hour	Summary of Events and Information	Remarks and references to Appendices
			Station at CONEY STREET near "CRUCIFY CORNER". This line was being continuously cut but an immense amount of duty at the "CAPS RANK" in order to maintain these lines. The Brickwork Visual Station was situated at W15b 4/2 when a dug out had been made. Another station was placed with them at W9 c 1/1 from which position a good view of the "FERME DE MOUQUET" could be obtained. One Officer, three N.C.O's and 10 men were on duty day & night throughout its operations. Other means of communication were as follows (3) Wireless - The two brigades in the line each had a Trench Wireless set with them fixed up in ready improvised — The Reserve Brigade had a Trench Wireless set up & working — this at Intervals to the 39th Division — The Corps "Power" set was situated at Q 33 c 5/1. (3) Visual each Battalion and each Brigade Headquarters was provided with a French portable Signalling lamp, in order to signal either to the Ground Divisional Signal Station or the Aerodrome. (3) CONTACT AEROPLANE — Each Battalion had a Ground Sheet, and a Marman flare and flares and magnesium candles, for making signals to the contact aeroplane. Each Brigade Headquarters had a ground sheet and a panneaux. (4) Pigeons — The two Brigades in the line had six pigeons each, and the Reserve Brigade a store basket of eight pigeons. (5) Despatch Riders. Relay system was arranged as follows. The Right and Reserve Brigades kept runners and their D.R.'s at W11 c 3/0 — When Relief wished to send a despatch to its	

T2134. Wt. W708—776. 500000. 4/15. Sir J.C. & S.

Army Form C. 2118.

WAR DIARY
~~of~~ INTELLIGENCE SUMMARY
(Erase heading not required.)

Instructions regarding War Diaries and Intelligence Summaries are contained in F.S. Regs, Part II. and the Staff Manual respectively. Title pages will be prepared in manuscript.

Place	Date	Hour	Summary of Events and Information	Remarks and references to Appendices
July 1st			Division. They sent runners to their O.P. which was a culvert underneath the railway, and from there the Brigade O.R. brought the message to Divisional Headquarters. When a message was sent to the Right Reserve Brigade from the Division a DR was despatched (g W11 c 3/0 and the despatch was taken on by Runner.	
			The Relay Post for the Left Brigade was in a Culvert under the main Railway at Q 35 d 3/2 and the same procedure of relay posts was adopted here as at the right + Reserve Bde.	
			Following is the Diary of the Headquarters Office:-	
	1.4.16	4.0 AM	L⁺ Kent repaired telephone line between the Visual Station and Report Centre faulty – Linesmen Steals + Hopkins. Wires sent out and line repaired.	
		4.0 AM	All telephone and Morse lines tested + found correct, except the lateral line to the 8th Division. Cpl Rivers and a Linesman sent out on this line, and an SG sent to 8th Division to send out their Linesman.	
		4.30 AM	Zero time to the Infantry attack. All lines correct except 8th Division lateral	
		2.20 PM	Line to the Adjutant's post of Left Grp. R.F.A. broken. Linesmen sent out. All other lines working	
		4.30 PM	Line to 8th Division working all lines except "Adjutants post" correct	
		5.20 PM	Adjutant's Post repaired all lines now correct.	
		5.40 PM	Lines to the Left Brigade + Left Front Artillery broken by Salt fire – manage a telephone communication	

Army Form C. 2118.

WAR DIARY
of
INTELLIGENCE SUMMARY.
(Erase heading not required.)

Place	Date	Hour	Summary of Events and Information	Remarks and references to Appendices
	July 1st		Through the lateral lines of the 97th & Right Brigade, Divisional lines sent out to show to "BUFF" lines, and the Divisional lines party sent out from 9th Bde. Headquarters to assist in mending its lines.	
	1/7/16	7.10 PM	Lines to the BUFF working again broken in two places by shell fire.	
	"	7.34 PM	All lines working	
	"	8.15 PM	All lines working	
		10.25 PM	Sounder hurt to the Left Bde broken	
		10.30 PM	Telephone lines to the Left Field Artillery and Left Infantry Bde broken. Also lateral line from Right to Left Bdes. Lines sent out & communication maintained by relay post.	
		10.30 PM		
	July 2nd	12.35 AM	Vibrator placed on K.O. 14 - worked splendidly forth.	
		12.45 AM	All lines to the Left Bde mended - & Vibrator kept on K.O. 14 in case of accidents.	
		7.0 AM	All circuits tested and reported Good.	
		7.10 AM	Sounder replaces Vibrator on K.O. 14 to Left Infantry Brigade.	
		9.20 AM	D.15. Division Signals sent an "S.G." saying they had relieved the 4th Division	
		1.0 PM	All lines correct.	
		8.30 PM	Line laid to the 15th Brigade in MARTINSART WOOD, and communication by Sounder established.	

Army Form C. 2118.

WAR DIARY
INTELLIGENCE SUMMARY.
(Erase heading not required.)

Place	Date	Hour	Summary of Events and Information	Remarks and references to Appendices
	July 2nd	1.10 PM	D³ Telephone replaces Sounder on the line to the 75th Brigade – as Signals are moving up to relieve 142nd Brigade into BLUFF.	
		9.22 PM	Latest line to 8th Division reported "dis". Linemen sent out.	
		11.20 PM	All lines correct except 8th Division latryal.	
	July 3rd	3.30 AM	Linesmen to the Left Brigade and Left Group Artillery "dis". Linemen sent out. Vibrators put on KO in the Boisunal Office and totally shot across from 142nd Brigade to the 75th Brigade to put an on new vibrator.	
		4.20 AM	The Right Brigade Signal Officer 'phoned and was taken over by to 142nd Brigade – this 92nd Punjabi. redirecting to BOUZINCOURT.	
		4.55 AM	Vibrator working both the Left Brigade. Telephone lines still broken.	
		5.5 AM	line to Captain's post at MESNIL reported correct – This line has been forward [?] with an intermittent dis.	
		7.0 AM	Exchange report all lines correct except Telephone line to Left Front Artillery and Left Brigade – Divisional Linesmen are out on the lines – which are reported as being badly smashed by shellfire.	

T/134. Wt. W708-776. 500000. 4/15. Sir J.C. & 9.

Army Form C. 2118.

WAR DIARY
or
INTELLIGENCE SUMMARY.
(Erase heading not required.)

Instructions regarding War Diaries and Intelligence Summaries are contained in F. S. Regs., Part II. and the Staff Manual respectively. Title pages will be prepared in manuscript.

Place	Date	Hour	Summary of Events and Information	Remarks and references to Appendices
July 3rd		8.0 AM	Failed to get the 75" Bde onto Vibrator, messages being disposed of by DR to the Relay Post.	
		11.00 AM	Attempts made to dispose of messages over the Vibrator, but not satisfactory. Two operators and a vibrator sent down to report to Lt Armytage at East Lancashire dump, also his visual signallers and a French lamp. Orders being that the vibrator should be tried until NOW in a tub box W of AUTHEUILLE. MARSH and his messenger transmitted by lamp. Lt Armytage and his men had been manning the lines across the Marsh, and were putting up an line and cutting out the track running through the marsh which was being continually hit by shells.	
		10.30 AM	Message sent to OC Signals 75" Bde to use his vibrator set and his pigeons. Message to 75" Bde being sent by west to MARTINSART WOOD and from there by orderly to the BLUFF being 75" Bde Leaving left a [relay?] station at MARTINSART WOOD.	
		11.30 AM	Vibrator down to 75" Bde working again. Telephone line still "dis".	
		1.15 PM	All lines correct.	
		5.0 PM	Telephone line to left Group Artillery "dis". Linesmen sent out.	
		5.30 PM	Telephone line to Left Group Artillery working again.	

WAR DIARY or INTELLIGENCE SUMMARY.

Army Form C. 2118.

Place	Date	Hour	Summary of Events and Information	Remarks and references to Appendices
	July 4th	8.0 AM	Instruments staffed by 25th Division operators – no faults on circuits – work disposed of without delay.	
		10.0 AM	D.R.L.S. Officer and Sounder three to 2nd Corps observers at CONTAY. BOUZINCOURT Division all offices hands over to the 25th Division – Captain Cleary Cpl Williams and L/Cpl Rewart remained behind to assist the 25th Division. Company moved to CONTAY.	
			The 14th Brigade are at SENLIS, 96th & 97th Brigades WARLOY. DR's for orderly room was as all instruments and the Strongly overhauled. DR's leave for hunts at Sunny clock have platting at 7.0 AM and about 9.0 P.M. Between the hours of 9.0 P.M. and 7.0 AM only B.D.R will be dealt with. A 155 B to C 150 SP 1344 = 4.53	
	July 5th		Captain Cleary returned from BOUZINCOURT. Sound troop brought in from SENLIS. 14th Brigade moved to 96th Brigade to HERMILLIERS and VARENNES. 97th remains in WARLOY.	
	July 6th		Capt Cleary and Lt Rawsford taking the company in handling of arms and company drill. 2d Armytage taking for exercise party – L/Kent and C.Q.M.S fitting up cable cart and light Spring Waite Wilson. The instrument repairs mechanics all instruments of the Company. Two swinging telephones handed over to L/ Sappers 25th Signal Coy. Surplus cable sent to W 31st 22 Escadrons at WARLOY.	

WAR DIARY or INTELLIGENCE SUMMARY

Army Form C. 2118.

Place	Date	Hour	Summary of Events and Information	Remarks and references to Appendices
July 7th			Capt Cleary - Sgt Beckett Capt Sulford Capt Williams taking the class of signallers from 1st & 11th Bde. L'Armytage exercise horses - L'Kent filling up cable wagons - Company parade under O.C. Bde. Hqs moved to the old Hq 4th Divn Headquarters location SENLIS aid HENENCOURT Mill at 7.0 p.m.	
July 8th			14th Bde in BOUZINCOURT - 96th Bde in VARENNES - 97th Bde in SENLIS. Capt Cleary sent to BOUZINCOURT with line drummer to look after 32nd Divn R.A. wires. L'Armytage taking the signal class from the 14th Bde. L'Kent filling up cable waggons. L'Forester in charge of the office. 32nd Divn ordered to relieve the 12th Divn - 14th Brigade relieves 21st Bde and 97th Bde relieves 36 Bde. Telephone pair and superimpose on K133 NORTH route to QUARRIE - Telephone pair to QUARRIE on K 133 SOUTH cable bridged over to C.G.U.2 A.P.O. to 25th Divn Signal Office. Telephone pair to C.R.A. 12 15 Divn who is covering our front. Telephone pair and sounder line to Capt L'Ransford sent down to QUARRIE to take over advance office - 12th Divn Signals upon forward lines to Bdes from Quarry not good. L'Armytage sent down to help L'Ransford. Line working correctly at 9.45 A.M.	
July 9th			Sp. Byyss sent on K 133 North Route for Rictorbon on K 133 South Route and also Steven Route. 14th Bde report they have established telephone communication to their two units in OVILLERS - also Battery hqrs	

T.2134. Wt. W708—776. 500000. 4/15. Sir J. C. & S.

WAR DIARY
INTELLIGENCE SUMMARY.
(Erase heading not required.)

Army Form C. 2118.

Place	Date	Hour	Summary of Events and Information	Remarks and references to Appendices
	July 9th		Established visual from OVILLERS breaking out in station ground line — Visual station at QUARRY established to 14th + 97th Bdes with a telephone line into Quarry — Lines working satisfactorily. A 210 B 50 C 300 DRLS 126 = 606	
	July 10th		Worked satisfactorily with "Paunch" set at 11-30 am by 11th Bde from Post DONNET. Visual established for Brigades from the "Paunch" "S.D." Cable detachment below Café into MEULES from the Quarries on their other line trained to bed — Sent out two 4/d of ladder D³ to OVILLERS to pushing troops into OVILLERS. A 222 B 16 C 180 DRLS 167 = 585	
	July 11th		Sent out 1 mile of ground line HETA³ Brigade to keep into OVILLERS — two telephones also sent to 11th Brigade. A pole cable line from the Quarry Office to "Sea View" - 96th Brigade which 11th Brigade will also be having two Cables to BOUZINCOURT as we move (bad to-morrow). A 219 B 31 C 184 DRLS 187 = 601	
	July 12th		Division moved to BOUZINCOURT at 9:45 A.M. Office closed at last hour in SENLIS and opened in BOUZINCOURT. All lines correct. (a) A Sounder line to the C of S (b) A Telephone from G to its C of S (c) A Telephone from G to CRA 12th Division (d) A telephone from G to its QUARRY exchange (e) A Telephone from G to its QUARRY exchange (f) A telephone from Q to its QUARRY exchange. Sent up one mile D³ to Fresleg (97th Bde) — Sent two more lineman to CRA 32nd Division above the	

WAR DIARY
or
INTELLIGENCE SUMMARY.
(Erase heading not required.)

Army Form C. 2118.

Place	Date	Hour	Summary of Events and Information	Remarks and references to Appendices
	July 12th		moving board – All lines working at BTR QUARRY office.	
	July 13th		Cleaning up wires from the village of BOUZINCOURT six drums picked up of different kinds of wire. Test dug out taken over by Corps. D.D.T.S. reserve army arrived 2.30 P.M. – was taken round office – QUARRY OFFICE – RIGHT BRIGADE HEADQUARTERS. Drums' exercise under L/Sergt. Visual class under Sergeant Foster. A 250 B 27 C 179 SRS 252 = 686 A 199. B 33. C 135 DRLS 200 = 567	
	July 14th		One detachment of S.O. moving Trench artillery line – The other attached with O.C. S.D. Section picking up arriers lines at the QUARRY OFFICE. L/Rent taking the driving parties. Sgt. Holt's party filling up cable waggon drums. Cpl Sharpe and party taking up cable at BOUZINCOURT. Sgt. Yates and L/Cpl Jordan instructing visual signallers (in Code)	
	July 15th		Advance party of 48th Signals arrived – 48th Division relieves 32nd Division tomorrow – S.D. cave section returns to X Corps. R.P. section arrived from 3rd Corps. L/Ransford sent to BENVAL to arrange communications.	
	July 16th		Hands over Signals to 48th Division at 10.30 AM. 32nd Division moved to BENVAL – Three lieutenants left at the QUARRY OFFICE to help 48th Divn Signals – with orders to report to Capt CLERY when they were no longer required, who is remaining with the 32nd Brit Artillery at BOUZINCOURT. 48th Divn move to	

WAR DIARY or INTELLIGENCE SUMMARY.

(Erase heading not required.)

Army Form C. 2118.

Place	Date	Hour	Summary of Events and Information	Remarks and references to Appendices
	July 16th		BEAUVAL – 97th Brigade to AMPLIER – 14th Brigade at SENLIS. Communications to Brigades and units of the division by D.R. and cyclist orderly. A telephone from G. Staff and a sounder to 3rd Army through which communication to all divisions and Corps was obtained.	
	July 18th		Division Hqrs moved to DOULLENS. 96th Brigade to NEUVILLETTE, 97th Brigade to SUS-ST-LEGER, 14th Brigade to HALLOY. Communication to 3rd Army by sounder, and telephone from G. Office to DOULLENS Exchange. D.R.L.S. post every two hours to Brigades and units of the division.	
	July 18th		Division Hqrs and Brigades remain the same as 17th.	
	July 19th		Division Hqrs moved to FLERS. Telephone direct to 3rd Army superintendent on the telephone bus to Sounder to 3rd Army. D.R.L.S. post every two hours to Brigades and units of Brigades. 96th Bde BLANGERMONT 97th Bde BONNEVILLE 14th Bde MONCHEAUX	
	July 20th		Division Hqrs moved to BRYAS. Telephone and superimposed Sounder to 1st Army arranged super centre. D.R.L.S. post every two hours to Brigades and units of 32nd Division 14th Bde MONCHY BRETON 96th Bde HUCHIN 97th Bde TANGRY.	
	July 21st		Division Hqrs moves to Chateau Philomel. Telephone line from to Lillers exchange. Telephone pair and superimposed Sounder to 1st Corps. Telephone pair and superimposed Sounder to	

WAR DIARY or INTELLIGENCE SUMMARY.

Army Form C. 2118.

Place	Date	Hour	Summary of Events and Information	Remarks and references to Appendices
	July 21st		96th Brigade at CAUCHY-EN- FONTAIN-LEZ-HERMANS. Telephone pair and subt circuit sounder to 97th Brigade at ALLOUAGNE. Subt circuit sounder to 145th Brigade who established an office at RAIMBERT leaving their Hqrs at CAUCHEY-LA-TOURS. A pair to G Office and also to Q Office.	
	July 22nd		Lines on two line exchange. (1) 1st Corps (2) KILLERS Exchange (3) KILLERS EXCHANGE (4) G Staff (5) 97th Brigade (6) 96th Brigade (7) Q Staff (8) 145 Brigade (9) Signal Office (Company) (10) Signal Master. Lt Ransford went out at 7.0 AM to extend 1/2 telephone pair PRR 1.2 from RAIMBERT Hqts 145th Bde Hqrs at CAUCHEY-LA-TOURS but to 145th Rde Hqrs but RAIMBERT midday so to extension had to be held up. Lt Armytage left at 7.0 AM with a detachment and extended the telephone pair PRR 5.6 from AMETTES to 96th Brigade Headquarters at FONTAIN-LEZ-HERMANS. Wireless office working for receiving press daily. — Electric light supply working satisfactorily. Q have been supplied to the CRA at ECQUEDECQUES his also to the Divisional School at TERFAY. Pump engine being put together by Corpl Grout for pumping water into PRESMEZ CHATEAU. A 107, B 13, C 88 Registered 39 - Unregistered 144 = 310	

WAR DIARY
or
INTELLIGENCE SUMMARY.
(Erase heading not required.)

Army Form C. 2118.

Place	Date	Hour	Summary of Events and Information	Remarks and references to Appendices
	July 23rd		Lt Rowsford takes command of A section. Lt Armytage takes command of B section. Signal class under Sgt Foster. Capt Williams, Capt Forder.	
	July 25th		Divine service after battle sent into HQ lawn from Coy Office. Lt Signal Officer visits up at 7:30 p.m. Cars use from work shops. Capt Cleary went into BETHUNE to arrange for signals for the move. Inspected the signal class at flag drill. A 168 B 17 C 125 Sprs R 87 UR 248 = 545	
	July 26th		Brit HQ moves to BETHUNE at noon. 97th Bde to BETHUNE. 96th Bde to MARLES. 14th Bde to RUITZ. Brit Engineers at ALLOUAGNE – C.R.A. ECQUEDECQUES – Divl School still remaining at FERFAY. D.R.L.S. posts from BETHUNE OFFICE to 1st Corps and Brigades at 8:15 A.M. 11:0 A.M. 2:30 P.M. 6:30 P.M. 9:0 P.M. – Sounder lines to 1st Corps, 96th & 14th Bdes – lines on the exchange (1) Signals Mess (2) G Office (3) Workshops (4) 96th & 14th Bdes (5) Advance Exchange – through which Brit C.R.E. and Divisional School can be obtained. (6) "Q" Office (7) O.C. Signals (8) A.D.M.S (9) 2nd Divn (10) 251 Coy RE (11) 3rd Divn (12) 97th Bde Brigade (14) D.A.D.O.S. A 170 B 8 C 93 Spr R 30 UR 158 = 373	
	July 27th		Nothing to report. A 142 B 10 C 115 Spr R 79 UR 175 = 521 - visited 1st Corps Signals	
	July 28th		Visited 16th Divn & 30th Divn Signals and 1st Army Signals. A 216 B 13 C 91 Spr R. 47 UR 210 = 581	
	July 29th		C.R.A. moved to MARLES from ECQUEDECQUES. 96th Bde moves to RUITZ. 14th Bde moved to BETHUNE.	

Army Form C. 2118.

WAR DIARY
or
INTELLIGENCE SUMMARY.
(Erase heading not required.)

Instructions regarding War Diaries and Intelligence Summaries are contained in F. S. Regs, Part II. and the Staff Manual respectively. Title pages will be prepared in manuscript.

Place	Date	Hour	Summary of Events and Information	Remarks and references to Appendices
	July 29th		Laid telephone pair from exchange to 1st/ Bde Hrs at RUE VICTOR HUGO. A Sec B. 1b C.111 SP = R.46 UR 2.95 - 6.65	
	July 30th		Nothing to report. A line B.12, C St SPRING UR 2.69 - 5.50	
	July 31st		Nothing to report. Section training under Section officers commenced.	

C. H. Walsh Capt.
O.C. Signals 2nd Division

T.134. Wt. W708—776. 500000. 4/15. Sir J. C. & S.

For operation Orders.

The methods of communication for the offensive are as follows.

(a) Telephone and Telegraph
(b) Visual (ground)
(c) Contact Aeroplane
(d) Wireless
(e) Despatch Riders and Messengers
(f) Runners
(g) Pigeons
(h) Visual (Balloon)

(a) (Sketch A) lines are laid as follows. "Buried" (These lines are in touch with either the DIVISIONAL REPORT CENTRE on the MEULES or BOUZINCOURT)

  (i) A telephone line to the 8th Division on our right
  (ii) A telephone line to the Divisional Siege battery in ALBERT.
  (iii) A vibrator line and a telephone line to the RESERVE BDE in dug outs at W 12 a 7.5
  (iv) A telephone line to the Right Infantry Brigade and a vibrator line to the Right Infantry Brigade at W 12 a 7.5
  (v) A telephone line to the Right Group Headquarters R.F.A who are with the Right Infantry Brigade.
  (VI) A telephone line and a vibrator line to the

Left Infantry Brigade at Q 36 C 7.7.

(VII) A telephone line to Left Group headquarters R.F.A. who are with the Left Infantry Brigade

(VIII) A telephone line to the 36th Division on the left.

(IX) A sounder line and two telephone lines to the 8 Corps at SENLIS

(X) A telephone line to the Heavy Artillery Group at Bouzincourt.

A system of Buried lines has been (Is being) laid from R.F.A Group headquarters to their Batteries and from batteries to OPs (sketch B)

Sketch C are the lines forward from brigade headquarters

(a) From the left Brigade headquarters No 1 is a lateral line to the Right Bde of the 36th Divn.

No 2 is a line running through JOHNSON POST up to the Russian Sap Thiepval point North. For use of Infantry

No 3 is a line running through JOHNSON POST up to the Russian Sap Thiepval point North for use of Artillery

No 4 is a line running to JOHNSON POST for use of the Heavy Trench Mortar.

No 5 runs through JOHNSON POST to the Russian Sap Thiepval Point South for Infantry use.

No 6. runs through JOHNSON POST to the Russian Sap Thiepval POINT SOUTH for Artillery use.

No 7 runs through CAMPBELL POST to Russian Sap

at TYNDRUM STREET for Infantry use.
No 8 runs to Russian Sap SANDA STREET. for Artillery use.
Nos 9, 10 are lateral lines between the Right and Left Brigades.

(b) From the Right Brigade headquarters.
  No XI runs to Russian Sap at Tyndrum Street. (Inf.)
  No XII runs to Russian Sap SANDA STREET for Artillery use
  No XIII runs to Russian Sap SANDA STREET for Infantry use.
  No XIV & XV Run to Russian Sap SANDA STREET for Artillery use from battery positions 17 and 18.
  No XVI Runs to the top of the NEW ROAD for Infantry.

The purpose of these wires is that directly after the first rush is made - three men each having a ½ mile drum of cable (who should be told off beforehand and instructed what to do) shall each join their cable onto one of these lines and take it into the enemy's front line (see dotted lines on sketch C). Infantry looking after their wires and artillery after theirs.

As the brigades move forward they will use these lines for communication back to division. In addition to this a party of 1 Corpl and four sappers will be attached to each brigade with a barrow and 2 mile drum of D⁵ cable to help in keeping touch with the division.

Directly Brigades HQrs leave their dug outs and go forward a vibrator is all that can be used. The sounder and the telephone will be left behind and handed over to the incoming Brigade.

(b) Ground Visual

A divisional "reading" station is established at W 15 b 6.3 call M.L.E. Landmark from the front - Between the two Southern trees on MEULES RIDGE. This station will be connected to the Report Centre by wire. Messages will be sent DD-OO three times and no acknowledgment will be sent from the reading station. There is also a reading station at Q 22 d 8.8 call BRK (36th Division) Landmark from the front - Single tree on MESNIL RIDGE. There is a third station at Q 29 c 2.4. call "AVU" Landmark MESNIL CHATEAU. (49th Division). These points should be pointed out to signallers of assaulting Infantry who should know how to recognise the direction of the reading stations from the front.

Messages must be limited to those of absolute necessity and be kept as short as possible. Lengthy and unnecessary messages hinder the transmission of other messages, which may be of vital importance.

(c). Contact Aeroplane

The contact aeroplane on 10th Corps front is a "BE 2 C" and will have a broad black band under the right hand bottom plane.

The following means of communication are to be used. Flares, and mirrors by advanced Infantry denoting "we have reached this point" - Three flares must be fired in a row at 3 or 4 paces interval. From Brigade and battalion headquarters, Panneaus, and ground sheets. A lamp should only be used in case of necessity.

The following code is to be used. The unit call. followed by "Y" means "Short of grenades"
"O" - "Barrage"
"H" - Lengthen Range
"X" - held up by Machine Guns
Z - held up by wire.

(d). Wireless
The Right and Left Bdes will have a wireless set (Trench) each - packed up and ready to go forward. the operator will be provided by the division. for each instrument four porters must be provided by Brigades for each instrument.
The 14th Brigade will have a wireless set working with them before they advance, Provided with its personnel by the 49th Divn. This set will not go forward. The "Parent" set will be working near MARTINSART and will be in telephone communication with the Corps.
Messages will be in Code, unless distinctly marked "in clear" and signed by the Staff Officer originating them.

(c) Despatch Riders & Messengers.

The following arrangements will be made for Despatch Riders connecting with messengers from Division to Bde and vice versa.

For the 97th and 114th and Right Group R.F.A. Bdes & Brigade Despatch Riders and Runners will be placed with railway culvert at W.17.a.2.9.

When a despatch is sent by Brigade to Divisional it will be sent by messenger to the culvert and taken on by Brigade D.R.

When sent by Division to Brigade the Divisional D.R. will proceed as far as the culvert and hand his despatch over to a messenger.

For the 96th Brigade and left Group R.F.A.

Brigade Despatch Riders and messengers will be in MacMahons Post signal dug out Q.35.d.5.9. Despatch from Bde to Division will be sent by messenger to McMahons Post and taken on to Division by DR

Despatch from Division to Bde will be taken by Divisional DR to McMahons post and from here to Brigade by messenger.

At least four messengers should be at each relay post.

(4). Runners.

(9). Pigeons

The 98th and 97th Bdes. will previous to the assault be supplied with 6 birds each, and the 166 Bde will have a stock basket of 8 birds.

Birds can be kept in stock baskets for 4 or 5 days - they should not be kept in the dark. Bdes in the line will fill up from the 166th Brigade in the first case.

Food must be carried forward for the birds - The number of pigeons is very limited and should only be used when all other means of communication have failed and then only for great urgency.

Birds should not be kept in the small baskets for more than 48 hours.

Those with Brigades in the line should be sent well forward and not kept with Brigade HQ. Pigeons cannot fly at night and must therefore be released in time to reach HQ before dark.

(h) Balloon Signalling.

The Sentis Balloon will be up night and day (weather permitting). This Balloon will take messages from Brigade Headquarters by lamp or helio - It will fly a red & white streamer below the basket when it is ready to take messages - And at night will flash a lamp every now and then to give direction. The procedure will be the

same as signalling to Aeroplanes. The Balloon will answer by lamp as follows.
RD = message understood
I.M.I = Repeat

precedes message case by Brigade or Battalion code letter.

Code Calls

The annexed list of code calls issued under G 91/5/7 will be used on all occasions during operations.

The code call will be used as a station call and also as a code name to denote a unit in the "address to" "text" or "address from" of a message.

The writer of any message emanating from or going into the forward area, and also of any message to be sent by visual, wireless or pigeon will be responsible for inserting the code name in his message.

Communications during a General Advance.

When troops are on the march few opportunities will occur for communication by telegraph or even visual.
Despatch Riders will be the main means of communication. Cable lines should only be

laid out when the situation is sufficiently definite to justify their use.

A vibrator line from Corps to Divisions and Divisions to Brigades is probably as much as can be expected.

Telephones and exchanges will have to be left behind and dumped with surplus stores.

C H Walsh Capt.
O C Signals 32nd Divn.

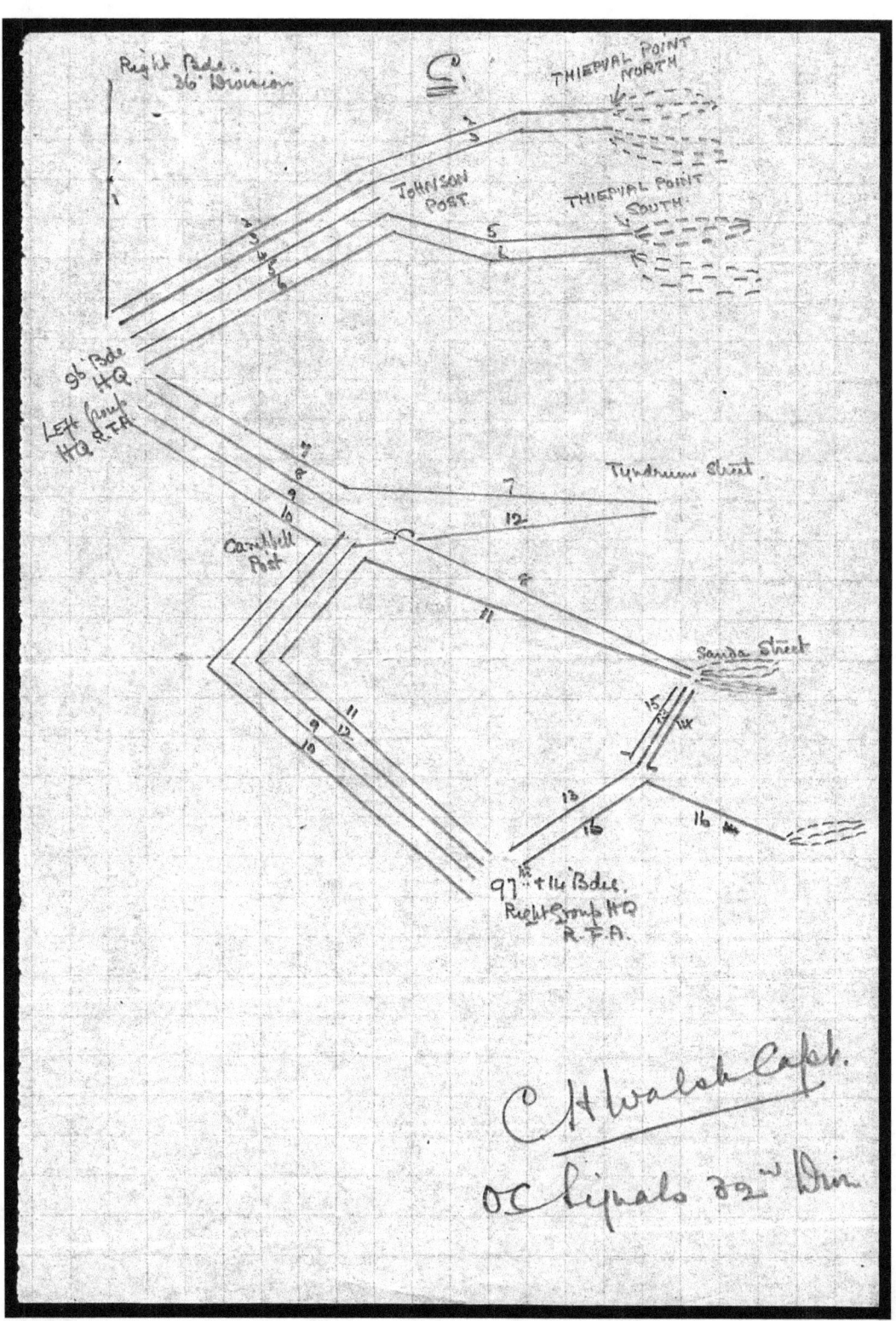

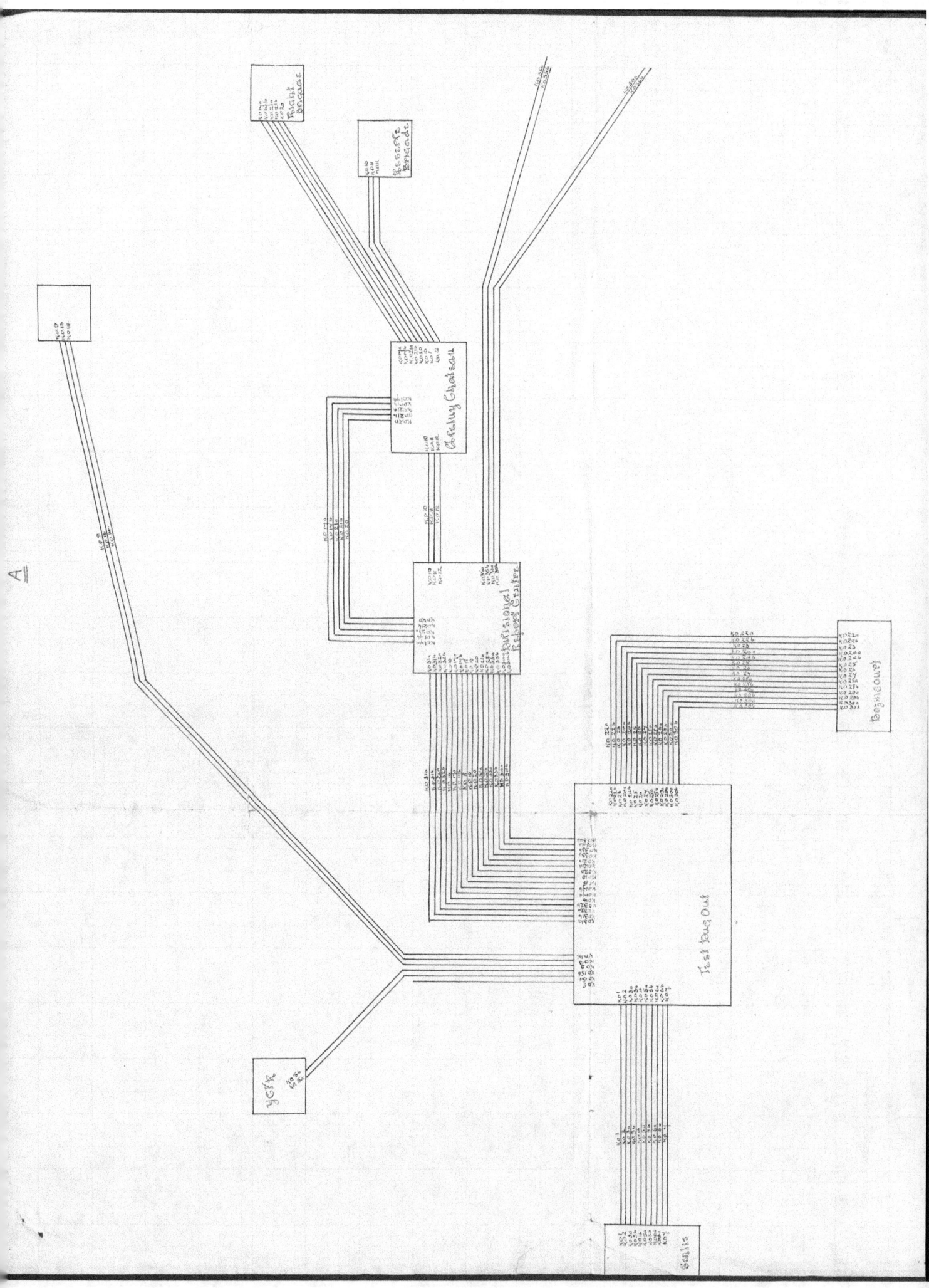

32nd Divisional Engineers

32nd DIVISIONAL SIGNAL COMPANY R. E.

AUGUST 1 9 1 6

Army Form C. 2118.

Vol 9

WAR DIARY
or
INTELLIGENCE SUMMARY.

CONFIDENTIAL
WAR DIARY.
of
32nd Divisional Signal Coy R.E.

from 1st Aug 1916 to 31st August 1916

WAR DIARY
INTELLIGENCE SUMMARY
(Erase heading not required.)

Army Form C. 2118.

Place	Date	Hour	Summary of Events and Information	Remarks and references to Appendices
	August 1st		Morning menu received that we shall be going into the line on Saturday-Sunday 5th/6th. A.D.A.S. arrives with secway - asked for the loan of his groom as am going to take over. A 164 B 3 C 85 SP R. 45 UR 259 = 761.	
	Augt 2nd		Lt McKinley arrived from 6th Divn with despatches - Visited LE QUESNOY and LE PREOL examining lines - Capt Clay + Lt Armytage went out with sergeant to see the ground which took us to the down to-morrow. Asked for officer to replace Lt Kent evacuated other than from A.D.A.S. 1st Corps - Lt Rawsford attached to 32 R.A. as Signal officer. Owing to the L.D. horses & men with a kind of sore throat which is said to be given by the stag standings - Evidently 7th Divn lost a number of animals from this same thing when they were quartered here. All has been stained for tonight and horse lines will be moved to-morrow. A 189 B 6 C 134 SP R 103 UR 251 = 653.	
	Augt 3rd		1. A detachment under Lt Rawsford assisting the R.A. this detachment was worked owing to right front not being able to decide on their Hqrs. 2. A detachment laying YCB I.A.B. to LE PREOL from LE QUESNOY. B section repairing telephone AM 23.46 AM 23.20 from LEQUESNOY to the DUG OUT. Curtis horse with sore throat, moved stable and A section + all driver to 139 RUE DE LILLE where horses where knick standing. Neither of Chatie horses or of trangen. A 174 B 6 C 124 SP R 21 UR 120 = 745	

Army Form C. 2118.

2

WAR DIARY
INTELLIGENCE SUMMARY.
(Erase heading not required.)

Instructions regarding War Diaries and Intelligence Summaries are contained in F. S. Regs., Part II. and the Staff Manual respectively. Title pages will be prepared in manuscript.

Place	Date	Hour	Summary of Events and Information	Remarks and references to Appendices
	Aug: 4th		2.A detachment building a line from Left Group R.A. Depot to the divisional dump/post. B section building a line from TOURBIERES to BEUVRY. Choke horses recovering. Nothing settled about the right Group R.A. or their work. Cannot proceed. Cpl Williams fixing up the office exchange. Infantry making threading in Firefies. 1.A detachment out with the Gunners laying Cable. A 149. B 10 C 115 SPR 75 UR 277 = 626	
	Aug: 5th		Stopping over all lines and getting lines ready — at 9.0 PM lines were as follows — (a) Saunters lines to (a) 1st Corps (b) 96 Bde (c) 97th Bde (d) and 14th Bde — The 14th Bde lines worked in circuit as the brigade was not strongly battalion. Telephone lines to Signal heads (a) G office (3) 1st Corps (4) 96 Brigade (5) Pathline — Lillers — Dud School supply Column (6) Q office (7) OC Signals (8) ADMS (9) 8 Divn (10) 251 Coy RE (11) 3q Divn (12) — (13) DAC 3q Divn (14) DADOS (15) CRA (Inner office) (16 — (17) CRA (Staff) (18) Left Group R.A. (19) CRA (20) Junction (1.A) Junction (2.A) Right Group R.A. (3A) 97 Bde (4.A) 14th Bde. A 135 B 10 C 139 DRLS R 18 UR 257 = 632	
	Aug: 6th		1.A sent out to repair line AM 3.4 to 6. B section sent out to temporary leave at limits for maintenance purposes. Cpl Williams and Corporal Pattinson off tonight terminal pole outside the office as leading in two lines. A.M. 3.4 Shoes contact 11.30 P.M. A.M. 10 still showing 20 volts difficult. Junk correct. A 197. B 18. C 131. D.R.L.S. R 52. U.R. 373 = 741.	

T/134. Wt. W708—776. 500000. 4/15. Sir J. C. & S.

Army Form C. 2118.

WAR DIARY
INTELLIGENCE SUMMARY.
(Erase heading not required.)

Instructions regarding War Diaries and Intelligence Summaries are contained in F. S. Regs., Part II. and the Staff Manual respectively. Title pages will be prepared in manuscript.

Place	Date	Hour	Summary of Events and Information	Remarks and references to Appendices
	Aug 7th		Visited 91st Brigade and 16th Brigade Headquarters - Between cables cut. Signal offices moved to new cellar except the orderlies. AM 3rd sitt. quiet from Me. A 183 B 21 C 142 DRLS R 75 UR 283 = 704	
	Aug 8th		2.B detachment reeling up derelict lines in Bethune. 1.A. and 1.B. cleaning up and overhauling their office. 2.A. laying Artillery wires. A 206 B 10 C 135 DRLS R60 UR 248 = 649.	
	Aug 9th		Visited Right & Left Artillery Groups and 1st Battalion Headquarters of the 91st Brigade. 2.B cleaning up derelict wires in Bethune. 1.A laying Artillery lines, lines being straightened into Signal Office. A 196 B 10 C 147 DRLS R 61 UR 220 = 634	
	Aug 10th		Reeling up derelict wires at LE QUESNOY CHATEAU for the divisional wires getting its wires through to new headquarters left Camb. A 176 B 23 C 127 DRLS R 39 UR 247 = 662.	
	Aug 11th		Lines laid to new hqrs of A.D.M.S. and C.R.A. - Moving the billets of the Company to the houses behind the Church. 2.B. repairing AM 2.3.4.B. - Cpl Williams and 1.A. finishing off the labels on wires at LE QUESNOY CHATEAU. 1.B repairing and reeling derelict wires onto drums. A 177 B 31 C 142 DRLS R 59 UR 262 = 673	
	Aug 12th		Moving Billets. A section reeling up wires from the LE QUESNOY CHATEAU. Laying lines to D.A.D.O.S. A.O 14 A.B. C.R.A. desks A.O 15 A.B. Infantry Bde Service A.O 16, CR2 moving him office. A 151 B 22 C 125 DRLS R 49 UR 303 = 650	

T.1134. Wt. W708-776. 500000. 4/15. Sir J. C. & S.

Army Form C. 2118.

INTELLIGENCE SUMMARY.
(Erase heading not required.)

Instructions regarding War Diaries and Intelligence Summaries are contained in F.S. Regs, Part II. and the Staff Manual respectively. Title pages will be prepared in manuscript.

Place	Date	Hour	Summary of Events and Information	Remarks and references to Appendices
	Aug. 13		1 A detachment reeling up derelict wire at LE QUESNOY CHATEAU. 1 B attending CRA create line and laying a pair b/t. Supply Column. 2 B reeling up derelict wires in Bethune. 2 A laying a pair b/t the D.A.C. ANNEZIN. A 123 B 19 C 103 DRLS R 43 UR 203 = 496.	
	Aug. 14"		A section mounted number attached to mounted brigade of. B section to leave to join Remounts of. A section reeling derelict wire out, drums and wet jointing. B section moved to Choquez connecting up to the 2nd Fuse Coy at PREDIN b/tn 1st Brigade H.Qrs. A 162. B 14 C 117 DRLS R 69 UR 299 = 666.	
	Aug. 15"		Connecting up the advanced dressing station Henley Smit to the advanced dressing station CAMBRIN and trying to K. reserve battalion in HARLEY Strat. Laying new emergency line to CRA and G Staff + attempt into the Signal Office from the C.R.R's office. On the whole rather long the work broken. A 125 B 30 C 112 D.R.43 R 40 UR 263 = 573	
	Aug. 16".		1 A detachment packing up Le1 horse bus Side bike line news to dust dug out. 2 A reeling up derelict cable B section rushi station Officers lectures at Each School. Are Signals + communication with division Exchange board moved again into portable duning the night	
	Aug. 17"		Position chosen for the wireless at A 26 b. 6. 8 Receiving Station. A 21 b. 6. 6 for left Sector, A 27 b. 3. 3. Right Sector.	

T/2134. Wt. W708—776. 500000. 4/15. Sir J. C. & S.

Army Form C. 2118.

WAR DIARY
or
INTELLIGENCE SUMMARY.
(Erase heading not required.)

Instructions regarding War Diaries and Intelligence Summaries are contained in F.S. Regs., Part II. and the Staff Manual respectively. Title pages will be prepared in manuscript.

Place	Date	Hour	Summary of Events and Information	Remarks and references to Appendices
	Aug. 17th		Visit from the D.O.A.S. Pigeon loft studied at MAISON ROUGE for the right Brigade. A 138 B.22 C 110 D.R.L.S R.65 UR 271 = 626.	
	Aug. 18th		Visited right sector for buried lines. Clery visited dug outs for the wireless stations. A 124 B 24 C 124 D.R.L.S R 7p UR 226 = 576.	
	Aug. 19th		Staff ride for the defence scheme at 6.0 A.M. Clery lecturing to Brigade R.F.A. on signals. Second party for immediate wireless station in position. Receiving Station A 26 b 6.2 Left sector. A 21 b 6.6 Right Sector A 27 b 3.3. A 122 B 25 C 115 D.R.L.S R.67 UR 285 = 594.	
	Aug. 20th		Nothing to report A 120 B 33 C 110 DRLS R 65 UR 607 = 534.	
	Aug. 21st		B section salvaging cable under Capt Clery's orders - A Section jointing and setting up salvaged cable. Inspection of the signal class - 96th Brigade relieved the 97th Bde in the right sector. A few shells near the station no wires damaged. A 130 B 13 C 116 DRLS R 60 UR 181 = 500	
	Aug 22nd		1 A detachment jointing & setting up derelict cable. 2 A setting up derelict wires for the Right Group R.A. B section setting up derelict wires in the left sector. Vice versa given for the signal class. A 139. B 24 C 102 D.R.L.S. R 110 UR 291 = 656	
	Aug: 23rd		1 A setting up derelict cable for the right group R.A. B section setting up derelict cable under Capt. Clery. 2 A jointing & setting up cable. Vice versa exams of the signal class. A 125 B 41 C 117 DRLS R 65 UR 172 = 578	

T.J.134. Wt. W708-776. 500000. 4/15. Sir J. C. & S.

Instructions regarding War Diaries and Intelligence Summaries are contained in F. S. Regs., Part II. and the Staff Manual respectively. Title pages will be prepared in manuscript.

INTELLIGENCE—SUMMARY.
(Erase heading not required.)

Place	Date	Hour	Summary of Events and Information	Remarks and references to Appendices
	Aug 24"		Square gallows erected over Divisional dug out - Temporary line to left Group R.A. less artillery lines moved. Attaching derelict cable with CAMBRIN area. A 158 B 41 C 131 DRLS 77 R UR 153 = 530	
	Aug 25"		Rake line had only spare gallows and divisional lines A0 20 a.b A0 36 a.b. than to left Group R.A. partly erected. Lines in BETHUNE being placed on insulated brackets. Derelict cable being used up. A 150. B. 38 C 141 DRLS R 71 UR 216 = 616.	
	Aug 26"		"L" Armytage went on leave. Sgt Stoilt & party facing lines for wiring up. Waggons being sides strengthened. Lines in BETHUNE being straightened. A 157 B 30 C 141 DRLS R 56 UR 295 = 679	
	Aug 27"		Rifle and Gas Helmet inspections — Cleaning and oiling cable waggons & light sprints — Battery parades — A 130 B 17 C 133 DRLS R 79 UR 322 = 681	
	Aug 28"		1.B. detachment reeling up derelict cable for Right Brigade — 2B reeling up derelict cable for the Right Group R.A. — A section jointing & reeling cable — Cleary reconnoitering ground for trestle line — A 142 B 45 C 1145 DRLS R 60 UR 325 = 720.	
	Aug 29"		1 A detachment jointing and reeling cable. 2 A detachment reeling up derelict cable for 1st Brigade. 1B detachment reeling up special wires, 2B detachment reeling up cable for the Right Group R.A. A 164 B 32 C 159 DRLS R 61 UR 322 = 761	

INTELLIGENCE SUMMARY.

(Erase heading not required.)

Instructions regarding War Diaries and Intelligence Summaries are contained in F. S. Regs., Part II. and the Staff Manual respectively. Title pages will be prepared in manuscript.

Place	Date	Hour	Summary of Events and Information	Remarks and references to Appendices
	Aug. 30th		2 A detachment reeling up airlrit cable for the Right Group R.A. 1 B detachment reeling up line with left sector - 2 B reeling up line for the 14th Brigade - 1 A joining and reeling cable. A 175 B 39 C 155 D.R.L.S.R.63 UR 260 = 692.	
	Aug. 31st		Same routine as 30th. A 174 B 35 C 134 D.R.L.S. R 49 UR 297 = 686.	

CH Walsh Capt
OC Signals 32nd Division

32nd Divisional Engineers

32nd DIVISIONAL SIGNAL COMPANY R. E.

SEPTEMBER 1 9 1 6

Army Form C. 2118.

Vol 10

WAR DIARY
or
INTELLIGENCE SUMMARY.
(Erase heading not required.)

CONFIDENTIAL
WAR DIARY
of
32nd Divl Signal Cy. R.E.

from 1st September 1916 to 30th September 1916

INTELLIGENCE SUMMARY.

(Erase heading not required.)

Instructions regarding War Diaries and Intelligence Summaries are contained in F. S. Regs., Part II. and the Staff Manual respectively. Title pages will be prepared in manuscript.

Place	Date	Hour	Summary of Events and Information	Remarks and references to Appendices
	Sept 1st		2. A detachment reeling up derelict cable for the 11th Bde. – B section reeling up derelict cable for the Right Group R.A. 1. A detachment brings the linesmen for not taking it and the remainder first & reel up salvaged cable which is brought in – A 157, B 23, C 119, DRLS R 65, UR 276 = 640.	
	Sept 2nd		A section jointing & reeling up cable – B section picking up derelict cable for the Right Group R.A. Cpl. Mitchell & Pte. Hall posted to 9th Bonyiade. A 127, B 39, C 121, DRLS R 56, UR 277 = 620.	
	Sept 3rd		Both sections overhauling their equipment & cleaning their wagons – Two parties jointing & reeling cable – Bathing parade at 11.15 P.M. A 143, B 22, C 112, DRLS R 77, UR 239 = 593.	
	Sept 4th		B Section reeling up cable for the Right Group R.A. A section jointing & reeling up salvaged cable. Horses moved to the 5/6 Royal Scots and one man 15th H.L.I. sent to No 2 Squadron flying Corps for instruction in contact aeroplane. A 173, B 37, C 119, D.R.L.S R 61, UR 276 = 666.	
	Sept 5th		Two men of B section proceeded to 9th Bde. to learn some forward lines. Remainder of sections jointing & reeling cable. L/Armytage returned from leave. A 137, B 33, C 122, DRLS R 63, UR 237 = 592.	

Army Form C. 2118.

INTELLIGENCE SUMMARY.
(Erase heading not required.)

Instructions regarding War Diaries and Intelligence Summaries are contained in F. S. Regs., Part II. and the Staff Manual respectively. Title pages will be prepared in manuscript.

Place	Date	Hour	Summary of Events and Information	Remarks and references to Appendices
	Aug 6th		Party under Corporal Jullord reeling up a derelict line to BEUVRY - Parties jointing and reeling cable - L/Armytage reconnoitring cables from ANNEQUIN to MAISON ROUGE and LEWIS KEEP - Beuvry line now approaching Nº 2 Siding. A141 B 42 C 139 DRLS R 73 UR 246 = 631.	
	Aug 7th		Moved the billets from 139 RUE DE LILLE 15 to the Barracks - leaving horses and drivers under L/Cpl Schofield at the old billet. A 162 B 24 C 117 DRLS R 66 UR 256 = 625.	
	Aug 8th		Went to 8th Divisional School to see experiment of shooting messages out of a Stokes mortar - fairly successful. Went to Josse q to arrange about a visual station - This there will make an excellent transmitting station visual from its front to the Josse and transmit back to the sand pits behind LEQUESNOY CHATEAU. Parties jointing & reeling cable. A 148 B 114 C 127 DRLS R145 UR 329 = 676.	
	Aug 9th		Mounted party reeled from 96th Bde - Coll onwards from 1st Corps to building from a trestle line from LEQUESNOY to the Dist dug out, L'Armytage reconnoitering the ground with Cpl Barclay for trestle line. 2A detachment reeling up cable to Right Group R.A. Inspection of visual class. Report sent in as to ventilators under French mortars A 124 B 19 C 128 DRLS Sg 59 R UR 310 = 635.	

T.J.134. Wt. W708—776. 500000. 4/15. Sir J. C. & S.

INTELLIGENCE SUMMARY.
(Erase heading not required.)

Place	Date	Hour	Summary of Events and Information	Remarks and references to Appendices
	Aug 10		Inspected the Signal class in Runagay work. Bullfield Riffles and Gas helmets - Rostering parade. Cpl Suffold and a party presently up ou list on line - Remainder chicken stew as cleaning wallpaper list 12.0 noon. A 145 B 19 C 113 DRLS R 66 UR 274 = 615.	
	Aug 11		Yvelle line from LEQUESNOY to 1st Cnps. Cable Sttn being towed at night under Cpt Clery parallel to MAISON Barclay from 1st Cnps. Cable Sttn being towed at night under Cpt Clery parallel to MAISON ROUGE ALLEY. Printing jointing trestling cable. A 148 B 43 C 117 DRLS R 32 UR 246 = 526	
	Aug 12		A fresh party on the trestle line all men with Company who can be spared have been put onto this for instruction number being 40. Remaining men jointing and testing cable A 139 B 27 C 112 DRLS R 56 UR 291 = 625.	
	Aug 13		Party of 16 working on trestle line again - Testing & jointing cable for the remainder. A 140 B 26 C 116 DRLS R 41 UR 148 = 471	
	Aug 14		Party of 12th hrs working on Trestle Line again. Wires laid from Tramentine Standard at LE QUESNOY as far as the Canal at LE PREOL. 6 pairs only put up as only 6 strainers available. Reeling and Jointing Cable for remainder. A 141 B 39 C 136 DRLS R 52 UR 164 = 532.	
	Aug 15		Captain Clery took over Command of Company from this date during absence of Captain Walsh on leave.	C.H.W.C.W

Army Form C. 2118.

INTELLIGENCE SUMMARY.
(Erase heading not required.)

Place	Date	Hour	Summary of Events and Information	Remarks and references to Appendices
	Sept 15th.		Party of 13th mat. on Trestle line again - Reling out Jointing cable for remainder. A 154 B 35 C 117 DRLS R 45 UR 24 = 615.	
	Sept 16th.		Party of 14th visit antreatle line again - Reling out jointing cable for remainder. Burst cable work ceased owing to the Pioneer battalion which provided the necessary digging parties being ordered to leave the area. A 146 B 41 C 154 DRLS R 70 UR 288 = 749	
	Sept 17th.		Party of 1 Officer (Lt Ransford) and 24 O.R. proceeded at 10 a.m. to XVII Corps H.Q. at LABUGNY AUBIGNY to attachment to XVII Corps Signals for buying cable. Rifle and Gas Helmet Inspection for Company at midday. Baths for Company in afternoon A 172 B 26 C 128 DRLS R 42 UR 281 = 648.	
	Sept 18th.		Party of 1 Offr and 26 men 17th N.F.s arrived and were billeted in CAMBRIN for cable trench digging. They started work in evening. A small party of Signallers carried on with trestle line. A 129 B 21 C 107 DRLS R 44 UR 266 = 556.	
	Sept 19th.		Owing to change in orders, 18 O.R. returned from AUBIGNY during the day, leaving Lt Ransford and 6 men still there. Small party at work on Trestle line as before. A 124 B 42 C 152 DRLS R 52 UR 327 = 660.	
	Sept 20th		Lt Ransford and 6 men returned from AUBIGNY. Capt LINTON A and S Highlanders arrived to take over duties of 2nd in Command from Captain Cleny. Full strength party of Signallers on Trestle Line. A 141 B 62 C 108 DRLS. R 69 UR 276 = 656.	

C H W a W.

INTELLIGENCE SUMMARY.
(Erase heading not required.)

Summary of Events and Information

Place	Date	Hour	Summary of Events and Information	Remarks and references to Appendices
	Sept 21st.		Usual Trestle party under Lt Armytage. Reading and Jointing cable for terminals A1+6 B29 C142 DRLS R46 UR 309 = 672. 7 Reinforcements for Company arrived	
	Sept 22nd.		Usual trestle party under C.S.M. Lt Armytage on 2.O.R attended gas course at BEUVRY in morning. A138 B33 C143 DRLS R64 UR 244 = 622.	
	Sept 23rd		Car returned from Workshops. Signal Clerks for infantry reported at 10.30am in Fly Work and at 12 midday in Buzzing by Capt Clery. Captain Linton shown over new buried route from BOYAU 4 to Railway Keep by Captain Clery. Working party 50 17th Northumberland Pioneers, who were due to start digging in evening under Corps Signals, were ordered to stand by & not to move by 1st Corps – hence no work done. A156 B34 C131 DRLS R67 UR 326 = 714.	
	Sept 24"		Capt Walsh returned from leave – Lt Osmonde Cpm on leave – Capt Clery took over command of 1st 8th Division signal Coy – Capt Linton becoming second in command of his company – A173 B37 C116 D.R.L.S R61 UR 256 = 643	
	Sept 25"		Trestle line being finished off – stays put in, wires tightened up, etc. Stag being drawn for staff & standings being forwards under C.Q.M.S, at Dq ROE DE LILLE. A153 B34 C.148 DRL3 R45 UR 334 = 714	
	Sept 26"		AD2o a,b which is two pair from LE QUESNOY to the right front RA Frontiers to the biloum	

C.H.O.F.A.H.

INTELLIGENCE SUMMARY.
(Erase heading not required.)

Place	Date	Hour	Summary of Events and Information	Remarks and references to Appendices
HQS	Sept 26th		pairs of the trestle have the remaining two pairs being handed over to the Brigade entire right. The old AO 20 a.b. & 39 a.b. being dismantled under Sgt Holt. States brought his states being under C.O.R.S. – No night digging party as the 6th Northumberland Fusiliers have been. A 176. B 31 C 141. DRLS 51 R 344 UR = 749.	
	Sept 27th		Sgt Holt carrying on dismantling AO 20 v 26 a.b. – Semi permanent line being built from BÉTHUNE to LE QUESNOY under Lt Williams & 1st Corps. Standups being made. A 138 B 26 C 120 DRLS R 70 UR 287 = 545.	
	Sept 28th		Semi permanent line to LE QUESNOY completed – permanent linemen making extensive for joining up. Cpl Peachey and party reels up 5 miles of D5 cable left by the 30th Division – Lt Litz continuing with the digging party of 60 cyclists. Contact scheme of 97th Brigade with contact aeroplane fairly satisfactory. A 110 B 32 C 158 DRLS R 39 UR 345 = 657.	
	Sept 29th		Lt Rancfora gone on leave. Party making new status. Permanent linemen yesterday AO 13. 20.21 22 a.b. on the semi permanent lines. L'Ermitage has taken over the R.A. twin vice L' Rancfora. E. L. Lorry set arrives from P.E.L. GHQ. A121 B 29 C 141 DRLS R 55 UR 257 = 623.	
	SEPT 30th		Telephone pairs to Right and Left Brigades and Right staff Corps R.A. transferred from the twin lines to the semi-permanent. The twin lines to Right & Left Brigades transferred from the twin lines to the RAILWAY ROUTE. A 136 B. 25. C120 D.R.L.S. 46 R. 348 UR. = 675	

C. H Walsh Capt
O.C L'ipsuits 22 J Diw

32nd Divisional Engineers

32nd DIVISIONAL SIGNAL COMPANY R. E.

OCTOBER 1 9 1 6

Army Form C. 2118.

WAR DIARY
or
INTELLIGENCE SUMMARY.
(Erase heading not required.)

32/ Vol 11

CONFIDENTIAL

WAR DIARY

of

32nd Div. Signal Coy R.E.

from 1st October 1916 to 31st October 1916.

Army Form C. 2118.

WAR DIARY
or
INTELLIGENCE SUMMARY.
(Erase heading not required.)

Place	Date	Hour	Summary of Events and Information	Remarks and references to Appendices
	Oct 1st		Party under C.Q.M.S. continue to build stabling at 129 RUE DE LILLE. Linesmen transferring labels from their old lines to the new lines which were altered 30.9.16. Rifle and gas helmet inspection. Bathing parade. Remainder of sections checking their stores, returning waggons, being inspected one by one. Lt LISTER 1st Corps Signals who is i/c of the Canad lines attached and living with this company has notice of leaving at VERMELLES. A 12b B 13 C 112 SP.S R 76 UR 262 = 60W.	
	Oct 2nd		Party under Sergt Hoult dismantling cannac lines across canal between BETHUNE and LEQUESNOY. Lt PERKS with G cable section relieved Lt LISTER with AE section. Digging party continuing. Scheme with aeroplane and 91st Brigade postponed owing to rain A 152 B 29 C 118 SP.S 78 R 353 UR 730	
	Oct 3rd		Sgt Hoults party out completing the dismantling of the air line. Aeroplane scheme again postponed owing to weather. 2 officers & 120 men of Corps cyclists dropping transport. A 166 B 89 C 128 D.R.L.S. R 80 UR 356 = 789.	
	Oct 4		Sgt Hoult and a party relying up a disused wire from CHICORY FACTORY to LE QUESNOY. Stable party carrying on under Quarter Master Sergeant. Straw mattresses for the men arr and issued. Night party finishing off village line wires and starting from right company to Right Battalion Hq at RAILWAY KEEP. A 148 B 44 C 148 D.R.L.S. R 66 UR 304 = 704.	
	Oct 5th		Party under Sergeant Major altering local wires. Party under Sapper Prentice making a suspension	C N Morton Capt

Army Form C. 2118.

WAR DIARY
or
INTELLIGENCE SUMMARY.

(Erase heading not required.)

Instructions regarding War Diaries and Intelligence Summaries are contained in F. S. Regs., Part II. and the Staff Manual respectively. Title pages will be prepared in manuscript.

Place	Date	Hour	Summary of Events and Information	Remarks and references to Appendices
	Oct 5th		Multiple cable to LEQUESNOY. Staff party continuing. Visited 1st Army report. A 175 B 40 C 166 D.R.L.S. R 60 UR 327 = 768	
	Oct 6th		Men on same works & parties at 5·10·16 - Jock Sergt buried over te permanent lines Walt and to be repaired from LEQUESNOY to LE PREOL via GORRE RAILWAY STATION. A 174 B 25 C 130 D.R.L.S. R 54 UR 392 = 775	
	Oct 7th		Works shifted as division is coming out of the line. Rating up & jointing cable - continuing with its horse lines - straightening wires in Bethune. A 158 B.135 C 29 D.R.L.S R 76 UR 385 = 782.	
	Oct 8th		G.O.C. inspected horse lines - Usual inspection of rifles - gas helmets & kits. Battery parades. A 138 B 29 C 127 D.R.L.S. R 62 UR 265 = 818	
	Oct 9th		Nothing to report A 161 B 36 C 127 D.R.L.S R 64 UR 294 = 672	
	Oct 10th		Rendred returned from leave. 14 Punjab moved to BUSNES. Communication to them by telephone and Superimposed Sounder. Otter Communication to same A 152 B 22 C 137 D.R.L.S R 51 UR 270 = 657.	
	Oct 11th		Staff party still continuing jointing and reting cable. 96th Bde now in BETHUNE relieved by telephone & Superimposed Sounder. A 154 B 32 C 134. No 95th Bde 5th Divn. Communication D.R.L.S. R. 64 UR 303 = 687.	
	Oct 12th		Sections at disposal of Section officers - Repainting wagons - jointing & reting cable - continuing	O.H. Morrison

T.134. Wt. W708-776. 500000. 4/15. Sir J. C. & S.

WAR DIARY or INTELLIGENCE SUMMARY

Army Form C. 2118.

(Erase heading not required.)

Place	Date	Hour	Summary of Events and Information	Remarks and references to Appendices
	Oct. 12/16		with Installer. A 192 B 30 C 185 DRLS R 56 UR 24hr = 108.	
	Oct. 13/16		Nothing to report. Same worker as 12.10.16.	
	Oct. 14/16		97th Bde relieved by 21st Div. - 97th moved into Ruisdh Gaulette communication with 14th Brigade.	
			97th Bnyards relieves by 21st Div. - 97th moved into Ruisdh Gaulette communication by telephone. Sections at Sections officers disposal checking stores and kits. A 208 B 40 C 115 DRLS R 63 UR 267 = 693.	
	Oct. 15/16		14th Bde moves to RAIMBERT communication by phone at 2.20 PM 96th Bde to DIEVAL telephone cine at 2.0 PM	
			97th Bde moves to LABEUVRIERE cine by telephone at 12.0 noon. Rifle + gun helmet inspection. Battery parades.	
	Oct. 16/16		Divl Hqrs moves to CHEELERS - 14th Bde to ROELCOURT - 96th Bde FREVILLERS - 97th Bde to MONCHY-BRETON	
			Communication with brigade by D.R. Sounder and telephone line to 7th Corps.	
	Oct. 17/16		Divl Hqrs moved to LE CAUROY - 14th Bde to REBREUVE - 96th Bde to MAIZIERES - 97th Bde to BONNVILLE - Communication to units of the division by D.R. Sounder + telephone to 3rd Army.	
	Oct. 18/16		Divl Hqrs to BEAUVAL - 14th Bde BEAUVAL - 96th Bde AMPLIER - 97th Bde HEM. Communication to units of divn by D.R. Telegraph office (Reserve Army) in BEAUVAL sending own messages also a phone pair onto their board.	
	Oct. 19/16		Orders for Divn to move to CONTAY cancelled - Divn in same position as 18th	
	Oct. 20/16		Division in the same place. Visited reserve army signals D.O.A.S. was out G.O.C.'s conference at 2.45 P.M.	

WAR DIARY
INTELLIGENCE SUMMARY.
(Erase heading not required.)

Army Form C. 2118.

Instructions regarding War Diaries and Intelligence Summaries are contained in F. S. Regs., Part II. and the Staff Manual respectively. Title pages will be prepared in manuscript.

Place	Date	Hour	Summary of Events and Information	Remarks and references to Appendices
	Oct 21st		Divn Hqrs moved to CONTAY – 96th Bde CONTAY – 97th WARLOY – 14th REUBEMPRÉ. Subsequently Somme to 2nd Corps – 97th – 14th Rlvs. Telephone rang tonight Rlvs.	
	Oct 22nd		Divisional positions Somme 21·10·16 – Visited HESSIAN TRENCH. Arrangements with 2nd Corps Sqdn for Divn Itineraries.	
	Oct 23rd		Divisions moved to USNA REDOUBT. 97th Bde BOUZINCOURT – 96th + 14th BRICKFIELDS AREA. Liaison to 2nd Corps but not to Brigades owing to mistake with 2nd Corps	
	Oct 24th		Lt Armytage sent out to fix up a Subsidiary office at BOUZINCOURT for ADMS. CRE DADOS on the phone with subordinate Borders. Capt Luton at fixing up W T/g Rlvs to Bouzincourt – Six mounted men out reconnoitering between OUILLERS and the NAB. DR's sent out & to find the RED CROSS FLAG at X 4 C 5.4 – Raining – A 158 B 39 C 114 DRLS R at UR 185 = 529.	
	Oct 25th		Pair laid to 24th Manchesters and Stores Line Albert. Visited ADMS. 2nd Corps and got buzzer leads and relief harness (30) for Brigades. – Raining – A 101 B 46 C 77 DRLS R 58 UR 62 = 444	
	Oct 26th		14th Brigade moved to CONTAY – 96th Brigade to WARLOY – both Brigades to supervise to B.C.O. Raining – Capt Luton + Lt Armytage out with works parties preparing future communications. A 64 B 56 C 93 DRLS R 54 UR 180 = 447.	C H Worsley

T/2134. Wt. W708–776. 500000. 4/16. Sir J. C. & S.

WAR DIARY or INTELLIGENCE SUMMARY

Army Form C. 2118.

Place	Date	Hour	Summary of Events and Information	Remarks and references to Appendices
	Oct 27th		Lt MUTCH sent out with visual party to survey the ground round IRLES - PYS - MIRAUMONT from future observations. A117 B81 C85 DRLS R65 UR 207 = 555	
	Oct 28th		Lt ZOLLERN TREACH Capt LINTON and Lt ARMYTAGE completing the communications to the Obsyntage and Lt Mutch erecting poled cable posn from E box to Wbox for the visual party. HUb being finished. Signal Office and Chaplains Office being moved. Communication orders issued to 2nd Rl Bde. Lieuten - Capt Little - Lt Armytage - Lt Mutch and to GI Staff for internally. A105 B45 C95 DRLS R51 UR 276 = 512	
	Oct 29th		Coy being efficient and signal office finished increase 1565 on the forward lines. A 58 B118 C91 DRLS R52 UR 164 = 440. Visual party practising with Lt MUTCH	
	Oct 30th		97th Brigade moved to RUBEMPRE. Luisieux test not altogether satisfactory. A104 B64 C118 DRLS R91 UR 267 = 613. Visual party practising under Lt MUTCH	
	Oct 31st		97th Brigade moved to CAMBLES - 96th Brigade moved to RUBEMPRE - 14 2d CONTAY all messages and QRLS through 13 CO - Luisieux tests all over except R29 C64. Visual party out under Lt MUTCH	

C.H. Lowell Capt
RE Signals 32nd Divn

32nd Divisional Engineers

32nd DIVISIONAL SIGNAL COMPANY R. E.

NOVEMBER 1 9 1 6

Army Form C. 2118.

WAR DIARY
or
INTELLIGENCE SUMMARY.
(Erase heading not required.)

Vol 12

CONFIDENTIAL

WAR DIARY

of

32nd Divl. Signal Coy R.E.

From 1st November 1916 to 30th November 1916.

Army Form C. 2118.

Instructions regarding War Diaries and Intelligence Summaries are contained in F. S. Regs., Part II. and the Staff Manual respectively. Title pages will be prepared in manuscript.

INTELLIGENCE SUMMARY.

(Erase heading not required.)

Place	Date	Hour	Summary of Events and Information	Remarks and references to Appendices
	Nov 1st		Officers looking out to make sectional sketches to the forward lines – 3p/40 discs between N and E dug out – 25th showing 10° of smoke – at Manchester Redt asked to be a line which will not be laid as by Staff did not approve it – Heavy showers all day. A q5 B n 2 C 79 DR&S R 49 UR 20½ = 49.7 Squadron OTC with regard to be working of keep time with Infty Brigade.	
	Nov 2 1		Capt Luke with party of Lewisers letting doors from H to E losses also keeping base and fire. Party laying field cable to 2nd Canadian Artillery. A q9 B 7 C 81 DR&S R 58 UR 33¾ = 60	
	Nov 3 rd		School with Off Bde – Contact aeroplane answering Zero Tune – tune take to essence French lamps at dusk to aid planes very effective and message exchanges at long distances. Brit lamps took a forward one but the aviaons found out each number. A 92 B 89 C 98 DR&S R 7b UR 224 = 330.	
	Nov 4		Testing surveillances on forward lines with telescope. Lamps are visible which shows not to the bare earth. All have test OR at sunset 25th which was shot on at which to the bare earth. H2 and P dug out 2 deaths had. A 100 B 84 C 77 DR&S R 20 UR 208 = 52	
	Nov 5		Inspection of rifles – ammunition – gas helmets – iron rations field dressings. Kernel Ryndalen with M'Pater. Anstone & Lt Lookert under General Saville A 111 = DRS Aq B L C 75 DR R 7b UR 210 = 535	CMEal

T2134. Wt. W708–776. 500000. 4/15. Sir J. C. & S.

Army Form C. 2118.

Instructions regarding War Diaries and Intelligence Summaries are contained in F.S. Regs., Part II. and the Staff Manual respectively. Title pages will be prepared in manuscript.

INTELLIGENCE SUMMARY.
or
(Erase heading not required.)

Place	Date	Hour	Summary of Events and Information	Remarks and references to Appendices
	Nov.6th		Lines tested correctly - Section drill under Section Officers - Laying of army wire Signal drill	
			Aeroplane party under Cpl Acheivld. Shortage of men - 9th Sumerians sent in.	
	Nov 7th		Output to Subcommanding officer. A 111 B 65 C 76 DRLS R10a UR 230=552	
			Lines tested all correct - Field cable Broads re many places by shell fire.	
	Nov.8th		A 82 B 84 C 69 DRLS R 85 UR 231 = 571	
			Bricks lines 25/26 handed over to 18 Divn (by orders of A.D.A.S. BCO. Tests show a certain amount of cuts on 39/1. A 87 B 80 C 83 DRLS R 51 UR 230 = 571.	
	Nov.9th		Visited BRAMLEY to lighting accommodation - Testing of lines shows a dis on 39/1 otherwise correct. A 71 B 82 C 76 DRLS R 87 UR 233 = 563. Weather fine. Cosmode for Heavy Artillery Group.	
	Nov.10th		Fault on 39/1 being located - informed Corps signals. Camouflage now Ida Signal Officer of 14th Bde. A 72 B 102 C 72 DRLS R 86 UR 142=471.	
	Nov 11th		Visited brigade stations - Inward lists as usual - Cautionary reconnaissance and making A.S. - Section whole. A 87 B 68 C 160 DRLS R 72 UR 240 = 552	
	Nov 12th		Preliminary bombardment - Inward lists as usual - Orders given for movement of parties when necessary	
			Twelve fire fighters arrived Mere from 2nd Corps - Carpenters been sent in for present under charge of Staff Capt. A 122 B 64 C 117 DRLS R 83 u 175 = 193k	

C.M.D.CPT.

Army Form C. 2118.

WAR DIARY
or
INTELLIGENCE SUMMARY.
(Erase heading not required.)

Instructions regarding War Diaries and Intelligence Summaries are contained in F. S. Regs., Part II. and the Staff Manual respectively. Title pages will be prepared in manuscript.

Place	Date	Hour	Summary of Events and Information	Remarks and references to Appendices
	Nov. 13		14th Bde. moved to BOUZINCOURT – 96th Bn. to WARLOY – 97th Bn. to CONTAY. Battle commenced 5.45 am. Message received 7.11 a.m. Troops progressing favorably. North of the ANCRE. No news South of ANCRE. 96th Bn. moved to PAISLEY DUMP – 97th Bn. PASSERELLE – 14th BOUZINCOURT A 119 B 71 C 132 DRLS R 5½ UR 18L = 56L	
	Nov. 14th		Arrived FORCEVILLE. 14th Bde moves to MAILLY MAILLET and 11th to ELLIS SQUARE. 96th Bn. PAISLEY DUMP. 97th Bde ENGLEBELMER. A 119 B 45 C 122 DRLS R 4½ UR 170 = 159. Sending over observer to BERTRANCOURT – visits 2nd Division Signals – Brought in office from BOUZINCOURT.	
	Nov. 16th		14th Bde ELLIS SQUARE – 96th Bn. Paisley Dump – 97th Bde WHITE CITY. Took over from 2nd Division at BERTRANCOURT. Lucla up at Q 2.b – Match out at visual station Q 3a.u. Great rush of work all day. Operation orders O.O.65 took a long time getting out to Brigades. 96th Bn. moved to MAILLY MAILLET in the evening. 14th Bde at ELLIS SQUARE 97th and 154th Bdes at WHITE CITY. A 213 B 102 C 213 DRLS R 7b UR 110 = 7½	
	Nov. 17		Battle commenced 6.10 a.m. – Pigeon message came in 8.39 a.m sent off by 11th Border Regt at 8.30 a.m Battalion held up at a strong point. Had aeroplane station out but it is no day for aeroplanes – low clouds and sleet, message received from 31st Division saying attack of 32nd Division appears to be going well. But no news from our own perhaps yet. Sgt Powell badly wounded – Cpl Picken ?	
	Nov. 18"			

Ch[signature]

INTELLIGENCE SUMMARY.
(Erase heading not required.)

Place	Date	Hour	Summary of Events and Information	Remarks and references to Appendices
	Nov. 19		Pte Lees wounded at White City – Spoke to W. Pde on phone who say they are trying to keep their lines out but are being kept getting broken.	
		11.0 am	Gave orders to Capt Huston to lay a wire from White City to 97" advanced report centre.	
		11.45 am	Gave orders to Capt Huston to see about the line from Q.2.b. to 1st advanced dressing station in Midley Pickles trench and to keep to M.A.R.	
		12.5 pm	Capt Huston reports that a forward line from 97" Pde at White City to 97" Pde advanced report centre is through. Gave him instructions to carry on with the wire.	
		12.35 pm	Capt Huston reports that he has the advanced dressing station wire through but cannot as no one familiar with it - has been sent spare ends to see station is this has been lost with consequently no lineman can get a lineman.	
			Wires up to ELLIS SQUARE and WHITE CITY held all right but lines in front of that did not hold. 97" Pde had several lines out between our HQ for half an hour - although lineman do their best to keep them through. No wires was managed to M.A.R. He has his party out its best from Q.2.a.11. but nothing happened. Azass B.180 C.253. DRLs R.7a UR 212 = 963. 5th Pde left BEAUSSART. 5th Pde left BEAUSSART tulan without warning us consequently no teleblus line two Sounds out - Sent up Saffer Bell to Hill get and fined LADs	C.W.C. Capt

T.134. Wt. W708-776. 500000. 4/15. Sir J. C. & S.

INTELLIGENCE SUMMARY.

(Erase heading not required.)

Instructions regarding War Diaries and Intelligence Summaries are contained in F. S. Regs., Part II. and the Staff Manual respectively. Title pages will be prepared in manuscript.

Place	Date	Hour	Summary of Events and Information	Remarks and references to Appendices
			asking for two operators - a lot of stray units here and no orderlies, 9th Div relieved 97th Bde with him - Brought L/Mutch back to BERTRANCOURT - to Summerhays. 9th Div is CAMPAGNE on a mule winter camps. Two runnouts in from HB Base. A 297 B 66 C 216 DRLS @ R 50 UR 283 = 837.	
Nov 20th			Visited BEAUSSART M/o Pioneers (Lloyd Notts Lancs) and R.E. dump on BEAUSSART road. Pte M⁶Gregor and 2 wounded based at BERTRANCOURT. Finished operation diaries and handed them into G. Staff. Head runner Dick Massey.	
			Shakey. to MARIEUX. Fine day. A 234 B 85 C 182 DRLS R 48 UR 260 = 813	
Nov 21st			Line to BEAUSSART broken by a train carrying a train - broke down six bays of semi-permanent, 5th Corps break down gang arrived late into evening but it was too dark to repair the line - they are relieving at dawn tomorrow. 4th Divn Signals came in to see about taking over Rizea also impossible this morning	
			trajets - so FAR DRLS will be carried by mounted orderlies commencing tomorrow which we are in this area - Corps have been asked to supply six mounted orderlies to assist. Very misty day and roads already bad Sir of the Corps dismounted orderlies been arrived here from the Divisional depôt etc.	
		to the Corps being no longer required. A Lqs 13 53 C 173 DRLS Q 58 UR 237 = 712.	
Nov 22nd			Cops break down gang reconstructed broken line over railway W of BEAUSSART. Road under WILLIAMS Wks 26 MAR. to leave the lines (11/5 Bn/S is now 15/7th Divn Signals) were seen taken over by 25 & 20th Bn HQ.	
			moved into BEAUSSART and on leaving BEAUSSART today to completed. A 240 Roz Civp DRLS R 89 UR 268 = 919	

Clifford Capt.

INTELLIGENCE SUMMARY.

(Erase heading not required.)

Instructions regarding War Diaries and Intelligence Summaries are contained in F. S. Regs., Part II. and the Staff Manual respectively. Title pages will be prepared in manuscript.

Place	Date	Hour	Summary of Events and Information	Remarks and references to Appendices
	Nov. 23rd		Sections off to Bde HQrs. Roads very bad and DRs taking a very short time to deliver messages back again.	
	Nov. 24th		R 205 B 115 C 223 DR's R 85 UR 247 = 930 14th Bde relieved by 20th Bde – 112th AD 96th Bde joined relieved by 97th Bde. Two army lines cut off on …	
	Nov. 25th		Advance to Doullens Packing. Coming closer …… MAR. A 210 B 179 C 217 DR's R 57 UR 238 = 901 Divn moved to DOULLENS - 14th Bde to AUTHIEULE - 96th Bde AMPLIER - 97th Bde BEZAINCOURT. Telegraph and telephone to V ARMY and 97th Brigade. A 119 B – C 83 DR's R 52 UR 101 = 355	
	Nov. 26th		Divn moved to CANAPLES. 14th Bde to PERNOIS. 96th Bde FIEFFES – 97th Bde BERTENCOURT. Telegraph & Phone to V – 97th Bde – Local phones G & Q Offices Signal Mess. A 103 B 1 C 93 DR's R 48 UR 93 = A168	
	Nov. 27th		Visited all four Brigades. Telegraph & phone to 96th and 14th Brigades – Divn Supply Column ……. from wireless course. A 191 B 16 C 115 DR's R 51 UR 215 = 570. Local phone circuits being laid to G.O.C. C.R.E. ADMS. DADOS. Company Office (Signals)	
	Nov. 28th		Capt Hunter to Div Cable in Car to get camp paint money and one mile of S Lake H.W. for electric lighting and how to … to DOULLENS to buy necessaries supplies – footballs. Boxing Gloves. Quoits. Darts. footballs obtainable of which we got six – nothing else could be procured. A 146 B 29 C 121 DR's R 97 UR 220 = 573	
	Nov. 29th		Who desired to try & get recreation kit – quoits – boxing gloves – shirts & shields wanted by the Brigade …… mentioned to join the Sparks for Cockney Training. Divn Paid to APM and CRE Visited 5th Army Signals to get S. Salisbury.	CMDCpt

T./134. Wt. W708—776. 500000. 4/15. Sir J. C. & S.

INTELLIGENCE SUMMARY.
(Erase heading not required.)

Place	Date	Hour	Summary of Events and Information	Remarks and references to Appendices
	Apr. 30th		Tit Electric lighting but could not get any - obtained 29 instead and the line (power) will have to be laid with an open wire. A119 B27 C111 D R=S R+0 VR 18H = 148.1. Company training orders. Hours of parade for Mounted Men 7.0-7.45 Stables. 10-11.15 Riding & Driving School. 11.15-12.45 Stables. 1.45-2.30 Cleaning Harness & Waggons. 4.15-6.0 Stables 6pm Night Guard mounts. Dismounted Men 7.0-7.45 Cleaning billets and any other work by parties that may be nis'd. 11.0-11.0 Section drill 11.0-12.0 Physical Drill. 12.0-12.45 Company drill. 1.45-2.30 Section drill 3.0-4.0 Lectures. Whole Company 6.30 am Reveille. 7.45-9.0 Breakfast & cleaning equipment & Kit. 9.30 am "Pee Cell" Inspection. 9.45 am. Officers Inspection. 1.0 Dinners. 5.15 pm Teas. A151. B14 C123. D 4 L=S R+1. VR 21H =552	

C H. Walsh Capt
O.C. 32nd Div'l Sig'nl Coy R.E.

32nd Divisional Engineers
9----------

32nd DIVISIONAL SIGNAL COMPANY R. E.

DECEMBER 1 9 1 6

Vol 13

CONFIDENTIAL
WAR DIARY
of
32ND. DIVL. SIGNAL COY. R.E.

from 1st December 1916 to 31st December 1916.

Army Form C. 2118.

INTELLIGENCE SUMMARY.
(Erase heading not required.)

Place	Date	Hour	Summary of Events and Information	Remarks and references to Appendices
	Dec 1st		Company Training - Electric lighting being arranged for the Chateau and G.O.C's private office. Telephone pair extended to O.C. Supply Column BERTEAUCOURT from 97 Infantry Brigade. A 116. B 33 C 116 DRLS R 41 UR 229 = 519	
	Dec 2nd		A 150 B 36 C 113 DRLS R 66 UR 168 = 533	
	Dec 3rd		Company Training. 2/Lt Summerhayes HOOD Broden left for Army Signal School LE THIAIS FARM as instructor for one month. Inspection of Company - Rifles - Ammunition - Iron rations. Gas Helmets. Football matches in the afternoon. D.D.O.R inspected pack mules for returning to remounts in place of L.D. horses for Mule Carts. A 135 B 27 C 104 DRLS R 33 UR 184 = 483	
D	Dec 4th		All pack mules going back to this Remounts except the Grey mule of 97 Brigade Company remained. A 123 B 22 C 92 DRLS R 37 UR 167 = 461.	
	Dec 5th		Pack mules marched to QUERRIEUX. Company Training. R.A. headquarters arrived at ST OUEN. Asked Army for a pair. A 116 B 27 C 117 DRLS R 41 UR 175 = 526.	
	Dec 6th		Cpl Hand went to ST LEGER with Lt QUENTIN engine to fix up electric lighting at PEDLARS [?]. Sergt HOAD proceeded to Army Signal School LA HAIE FARM via Capt Yorden who returned - Visual instructors not required at the School. Company Training. Pack mule cart & harness Confetti handed over to 97 Brigade section. CMS Capt

INTELLIGENCE SUMMARY

Place	Date	Hour	Summary of Events and Information	Remarks and references to Appendices
	Dec 6th (Cont)		Following train to ST OUEN (from to Army) BRCP 7/8 - SRBR 7/8 - SRSO 5/9. A135 B47 C112 DRLS R40 UR 162 = 496.	
	Dec 7th		Line to C.R.A. not very satisfactory with has been tried on to lt Col Luis — a separate pair is absolutely necessary. Company training. Cavalli pair from Army for C.R.A. A118 B35 C107 DRLS R48 UR 228 = 526.	
	Dec 8th		Company training — Rains most of the morning. Lt Rawford with No 2 detachment A section returned from BERTRANCOURT. A151 B30 C105 DRLS R40 UR 234 = 560.	
	Dec 9th		Company training — Rain most of the day. A135 B27 C92 DRLS R46 UR 244 = 572.	
	Dec 10th		Line through to Divisional School MONTRELET via 96th Pole exchange. Inspection of animals, gas helmets — Iron Rations — Box Respirators & Iron dressings. A126 B27 C100 DRLS R43 UR 255 = 551.	
	Dec 11th		Company training completed this day — Corupa in landed over to Capt Linton — A147 B17 C84 DRLS R35 UR 175 = 458.	
	Dec 12th		Rain torrow most of day — Pole sections returned to Bolso — HQ + Cable section training commenced — Lt Rawford and class of 30 gunners from RA arrived — Line to V corps died at 8.45 AM. fault partially corrected 11:30AM fully at 12:20 PM. A169 B34 C100 DRLS R24 UR 193 = 520.	CHWGH

INTELLIGENCE SUMMARY.

(Erase heading not required.)

Place	Date	Hour	Summary of Events and Information	Remarks and references to Appendices
	Dec 13th	(am)	HQ & Cable sections training continued. RA Class commenced training. A 128 B 37 C 95 DRLS. R 30 UR 216 = 506	
"	14th		HQ & Cable section +RA Class cont. training. Rained in aft. A 105 B 27 C 87 DRLS R 43 UR 200 = 462	
"	15th		HQ & Cable section +RAClass cont training. Wet all day. A 140 B 28 C 110 DRLS R 29 UR 216 = 523	
"	16th		HQ & Cable section +RAClass cont training. 97 Bde moved to Rubempré after Close Parloir Conf. 9.30 AM. Opened R. 1.45pm Comtin by DRLS + Phone thro' Corpo Army + Hennicourt exchge. A 107 B 13 C 107 DRLS R 44 UR 208 = 519	
"	17th		HQ & Cable section Cont +RAClass Cont training. Direct line thro' to 97 Bde phone to runner inn return field drawing at 11:35 AM. Inspection of Arms Amctn Gas Helmets. A 165 B 22 C 11 DRLS R 40 UR 187 = 525	
"	18th		HQ & Cable section training +RAClass Cont. Lt Rawstre proceeded on leave after midnight 18/12/16. G.O.C.'s phone reported faulty 6.30 pm tested thro' this Office 7/15 OK. A 152 B 20 C 118 DRLS R 49 UR 225 = 564	
"	19		HQ + Cable section +RA Class cnt. A 143 B 20 C 113 DRLS R 32 UR 204 = 512	
"	20th		HQ Cable section +RA Class Cont. repair of RA batteries completed. Work commenced on 96 Bde hut. A 124 B 28 C 109 DRLS R 27 UR 203 = 4[?]6	

J W Carbb

INTELLIGENCE SUMMARY.

(Erase heading not required.)

Instructions regarding War Diaries and Intelligence Summaries are contained in F. S. Regs., Part II. and the Staff Manual respectively. Title pages will be prepared in manuscript.

Place	Date	Hour	Summary of Events and Information	Remarks and references to Appendices
	Dec 21st		HQ + cable section Training. Cont. also R.A Class. Showery. A 116 B 20 C 116 DRLS R 35 UR 229 = 516	
	22nd		HQ + cable sections + R.A class cont'd. R.A. Instrument Returned. A 116 B 15 C 27 DRLS R 34 UR 201 = 503	
	23rd		Company taken over from Capt Walsh on return from leave by 2nd Field Ambulance through 97th Bde. Working at 10 p.m. Lieut Longfellow did at 4.45 p.m correct at laying across the road at BONNEVILLE. Training of classes continuing. Rain rest of day. 14th Bde section to AMIENS under Lt Summerhayes A 127 B 17 C 129 DRLS R 34 UR 236 = 542	
	24th		Capt Walton proceeded on leave till 3/1/19. Inspection of rifles - Gas helmets - 2nd Field dressing - Iron Rations - a few differences which are being made up. Church parade - Battalion Signals defeated Divisional Headquarters in the 1st Preliminary round of the football Cup by 5-0. A 201 B 13 C 111 DRLS R 34 UR 236 = 595	
	25th		Christmas Day - Routine as for Sunday - Company had their Christmas dinner in the evening at 5:30 p.m. Showery day - A 90 B 20 C 158 DRLS R 128 UR 178 = 225	
	26th		Routine and training in morning as usual - afternoon area holiday - Batt. Officers as usual afternoon drawn area holiday - Bat. Officers	

Instructions regarding War Diaries and Intelligence Summaries are contained in F. S. Regs., Part II. and the Staff Manual respectively. Title pages will be prepared in manuscript.

INTELLIGENCE SUMMARY.
or
(Erase heading not required.)

Place	Date	Hour	Summary of Events and Information	Remarks and references to Appendices
Bac	26/12		Returned to the Brigade and Brigade Signals Class returned to Division. Signal Coy defiled by A.S.C. 1-0 with the second round of Platoon Cup Ties. Rain most of the day. A 101 B 26 C 102 DRLS R 24 DR 1555 = 4074	
"	27 "		Training of sections telegraphy as usual. Went over to Bus + A/MOTCH - to get an outline of 3rd Division lines - Wet ribbons 2nd Divn - Did not go to Bus as Car smashed a spring. Army B16 C 103 DRLS R35 UR 246 = 627	
"	28 "		Inspects of the Signal Class at Hq mill. Inspected two cable detachments at cable drill - Lectures to the Divisional School on Communications in the field - Company lorry carting cinders to horse lines - Wheelwrights overhauling cable waggons. Targets finished for Divisional range - Three blackboards + seventeen signboards finished for Divisional School. A 124 B 32 C 110 DRLS R 42 UR 208 = 517	
"	29 "		Visited III Division at BUS - getting two new Battln Intnd Schemes out of Army on the way through. Routine Training as usual A 131 B 26 C 126 DRLS 42 R 216 UR = 539.	
"	30 "		Inspects RA Signal Class at Vinal. Trials with the "Lucas" Signal lamp being carried out - V Rumped returned from large Stirptown offeren sent into DDS 5th Army, A 132 B 39 C121 DRLS R 39 UR 244 = 625.	
"	31 "		Church parade - Inspection of cable - box upridon (small) etc. Visited 96th Bde + AD Cynals 5th Corps. A 149 B 32 C 96 DRLS R 44 UR 2qy = 550	

A Walshabit
D.C. Signals 32nd Division

Army Form C. 2118.

Vol/4

WAR DIARY
or
INTELLIGENCE SUMMARY.
(Erase heading not required.)

CONFIDENTIAL
WAR DIARY
of
32nd Civil Engineer Coy. RE
from 1st January 1919 to 31st January 1919

Army Form C. 2118.

WAR DIARY
or
INTELLIGENCE SUMMARY.
(Erase heading not required.)

Instructions regarding War Diaries and Intelligence Summaries are contained in F. S. Regs., Part II. and the Staff Manual respectively. Title pages will be prepared in manuscript.

Place	Date	Hour	Summary of Events and Information	Remarks and references to Appendices
	Jan 1st 1917	8.30 a.m.	No 1 detachment of B section marched under Lt Rawford to BERTRANCOURT at 8.30 a.m. - detachment i/c of Corpl McGowan. Pt Prof Stannes for building stables. Cpl Powell appointed instructor to visual class to assist Cpl Sowden. A 129 B 35 C 137 DRLS R 56 UR 247 = 614.	
	Jan 2nd		Visited 97th USA Signal Class and 5th Army Signals. Stable party commenced fitting up overhead cover for horses. R.A. moved from their rest area up into the line - R.A. headquarters being at LOUVENCOURT and the Artillery Brigades under the orders of the 7th Division at BERTRANCOURT. A 134 B 25 C 113 DRLS R 52 UR 216 = 540.	
	Jan 3rd		Erecting overhead cover for stables - finished. Altitude parts round the water troughs also the ramps up to the horse lines from the road. A 174 B 29 C 108 DRLS R 44 UR 195 = 552.	
	Jan 4th		Capt Linton returned from leave. Training of R.A. class and cable sections. A 165 B 43 C 185 DRLS R 44 UR 228 = 645.	
	Jan 5th		Cleaning up & preparing for the move. Capt Linton took over charge of Signal Office and linen. Suspected case of mange into lines - animal separated. One 3 ton lorry from ADAS and one from Q division to move to morrow. A 179 B 50 C 129 DRLS R 46 UR 240 = 644.	
	Jan 6th		Divl HQ to MARIEUX - 14th Div BEAUVAL - 96th Div BEAUQUESNE - 97th Div RUBEMPRÉ - All brigades are	

2353 Wt W2544/1454 700,000 5/15 D. D. & L. A.D.S.S./Forms/C. 2118.

Army Form C. 2118.

WAR DIARY
or
INTELLIGENCE SUMMARY.
(Erase heading not required.)

Instructions regarding War Diaries and Intelligence Summaries are contained in F. S. Regs., Part II. and the Staff Manual respectively. Title pages will be prepared in manuscript.

Place	Date	Hour	Summary of Events and Information	Remarks and references to Appendices
			on the phone. 5th Corps on the phone. Our acting horse at Hq Section has had the left behind under Pte Mathews. Otherwise more carried out satisfactorily - Billets in MARIEUX fillthy dirty. Lt Grady went on urgent leave this evening. A 115 B 7 C 117 DRLS R 18 UR 144 = 110 w.	
Jan y 7th			9th Ade moves to BUS - 97th Bde moves to COURCELLES. - Camp being cleaned up in MARIEUX. Captain Newton with advance party moved to BUS. Visited A.D.A.S 5th Corps A 120 B 1 C 94 DRLS R 26 UR 188 = 433	
Jan y 8th			Sgt Penney with another party went over to BUS. 114th Bde moved from BEAUVAL to COURCELETS. St Spratt sent over to 32nd Div.L School MONTRELET to put the Telephone straight. Visited BUS with C.Q.M.S. to look round.	
Jan y 9th			Division moves to BUS taking over Command of his Area at 11.0 a.m. - Put down new duck boards from Signal Office to Camb - Compain Lorry returned from 7yrs Press DOULLENS. All hire working - line to C.R.E going slight trouble. A 154 B 51 C 114 DRLS 30 R 125 UR = 574.	
Jan y 10th			Visited 114th + 17th Bdes and 13th Corps Dug Out Coopentie completing Signal Office - trunking - Commenced work on the Cart horse and stables. Aeroplane hickup out all day - no messages dropped. A 191 B 65 C 1524 DRLS R 55 UR 198 = 563.	
Jan y 11th			Inspected local lines with Serjt Adams. Put down duck boards - Continued cook house rotation. Showers being put through.	

Army Form C. 2118.

WAR DIARY
or
INTELLIGENCE SUMMARY.
(Erase heading not required.)

Instructions regarding War Diaries and Intelligence Summaries are contained in F. S. Regs., Part II. and the Staff Manual respectively. Title pages will be prepared in manuscript.

Place	Date	Hour	Summary of Events and Information	Remarks and references to Appendices
	Jan'y 11th		To Divisional Supply Column Downcourt. Gas alert from G office 6.10 p.m. A 201 B 78 C 133 DRLS R 41 UR 276 = 729	
	Jan'y 12th		Line through to 218th Field Coy R.E. on Southern Portade Road – Sent in for part of G.S. Wagon to the Ordnance Workshops but they could not take it. Gas alert 0H 9.0 a.m. A 129 B 58 C 116 DRLS R 33 UR 341 = 687	
	Jan'y 13th		Inspected Signal Clan in flag and buzzer work. A.D.A.S. 5th Corps arrived 11.30 a.m. Spoke about pigeons - permanent ranks to COURCELLES - 9 had covered cable to C.R.A and other village lines. Straining up the BUCL route. Bde and Inkerman lines giving a bit of trouble. Line working to Dixt. Tramways. Line through to COLINCAMPS during Stn - Rally Concentrated on Stables from 9.10-12.10 - Inspection of Rifles - Gas Helmets - Ammunition etc. 12.30 p.m. Company bathing miles afternoon. 96th Bde relieved 97th Bde into line. A 141 B 86 C 130 DRLS R 47 UR 295 = 699	
	Jan'y 14th		A 116 B 107 C 122 DRLS R 45 UR 291 = 681	
	Jan'y 15th		Business busy all day on ORL route - one line put through - not enough wires for the system. PU Mallitiers with lines have arrived from CANAPLES. A 176 B 81 C 157 DRLS R 32 UR 226 = 670 Visited 116th & 1/10th Punjabis.	
	Jan'y 16th		Rally sent out to 116th Idle Wilks from 1/4 mile Knyfles armoured fund, from 1/2 mile Knyfles armoured train to complete his ORL lines. Went over to see Lorries at Bertrancourt, about lines to Q.b. Spoke to Casey - Morris about the Corps cable section here in BUS going to BERTRANCOURT to take care of lines etc. Wish Luck.	

Army Form C. 2118.

WAR DIARY
or
INTELLIGENCE SUMMARY.
(Erase heading not required.)

Instructions regarding War Diaries and Intelligence Summaries are contained in F. S. Regs., Part II. and the Staff Manual respectively. Title pages will be prepared in manuscript.

Place	Date	Hour	Summary of Events and Information	Remarks and references to Appendices
	Jan'y 16th		Reported this arrival from 5th Army Signals. A 154 B 84 C 142 DRLS R 50 UR 276 = 736	
	Jan'y 17th		"L" Lock boiled to B cable section - "U" Mulch boiled to A cable section. Snows have shown night. Cpl Juper busy again out on OPL lines. Sgt Richardson connecting up 20 line exchange in RA Office. Capt Brownfin reports his arrival from England for a fortnight attachment. Visit from DDAS. Also interviewed 2nd Sinclair about a transfer to the Signal Service. A 177 B 72 C 172 DRLS R 48 UR 259 = 706.	
	Jan'y 18th		Went over to see 7 Divn Signals and Corps Heavy Artillery Signals. A 208 B 62 C 157 DRLS R 42 UR 302 = 773	
	Jan'y 19th		Visited 4th + 16th Vidus at Courcelles. Continuing with the studies. A 179 B 59 C 149 DRLS R 60 UR 209 = 696.	
	Jan'y 20th		Remounts came in seven riders and two light draft - slipped stocking train + looked up. A 173 B 65 C 143 DRLS R 65 UR 250 = 696.	
	Jan'y 21		A.R. Section moved over to Behancourt. 113 detachment sent a Mulch on works for Lt Rawford. 96 Bde Courcelles - 4th Bde Beaumont - 97 Bde Q2b. Montpenny O.C. 62nd Signals came over to Bus to look round. A 176 B 110 C 168 DRLS R 57 UR 310 = 82.3.	

WAR DIARY or INTELLIGENCE SUMMARY

Army Form C. 2118.

Place	Date	Hour	Summary of Events and Information	Remarks and references to Appendices
	Jan 22nd		Capt Jessop reports his arrival - one officer and 7 men arrived from 61st Signals to take over - SA panic roots completed from Signal Office to RA wire village conflict & latrine "SA 1-12". Morning steen and cleaning up 1st Camp. Company lorry out of action borrowed a GS to draw our rations. A 201 B Sqn C 165 DR&S R 33 UR 358 = 846.	
	Jan 23rd		Division moved to Bertrancourt. Visited 16th Pde Hqrs, 62nd Divn arrived in Bus. A 290 B 117 C 161 DR&S R14 UR 194 = 801	
	Jan 25th		Party laying lines from Dyhem Camp to Rotrancourt exchange and from 1st barracks 318 Northumberland Fusiliers onto Divl exchange. Visited 96th Bde. A 165 B 138 C 142 DR&S R 26 UR 201 = 708	
	Jan 26th		Visited 9 Pde Sgts, not in. Paty out with ob Pde Horyes lines. Standard cars escorted of sts Company to Englebelmer forest. A 172 B 122 C 162 DR&E R 35 UR 247 = 738 ADS igs V Corps visited Bertrancourt. Asked him for an open wire route to Gr duy wik, sent other to COURCELLES. Discussed Burid lines. Visits 14th Bde, discussed forward lines with Lt Armytage. A 256 B 142 C 194 R 36 UR 342 = 970	
	Jan 27th		Visited 96 Bde + discussed lines with staff, promised Summerhayes new telephone to pacify his B.M. shifted all billets from X Camp into village. A 260, B 151, C 165, R 8, UR 323 = 947	

Army Form C. 2118.

WAR DIARY
or
INTELLIGENCE SUMMARY.
(Erase heading not required.)

Instructions regarding War Diaries and Intelligence Summaries are contained in F. S. Regs., Part II. and the Staff Manual respectively. Title pages will be prepared in manuscript.

Place	Date	Hour	Summary of Events and Information	Remarks and references to Appendices
	Jan 29th		97 Bde move to Mailly-Maillet. 1 Officer & 6 OR to 96 Bde, 6 OR to 97 Bde from 62 Dn for attachment. Lieut E. F. CHURCHILL reports to A.D.S.G. II Corps to take up of 6 HQS.	
	Jan 29/30		Visited Beaumont Hamel with Staff Geog page. A221, B132, C163, AHD, UR378 = 939. Visited 96 Bde & went round Battalions with Lt Summerhayes. Visual to be installed where possible. Arty's to 2nd pigeon message daily, another line regd to R.Bn. Newgate St to be reconnoitred. A232, B120, C173, R55, UR 298. Total 879.	
	Jan 30th		Started line to R Bn of 96 Bde from N dugout. Laid line from Takegent to R Bn of 14 Bde. Capt Walsh left and reported to DD Sig. A225-B189-C169-R61-UR 362 - Total 1009.	
	Jan 31st		Went round Battalions 97 Bde with Lieut Graty. New line regd between Q213 + V3 test point in Beaumont Hamel. Car broke ball bearings right front wheel. O/C P.E.L. inspected E.L. act & reported favourably. A279/B74/C181/R5/OR 303 = 993. Lt in 30th I Lt A.D. SINCLAIR, 17th H.L.I. reported for 1 months attachment.	

31-1-17

A W Jesson
Captain,
O.C. 32nd Divisional Signal Coy., R.E.

Army Form C. 2118.

WAR DIARY
or
INTELLIGENCE SUMMARY.
(Erase heading not required.)

Vol/5

CONFIDENTIAL

WAR DIARY

of

32ND DIV: SIGNAL COY RE.

from 1st FEBRUARY 1917 to 28th FEBRUARY 1917

Army Form C. 2118.

WAR DIARY
or
INTELLIGENCE SUMMARY.
(Erase heading not required.)

Instructions regarding War Diaries and Intelligence Summaries are contained in F. S. Regs., Part II. and the Staff Manual respectively. Title pages will be prepared in manuscript.

Place	Date	Hour	Summary of Events and Information	Remarks and references to Appendices
	1/2/17		Laid line. Q2B test station to AVB test station in Beaumont Hamel. IILieut. Mitch went home on leave. Capt Bloomfield returned to M. of S School Grantham.	
	2/2/17		Supply Coe fitted new gudgeon pin & bearing to Quentin F.L.i set — obtained pair ball bearings for car. A/242, B/163, C/165, RAH, UR318 = 988. Pigeon Class assembled. 2 men per battalion. Supply Column finished repairs to car — Quentin set running well. A/257, B/191, C/157, R/50, UR/409, Total 1064	
	3/2/17		96 Bde handed own front last night to 57 Bde. Disarmed with 8, 95, 97 & 14 Bde scheme of signalling for future use. Visited Corps and Army wireless officer & returned. Loan of wireless set and power buzzer set. A/295; B/200; C/219; R/66; UR/296 = 1075.	
	4/3/17		Corps wireless officer arrived with power buzzers & listening set. I NCO & 1 Pte instructed in use. Visited 14 Bde & II-B wireless station. II Lieut AF CUMMING reported for attac' e home from 5th Army Sig. A/229, B/234, C/159, R/35, UR/348 = 1005.	JM

WAR DIARY
or
INTELLIGENCE SUMMARY

Army Form C. 2118.

Place	Date	Hour	Summary of Events and Information	Remarks and references to Appendices
	5.3.17		Lecture by Lieut Rowe of 5th Army Signal School in Fullerphone at Mailly. Class 2. 1 man per Battalion, still infantry Laisance men as before from Brigade sections and from men. Pigeon class finished, visited Same, also 97 Bole and Fullerphone Lecture. A/262, B/203, C/154, B/45, UR/310, = 974.	
	6.3.17		Laid 3 pairs cable Q2B - White City to replace faulty buried lines, visited this party. Pinto went on leave. MCs from 5th Army Signal School continues Lectures in Fullerphone A/207, B/172, C/160, R/34, UR/317 = 890.	
	7.3.17		Tested four buzzers 4 got good Signals at 2,300 yds in spite of frozen ground, which made good earth difficult. Cylinder of Quentin E.L. engine cracked owing to non compliance with orders. Visited 97 BS - Gough just a Co. HQ Bn in this area. Il Rent Luck with party started overhaul of buried route Q2B - White City. A/249, B/202, C/167, R/67, UR/350, = 1035	
	8.3.17		Visited Corps + Army. Left Quentin cylinder with 5th Bde RFC workshops to be repaired	

WAR DIARY
or
INTELLIGENCE SUMMARY

Army Form C. 2118.

Place	Date	Hour	Summary of Events and Information	Remarks and references to Appendices
	9.2.17		A/24H, B/173, C/160, R/45, UR/295 = 887	
			II Lieut Luck reports Q2B - WHITE CITY buried route hopelessly faulty between Q2B and 1st test box, a distance of about 16 yds.	
			Arranged final details for tomorrow's operations with 97 Bde Signal Officer and Corps wireless officer.	
			Visited Beaumont Hamel, selected routes for lines to be laid at last minute.	
			Arranged two extra pairs to MAILLY MAILLET for use by 96 Bde.	
			Arranged for loan of chaff cutter, three forage reduced to 4 lbs corn. Feeds in future to be 2½ lbs corn, 2 handfuls of chaff a day at 8.30, 12.30, 4.30 & 8.30. A/31, B/168, C/175, R/92, UR/321 = 1307	
	10.2.17		Despatched to 97 Bde sigs — 1 visual station, 2 Power buzzer stations, one listening set, 2 wireless stations, a second DR.	
			Laid lines from Point 88 (A/7 Bde R.C.) – Cemetry (R.B.R.) – Walker Quarry (L.B.F.H.)	
			and — " — – AV3 (Test point) –	
			also (at dusk) Tank (about 97 Bde R.C.) to forward position of attacking Battalion	
			Lines held well during night, operations most successful. Only wrong unit	
			G' direct line A/241, B/230, C/185, R/82, UR/298 = 1216.	
			II Lt Cumming moved to wireless corner for 5 days	

Army Form C. 2118.

WAR DIARY
or
INTELLIGENCE SUMMARY.
(Erase heading not required.)

Instructions regarding War Diaries and Intelligence Summaries are contained in F. S. Regs., Part II. and the Staff Manual respectively. Title pages will be prepared in manuscript.

Place	Date	Hour	Summary of Events and Information	Remarks and references to Appendices
	11.2.17		Sent small party to run through our lines between Post BP & TY & X telephone. Visited Q2B wireless, Milly Pigeons, Adv 97 Bde, 97 Bde Post. All communications of 97 Bde apparently worked well last night, a few forward lines only being cut, except power buzzers. Them at Gough Post was correct, aligned & connected though the base might have been longer. A/279, B/470, C/188, R/58, U.R./292 = 1277.	
	12.2.17		I.L.t Lucks having failed to make anything out of buried route Q2B - White City, sent out Capt Linton with larger party. Results more satisfactory, the route being in very fair condition from Q2B to sunken road. Power buzzers called in, being of no use. Forward wireless also came in, apparently without orders. A/248, B/452, C/181, R/55, U.R./293 = 1229.	
	13.2.17		II Lt Mulch returned from Crowe. 14 Bde move to BUS. Laid new line T dugout - D.S. Continued repairs to Q2B - White City buried route. 186 Bde took over from 14 Bde, who moved to Bus. Visited 96 & 97 Bdes. Latter having slight trouble with lines cut by our fire. Sent up flying squadron. A/236, B/197, C/202, R/91, U.R./331 = 1107	

MG

WAR DIARY
or
INTELLIGENCE SUMMARY.
(Erase heading not required.)

Army Form C. 2118.

Place	Date	Hour	Summary of Events and Information	Remarks and references to Appendices
	14.2.17		96 Bde move to Louvilliers. Apparently the people relieving them at Mailly are none too happy, so tell Lt Summerhays to send another man back to help. Lieut. Lant II Corps H.A. D.C. in am: to help owing to bad Roads. Visited 97 Bde, who are looking forward to coming out tonight. A/210, B/422, C/150, R/145, V.R/272 = 1116. Handed over to 62 Div at 9 a.m.	
	15.2.17		Visited Corps & saw 1st Summerhayes at Louvre. Have still 4 men at Mailly Maillet, 1 at an Bde & an NCO at Walker Quarry, in addition to men at Lt Mailly Maillet, Acheux & Quarry. These Removed afternoon. A/177, B/126, C/96, R/148, V.R/236 = 683 Sent Capt Linton & advance parties to VILLERS BOCAGE, & two 3 ton lorry loads stores.	
	16.2.17		14 Bde contracted to CONTAY exchange. Bde à dieux to ADS, 9 II Corps. A/170, B/50, C/82, R/147, VR/225 = 580	

WAR DIARY
or
INTELLIGENCE SUMMARY.

Place	Date	Hour	Summary of Events and Information	Remarks and references to Appendices
	23.2.17		Lectured to Officers of Divisional School at MONTRELET. A/143, B/161, C/72, R/62, U.R/197 = 490	
	24.2.17		Went round RA Bde & batteries with R.A Signal Officer. Work on line LEQUESNEL-WARVILLERS continued; it being hard open work in part buried in rather difficult trace. Led in 7 pairs from permanent route to LA RAPERIE Office. More lines laid for 96 Bde. Stables, horses, harness much improved.	
	25/2/17		96 Bde take over at WARVILLERS & Trunks & a more line. Visited HANGEST & DAVENESCOURT to see Sig. Offr French Div. He apparently passed me en route for Jonk, met him on return. He stayed to tea & arrange duct trunk to Div. Connected DSC to BEAUCOURT (Russ. Bde) Exchange. Line to WARVILLERS completed. RE Yard & RE Tram hut on exchange.	

Army Form C. 2118.

WAR DIARY
or
INTELLIGENCE SUMMARY.
(Erase heading not required.)

Instructions regarding War Diaries and Intelligence Summaries are contained in F. S. Regs., Part II and the Staff Manual respectively. Title pages will be prepared in manuscript.

Place	Date	Hour	Summary of Events and Information	Remarks and references to Appendices
	25/2/17		A/143, B/54, C/103, R/50, UR/168 = 498 Load cables for lines R.Bde - R.Div + R.Bde - B.Div R; latter not through owing to fault. French attacking.	
	26/2/17		Cable running very low. Replaced D.S. in villages with Trench D.I. Buried scheme in rear. Visited new ATD S.g.p. in cable pit in evening. A/171, B/56, C/138, R/62, UR/291 = 638	
	27/2/17.		Had 2 prs STRASSBOURG - LE QUESNOY for extending lines to R.Bde when it moves. Recovering cable and tracing out + making good French buried routes. Visited ATD S.g.s fogt cable with no success. 96.Bde moved to ROUVROY. A/182, B/98, C/141, R/80, UR/291 = 772.	
	28/2/17.		96 Bde returned from ROUVROY to WATIVILLERS. 2 Parties tracing out French buried and trench routes. Visited 96/116. Bdes + working parties. 14 Bde moved forward to LE QUESNOY. A/172, B/118, C/104, R/56, UR/228 = 676.	

H.P. Jervon
Capt RE
O.C. 32 Div Signal Co.

2/3/17

14 Bde HQ
5/6 Royal Scots
1st Dorsets
15 HLI
14 S.& G Tey
97 Bde HQ
11 Borders
2 KOYLI
16 HLI
97 M G Cy
A D M S
90 Fld Amb
91 " "
92 " "
72 San Sect
C R A
161st Bde RFA
168 " "
D. A. C.
V32 T.M.B.
Z32 T.M.B.
Y 32 T.M.B.
X 32 T.M.B.
C R E
206 Fld Cy
218 " "
219 " "

Do Train
D. H. C.
D. H. D. C. S.
42 1906 Nights
Signal

Army Form C. 2118.

WAR DIARY
or
INTELLIGENCE SUMMARY.
(Erase heading not required.)

CONFIDENTIAL

WAR DIARY.

of

32nd Divisional Signal Coy R.E.

for

1st March 1917 to 31st March 1917.

WAR DIARY
or
INTELLIGENCE SUMMARY.
(Erase heading not required.)

Army Form C. 2118.

Place	Date	Hour	Summary of Events and Information	Remarks and references to Appendices
	1/3/17		Line put through from CRA to 62 HAG Beaufort.	
	"		14 Bde to STRASSBURG (Shrewsbury)	
	"		WARVILLERS – ROUVROY (French Trunk Line) Visited HESDIN for Luminous course.	
	2/3/17		2 Pioneers sent to Army Signals School HESDIN for Luminous course. Visited R Bde, R Bn & R Co with I/Lt Sinclair, and A D Sigs IV Corps. A/169, B/168, C/145, R/57, VR/219 = 758. Arranged for reeling up parties as follows:— 1 NCO (Signal) + 4 battln signallers from R's Bde and 1 NCO (Class a) + 4 battln signallers from Battns in line on each Brigade front. 2 RA parties also at work + party under Sgt Head. Carrying on with trench & buried French lines. Visited Left Bn of French, arranged for repair of line to our Right Battln. I/Lt Sinclair reports to Sig 14 Bde, who is somewhat overworked owing to many moves. Today's move is from LE QUESNOY to STRASSBOURG. A/191, B/92, C/118, R/54, VR/025 = 650. Arranged for two parties Reserve Bde Signals to run through cable reeled up. Visited both Brigades in line to instruct them to push forward reeling up.	
	3/3/17			

Army Form C. 2118.

WAR DIARY
or
INTELLIGENCE SUMMARY.
(Erase heading not required.)

Instructions regarding War Diaries and Intelligence Summaries are contained in F. S. Regs., Part II. and the Staff Manual respectively. Title pages will be prepared in manuscript.

Place	Date	Hour	Summary of Events and Information	Remarks and references to Appendices
	4/3/17		1Lt Luck's party put through French trench/pair WARVILLERS – ROUVROY v reel in D5 pm. Sgt Stodd's party rel in 1¾ mile French D5 v ¾ mile D1, they also twin extn. A/183, C/170, C/153, R/60, UR/236 = 802. I gr much party cleaning earth of line RAPERIE – STRASSBURG. I gr much party. 2 batteries in line wearing tar. 1Lt Luck with remainder reeling up cable. Visited new line in morning + seed myself. A/203, B/118, C/140, R/58, UR/228 = 747.	
	5/3/17		Work as yesterday. Harness inspection shows that very considerable improvement has been made. 2 Battalions in town joined up to Div exchange. A/219, B/169, C/184, R/151, UR/139 = 805.	
	6/3/17		Laid Company lateral to French for 14 Bde. Maintaining French lines to 14 Bde. Recovering cable. Visited front line with 2Lts Luck + Sinclair to survey communications that may be required.	

WAR DIARY
or
INTELLIGENCE SUMMARY
(Erase heading not required.)

Army Form C. 2118.

Place	Date	Hour	Summary of Events and Information	Remarks and references to Appendices
	7/3/17 8/3/17		Worked as yesterday A/149, B/152, C/145, R/52, UR/222 = 770. Walk reconnaissance. Visited front line walk to T.J.J. to reconnoitre route for buried lines. ADS'n visited Dw re buried routes, but unable to do anything owing to adverse lack of men for digging. A/142, B/102, C/149, R/65, UR/196 = 604. Maintenance of him to Strasbourg. Started putting through an old French route to KARNEELERS. Visited both brigades in turn to arrange for more alternative routes to be laid to 13 Battalions. Visited reserve bde Hd arrang for BTCn signallers in cct to get instruction in signalling. A/170, B/156, C/110, R/59, UR/233 = 728. Put through line BORDEAUX (mb. rgt. btn) to Labyrinth (French exchange)	
	10/3/17		DC 62 (Tunnel) DwSig's came to lunch & discussed Refort. Lustus & communication to them. Put through another line to STRASBOURG, partly buried cable, partly open wire. Rec'd. sig. up & running thro' cable. A/222, B/176, C/120, R/57, UR/289 = 864	
	11/3/17		over	

Army Form C. 2118.

WAR DIARY
or
INTELLIGENCE SUMMARY.
(Erase heading not required.)

Place	Date	Hour	Summary of Events and Information	Remarks and references to Appendices
	11/3/17		DDSignals Fourth Army visited HellQrs + interviewed Sgts Hayward, Brown, Beckett + Cpls Thorpe + Williams, all candidates for commissions. Visited Battalion Hd Qrs of Keys Marne, insufficient men are being employed as signallers to keep lines in decent condition, + to brightest liverregd. A/147, B/128, C/125, B/54, U.R./017 = 68.	
	12/3/17		Visited BOUVINES, Trenches very bad. ADSignals commenced in afternoon. Started tracing lines in dug out in Chateau grounds. Existing lines will be dug little used too no. Remainder. Coy packing up + running through cable. A/168, B/156, C/143, R/88, U.R./206 = 761	
	13/3/17		Reding m's overloading cable. Trouble with lateral to Trench which unfortly put through wet in this area, at points faults do it without them. Laid a company lateral to Trench. A/175, B/146, C/131, R/65, U.R./278 = 795	

Army Form C. 2118.

WAR DIARY
or
INTELLIGENCE SUMMARY.
(Erase heading not required.)

Place	Date	Hour	Summary of Events and Information	Remarks and references to Appendices
	14/3/17		Completed two lines (armoured wire) from Australits to Sap 4, also one from Australits to Ryl Road to be connected to a french line from Vandrin.	
			Commenced armoured wire Strassburg–Australits.	
			Visited working parties above, traced company extral to French & endeavoured to discover their left Battalion report centre without success.	
			14th Bde return 9th at Wanquetin. A/145, B/178, C/121, R/62, U.R./224 = 720.	
	15/3/17		Completed Strassburg – Australits line.	
			Ceased nailing up cable. A total of about 100 miles have been nailed up & run through. Pushed on with cleaning manure out of fields, in many of which it seems to have accumulated for months.	
			A/141, B/180, C/131, R/147, U.R./237 = 776	
	16/3/17		Extended an open wire pair along permanent route from RAFFERIE to far side of BOUCHAIR & led in to STRASSBOURG.	
			Fixed 60 200 on D111 rifle range & tested cables correct.	
			Promulgated sentence of courtmartial on Pioneer Evans for breach of censorship	

2353 Wt. W2544/1454 700,000 5/15 D.D.&L. A.D.S.S./Forms/C. 2118.

WAR DIARY
INTELLIGENCE SUMMARY
(Erase heading not required.)

Army Form C. 2118.

Place	Date	Hour	Summary of Events and Information	Remarks and references to Appendices
	17/3/17		regulation, 42 clays R.T. No. 2. "Imms but though 15/14 C/ps from D.W. Dw. R.A. A/302, B/186, C/190, R/131, UR/283 = 1092. Regulated permanent lines through BOUCHOIR. One NCO & 2 men sent to AUSTERLITZ to look after Divl Cinema. 97 Bau move to DRAPERIE. 96 Bau move up to AUSTERLITZ. Great pressure of work. Spent night with 96 Bau. A/525, B/112, C/209, R/77, UR/214 = 1137.	
	18/3/17		Parties out at dawn extending Bde limits TO QU ESCOURT & PARVILLERS. 96 Brigade having trouble with battalion lines, due largely to battalions not reporting when they move, neither adjutants nor sgnl sergeants informing brigade before they take off their instruments. HQ moved to WARVILLERS, Bn 14, '96 Bdes move to LIANCOURT, 47 to Manin. Through to 2/Armee about 4 am. A/324, B/624, C/144, R/37, UR/147 = 764.	

WAR DIARY
or
INTELLIGENCE SUMMARY.

Army Form C. 2118.

(Erase heading not required.)

Place	Date	Hour	Summary of Events and Information	Remarks and references to Appendices
	19/3/17		1 Sec. New pair run by OO Cable Section through to LIAUCOURT. Handed to LIAUCOURT; 13 due 14/96 NESLE, 97 HERLY. Through to all towns. F/19 3; B/70, C/118; B/39, UR/73 = 403.	
	20/3/17		Moved to NESLE, took over 14 MESNIL-ST-NICAISE, 96 LONGUEVOISIN, 97 NESLE Bde H.Qrs in NESLE being changed. Slight delay in getting through at first owing to H.Qrs in NESLE being changed at 9 am, but through to Corps all lines by 11.30 am, (8 wherewhires on 9 p.m... 3 circuits apparently wilfully cut, reported matter. 96 Bde Fullerphone faulty, due to wrong connections. cleared them. A/278, B/Ahi, C/148, B/35, UR/12 = 617. 3 SDWRA connected. 2nd line to Roses laider 1st line held.	
	21/3/17		Bde move to VOYENNES. Lme ex tended & old part paid. Trouble with Corps line, wireless used at intervals. Collected a lot of German D scale with aid of infantry party. All battalions doing same, the shortage of cable being very serious. A/290, B/20, C/156, R/53, UR/118 = 657.	

Army Form C. 2118.

WAR DIARY
or
INTELLIGENCE SUMMARY.
(Erase heading not required.)

Instructions regarding War Diaries and Intelligence Summaries are contained in F. S. Regs., Part II. and the Staff Manual respectively. Title pages will be prepared in manuscript.

Place	Date	Hour	Summary of Events and Information	Remarks and references to Appendices
	22/3/17		Second line that through to 14 Bde at VOYENNES. Line laid from 96 Bde to OFFOY extended by thin wire to TOULLE Ferme by thin wire cable to CORPS MTD TPS at GERMAINE. Visited these two parties then went on to see possible Divl HQ at AUBIGNY. Party sent back to reel up D5 cable left behind. 2nd line through to CORPS. A/252, B/90, C/153, P/55, UR/182 = 719.	
	23/3/17		To Cable Section day about line D to E.M.T. Visited front line to see that all wires are cut. C.M.T. will attend to machine though it is well in hand at present. Put through line 14 Bde to TOULLE along permanent wires. Traced out permanent line radiating from AUBIGNY. Joined up DAC at CURCHY. A/243, B/78, C/169, R/49, UR/238 = 777.	
	24-3-17		Line (earth return) laid to Detnt of No 7 R.F. Squadron. Reeled up 6 inch cable on Roye Rd. Called hp pers on Hesly Rd. The two lines to 14 Bde at Voyennes transferred to Perm route as far as heavy strinaing, remainder of Route Poled. Return lines from 96 Bde at Lesquielinin	G.W.Q.

2353 Wt. W5544/1454 700,000 5/15 D. D. & L. A.F.S.S./Forms/C. 2118.

WAR DIARY
or
INTELLIGENCE SUMMARY.
(Erase heading not required.)

Army Form C. 2118.

Place	Date	Hour	Summary of Events and Information	Remarks and references to Appendices
	24-3-17 (am)		Ptd. line to C.M. Troops dis 4 pm. night 5 xpm line cut by Inf working party. Capt H.P. from R.E. handed over command of Coy to Capt S.H. Seelegh M.C. R.E. A30 S B122 C167 DRLS R57 OR 236 = 887	
	25-3-17		Corps brought up new pair to Corps + pair to 3.6 DW. 4 Pair cable erected to bridge over gap in AR UG Route & commenced re-regulating route. 11 It truck completed poling of lines to 1/4 Bde. Reeled up cable between Neail St N + Neale returned to Div HQ. hit his section. Line laid to Wireless Stn. Neale. Party relief Bozeh D.st recovered poles. Summertime came into force 11pm. A.I.S.M. & Ruton Party line with SADos. lines straightened out & labelled outside Sig. Office. A292 B140 C166 DRLS R 68 OR 220 = 886	
	26-3-17		11th hutch proceeded to Chateau Auroir as an advanced party to lay local circuits, straighten out perm Route Rly line to new Pde HQs. Picked up + overhauled cable Corps line giving a good deal of trouble between Neale + Rosieres. 10th/5th Pde on exchange trouble working 2.30 pm. CM Troops line dis 6.30 pm this 7.30 fault between Genevain + Souilly. Lorry pleased to be Queried & reflected L/C Hayes. Tell stores dumped there. 673 wagons supplied by DAC for this purpose. Pigeon loft arrived. Overhauling + picking up cable. A 258 B162 C176 DRLS R 53 OR 254 ~~875~~ = 903.	
	27-3-17		~~Gripping off~~ 11th truck with his section + advanced party proceeded to Chateau Auroir. AM OC's vis. Lieut Doubletl, / air Neale + Gnevain (NLVN 3/4) Advanced corps lorry arrived. F2 56 B238 C165 DRLS 95 OR 278 = 1662	

WAR DIARY or INTELLIGENCE SUMMARY

Army Form C. 2118.

Place	Date	Hour	Summary of Events and Information	Remarks and references to Appendices
	28-3-17		Capt. Sn Sodery and Bar. me Relief. Remainder of Coy'n proceeded to Chateau Aurion. Another relief arrived from corps. Laying of new lines & regulating of Penn Route station continued. 97 Bde not closed Neale noon opened Stn de Huntzville same hour. 14 Bde closed Voyennes opened	
	29-3-17		Juvinier same hour. Line 96 Bde dis Stn this 5-49 pm. A261 B100 C161 DRLS R77 UR348=1042. PN Cable section completed Pain Neale-Aurion. Rs station on wireless. 96 Bde closed Languevoisin 9 am opened Sorilly same hour. Div Office closed noon opened Aurion 11 am. 4 Corps Office opened Neale 12 noon. Pigeon loft proceeded to Aurion. Reeled up cable & regulated lines. Cable supply very low. A191 B182 C130 DRLS R43 UR152=698. Putting thro lines on AR DO VX Route. Single D5 laid but to Chateau Pommery. New line laid to	
	30-3-17		C.R.E. Lateral 14 Bde to 161 Div thro' 4 pm. Viso to 62 HAG 6pm. Work on AR DO VX AR DO RY Route unbroken, continued. A164 B72 C114 DRLS R55 UR160 = 557. 97 Bde opened Adv Stn. Chateau Pommery. DAC line thro' on 96 Bde exchge. At twitch with his Section proceeded to Pommery taking wireless set with him. Conference with Sigs RA & Bde Sig Offrs 9 Am. Line b159 Bde at Pargnieres. Linemans post established	
	31-3-17		at Dorcuty. O.P. erected at Aurion. Line laid to Dressing Stn Foreste. A241 B98 C154 DRLS R115 UR268 = 906.	

Army Form C. 2118.

WAR DIARY
or
INTELLIGENCE SUMMARY.

(Erase heading not required.)

Vol 17

CONFIDENTIAL

WAR DIARY of

32nd Divl Signal Coy R.E.

from 1st April 1917 to 30th April 1917.

Army Form C. 2118.

WAR DIARY
or
INTELLIGENCE SUMMARY.
(Erase heading not required.)

Place	Date	Hour	Summary of Events and Information	Remarks and references to Appendices
	1-4-17		DS line laid to Pommery this 4:20 AM. 3rd DS line laid to Pommery this 10:51 AM 15th & 16th BUR 79. # Bee closed — Quinies 10 AM opened Grenouine same hour. 9th Bee closed Douilly 12 noon opened Pommery same hour. 2nd DS line to PY dis 10:45 this 12:40 - shell fire Corps line troublesome all day. 2nd line this to Corps 9:30 PM. Party regulating Corps Route ARDO Route regulated & moved as far as Pole in Douilly. Route DO RY regulated (14 & 15 Bde) The Pommery line very troublesome. Cable supply very low. A241 B98 C154 DRLS RIIS UR268 = 906 line put this on ARBS Route to 23rd Manchesters. Adelphi moved SAVY 12-45 this (14 Bde) two DS line laid with 14 Bde at SAVY from Pommery this 12-45 PM 10 Corbeau Bd. established Pommery. Dir.Train Con at Bussy. Corps HA ex CR - 1st Bde est. Fin de Montigella 3:30 PM. Line Pts ont to KBS. the line use torn en CSE but not <u>connected up</u> by KBS very heavy gale (Wind & Rain) started 4.40 PM 6 1st line down Corps Lindown this 7.56 CRE Lindown 6.30 this 6.50 2 phone line to Pommey & Fullerphone this 10:30 PM, 1 phone this 11 PM 2nd this 12:30 AM working in ARDO Team pole clearing back contact - staying line to French Div (56th) dis 5 min uts. A314 B196 C158 DRLS RSS UR176 = 899	
	2-4-17			

WAR DIARY
or
INTELLIGENCE SUMMARY

Army Form C. 2118.

Place	Date	Hour	Summary of Events and Information	Remarks and references to Appendices
	3-4-17		Poled D5 line to Pommery. Staying Poles irregularly on AR & G Route - Straightening out leads to Eastroad - 3rd line to Pommery this 1.30am. Telephone line OR 7am - 157 Bde R7A line giving trouble - Corps lines bad and unreadable telegrams disposed of by phone, D3 + DR. 54 R DS joined up - Such used on telephone set to G.O. Pommery. D.R.'s got. Weather heavy + squally - cable supply very low. A 249 B 176 C 148 DRLS R 45 UR 167 = 785	
	4-4-17		3 Met Cols put two to Pommery - two by Open wires to Vaux - one by D5 - one by Open wires to Rouvroy - one by D5 - one pair superimposed on - reeled up two direct D.C. lines ARD O Pole stayed back. Snowing all day. D.A.C. phoned S7 order. attended to Corps line troubleaux - cable situation serious. A 273 B 206 C 166 DRLS Reg 67 UR 178 = 890	
	5-4-17		from Vaux. Corps ends interrupted by line tests - 1 leg perm line extended to 167 Bde at Attilly on Katteillers + Streuilles to x 15a by D3 - 1 leg extended from Vaux to 159 Bde at Ettreillers + in to x 15A D5 - one D3 line laid Streillers to Savy - D1 + D3 line laid Savy - x 15a. Pieced up D5 line Savy to Offury + Truille to Donilly - Erected Comic route Poles G1 hop Poles + others D12 B 63 to	1007

WAR DIARY
or
INTELLIGENCE SUMMARY
(Erase heading not required.)

Army Form C. 2118.

Place	Date	Hour	Summary of Events and Information	Remarks and references to Appendices
	5-4-17		Guizancourt bct Div line now working. Metallic on far air X 12 & 32 when one leg goes to earth, other leg slung carries short in metallic section. DRH 4th Airline section which arrived aft of 4-4-17 thoroughly overhauling [Penn route ARDO Dove]. Aerial labelling. A314 B262 C194 DRLS R75 UR 253 = 1098	
	6-4-17		Cpl Fuld transferred to No 2 section vice Sgt Bankett recalled to No1 Section. 2 pairs extended from Vaux to Attilly via Streillers (open wires = able DS) one pair Attilly & Streillers (open wires DS). One pair twisted DS from Guizancourt + two pairs twisted DS from Quivieres to Penn Route at D12 to reeled up. 44 Airline Party carried on with ARDO Dove Routes. DS to Beauvois Dueman sent out & reported all air lines to No cable out near Foreste Criterion closed Pommery 3.0 pm opened Attilly 4.30 pm. Diricle on Criterion exchge. A304 B208 C179 DRLS R89 UR 203 = 983	
	7-4-17		Reeled up 1½ pairs DS Pommery to Vauxpole leaving ARDO ¾ Wires to PY - ARDO 2/6 extended hot tied up to 97 office at Attilly. Reeled up DS Vauxpole to crater outside Streillers. Reeled up D3 single Beauvois towards Foreste. 62 MAG. Single line joined up to 1 leg of ARFT 2 other leg earthed at pole	/AT

A.D.S.S./Forms/C.2118.

WAR DIARY or INTELLIGENCE SUMMARY

Army Form C. 2118.

Place	Date	Hour	Summary of Events and Information	Remarks and references to Appendices
	7-4-17 (Con)		14 Bde closed down STM opened Germaine same hour. Twisted D3 from V. Morden HA to F. Mats Stm reeled up. Sin C.O. D3 to reel & Stn to Sig Office reeled up. D3 (Scrumy) reeled up in forests. Cleaned up camp. Struck surveyed proposed route Rompy to X18a. & buried stag block ready to stay f Taus pole. Collected top poles. Found Sixmen dump of top + semi perm poles + collected some - also G1 + Staguina. A 302 B 178 C 169 DRLS R 62 UR 272 = 933	
	8-4-17		Fine rain. AR/DO/RY route extended few wires Rompy to X18a. 161 Bde RFA good sigs 7.30pm. Boche perm Route surveyed Vaux – Streillers – Attilly – Streilles – Savy. First two comparatively good. 3rd no good. Overhauling cable. Airline Route 44 Airline section completed work on AR to VX Route. 161 Line dpartedtcls 515pm. Fault found the hut in 181 Stries. A247 B 232 C 171 DRLS 55 UR 179 = 884	
	9-4-17		Diverted AR&Y Route (2 prs) from AR.DO Route – Reeledup Broek D3 Dieup P.O. to Beauvin. Collected poles h/p, Comie, Demi Ferm – Herleville cable. 44 MAC commenced work on VX & ES Route regretting & pulling thro & pairing – A 330 B 238 C 177 DRLS R 67 UR 232 = 1084	

Army Form C. 2118.

WAR DIARY or **INTELLIGENCE SUMMARY.**
(Erase heading not required.)

Instructions regarding War Diaries and Intelligence Summaries are contained in F.S. Regs. Part II. and the Staff Manual respectively. Title pages will be prepared in manuscript.

Place	Date	Hour	Summary of Events and Information	Remarks and references to Appendices
	10-4-17		Erected 3 bottle comic route (60 U.G) 96 Bde new HQ at Quarry X27 d.3.6 one leg earth return been line other pin extended to meet X2 & 3.2 to 159 Bde RFA. VX 15 Route by D3 Serman. one pair D3 Serman laid 159 to VX 15 Route. one pair pair put thro Roupy to & 15a Tied in by cable. Reeled up cable X15a to Savy to Pommery. Cleaning Savy generally. 4.4 M.a.L. completed. been pain Vx to Streillers. Paid company. Very rough weather all day snow sleet storms. A 306 B158 C185 DRLS R81 UR263 = 973	
	11-4-17		Two lines to Pommery dived at VX hole one put thro to 159 at Streillers other thru 96 Hqs at Savy Quarry. 96 closed Pommery 12 noon opened Quarry same hour. Looking in pain Roupy to Quarry rQuarry X15a - tested D5 laid Attily to new Criterion at X16a. 44 M.a.L. Malcing good P. line to Streillers. Eighteen closed down at X16a. 2 pm Proceeding to Villeverque - 182 Bde opened Fm de Montzeville 4.6 pm - 35 Div Report centre opened Beauvois 5-10 pm. Very high wind causing a good deal of trouble. A225 B198 C137 DRLS R67 UR191 = 813 Reeled up phno cable	

Army Form C. 2118.

WAR DIARY
or
INTELLIGENCE SUMMARY.
(Erase heading not required.)

Place	Date	Hour	Summary of Events and Information	Remarks and references to Appendices
	12-4-17		Work continued on Vaux attack Route & Reserve being put thro' to Arras. Roupy × 150 Route 2 pairs - Straightening of Fresh Route. Commenced erecting horse shelters. Two to 3rd Div Rear W36m, 14 Bde relieved 96 at Savy Quarry 96 to Serume — Contact on DoV × AT Route Grand + Criterion especials A294 B176 C 3.09 DRLS R82 UR 283 = 1044	
	13-4-17		Capt Rudolph + Pauls out cleaning Contact DoV × 1st Route 1.10pm Criterion Grand + Adolphi lines) later thro' Criterion + Jude in view few contact afterwards let thro' two — D5 interruption cable had been deliberately cut out Stricklers — Pain put thro' to 3rd Div on AR BS1 — route in very bad order where 3rd K.B.S. had cut R.E. cables & Ropes in — trajum both sides gone back to 2pm D3 interruption cable from Foucle - Douilly Rd to Suenne needed up by some unit unknown app 97 Bde moved to ×152 — Dandy lines on by app. D10 other earth Adolphi lines in contact with dandy. Work on Phiens Wheeler & Hells cont'd. ton Roup Savy ×180 Realeluf DS Wheeler Vaux & S1 1½ mile put in view drums to length. A309 B130 C 215 DRLS R51 UR 218 = 956	

Army Form C. 2118.

WAR DIARY
or
INTELLIGENCE SUMMARY.
(Erase heading not required.)

Instructions regarding War Diaries and Intelligence Summaries are contained in F.S. Regs., Part II and the Staff Manual respectively. Title pages will be prepared in manuscript.

Place	Date	Hour	Summary of Events and Information	Remarks and references to Appendices
	14-4-17		Party out clearing contact ents on Doux AT Route to 159 — 14 — 97 + 158 — all clear 7 A.m, one leg of new P.L (not in use at present) found cut — lines to Adelphi (Y 4.13.60) + 97 Bde via nonpy apparently in contact, found 2 to crossed — 96 Bde moved to Attilly 16 A.m took to Germaine again + repair 3 bottle Cornie thoroughly stayed new pole put in — Work cont'd on RY-Y 153 route + Etreillers. Attilly Route — Reeled up interruption cable on Etreillers. Satry Attilly route — 85 men J Coy billeted at Germaine — A 268 B 104 C 163 SRLS R 58 UR 16D = 753	
	15-4-17		4.4 M.A.L at disposal of Sctn Officer to overhaul — Rain D5 — Rain Attilly to 150 to extend pair on Penn Route + pair 15 laid X 15a to 16b at X 12 a 16-8 moved Attilly to X 12 a — 96 Bde relieved 97 at X 15a — 97 took to Germaine — Work cont'd on Penn Route Rouby — Attilly — Contact via Adelphi + X 15a Line no Rouby front found the due to tightly strained Bronze wire erected by French in same poles — Uneven cut-out on toy + Uneven above recented — Work on Foreste Route Cont'd — A 269 B 148 C 145 SRLS R 58 UR 782 = 87 —	

Army Form C. 2118.

WAR DIARY
or
INTELLIGENCE SUMMARY.
(Erase heading not required.)

Place	Date	Hour	Summary of Events and Information	Remarks and references to Appendices
	16/4/17		Wiring of Auroir X15a Route cont'd — 2 single Ds lines laid up to Bde to adv 14 Bde HQt at S.1.6 central — an English aeroplane was brought down near the party. The Officer i/c rendered potent remains to ambulance for wounded observer & body of pilot though in trains. Guns, maps etc. reported walter to G— and h.l. confirmed mining Arttly Route on far as brittany in Artilly — Work on Front Route cont'd parties collecting & burying Ammo — A 193 B100 C 137 DRLS R42 UR 260 = 712	
	17/4/17		Wiring of Auroir — X15a Route cont'd — Work cont'd on Penn Route Attily x/15a — OC. Sig. 61 Dir. Came over with his 2nd i/c & took round — Overhauled cable — Completed trunk on Front Route — collected & burying Ammo. A 208 B 82 C 138 DRLS R67 UR 227 — Some running work cont'd by 44 bud on Attilly X15a Route — also work cont'd on Ronby x15a Route — Clearing of AR YSC & ARmE Route commenced New Tram Pole up — Overhauled cable — A 188 B 88 C 152 DRLS R73 UR 202 = 703	
	18/4/17		1st Bde Moved to Fermoring 97 Moved to Beny — Work cont'd on Attilly x/15a Route — Collecting ton X15a Auroir route — diversion of ARmE Route cont'd — collecting	
	19/4/17			

Army Form C. 2118.

WAR DIARY
or
INTELLIGENCE SUMMARY.
(Erase heading not required.)

Place	Date	Hour	Summary of Events and Information	Remarks and references to Appendices
	19-4-17	(con)	Ammo etc. Overhauling Cable. Sig 61 taken round lines & Rdes — Enemy shelled heavily in the evening & lines broken down — Party out most of night putting this — A 278 B 116 C 169 DRLS R 57 UR 319 = 777	
	20-4-17		Interruption cable put in at army heading division S route — Division S route commenced — 154 Bde moved to Attily — later 96 Bde moved × 15a to Attily — now to servicing — ARMIE Route carried on the overhauled cable — visited Voyennes — 182 Co Sny 14 Bde to Pro de Montigny A 213 B 188 C 144 DRLS R 57 UR 116 = 818	
	21-4-17		Division I) AR × A Route completed trunk carried in with on × 18a AR eta 2 pairs — 12 pairs J5 Attily — × 15a trans forced to open line & needed up — 1 Cable section sent on manoeuvre to Voyennes under Lieut Thurtle to recon cables etc — 96 Bde moved to Endomont on to Attila — A 212 B 224 C 188 SPLR R 28 UR 261 = 873	
	22-4-17		AR × A Route blown up & Enemy party sent out & recovered from out H.M. landed over to 61st DIV 10 am ace line OR except sig route — took over lines at Voyennes in Sprl on division — A 132 B 112 C 114 DRLS R 37 UR 176 = 571	

2353. Wt. W3544/1454 700,000 5/15 D. D. & L. A.D.S.S. (Forms/C. 2118.

Army Form C. 2118.

WAR DIARY
or
INTELLIGENCE SUMMARY.
(Erase heading not required.)

Instructions regarding War Diaries and Intelligence Summaries are contained in F. S. Regs., Part II and the Staff Manual respectively. Title pages will be prepared in manuscript.

Place	Date	Hour	Summary of Events and Information	Remarks and references to Appendices
	23-4-17		Overhauling stores, cleaning wagons etc. F.S. hostel 97 E. Bde Signal A 164 B 124 C 107 DRLS R 38 VR 274 = 704	
	24-4-17		Overhauling & cleaning wagons, stores etc. F.C. hostel 176 Bde 10 Officers Arrived Battalion Battalion Sig. Officer course. A 143 B 94 C 141 DRLS R 37 VR 25 = 646	
	25-4-17		Overhauling stores - cleaning harness etc. Dt. visits 14th & 96th Bdes. A 158 B 98 C 95 DRLS R5 30 Lurries 306 = 687	
	26.4.17		Cleaning harness, overhauling stores etc. All horses inspected. Capt Linton left the Coy & proceeded to 4th Army Signal School at Le Quesnoy. 11 hrs from AN Cable Section RE joins the Coy Summerhoff No 3 Section presents in leave. Riding School from 2 to 3 every day for Balt: Signal Officers. Canvas trenches near Coy Hd Qrs. Lectures - gas A 101. B 112. C 89. DRLS. A 37. Lurries 198 = 537 A.D.S.S./Forms/C. 2118.	

WAR DIARY
or
INTELLIGENCE SUMMARY.
(Erase heading not required.)

Army Form C. 2118.

Place	Date	Hour	Summary of Events and Information	Remarks and references to Appendices
	27.4.17		Grooming, cleaning harness etc. Horses inspection. Riding school in afternoon. Store-taking etc. A 119 B 100 C 109 DRLS R 40 UR 252 = 610	
	28.4.17		Running his cable, overhauling stores etc. two infection on Aeri- officer clears Signals lectures & Baths (in) "Pigeon Service" weather B 121 B 156 C 82 DRLS R 37 UR 298 = 694	
	29.4.17		Stables harness cleaning etc. Church Parade. A 119 B 120 C 85 DRLS R 35 UR 229 = 568	
	30.4.17		Grooming harness cleaning horses etc. Horses inspection. Horses to MONTIZEUSE mounted patrol Shoeing Steaming Farm. A 118 B 156 C 99 DRLS R37 UR 233 = 613	

Stratton. 1t
for Major
OC. 32nd Div. Sig. Cy. R.E.

Army Form C. 2118.

WAR DIARY
or
INTELLIGENCE SUMMARY.
(Erase heading not required.)

Vol 18

CONFIDENTIAL

WAR DIARY.

of

32nd Divisional Signal Coy R.E.

From 1st May 1917 to 31st May 1917

Place	Date	Hour	Summary of Events and Information	Remarks and references to Appendices

Army Form C. 2118.

WAR DIARY
or
INTELLIGENCE SUMMARY.
(Erase heading not required.)

Instructions regarding War Diaries and Intelligence Summaries are contained in F. S. Regs., Part II. and the Staff Manual respectively. Title pages will be prepared in manuscript.

Place	Date	Hour	Summary of Events and Information	Remarks and references to Appendices
	1.5.17		Grooming, cleaning harness, exercising horses etc. Company Drill. Kind weather. Patrols patrolled by mounted patrol. Weather very fine.	
	2.5.17		Inspection of horses & harness etc. Exercises etc. a Cricket match was played between the Battalion Signal Officers Course to the pukes from the Signal Coy. Signal Coy own. Weather very fine	
	3.5.17		Grooming, cleaning horses etc. Company Drill Exercising 15 minutes patrol along the line MONTIZELE FARM. Weather very fine	
	4.5.17		Grooming, grazing etc. The remounts & horses Cleaning & burnishing harness ready for inspection of Company by Divisional Commander. Weather very fine.	
	5.5.17		Cleaning & burnishing near & for inspection. Major General Shute inspected the Signal Commander & Company & expressed himself as being very pleased	

WAR DIARY
or
INTELLIGENCE SUMMARY

Army Form C. 2118.

Place	Date	Hour	Summary of Events and Information	Remarks and references to Appendices
	5.5.17 (cont)		with the smartness of the turn out the also Frankles the Company for the work they had done in heated very fine 2/Lt Mitch speaking of the Division. Grooming, grazing etc. Church Parade 5 GHQ holder hence	
	6.5.17.		Grooming, grazing etc ATHIES. Weather very fine	
	7.5.17.		Cleaning harness etc Grooming grazing wagons etc. Drivers (Dvr McGrath (Steinkamp) to GHQ for shoeing course had Ernst stains from Leave. Lt Handle to the first visits all Battalion Signallers in 97th Brigade wear his Grooming harness & Grazing etc weather very fine	
	8.5.17.		Stables, horses, wagons etc	
	9.5.17.		3 recruits L.D.H. Train from Div Amm Col Cleaning wagons, grazing, grooming. arrived at Sordell hay and animals of St Beckett leaves from Co Vm to St Pol & tm HQ Can Kum Forees Spruls hrs in which he TANKS. Demand of	

Army Form C. 2118.

WAR DIARY
or
INTELLIGENCE SUMMARY.
(Erase heading not required.)

Instructions regarding War Diaries and Intelligence Summaries are contained in F. S. Regs., Part II. and the Staff Manual respectively. Title pages will be prepared in manuscript.

Place	Date	Hour	Summary of Events and Information	Remarks and references to Appendices
	9.5.17		The Company trek well represented races breaths very fine.	
	10.5.17		Stables, grazing, grooming horses etc. Weather fine. O.C. + Hbreth to 14th Brigade	Cleaning wagons and harness. Batts Signallers of
	11.5.17		Grooming, grazing horses. O.C. + 2nd i/c @ general battalion Squadron Brigade on parks inspections line to Langouvoisin transport lines, in cops line to IGNY. O.C. 2 i/c + H. Lieut to NESLE to see A.D. Sigs IV Corps.	cleaning etc. Squadron of 26 breths hair A.D. Sigs IV Corps
	12.5.17		Stables, grazing, cleaning harness etc. Cpl Welsh Jones the Company from "A" + "B" Cable Section R.E. O.C's No 2, 3 + 4 sections to YONENNES breath changed.	K. Nesle
	13.5.17		Grooming grazing, burnishing harness to Church Parade Lt Scott acting as Div Sig Officer for the day O.C. 2-in C. + H Luck to NESLE to see A.D. Signals IV Corps	

WAR DIARY
or
INTELLIGENCE SUMMARY.
(Erase heading not required.)

Army Form C. 2118.

Place	Date	Hour	Summary of Events and Information	Remarks and references to Appendices
B.S. 17			Horses + Harness to BEAU COURT + arms was cleaned. Officers + men to BEAU COURT to take over new Signal Office & Stables. Willis eto. breakfast.	
14.5.17			Horse & Stallion furnishing it. "B" walked with 16th Brigade. R.F.A. Communication Cable Section maintained by D.R. to FONCHES. 30 Carts + harness. 2 journeys to BEAU COURT with Shoe horse brakes. Changed makes its men & horses cleaning up.	
15.5.17			Stables. Little et Hot Brigade R.F.A. move to FOLIES. Communication Section by D.R. B Cutts went Cable Lines from FONCHES — BEAUCOURT — DMIE COURT Lines NESLE - CHAULNES Company. B Cuts put up places with "D" R.A. 97th Brigade lines to FONCHES 14th Brigade move to BUNY + took over Communication of 97th Brigade. B Cable Section prevent to BEAU COURT then 1/Res	

A.5834. Wt. W4973/M687 750,000 8/16 D. D. & L. Ltd. Forms/C.2118/13.

Army Form C. 2118.

WAR DIARY
or
INTELLIGENCE SUMMARY.
(Erase heading not required.)

Place	Date	Hour	Summary of Events and Information	Remarks and references to Appendices
	15.5.17		Moved to BEAU COURT. Horses made 2 journeys to BEAU COURT and stores. Conveyance for stores CSM	
	16.5.17		K BEAUCOURT. Headquarters transport + 1 detachment of A Cable section marched to BEAU COURT leaving VOYENNES at 4 AM. 1 Detachment of A Section rail at they to ATHIES + 2 lines to BUNY. Divisional H.Q. move from VOYENNES to BEAU COURT. Signal Office closes at VOYENNES at 12 noon + opens at VOYENNES. Same hour. Small exchange eft at VOYENNES for communication by wire to 168 Brigade R.F.A. Communication established to — 14 Brigade at FONCHES 96 do at OMIECOURT 97 do at CAIX 4 Corps at NESLE CRA at BUNY Weather being wet.	

WAR DIARY
or
INTELLIGENCE SUMMARY.
(Erase heading not required.)

Army Form C. 2118.

Place	Date	Hour	Summary of Events and Information	Remarks and references to Appendices
	17.5.17		Parties out putting lines to VILLERS-AUX-ERABLES, CAYEUX, WARVILLERS, THEZZY. Communication established by wire to 14 Brigade at WARVILLERS 96 Brigade at CAIX 97 Brigade at THEZZY 2nd in C & A buck to NESLE VILLERS CARBONNEL and VILLERS BRETTENEAUX re about lines etc. Grooming, grazing, cleaning horses, marques etc. weather changeable cats.	
	18.5.17		Parties out putting thro' lines VILLERS BRETTENEAUX, DEMUIN to LE QUESNEL. Communication by wire established to 14th Brigade at LE QUESNEL, CRA at DEMUIN. 161 Brigade RFA at HAILLES line got through from DEMUIN to 97th Brigade exchange at THEZZY.	

Army Form C. 2118.

WAR DIARY
or
INTELLIGENCE SUMMARY.
(Erase heading not required.)

Instructions regarding War Diaries and Intelligence Summaries are contained in F. S. Regs., Part II. and the Staff Manual respectively. Title pages will be prepared in manuscript.

Place	Date	Hour	Summary of Events and Information	Remarks and references to Appendices
	19.5.17		Grooming cleaning harness etc. Lines gut through 4th Army Exchange at VILLERS BRETTON EUX D.A.C. at DEMUIN 108 B&E RFA at IGNAUCOURT.	
	20.5.17		Stables grooming harness exercise etc. Church Parade. Spraying vehicles along lines to THEZZY. LE QUESNEL, VILLERS BRETTONEUX, IGNAUCOURT + DEMUIN. 'A' 'An' Cable Section + 40 briders dep Section report from IV Corps. 4 Lack procees on leave to U.K. Lines holidae. Inspection parade hethers ... It.	
	21.5.17		to VILLERS BRETTONEUX - DEMUIN.	
	22.5.17		Grooming grazing exercise etc. Mounts parade along Lines to IGNAU COURT, VM DORE, CHENUM VEGT + DEMUIN. Installation of 1 Company stat...	

WAR DIARY
or
INTELLIGENCE SUMMARY.

Army Form C. 2118.

Place	Date	Hour	Summary of Events and Information	Remarks and references to Appendices
	23.5.17		Inspection parade etc. Grazing etc. Distribution 1 section detailed for the Company to accompany the Divisional Artillery	
	24.5.17		Morning grazing etc. Minute police along line	
	25.5.17		Stables, grooming, cleaning harness, wagon etc. Grazing exercise. Minute to total Painting along line is	
VILLERS BRETTON EUX			Painting all wagons. Cleaning	
	26.5.17		Grooming, grazing etc. Church Parade. Cleaning wagons. Overhauling cable	
	27.5.17		Church Parade, painting all hauling wagons overhauling Stables, grooming, cleaning harness etc. Painting	
	28.5.17		Stables, Grooming, cleaning harness etc. Painting wagons etc. Overhauling cable. Instruction of near personnel. Divisional Visual Scheme started 30 specialists	

Army Form C. 2118.

WAR DIARY
or
INTELLIGENCE SUMMARY.
(Erase heading not required.)

Place	Date	Hour	Summary of Events and Information	Remarks and references to Appendices
	28.5.17		From each battalion in the Division. Demand Commanders came round clothes at scheme.	
	29.5.17		Unveil scheme continued till noon. Stable groom him gym this to VILLERS BRETTONEUX etc. and MARCEL CAVE	
	30.5.17		Stable grooming went Brushing up wagons etc. Communication established to VILLERS BRETTONEUX 97 Bde at MARCEL CAVE 1st Bde at being hones over an Advance party BERQUIN OO there by Car. VIEUX BERQUIN. hourly cleaning wagons Stable grooming etc	
	31.5.17		preparing generally for move.	

Malhew Capt.
East Yorkshire Regt.
W.O.C. 33rd Divisional Cyclist Corps R.E.

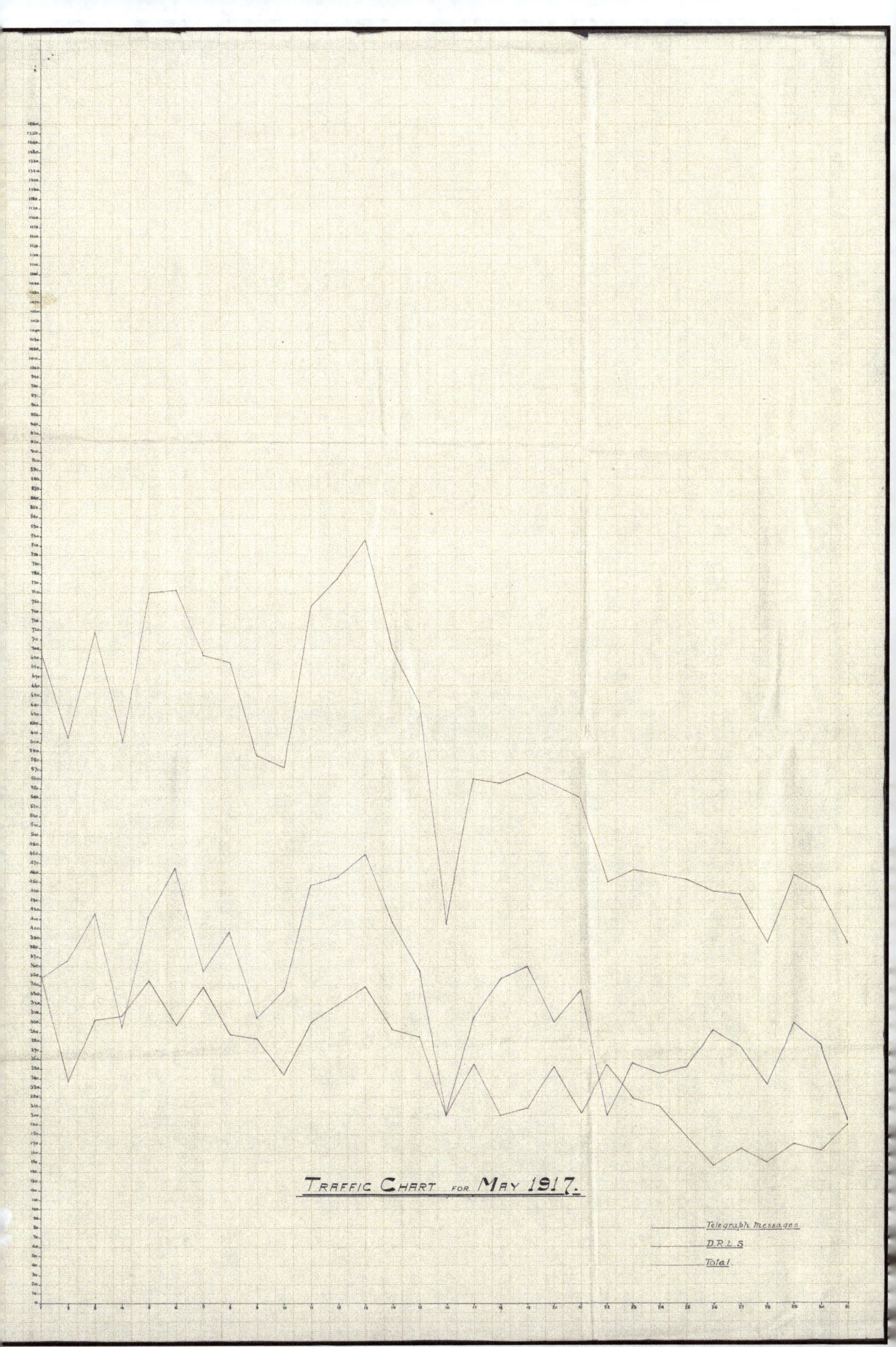

Army Form C. 2118.

WAR DIARY
or
INTELLIGENCE SUMMARY.
(Erase heading not required.)

Vol 19

CONFIDENTIAL
WAR DIARY.
of
32nd Divisional Signal Company R.E.
from 1st June 1917 to 30th June 1917

WAR DIARY
or
INTELLIGENCE SUMMARY

Army Form C. 2118.

(Erase heading not required.)

Place	Date	Hour	Summary of Events and Information	Remarks and references to Appendices
	1.6.17		Entrained at GUILLASCOURT station. Left Formow [?] till March to station near Formow [?]. Rethinking 9 [?]. on officers train in rear. Spent in travelling.	
	2.6.17		Arrived at CASTRES (Somme). Marched from station to billets. HQ and HQ Coy at BERQUIN. Battalion by Coys as follows:– A Coy at DUBLIEU, B Coy at GARONNE, C Coy at JOULIEU. Commenced general cleaning up with its settling in.	
	3.6.17		Settling in. Cleaning up. Church Parade in the morning. General cleaning etc. Sermon in the new "Kerryowo [?]" in the afternoon.	
	4.6.17		Cleaning stables. Cleaning along lines to all the billets [?] Parades.	[sig]

Army Form C. 2118.

WAR DIARY
or
INTELLIGENCE SUMMARY.
(Erase heading not required.)

Place	Date	Hour	Summary of Events and Information	Remarks and references to Appendices
	5.6.17		Stables grooming cleaning harness etc. Exercise of all horses. Parties out fatigues. OC & 2/Lt Amey began uf Company Carpenters busy fitting the S-L wagon of as a mercury signal office. Capt. Mullis & Lieuenen aspiration rehearsed rehearsing of scent from	
			VIEUX BERQUIN to FLETRE.	
			all battalion Expedition 96th F. Bar Exbr by 2 i/c.	
	6.6.17		Stables grooming cleaning harness etc. Exercise all held arm sprinklers in firing lines on by 2 i/c. Park rehearsing of firing lines on ris-0911 BERQUIN taken by FLETRE and by Enly evacuated sick Stables (Empty) who & section harness to rearer. Grooming sent to 68 Bre A.D.D. All	
	7.6.17		6 Riders Confines broomits callas and	
			Company Callas in Cur the horses K men pass the	

WAR DIARY
or
INTELLIGENCE SUMMARY.
(Erase heading not required.)

Army Form C. 2118.

Instructions regarding War Diaries and Intelligence Summaries are contained in F. S. Regs. Part II. and the Staff Manual respectively. Title pages will be prepared in manuscript.

Place	Date	Hour	Summary of Events and Information	Remarks and references to Appendices
	7.6.17		Troops attacking the MESSINES – WYTSCHAETE ridge. This Brigade is not to be used during the day.	
	8.6.17		Stables, grooming etc. Cleaning harness, wagons etc. fifa inspection etc. Party went to the VIEUX – BERQUIN – FLETRE road. Confined to billets in area.	
	9.6.17		Stables, grooming etc. Church services all Speakers, 1 battalion in T.S. B.S. taken by 2nd in C. at Grazies Church Parade.	
	10.6.17		Stables, grooming etc. Completed G.S. wagon – amplets as Regml. offrs.	
	11.6.17		Stables, grooming, cleaning harness, wagons etc. All majors etc. Trucks preparation to Capt & Reveillé moving to new area.	

Army Form C. 2118.

WAR DIARY
or
INTELLIGENCE SUMMARY.
(Erase heading not required.)

Instructions regarding War Diaries and Intelligence Summaries are contained in F. S. Regs., Part II. and the Staff Manual respectively. Title pages will be prepared in manuscript.

Place	Date	Hour	Summary of Events and Information	Remarks and references to Appendices
	12.6.17		Lt Luck with all men & BA Cable Section transport all moved to WORMHOUDT. Communication by wire established with all Bdes & RA in new sectors	VIEUX BERQUIN
	13.6.17		At Bde ent. Transport & BA Cable Section moved to COUDEKERQUE. Communication with all Bdes	
			& RA maintained. OC went into new area from WORMHOUDT to recce for night.	
	14.6.17		Lt Luck with Coudekerque to hospital. BA Cable Section proceeded from COUDEKERQUE - BRANCHE. Billets & General Buck Camp with Men & Cleaning up & settling in communication with 11st Bde at COUDEKERQUE - BRANCHE	
	15.6.17		Lines & 1st Bde at RUDYCOOTE. Officer patrol pushed forward from VIEUX BERQUIN to reconnoitre.	Kent

Place	Date	Hour	Summary of Events and Information	Remarks and references to Appendices
COUDEKERQUE-BRANCHE	15.6.17		Signed office at our HQ. Closed down tents after cleaning up. [illegible] with 2-i-C. [illegible] of Company's procedure & run Signal office. Opened a new HQ office to [illegible]. The S.S. group which her home littered as a [illegible] initials signal office was [illegible] very Satisfactory.	
	16.6.17		Stables. Drooming etc. Generally [illegible] house-keeping. Unnecessary all lines have been laid. Connect with 97th Bde at CHATEAU near FORT MARDICK - CAPPELLE "locale" lines put up.	
	17.6.17		Ord out. the mend 2/Lt Leek & "B" Section for a cable line finish to OOST DUNKERQUE communication with 1st Bde. On line to COUDEKERQUE BRANCHE	MM

Army Form C. 2118.

WAR DIARY or INTELLIGENCE SUMMARY.

(Erase heading not required.)

Place	Date	Hour	Summary of Events and Information	Remarks and references to Appendices
	17-6-17		Rules at by "A" Section. Remainder stable, grooming etc.	
	18-6-17		Pit truck with its Medium Lorry out local lines from Signal Office at new dromes at COXYDE-BAINS, generally settling down to new HQ. Remainder of horse transport under C.G.M.S. proceed from old HQ to new HQ.	
	19-6-17		On the Ammunition of the French from there taking over — see Kems to Coy inclosed drivers from Jn HQ to 20th Single cable lysotis in the line to a gallant platoon team with his HQ with "B" Section lay down lines from his HQ to OOST-DUNKERQUE BAINS & the lateral antennae lines between OOST DUNKERQUE & NIEUPORT advanced BdeHQs in NIEPORT ans firm	

Army Form C. 2118.

WAR DIARY
or
INTELLIGENCE SUMMARY.
(Erase heading not required.)

Place	Date	Hour	Summary of Events and Information	Remarks and references to Appendices
NIEUPORT BAINS.	19.6.17 20.6.17		Divisional HQ moved out of rest at GIVERLE - BRANCHE into the line at COXYDE - BAINS. Lywel office closes at Old HQ & opens at new HQ at 9 AM. Communication established with Inf. Bde at ROSARY (OOST DUNKERQUE) 96th BDE at KING ELECTRIQUE (OOST DUNKERQUE BAINS) CRA at COXYDE BAINS 97th BDE at ZUYDCOOTE Slates cleaning, repairing & mopping etc. Remainder Coy 12-in-c Forces Officers apart of obs to man the lay any Fothergill Officers apart of duty with airplane Lt Jackson from 16th Lancs Fusiliers 2/Lt M.E. Parsons - R.S. Castle Lithuan.	

Army Form C. 2118.

WAR DIARY
or
INTELLIGENCE SUMMARY.
(Erase heading not required.)

Place	Date	Hour	Summary of Events and Information	Remarks and references to Appendices
	21.6.17		Stables. Grooming. Cleaning harness & equipment. Inspection Parades at 9 p.m. Ammunition established with Cox & Co Ville.	
	22.6.17		11 thick and 96 H B.Des. to B.HNS Coyle to Lt Coy Coote. Stables. Grooming. Cleaning harness & equipments. 2 hr mounted drives. Patrols by mounted party to his lines and 96 H B.Des. Lt Jackson takes over Command of A Section.	
	23.6.17		Stables. Grooming. Et or march. Single cable line Laid to GHYVELDE. ADMS put in the telephones.	
	24.6.17		96 H B.De. move to GHYVELDE. 1 Communication established. 1 truck & party got thus & horses from Cox ?AE	

Army Form C. 2118.

WAR DIARY
or
INTELLIGENCE SUMMARY.
(Erase heading not required.)

Place	Date	Hour	Summary of Events and Information	Remarks and references to Appendices
	24.6.17		15 AMIRAL Exchange. Lt Parsons & party lay a line of cables from OOST DUNKE RQUE to NIEUPORT via NIEUPORT Bains. Ych Schofield for seven cart for 3 days to 15th H.L.I. Clearing French wires out of the trenches in his sector. occupies premises lay a 1st Divisional HQ. Bde.	
	25.6.17.		Browning statty at an wurd. Hunter inspects Lt Jackson & party lay a pair of cables from AMIRAL to Bois TRIANGULAIRE. AMIRAL Lt park carries on with work as yesterday. Lt Parsons moves into the line with HQ 97th Bde. Communication establishes link from at NIEUPORT. to Bois TRIANGULAIRE And 161 Bde RFA	[signature]

Army Form C. 2118.

WAR DIARY
or
INTELLIGENCE SUMMARY.
(Erase heading not required.)

Place	Date	Hour	Summary of Events and Information	Remarks and references to Appendices
	26.6.17		Stables morning etc as usual. Lt Jenkins with section went in lieu of COXYDE BAINS to OOST DUNKERQUE BAINS & NIEUPORT BAINS. Mounted policy duty lines to 97th Bde. Lt Perran spent morning cleaning line to 97th Bde & faults. Party running wire Gate Mans from ROSAPH to AMIRAL Communication. 14th Bde move to 168 Bde FA about 200 yds established cable S. of AMIRAL.	
	27.6.17		Stables morning etc as usual. GS. CV work late cut & labelled. 1 NCO + 2 men Ah! by army large with Bde for work. Running line cable. O.C. ment trenches. Cpt Heath + 3 men hand to 2nd KOYLI & class are 1 Drunk iron to 101 Bde which been Rouck Directing line by field-line repeatedly token	
	28.6.17			

WAR DIARY
or
INTELLIGENCE SUMMARY.

Army Form C. 2118.

(Erase heading not required.)

Place	Date	Hour	Summary of Events and Information	Remarks and references to Appendices
	28.6.17		Lt Jackson took Patrol lines to 96th Bde. Spr Richardson lent to 14th Bde signals Jellyphone.	
	29.6.17		Stables, grooming etc as usual. Lines patrols by mounted parties to D.A.C. 96th Bde and 161 Bde R.F.A.	
	30.6.17		Stables, Grooming etc as usual. Lt Painter arranged the Military Rest. Hunts hosts Cath. Park meeting in cable in COXYDE BAINS. Cpl Brooks to Lumen out and to establish a Lumensis pot at ROSARY. OC. Lt Jackson with Painter recons. recounter near Ene NIEOPORT. D.a.-c new ...... Abraham Capt R.E. OC 32nd Signal Coy R.E.	

Army Form C. 2118.

Nov 20

WAR DIARY
or
INTELLIGENCE SUMMARY.
(Erase heading not required.)

CONFIDENTIAL

WAR DIARY
of
32nd Divisional Signal Coy R.E.

from 1st July 1917 to 31st July 1917

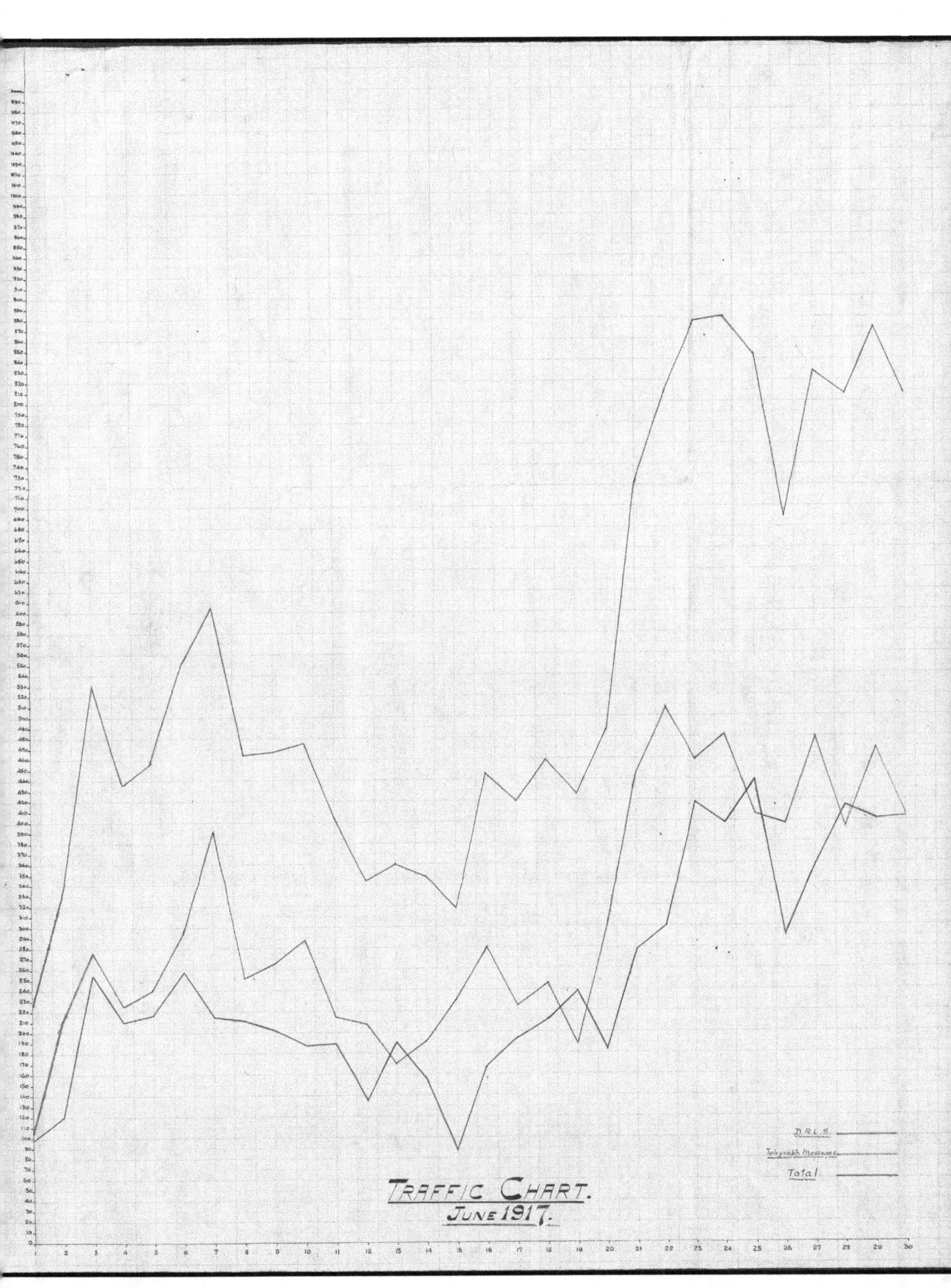
TRAFFIC CHART.
JUNE 1917.

WAR DIARY / INTELLIGENCE SUMMARY

Army Form C. 2118.

Place	Date	Hour	Summary of Events and Information	Remarks and references to Appendices
	1.7.17		Staff improving, cleaning harness etc. 11 truck of party put at a D's [Disposal] from ATTACK to DEFENSE. NIEUPORT VILLE The byke bere extends back a permanent line to General Signal Office line has had un circuit an count of 97 th Bde. Owen to high wind the wires a Bd q trouble owing to contacts in French permanent route. Lt Jackson with Parsons party examining + planning Severs in NIEUPORT VILLE. Cpl Brooke spent patrol report + strengthen line to 96 th Bde OC 2nd AD Sigs XV Corps. 97 th Bde has a certain amount in their battalion lines owing to shell fire. 14 th Bde lines OK.	[signature]

WAR DIARY
or
INTELLIGENCE SUMMARY

Army Form C. 2118.

Place	Date	Hour	Summary of Events and Information	Remarks and references to Appendices
2.7.17			Stables grooming harness etc. Kennen parade inspection. Cleaning. Exercise. Lt Jackson + party carry on reconnoitring demos of NIEUPORT VILLE. Party dilling on spare cables in two table. Running 26th Divisional expert by Co. 405 Bttns. 2 in C and his lines by 2 ins C. supply names with ratt in a place for OC & Lt Parsons. Ammed Exchange amount of work in lines many Constables causing controls at in trench to permanents with Bugart Curran Curtis in the white any mouth by stating had been taken Battle HQ. OC 1 & 2 i/c aux'l	16.1.44

Army Form C. 2118.

WAR DIARY
or
INTELLIGENCE SUMMARY.
(Erase heading not required.)

Place	Date	Hour	Summary of Events and Information	Remarks and references to Appendices

3.7.17 — Fitter gunning cleaning harness etc
Lt Fuch stomach claim reports wires mend
Battn HQ.
Lt Dawson)
Lt Gray   ) for 8th Corps in duty
Lt Jackson) returns from hospital
Party getting new Guns to Moetanicker in Out
Same to Pyram L/t at St IDESBALVE nothing at
St Reynt route. At tip XV Corps called forward
at with GSO I masters French amt. Air O/L
Bde.   haulea attack 31.7.17
Cotton arrived of Thunder on the lines every
to shell — tin   & Bde taken at
two of driver Guns
OOSt Dunkerke by shell fire

Army Form C. 2118.

WAR DIARY
or
INTELLIGENCE SUMMARY.
(Erase heading not required.)

Instructions regarding War Diaries and Intelligence Summaries are contained in F. S. Regs., Part II. and the Staff Manual respectively. Title pages will be prepared in manuscript.

Place	Date	Hour	Summary of Events and Information	Remarks and references to Appendices
4/7/17			Steady grooming exercise etc. Cleaning horses began 9.5. H had hats taking & starting trench new arms - permanent route from BX+SE-BAINS to BATTLE HQ. In addition to find routes there in old trench line from NIEUPORT VILLE 1.L. Panama obrum from 66 Hy Coy RE. Rams forward lines. Parks alley in the trench ST. IDESBALDE. COXYDE-BAINS and this is traceable. Party running lines a few good in all way.	

Army Form C. 2118.

WAR DIARY
or
INTELLIGENCE SUMMARY.
(Erase heading not required.)

Place	Date	Hour	Summary of Events and Information	Remarks and references to Appendices
	5.7.17		Morning Stables etc. Cleaning harness etc. Lt Jackson Party Carrying on with renewing Lt Luck Carrying on with constructing semi-permanent tents. Parties running this Cable + collecting its return wire. Went to YPRES/LILLE. Lines running all day. 96th Relieving with B.X.	
	6.7.17		Morning Stables. Cleaning harness etc. Lt Jackson Party carrying on. Lt Luck Party Party carrying on with 161 Bde R.F.A. Private Party running their Cable to collecting all Patrol Cars. Running their lines now in use good.	
	7.7.17		Morning Stables etc. Cleaning harness etc. Lt Luck Party Carrying on with semi-permanent tents. Party running line cable out on [?]	[sig]

Army Form C. 2118.

WAR DIARY
or
INTELLIGENCE SUMMARY.
(Erase heading not required.)

Place	Date	Hour	Summary of Events and Information	Remarks and references to Appendices
	7.7.17		CB – OE Roots which were broken by shell fire. Double in Divn'l lines owing River Avant. Considerable time in B.E. lines owing to shell- fire. "H" amb. Lays moved on leave to U.K. + Lt. Staff afloat him in hos 2 Lister until his return.	
	8.7.17		Stables grooming etc. Church Parade. Lt Lock Kait. Carry on with him personal kuntz. OC + Lt Parkins looking at Attchiad. Conspicuous hurts in Cart to 97th Bde army to Capt Meevies apparently Attang in honours. Sent Cleared Gift to Bde lives repeatedly all by enemy Shelling. 96th Bde lines Hutt required the again.	

A5834 Wt. W4973/M687 750,000 8/16 D.D. & L. Ltd. Forms/C.2118/13

Army Form C. 2118.

WAR DIARY
or
INTELLIGENCE SUMMARY.
(Erase heading not required.)

Instructions regarding War Diaries and Intelligence Summaries are contained in F.S. Regs., Part II. and the Staff Manual respectively. Title pages will be prepared in manuscript.

Place	Date	Hour	Summary of Events and Information	Remarks and references to Appendices
	9/7/17		Stables grooming etc. Exercise by truck & spring sling. Our usual from Adv HQ to Apirah 2/5 Lieut Ainlay with [?] party returning first of him to Adv HQ & 161 Bde J.H. 97th RFA	
	10/7/17		Our King Col by Army Headquarters, all Officers NCO's & men sent up to get lines this [?] bed saturating out again. Cpl Jackson D.R. returned on motor cycle and thrown off, but managed to carry on with message. Since France [?] taken recently Jerperne and Western Egypt and Gas furnaces very heavily shelled all day. Communication ceased through by pigeon and D.R's. Horses were taken off the lines because of the shelling, a Corps de Rein.	

WAR DIARY or INTELLIGENCE SUMMARY

Army Form C. 2118.

Place	Date	Hour	Summary of Events and Information	Remarks and references to Appendices
	11.7.17		3 A.M. Got time though to arrive. Patrol out under Lt. Luck, 2/Lieut. Cpl. Le Bon – C.Q.M.S. – 97th Bn. Cpl. Blake – 96th Cpl. Hoad – 94th K/Bn. Shellfire less violent than yesterday. Bde formed lines frequently as throughout the day and night. Cpl. Bern outposts (slept 3AM) laying around Quad in the canal from Pelican, noon thy Farrier. Capt. Walton and 2/Lieut. Raven keeping guard from defence to canal, out all night. 14th Bde. moves up from Rhyolite to relieve 97th Bde. 97th Bde moves to Camp Jennings. Party will out under Capt. Walton and 2/Lt. Raven arrived at 12.05 p.m. Cpl. Bern	
	12.7.17		2 A.M. 8 A.M. Cpl. Bern joins up from offices with Truck D5 to and party returned. Armoured good laid previous day, returned 5.20 p.m. All wires being frequently patrolled. Forward lines frequently dis: Capt. Walker + Lt. Jackson went today at Pelican M.W.	

WAR DIARY
or
INTELLIGENCE SUMMARY

Army Form C. 2118.

Place	Date	Hour	Summary of Events and Information	Remarks and references to Appendices
	13.7.17		Capt Walton still at Pelican. Lieut Jackson proceeded to Cappaqu to test in wireless comms. ~~[struck through]~~ 3 Ton Lorry under Capt Rawson and Lieut Shook with 6 men moving up sup experiment Digging trenches for huts & line Party returned 6 A.M. 30 cwt lorry left at 9.30 A.M. with Sgt Hill and 19 men for repairs to Capt Rawsons unsafe truck for work at Party returned at 12.35 p.m. 161 Sct R.F.A. 3 ton lorry Lieut Robson and 16 men left. Line Patrol as usual on repairs. Staff Routine. Line patrolled.	
	14.7.17		Capt Walton still at Pelican enroute toward ~~[struck]~~	

Army Form C. 2118.

WAR DIARY
or
INTELLIGENCE SUMMARY.
(Erase heading not required.)

Place	Date	Hour	Summary of Events and Information	Remarks and references to Appendices
	15.7.17	10.0 A.M.	Shell Parade as usual. Church parade 10.0 A.M. Sgt Hooke ans party out at Wireless post and station party. 2 p.m. running 9.7 Cable extension work same as yesterday. Lieut Snow, Cpl Evans and Sapper Murphy out in Car on Recons Ride. Sgt Ross and 2 men out at 6 a.m. with lorry returned 3 p.m. completing route, abandoned when Lieut Pearson yesterday.	
	16.7.17		Inspection parade and ashes down as usual. 4 pairs supports leave for S.W. to D.A.C. — RNAS station + Field training post track. 9th D.A.C. Lieut Pearson lives in D.7 Cable pair from Sig to F. Group R.F.A. Lieut Snow with Cpl Evans and horses out checking route from Group HQrs for Pelusium to R.N.A.S. Station.	

WAR DIARY
or
INTELLIGENCE SUMMARY.

Army Form C. 2118.

Place	Date	Hour	Summary of Events and Information	Remarks and references to Appendices
	17.7.17		Lines, Horses etc. inspected by A.D.A.S. Emperors House & Stables given a repaint.	
			Lt Parson & Sgt Hood laid 4 pairs from on French loop to Roary Pence to Roary trestle and arrival to P.C.A.L. & picked up 4 pairs picking up 4 pairs being issued there by 49th Div. as far as LL thence through n. & pairs to YCB exchange	
			Cpl Beatrice and 6 men out recovering 2 pairs along the LLCB trestle route.	
			Lt Inch and 11 men and lorry. two pairs in canal for Pont Pelican to X22A	
			B2 Cable Section parties 2 pairs from X22A to YCB.	
			Sgt Holt and party overheadx & recovering cable.	
			96th Inf Bde moves fwr to Craije	

Place	Date	Hour	Summary of Events and Information	Remarks and references to Appendices
	18.7.17		Parade and inspection parade as usual.	
			B2 Cable section completing work on [?]	
			A Cable detachment setting up Angle Cable from H.Q. to Airieul	
			B " " " " " "	
			Officer relief with C.S.M. proceed on advance party to new H.Q. in village	
			new signal office.	
			Line through to G. Office, G Office, at 10.45 p.m. 14th Div. Bde moved H.Q.	
			to Seffincourt	
			Capt Walker and party) N.C.O. & one man getting line through to 14th Bde.	
	19.7.17		Coy. moved to new H.Q. Cable laid Heavy for new H.Q. to Div. H.Q.	
			[?] D.7. Cable laid Heavy for new H.Q. to Div. H.Q.	
			New Sig. Office opened at 12 [?]	

Army Form C. 2118.

WAR DIARY
or
INTELLIGENCE SUMMARY.
(Erase heading not required.)

Place	Date	Hour	Summary of Events and Information	Remarks and references to Appendices
	20.7.17		Stables. Inspection parade, grooming and clearing harness and equipment. Party under C.S.M. Harry head lines, camp lines & H.Q. D.S. train & C.R.E. D.A.D.O.S.	
	21.7.17		Stables & Inspection parade as usual. Straightening up lines at new H.Q.	
	22.7.17		Stables & Inspection. Harness as usual. Church parade under Capt. Walton at 10.0 A.M. at Div H.Q.	
	23.7.17		Stables & Inspection parades as usual. Shingling up troop lines. Award S.M. to Military Medal to Sgt Powell, Sapper Gordon, Sapper Brown, Sapper Gemmill. Congratulations for Divl. Comdr. [signature]	

WAR DIARY
or
INTELLIGENCE SUMMARY.

Army Form C. 2118.

Place	Date	Hour	Summary of Events and Information	Remarks and references to Appendices
	24.7.17		Stable and inspection parade as usual. Overhauling and sorting of cable next G. Park. Instructed 1 N.C.O. and 2 men future time to 4th Bde.	
	25.7.17		Stables & Inspection Parade. Batty parade (horse) Party overhauling & renewing cable as y'day. 1 N.C.O. and 2 men actg. time to 14" Bde g.p.	
	26.7.17		Stables, Gun & Inspection parade as usual. Heliographer & linemen Party renewing cable as y'day.	
	27.7.17		Stables & Inspection parade as usual. Y. Jackson returned to duty Sgt Hirth & 16 men relieved Spl Hodges party at Croizer Barn from 9Dr. 96th Inf Bde.	

WAR DIARY
INTELLIGENCE SUMMARY

Army Form C. 2118.

Place	Date	Hour	Summary of Events and Information	Remarks and references to Appendices
	27.7.17.		Parade under Cpl. Prentice for instructions in personal hire work. Line pl through to O.P. D.S.	
	28.7.17.		Stable & Inspection parade & morning. Instructional ride under Cpl. Prentice a.y. day. Cpl. Bearer and harness parts relating to D.8 reins for X reins at Co. 7 & 9.7 to consist of lectures by master the Stable & Inspection Parade as usual.	
	29.7.17.		Church parade at 10.0 A.M. Instructional parts continues as before	N.M.T.

WAR DIARY
or
INTELLIGENCE SUMMARY.

(Erase heading not required.)

Army Form C. 2118.

Place	Date	Hour	Summary of Events and Information	Remarks and references to Appendices
	30.7.17		Stables. Inspection Parade as usual. Cleaning wagons & harness. Cpl. Blake and 11 drivers reported to Habarren at Coigneux-Bas as advance party.	
	31.7.17		Stables & Inspection Parade as usual. Cleaning wagons & harness. Packing up. Party of 6 men feeling & overhauling saddles.	

Amatin
Capt
for O.C. April 32nd Coy

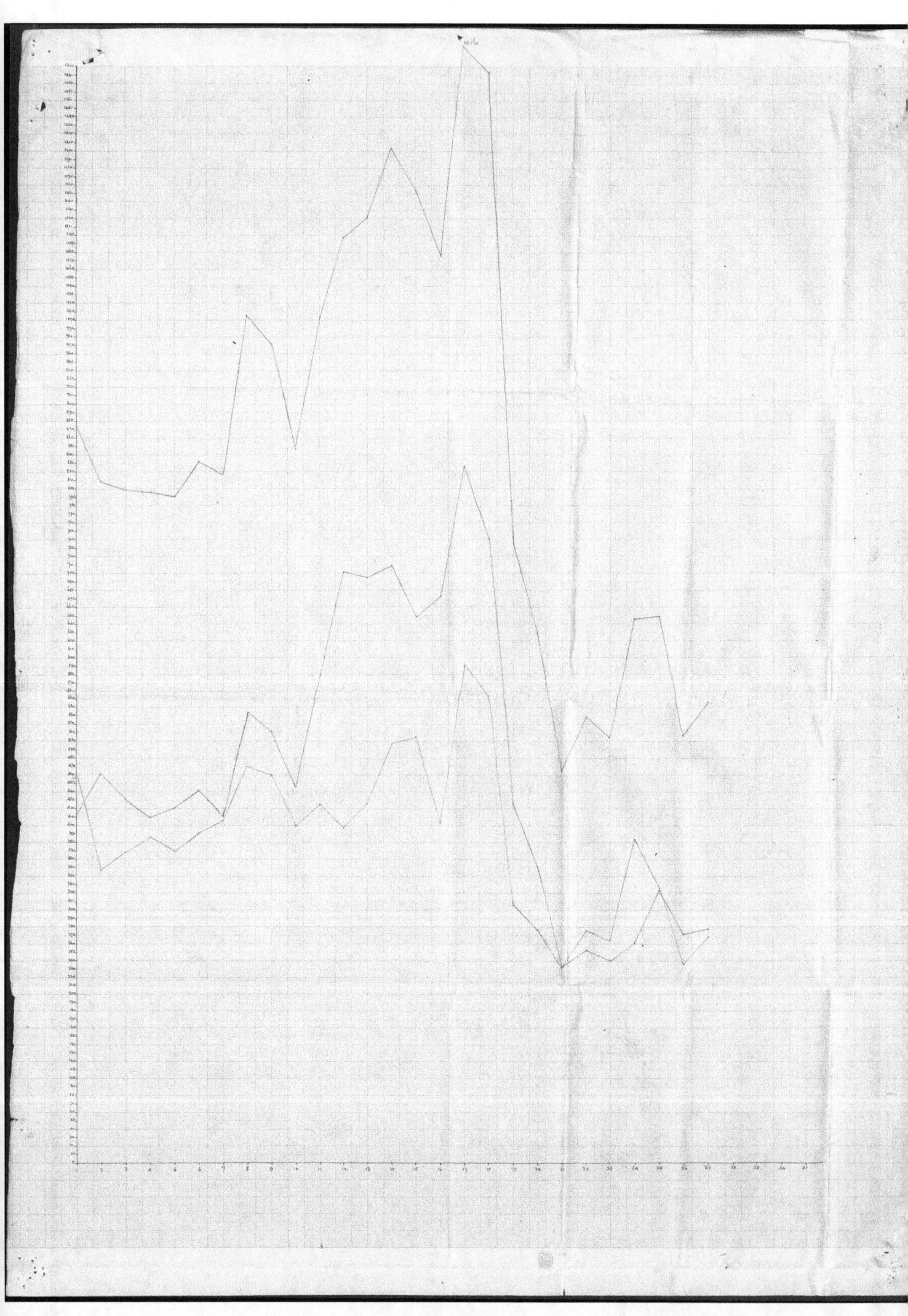

Army Form C. 2118.

WAR DIARY
or
INTELLIGENCE SUMMARY.
(Erase heading not required.)

CONFIDENTIAL.

War Diary

of

32nd Divl. Signal Coy R.E.

from 1st August 1917 to 31st August 1917

Instructions regarding War Diaries and Intelligence Summaries are contained in F. S. Regs., Part II. and the Staff Manual respectively. Title pages will be prepared in manuscript.

WAR DIARY
or
~~INTELLIGENCE~~ SUMMARY.

(*Erase heading not required.*) 32 Div Sig Co RE

Army Form C. 2118.

August [illegible]

Place	Date	Hour	Summary of Events and Information	Remarks and references to Appendices
[illegible]	1 Aug		Company moved into [illegible]	
	2nd		2/Lieut Bodak Smith, R G A(T) reports his arrival and was posted to [illegible] as supernumerary officer under 2/Lieut Geake RE	
	6		Lieut R.H. Jackson 3rd R W F reports his arrival and is attached for duty from this date.	
	8th		8 single [illegible] lines run from VCB to YBAR to provide telephone circuits to arty Groups	
	9-18		General work in maintaining lines in forward area. Considerable shelling each day and maintenance of communications [illegible] difficulties.	
	18		Co moved into rest in back area	
	19-28		Coy employed in cleaning harness and equipment. Men sent on leave at the rate of 2 per day. [illegible] wounded [illegible] one dead	
	29		Co moved into line	
	29-3[illegible]		Coy employed in maintaining lines in forward area	

E. N. Evelegh
Major RE
O.C. Signals
32nd Division

A5834 Wt. W4973/M687 750,000 8/16 D. D. & L. Ltd. Forms/C.2118/13

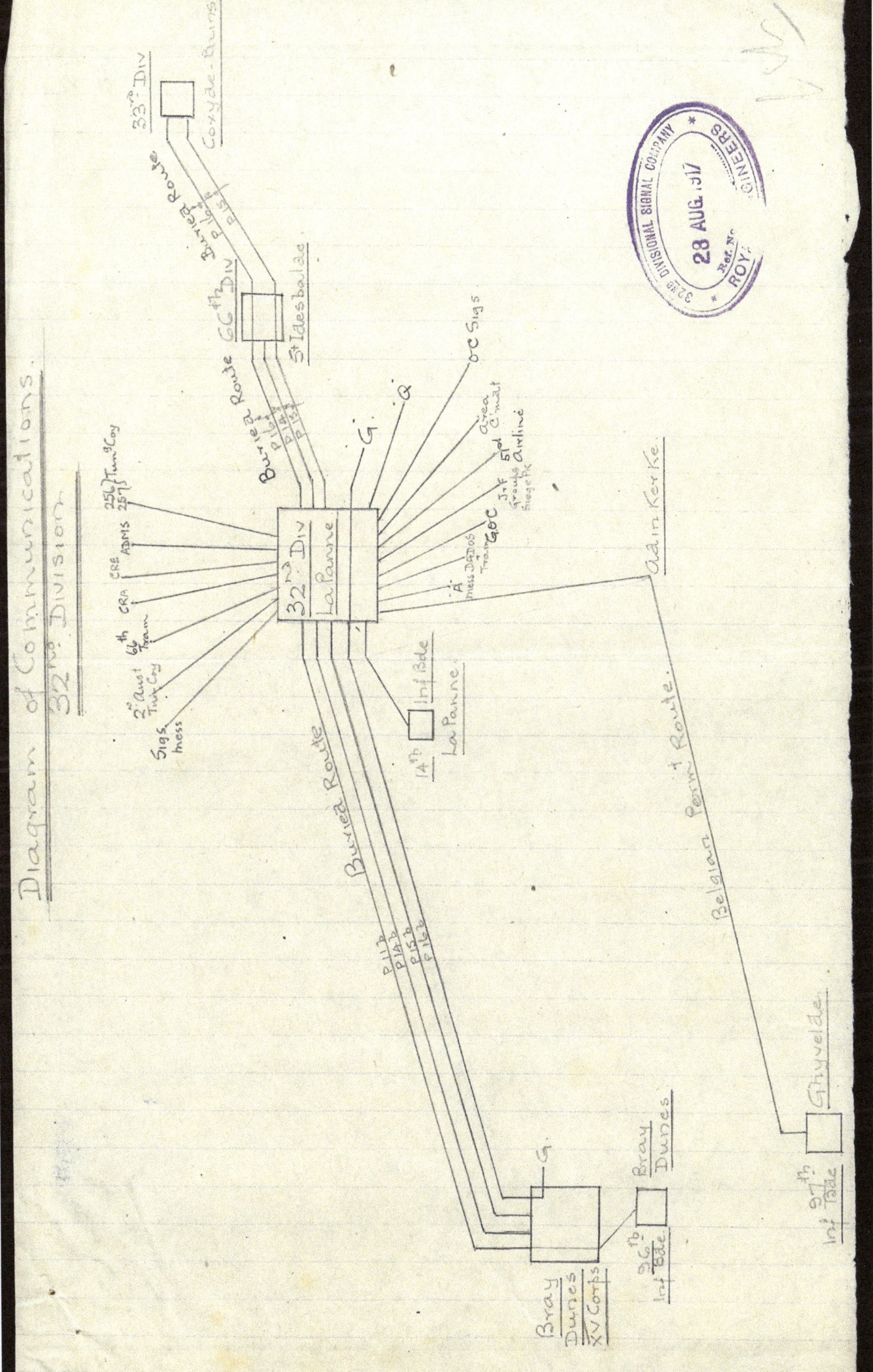

Telegraphs ———
DR.LS & Telegraphs ———

TRAFFIC CHART FOR
AUGUST 1917.

WAR DIARY
INTELLIGENCE SUMMARY
(Erase heading not required.)

Place	Date	Hour	Summary of Events and Information	Remarks and references to Appendices
			[illegible handwritten entries]	
	6			
	11			
	12-13			
	14			
	17			
	18			

Army Form C. 2118.

WAR DIARY
or
INTELLIGENCE SUMMARY.
(Erase heading not required.)

32nd Div. Signal Coy R.E.

September 1917

Page 2.

Instructions regarding War Diaries and Intelligence Summaries are contained in F.S. Regs., Part II. and the Staff Manual respectively. Title pages will be prepared in manuscript.

Place	Date	Hour	Summary of Events and Information	Remarks and references to Appendices
Field	19.		Wireless system of communication reorganised so as to provide a chain from Battalion HQ back to covering artillery & by S.M.C. & thence to Div. H.Q. Salvage of the cluster & pickets.	
	20.		Vicinity of Pelican Exchange somewhat heavily shelled but most of the blind hits & no unit was completely des. Carried on trekking hostiles.	
	21.		Pres. Grubble promoted to C.S.M. in place of C.S.M. Nielson who was evacuated sick. Sgt. Stiff promoted to Pres., promotions dating from 21.9.17. Routine work carried on. Sgt.	
	22.		Lieut Parsons surveyed route for laying cable in the open from the dockers to the Pelican. Work postponed owing to the sinking of the boat.	
	23.		Cpl. Bell (motor cyclist) badly wounded by shell fire while collecting papers from the Sgt. at Post Dunkerque & Spr. Cooper wounded by shrapnel while repairing telephone wire. Capt. Ransford & Lieut Parsons spent in search of a route reported to be at Gorge St. that was unsuitable for the work of laying cables in the open	
	24.		V.V. cable sections attached to the Company.	
	25.		Company employed maintaining lines & packing Staffs. Sgt. Kelly 1 ——— No. 2 station somewhat badly wounded by shell fire (in the Leg) & Sapper	
	26-30		Company employed on burying station, running through cables and repair of air cable (35 pairs and 6 Pairs)	

O.C. 32nd Divisional Signal Coy. R.E.

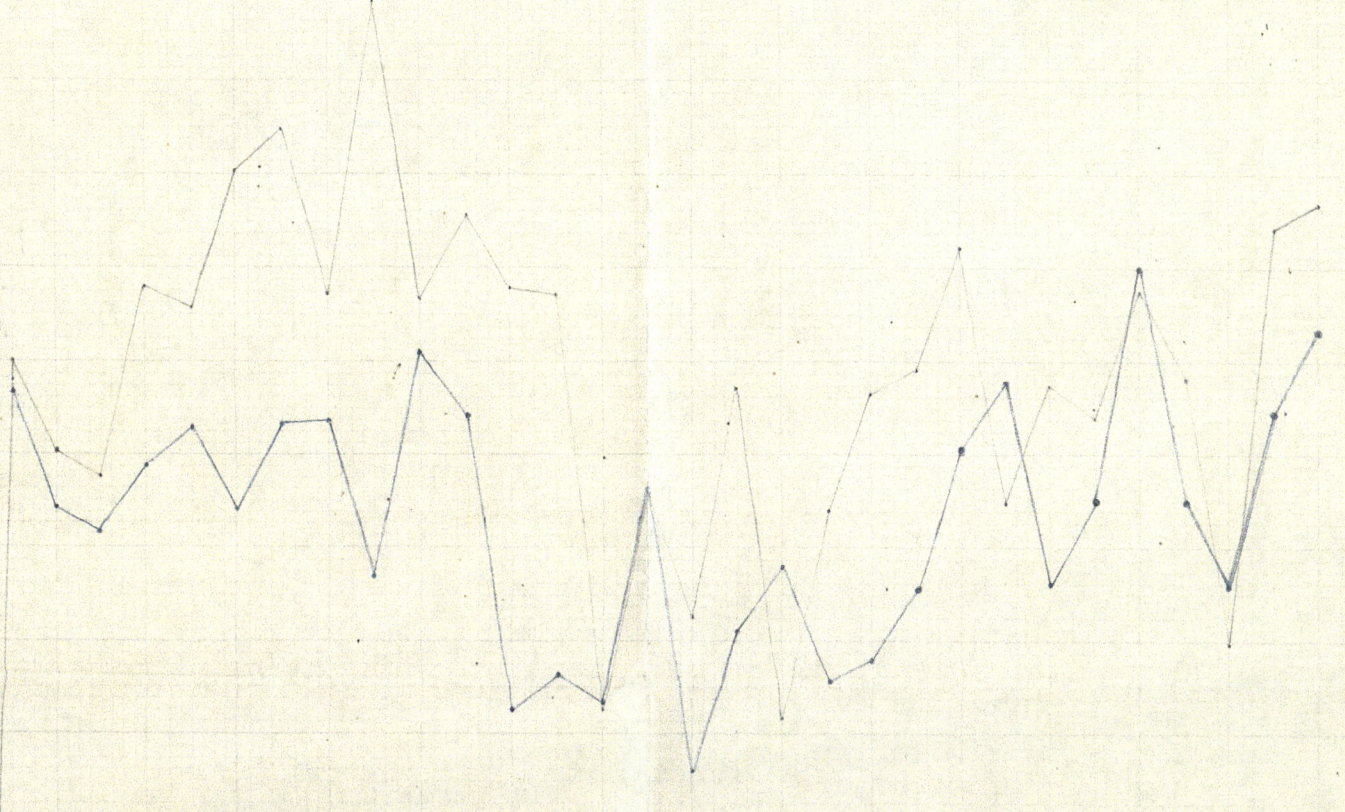

SEPTEMBER TRAFFIC CHART

KEY: TELEGRAMS. ———   DRLS. ———   TOTALS.

War Diary.

Army Form C. 2118.

WAR DIARY
or
INTELLIGENCE SUMMARY.
(Erase heading not required.)

Vol 23

Place	Date	Hour	Summary of Events and Information	Remarks and references to Appendices
Fins	Oct 1st		Enemy aeroplanes over Sapers and Essomes	
	3rd			
	6th		Enemy pressing to rear	
	7th		Enemy mind & back areas on relief by 2nd Div. 4th opened at new place at 10 O'c. All lines through that known	
	10th		Company Horse transport moved to Rocquent in preparation for move to Fins	
	11th		This HQrs opened at Rocquent	
	11-22rd		Company employed in clearing up billets	
	23		Coy moved to Cepry Camp & is under orders	
	26		Coy moves to Lieregate	
	31		Coy still at Lieregate	

E Moseley
Major RE
Comdg 22nd Army Troops Coy RE

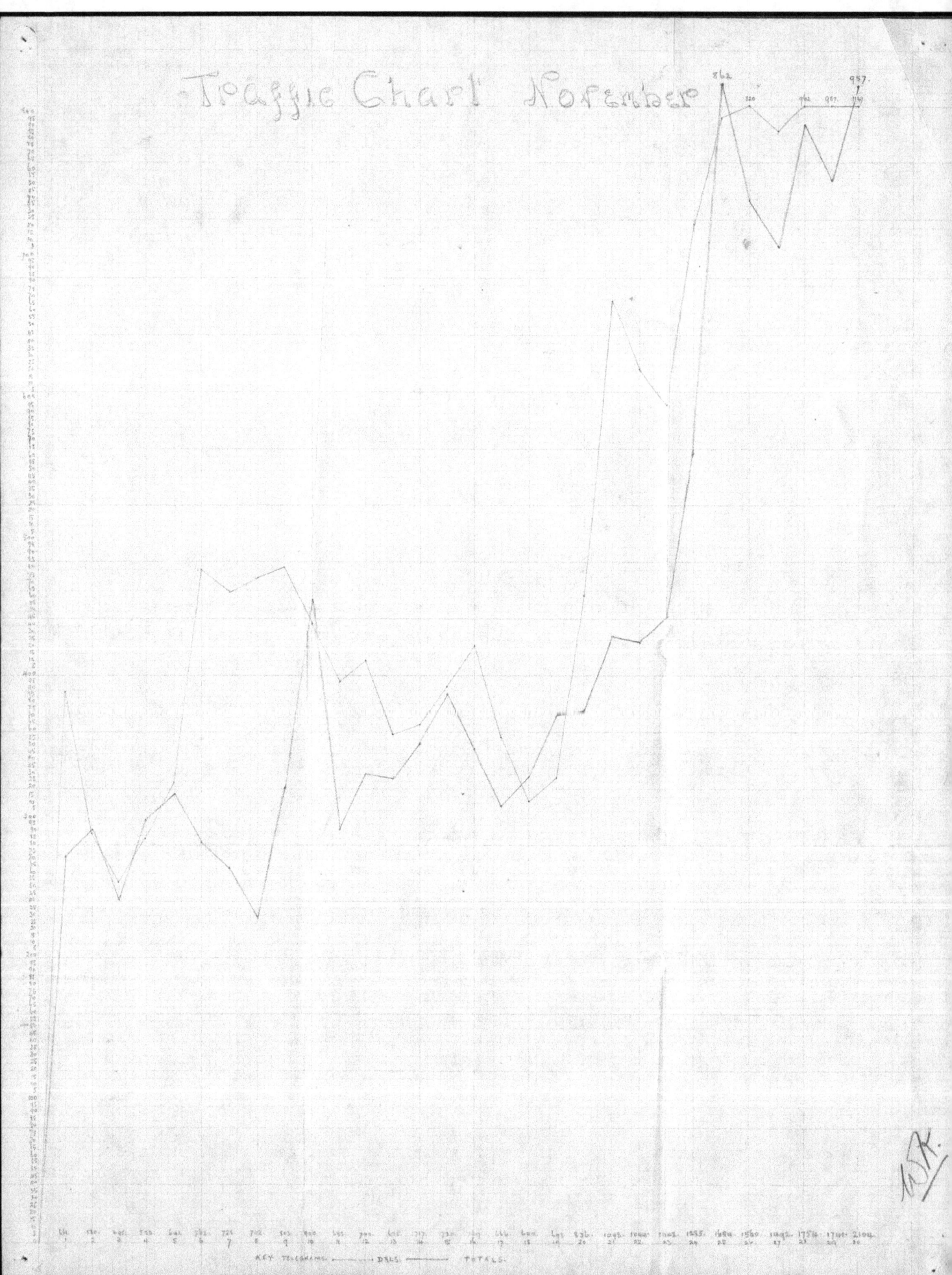

WAR DIARY
or
INTELLIGENCE SUMMARY

Army Form C. 2118.

Page 1.

3rd Adv Dep. C R6   Nov 1917

Place	Date	Hour	Summary of Events and Information	Remarks and references to Appendices
WD	1/11/17		Coy proceeded to prepare and complete equipment ready to leave to time scheduled from Adj Dixon transport to Coy at Peppino (CR73844)	
	11		Coy moved off as ordered	
	20		CO returns from leave in UK.	
	21		Lt Sgt Piggott brought 2/Lt B.? and Coy in place. Transport in next 3 days	
	4th	30	Burying commenced by platoon dumps at an average depth lower than 2 feet owing to water. 1 Officer and two men B.S. Cable detachment attached for assistance on forward lines. Don't carried on til 11" No casualties. Rifle for Principal. Gate regums only short taps more. taken being drawn on as average.	

E.W. Rider?
OC 32 Bn 3rd ? RG

Army Form C. 2118.

WAR DIARY
or
INTELLIGENCE SUMMARY.
(Erase heading not required)

32 Div Sig Co R.E. Oct 1917   Page 3

Place	Date	Hour	Summary of Events and Information	Remarks and references to Appendices
	Oct 17th		Corps Commr awards Military medal for gallantry and devotion to duty during operations 1-3rd to No 103133 Cpl(A/Sgt) Engelsdale J and No 103283 Upholland F.H.	
	28th		2nd Lieut J.E. Risley (No 2 Section) severely wounded by enemy M.G. fire - evacuated to 64th CCS.	
	30		Transport commenced to move to rest area	
	31st		Remainder of company moved to rest area. Common cabins established. Roads in bad condition owing to snow and frost, but whole of move completed without a casualty to transport	

E.M. Risley
Major R.E.
O.C. 32 Div Sig Co R.E.

WAR DIARY or INTELLIGENCE SUMMARY

Army Form C. 2118.

Page 1

32nd M.G. Co. 6 Bde. November 1917

Place	Date	Hour	Summary of Events and Information	Remarks and references to Appendices
	1		Coy HQ now increased post established along ladders lines from Chedder to Kronprinz and Kansas Cross to Kronprinz. Visual communication established as tested from Bn HQ to Kansas Cross and Kronprinz. Willis communication established and tested to Kronprinz, Bell line, Chedar Pillar. 97 Bde now to Kronprinz at 3pm and the M.G. Bde HQ established at Kansas Cross. Considerable difficulty in speaking to 97 Bde from touch 9pm. During this prior speaking was so faint that Burgess messages had to be resent to after considerable amount of work and ladders line which has been badly cut speaking became good and remains in use Bde left.	
	20		This Army HHers 8th Bn ad Kansas Cross cut 2 hours prior to zero. Enemi ran out emergency cables over the broken	

Army Form C. 2118.

WAR DIARY
or
INTELLIGENCE SUMMARY.
(Erase heading not required.)

32 Div. Sig Co. R.E. Sept 1917   Page 2

Place	Date	Hour	Summary of Events and Information	Remarks and references to Appendices
	21		point and re-established communication. Leaders wire kept throughout operations and found of great value. Communication maintained by telephone with all Brigades and forward arty groups without break throughout operations, and also throughout the period of the enemy counter attack. During this period the linesmen at forward posts were working continuously and under heavy shell fire as the maintenance of telephone communications was due to their exertions. Visual signalling and runners also works exceptionally with Corps connections during the attack. 4 O.R. killed and 3 wounded.	
	22		Conditions reported normal	

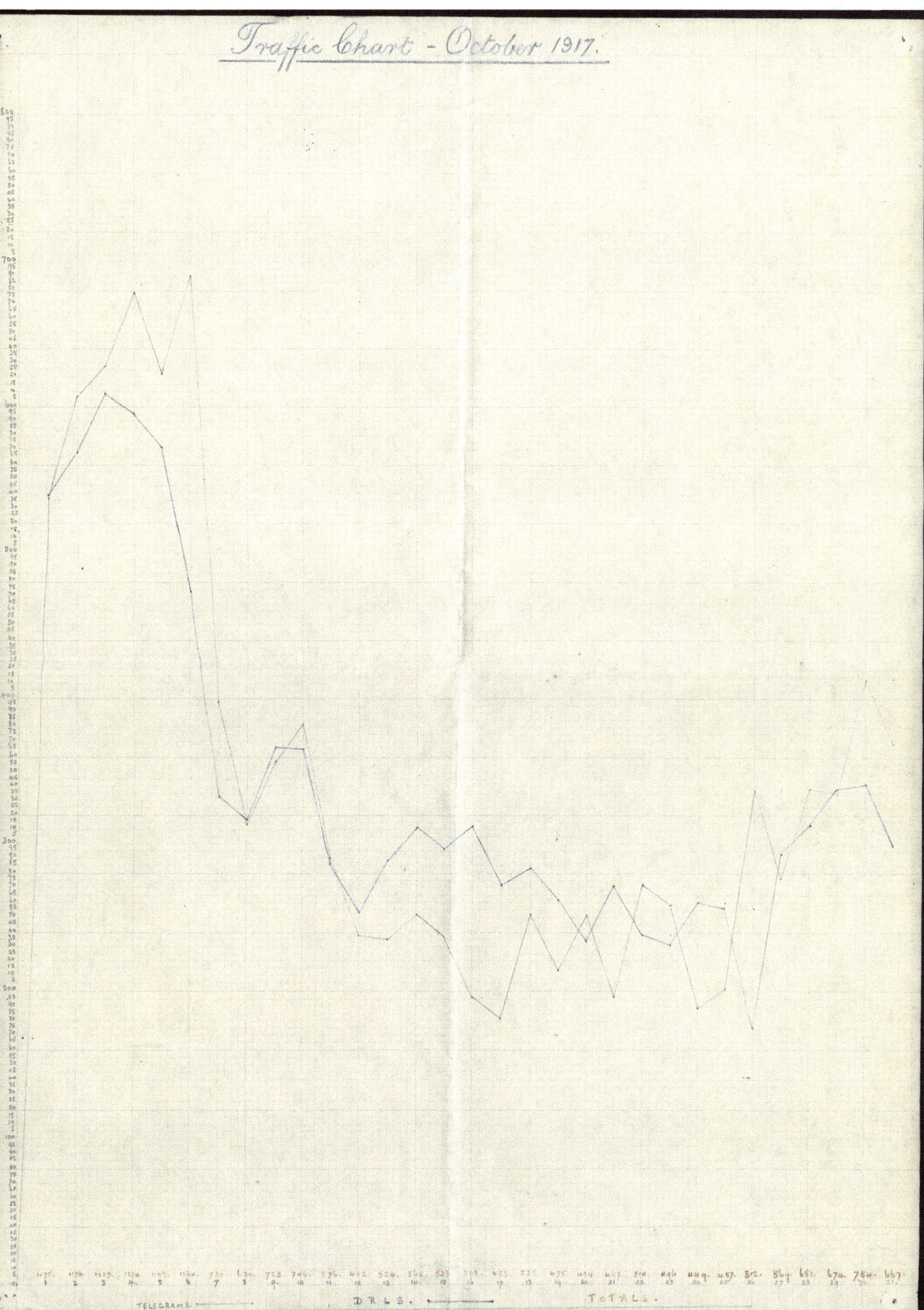

DAOMG 325 Jamieson

AAOMG
40 325 Jamieson

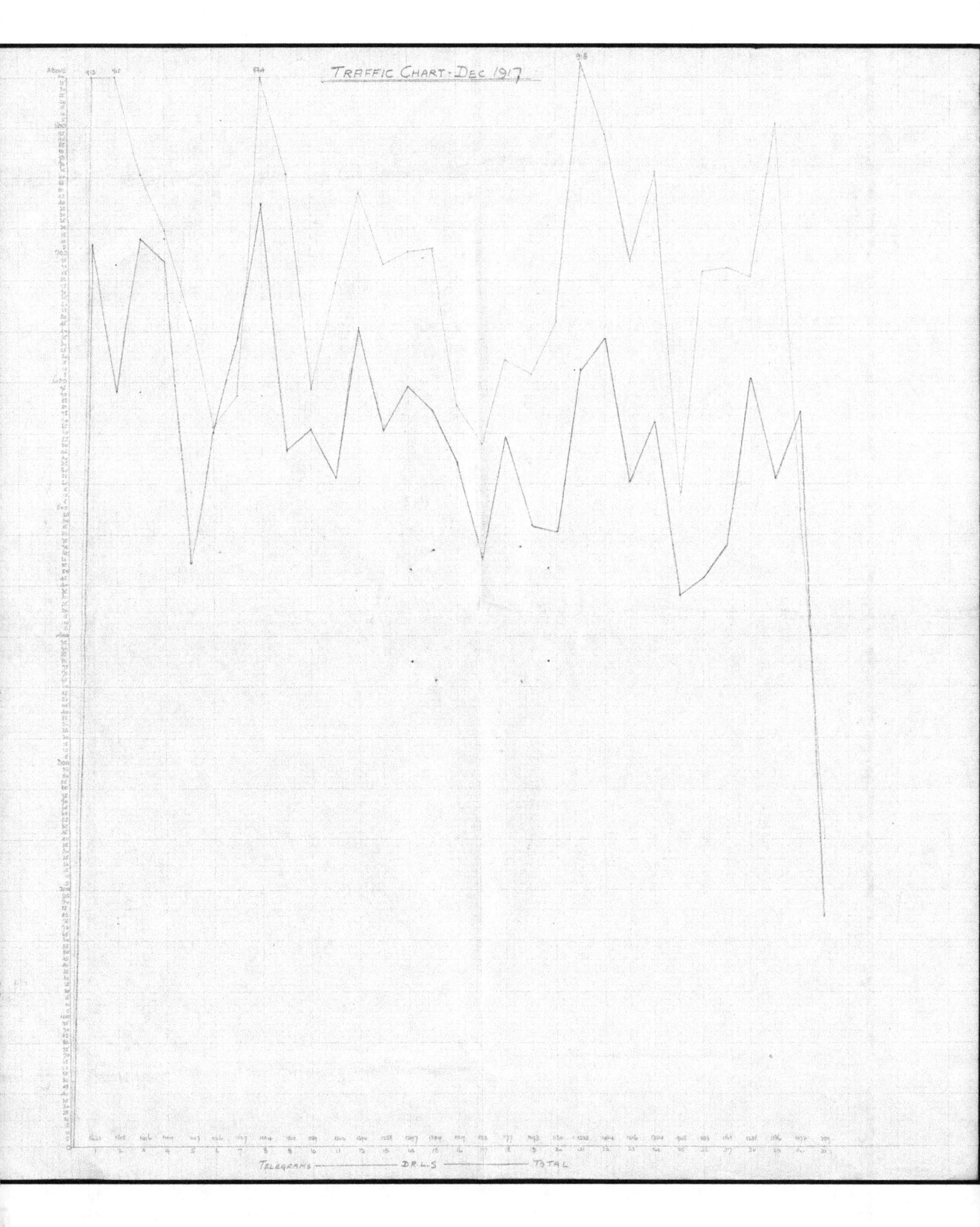

D. A. A. G.
HQ. 325 Division

D. A. A. G. HQ. 325 Division

Army Form C. 2118.

WAR DIARY
or
INTELLIGENCE SUMMARY.
(Erase heading not required.)

32 Div Sig Co. R.E. January 1918

Vol 26

Place	Date	Hour	Summary of Events and Information	Remarks and references to Appendices
	Jan 1918			
	1		Company employed in overhauling equipment	
			Destination of Divisional Signal Coy vacated by Major E.N. EVELEGH	
			M.C. R.E. Chingecto 1/1/18	
			Military Cross awarded to Lieut E.H. BINDLOSS R.A. (S/C 164	
			Bde R.F.A. Authorization (Kenhingecto 1/1/18)	
			Westong series General Marshal awarded No 1031279 Sgt. E.W.	
			FULFORD No 2 Section Changecto 1/1/18	
	2		Company employed in overhauling equipment	
	3.20		Shaped in ambulances and prints.	
			General overhaul of equipment	
	6.30		Squadron sent to Brigade Base	
	23-05		Occupied in preparations for telephones Whitington Cov Rd	

WAR DIARY
or
INTELLIGENCE SUMMARY.

Army Form C. 2118.

(Erase heading not required.)

Place	Date	Hour	Summary of Events and Information	Remarks and references to Appendices

Traffic Chart Jan 1918

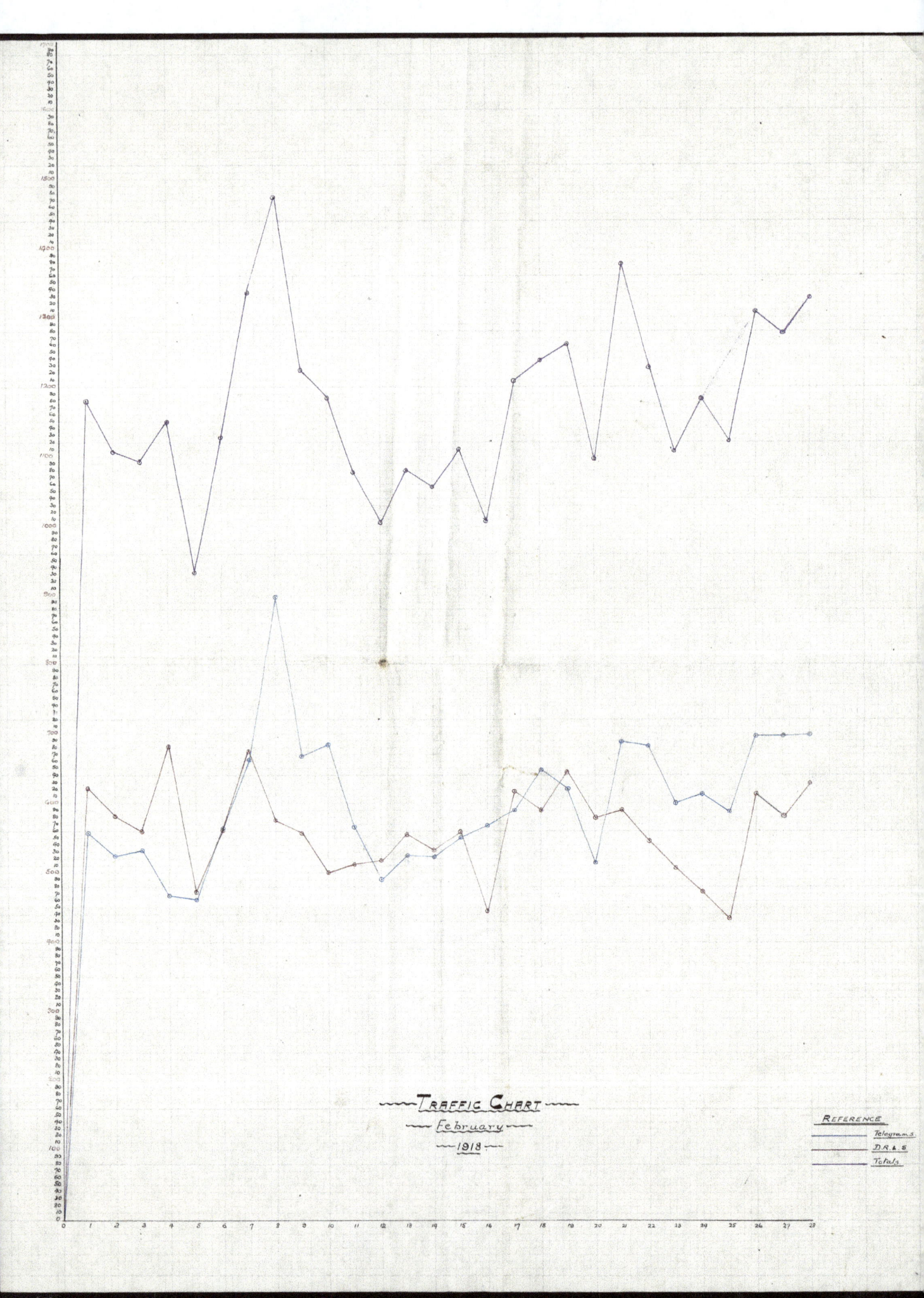

Army Form C. 2118.

WAR DIARY
or
INTELLIGENCE SUMMARY.
(Erase heading not required.)

32nd Div Sig Co R.E.
February 1918
Page 1

Place	Date	Hour	Summary of Events and Information	Remarks and references to Appendices
Luid.	1-5		One party laying and regulating top pole route erected by released Div. Other parties on maintenance of local lines and transport cleaning.	
	6th		Two pairs iron arm laid to new R/P Pole Hqrs & connect with lines in town. Transport cleaning.	
	7-10		Parties employed on cleaning up local lines in camp, cleaning harness and transport. Laid 6' cables Bany. Gridfield reports armed & posted Hqrs 4 Section 7/2/18. Two pairs D8 laid to new Arty Bde Hqrs on left connecting with Left Sector Bany.	
	11th		General maintenance of lines & equipment. No 530233 Spr Brooks Y. revoked to Depot by order of Corps Commdr 6/2/18.	
	12th		Right arty Bde new Hqrs connected both to Y. train & Left Sector Bany.	
	13-14th		Existing lines marked. General maintenance of lines & equipment.	
	15-21		New Div O.P. connected to Right Bany. Spare lines reeled up. General maintenance of lines & equipment.	Wadenport Capt R.E. (cont) OC 32nd Div Sig Co RE

Army Form C. 2118.

WAR DIARY
or
INTELLIGENCE SUMMARY.
(Erase heading not required.)

32nd Div Sig Co /26
Page 2

February 1918.

Place	Date	Hour	Summary of Events and Information	Remarks and references to Appendices
Field	22		New Bury commenced from Regtl Bde & connected with existing Right Actor Bury. Wtpairs laid. Work very slow owing to few men (50) only available for digging.	
	23-28		Continuing with new Bury. General maintenance of lines, equipped Harness & waggon cleaning. No 103101 Spr Watt A (No 3 Section) to be awarded Military Medal awarded to duty in action (CRO 1312 20/1/18)	

WH Ramford Capt R.E.
O.C.
32 Div Sig Co /7/18

32 Div Sig Co /7/18

32nd Divisional Engineers

32nd DIVISIONAL SIGNAL COMPANY R. E.

MARCH 1 9 1 8

WAR DIARY or INTELLIGENCE SUMMARY

Army Form C. 2118.

32nd Divl Sig Coy R.E.

March 1918.   Vol 28 page 1

Place	Date	Hour	Summary of Events and Information	Remarks and references to Appendices
V.J.T	March 6		Carrying on with new establishment. Busy of 60 pairs & Right Sec. Work very hard owing to small number of men available for digging. Maintenance of lines generally and cleaning harness and wagons.	
	7		Military Cross awarded Lieut Lieut R. Summerhayes R.E. (OR.O 2834 of 6/3/18). Leave allotment of 5 per day granted with effect from 6th.	
	8		All horses dipped. 69 men of DADVS in very cold weather detrimental to their condition. Enemy attack in early hours of morning and counter attack with heavy barrage lasting until midday. All wire lines to Battns and communication from forward positions maintained throughout by Visual and Power Buzzer.	
	9		Establishment of Wireless Station increased to one Sergeant present Cpl being promoted to complete establishment	E.N. Rudd Lt. RE OC 32nd Divl Sig Coy RE

Army Form C. 2118.
11.

WAR DIARY
or
INTELLIGENCE SUMMARY.
(Erase heading not required.)

Place	Date	Hour	Summary of Events and Information	Remarks and references to Appendices
	23/6/15		After assault casualty Claude retired to their trenches; enemy made no attempt to counter attack.	
			Day + night Much + refining damage caused to trenches by last nights bombardment. Quiet day as regards shelling. Enemy put up rocket lights about opposite e 5 Wells. They try to retaliate, They also put up red + white artillery screen in front of their trenches evidently with the idea of causing our arte. not to fire on their trenches. Casualties Wounded O.R. 1.	p/p
	24/6/15		A good deal of enemy shelling to day, probably registering on our trenches + H.Q. dug-outs. New gun used against us to day 13 c.c. high velocity field gun; very unpleasant because one can't hear the shell coming, on account of its speed. Battalion relieved by 6th Somerset L.I. 43rd INF BDE in trenches. First party of Relief should have arrived at our H.d. Qrs at 10 pm = did not arrive till 11.30 pm; delay caused by our guides leading relief up communication trench instead of the road, which was quite fairly safe, then being practically no shelling. Relief completed by 2:30 am. Reliefs came up by platoons 20 minutes between each, + were led by guides direct to their trenches. Orders for Relief Appendix 5.	p/p
			Casualties killed 6. O.R. 2. Wounded O.R. 6.	Appendix 5

Army Form C. 2118.
/2

WAR DIARY
or
INTELLIGENCE SUMMARY.
(Erase heading not required.)

Instructions regarding War Diaries and Intelligence Summaries are contained in F. S. Regs., Part II. and the Staff Manual respectively. Title pages will be prepared in manuscript.

Place	Date	Hour	Summary of Events and Information	Remarks and references to Appendices
Billets near POPERINGE	25/6/15		Battalion marched west by Coys independently & formed up 1 mile W of YPRES. Bat. met Brigade just W of VLAMERTINGUE. Marched through POP- ERINGE to billets - fields & farm 3½ miles N W of that place.	BP
"	26/6/15		Day spent cleaning up, & checking casualties etc. Divine Service at 11.30 am. Several showers of rain.	BP
"	27/6/15		Practice filling & placing of sandbags. Drill & skirmishing. Cold wind from S.W. Day dull & cloudy.	BP
"	28/6/15		Bombing School started under 2nd Lt CUPPER, Brigade Grenade Officer. 32 men trained in the Battalion, to be increased eventually to 64 per Coy.	BP
"	29/6/15		All Coys practiced attack on trenches with bombers standing. Men were instructed that any one duty a communication trench had to proceed up it at once with sandbag men & bombers to make this a formed rule & not- up. It was explained that to make this a formed rule & not- detail special parties to the task beforehand, as the little might not strike the communication trench.	BP
"	30/6/15			BP

Bomb party ~~crossed out~~
10 men with bombs   9ᵗʰ R.B.
~~crossed out~~
6 men with wire cutters   5ᵗʰ Oxx Bucks L.I.
Nº 9 platoon. (44 NCOs & men)
~~crossed out~~

This column will be formed up in C5 & will advance & attack the redoubt at the point I.12.a.0.4.

The

The assault will be made with no noise but with the utmost rapidity, and the parapet will be rushed. As soon as the work is entered, the platoon & section commanders will rally their men & set to work at once preparing the redoubt for defence, which will be held at all costs.

3. At the same time as the assaulting columns advance, covering bomb parties will accompany them, whose duty will be to clear & barricade all trenches leading into the redoubt. The object of these parties is to cover the work of the assaulting columns; & give time for the redoubt to be put in

Copy No. 2

5th OXFORD & BUCKS LT INFANTRY Order No. 1

Ref: ZILLEBEKE 1/10,000
(TRENCH MAP).

Appendix 1

1. The redoubt at I.12.a.0.4. just E of RAILWAY WOOD will be captured this evening.

2. The attack will be made by two assaulting columns, composed as follows:
   No I Assaulting Column
         Commander 2nd Lieut J. N. JACKSON.

   Bomb party.

         10 .. with bombs. 9th R.B.
         6 men with wire cutters 5th Ox & Bucks L.I.

         carrying 2 filled sandbags

         No 10 Platoon - 44 NCO's & men
         No 4 Section 62nd F¹ᵈ Co RE

   This column will advance from the barrier at the eastern end of the sunk road (at I.11.b.9.2) and moving up the sunk road will attack the redoubt at I.12.a.0.3.

   No II Assaulting Column
         Commander 2nd Lieut I.T. DAVIS.

4. Fire trenches will be dug as follows
 (1) To connect the redoubt with the existing fire trench at I.12.a.1.1.
 (2) To connect the redoubt with the southern portion of enemy trench running S from I.12.a.0.8 which we now hold.

Further work the following units will find parties as follows:
for (1) B Coy 5th Oxf & Bucks Lt Inf.   100 men.
        Kings Liverpool Regt.   90 "

    (2) Kings Liverpool Regt   30 "
        A Coy 5th Oxf & Bucks Lt Inf   50 "

Covering party for (1) 1 platoon (50 men)
    B Coy 5th Oxf & Bucks Lt Inf.

Covering party for (2) 1 platoon (50 men)
    A Coy 5th Oxf & Bucks Lt Inf
    & a bomb party in left of C.5.

a state of defence, & to allow the
digging mentioned in para 4. to be
completed.
These parties must on no account go
further than the points indicated.

With No I Assaulting Column there will
be 2 Covering bomb parties. Each
party will consist of
    1 NCO - bayonet   5th Ox & Bucks L.I.
    3 men
    10 men with bombs   5th Ox & Bucks L.I.
    6 Sappers 5th Ox & Bucks L.I. each carrying 2 sandbags
                                                half filled.

One Covering bomb party will clear and
barricade the trench running into the Redoubt
from the East at I 12.a.1.4
The second party will clean & barricade
the trench at I 11.b.9.3.

With No II Assaulting Column there will
also be two Covering bomb parties.
One will clean & barricade the trench
running into the Redoubt at I 12.a.1.5.
The second party will clean & barricade
the trench running in at I 12.a.3.6.

Report on attack of Redoubt 22/6/15
42ⁿᵈ INF BDE   Appendix 2.

With reference to your BM 136 I
forward report herewith.

1. I attach a copy of my orders.

2. The Artillery bombardment ceased
at 8 p.m. Owing to the fact that
I had to evacuate the front line
of trench during the bombardment
of the redoubt, I was unable at
8 p.m. to rush over the parapet
and attack the redoubt. The
assaulting columns had to be
put under cover in trenches behind
the front line trench, & to get
them out of there & in position
ready to move took some time.
    This enabled the enemy
to return to the redoubt and
re-occupy it.
    From 7.30 p.m. to 8 p.m. the
whole of my line of trenches
were subjected to a very heavy
bombardment of all kinds of
Artillery, which did considerable
damage. When the enemy
bomb parties & the columns

turned at 8 pm they did so under
very heavy fire indeed.
The two columns acted according
to orders, but when No 1 assaulting
column had gone some little way
over the barrier, they were met
with very heavy fire from a
work (B) in low ground to their
front, in addition to their heavy
machine gun fire. This was about
8-15 pm.

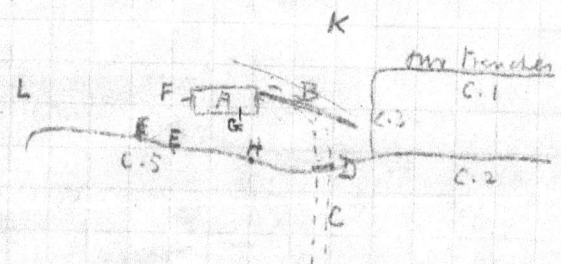

In the above sketch A is the German
work. B a new German sap.
C sunken road running through our
barricade D
The column struck the sap at the
point B.

No 2 column emerged from E
& should have struck the work

5. The remainder of C. Coy will hold the line of trench C.5. As soon as the assaulting columns reach the redoubt, ½ of this party will carry all the tools, trench bridges and sandbags to the redoubt.

D Coy & the remainder of A Coy will man their respective lines.

Local reserve (A Company 9th R.B) will man C. Coy support trenches.

All tools & spare loophole plates will be collected at the barrier in the Sunken Road.

6. The Regimental Aid Post at CAMBRIDGE ROAD dug-outs.

Stretcher bearers at the barrier in the Sunken road.

7. The attack will be prepared by an artillery bombardment which will cease at 8 pm, when the assault will take place.

8. Reports to ~~dug out in centre~~
   ~~of C.T.~~ CAMBRIDGE Rd dugouts

22/6/15   B Paght Capt adjt
                       5/ Oxf + Bucks L.I.

Copy No 1   plied
       2   A Coy
       3   B "
       4   C "
       5   D "
       6   MO 5/ Oxf & Bucks L.I
       7   62 Coy R.E
       8   Res. Coy. (9th RB)
       9   Coy Kings Liverpools
      10   42d Inf Bde.

4.

1

Lt BARLEREN 62nd Coy R.E. hearing this shouted to the men not to retire, and rallied around him what men he could, but finally he had to go back bringing the men back. I heard this story from this officer last night, & I have had it corroborated by 2 or 3 men this morning.

The column returned to the first trench which they had subheld.

There is no doubt from all accounts that the Germans were in strong force in the redoubt. Cpl Webb says a man is good on the parapet, & the parapet of the work seems to have been undamaged by our shell fire.

I have been unable to locate the position of the enemy's machine guns, but my machine gun officer Lt MAUDE who was watching for them last night, & he heard the fire of what he estimates to be 4 guns from the direction of the though he did not see flashes. Captain WEBB is of opinion

3.

at the redoubt at the point F. but they actually struck it at G.

Capt. A. WEBB, Commanding the Coy, was superintending the operation from H. When he saw that No II Column was going wrong he ran out & tried to divert it.

2nd Lt Davis & a few men reached the redoubt, which was strongly manned. No I Column probably did not get further than the point B - though there is a difference of opinion upon this point. Some say they reached the redoubt, & that Lt Jackson was actually firing at the men in it with his revolver. I am inclined to think however that they were wrong & that in the excitement they mistook B for the redoubt.

From evidence I have gathered there is no doubt some one shouted "Retire". The men had all been warned of this "Ruse de guerre", but it took effect on some of them.

By now both Lt Davis was dead & Lt Jackson severely wounded. Capt Webb had not reached his Company yet.

5.

that more guns were in the direction of K.

The first news that I received of anything came from a wounded man, who said that the assault was held up & could not get on. I sent 2 platoons of B Coy at once up to my front line. Soon after I heard from Major W.F.R. WEBB, whom I had sent up to ascertain what was going on, that the line was being easily held & he had not asked for reinforcements.

While our bombardment was going on I received information from the left of my line, on the railway, that large parties of the enemy were moving along trenches from the direction of the redoubt towards the railway. This I assumed to be the Germans evacuating the redoubt to escape our shell fire. & this is what makes me think that they reoccupied it again afterwards between the time of the cessation of our bombard-

6.

ment (8 pm) & the actual start of my assault (8-15 pm)

I received great assistance from No 4 Section 62nd Field Co R.E. who when the column was held up, threw down their tools & charged in with my men.

C H Cook Lieut Colonel
Commanding
5th OXFORDSHIRE & BUCKS LT INFY

23.6.16

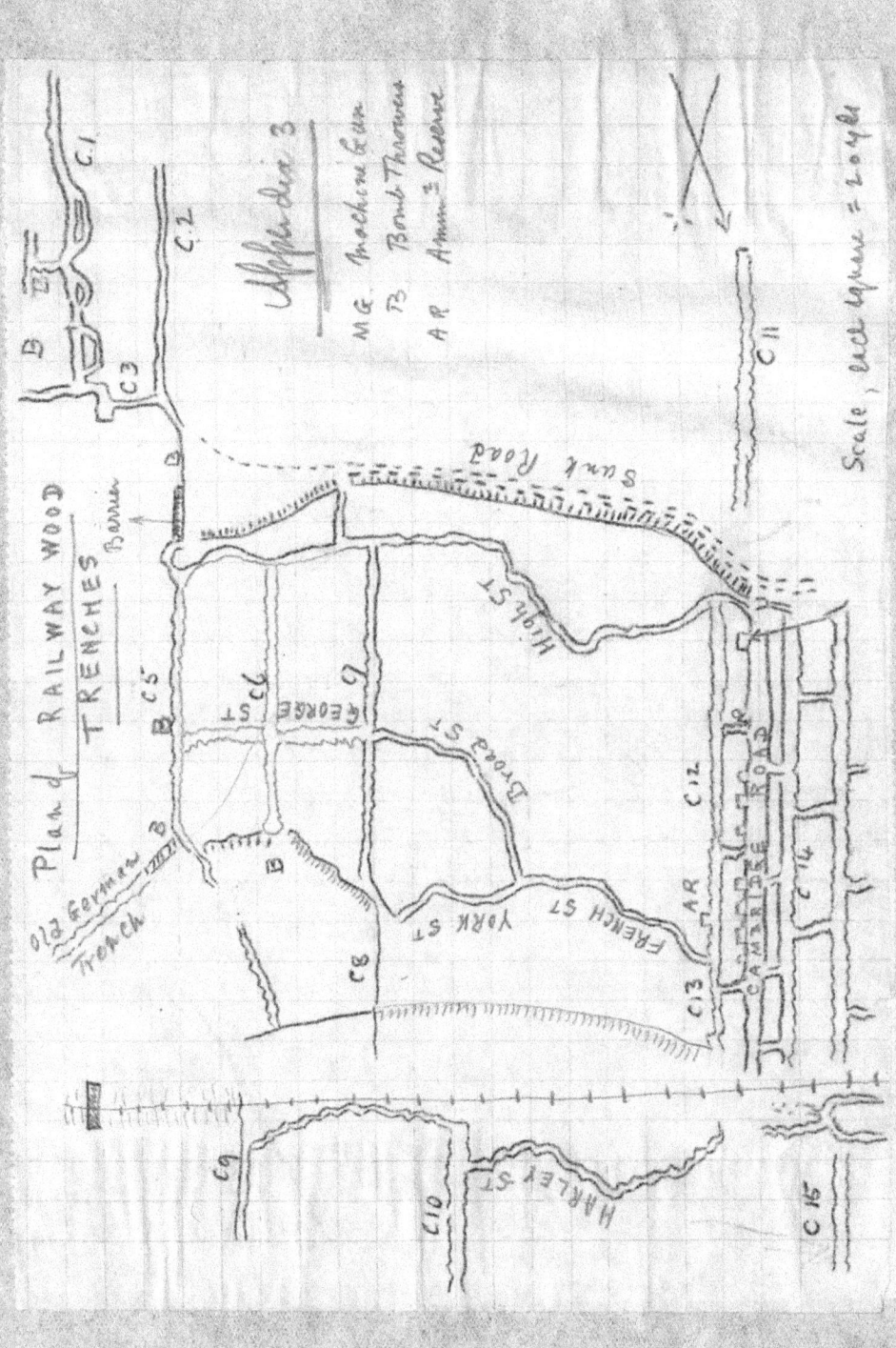

Appendix 4

O.C. 5th Oxf + Bucks L.I.
5th Shrops L.I.
9th Rif Bde.

42ND INFTY. BRIGADE
SECRET
Date 20.6.15.
No. O.O.8.

5th Corps wires "Intelligence reports indicate that enemy may have been withdrawing troops from NORTH to SOUTH during the last two days AAA. Army Comd" wishes you to carry out a reconnaissance to ascertain if hostile trenches on your front are still held in strength."

5th Oxf + Bucks L.I. + 9th Rif Bde will each send out 2 officer patrols consisting of one officer + two men each. 5th Shrops L.I. will send out one similar patrol to secure this information.

Troops + bombing parties will be held in readiness to make any forward move that may be possible.

Artillery have been warned not to shell enemy positions.

Report progress as often as possible. Final report must reach this office by 4 a.m. tomorrow.

O.C. Battn will inform Battn on their right + left that patrols will be out.

Report time patrols go out.
Acknowledge.

20-6-15

"A" Form. Army Form C. 2121.
MESSAGES AND SIGNALS.   No. of Message_____

About	40	of	the	enemy
at	dawn	advanced	against	our
[?]	post	of	this	post
but	were	[?]	and	left
3	dead	[?]	[?]	[?]
[?]	behind	them		

From Place: 5th Ox & Bucks L.I.
Time: 5.45 am

"A" Form. Army Form C. 2121.
MESSAGES AND SIGNALS.

TO: O C 9ᵗʰ R B

Sender's Number: OX-1
Day of Month: 21
AAA

My	left	patrol	has	returned
&	reports	enemy	hold	trench
S	of	Y7	facing	South
AAA	also	in	the	Eastern
of	the	two	trenches	running
South	from	Y7	and	the
tuktrn	and	our	railway	of
trench	in	of	Y7	AAA
He	estimates	enemy	force hidden	to
be	strongly	held	by	the
first	shuck	in	running	from
Y7 wn	and	French	moving	to
up	between	the	two	trenches
running	S	from	Y7	AAA
The	post	E	of	the
Y	in	RAILWAY	WOOD	is
held	by	about	10	men

From
Place

The above may be forwarded as now corrected. (Z)

Censor. Signature of Addressor or person authorised to telegraph in his name

*This line should be erased if not required.

"A" Form. Army Form C. 2121.

MESSAGES AND SIGNALS. No. of Message_____

Prefix	Code	m.	Words	Charge	This message is on a/c of:	Recd. at_____m.
Office of Origin and Service Instructions			Sent		_____Service.	Date_____
			At_____m.			From_____
			To		(Signature of "Franking Officer.")	By_____
			By			

TO { 42ⁿᵈ Inf B___

Sender's Number.	Day of Month.	In reply to Number	AAA
GR 2	21		

My	Party	Patrol	Started	About
	evening	was	late	
			the	which
of	BELLEWAARDE	FARM	AAA	My
left	patrol	found	the	morning
was	holding	the	wood	5
	47		South	
the	Easternmost	of	the	two
houses	running	North	from	
to	13		11	
	AAA	The		
	with			AAA
Apparently	from	the		the
enemy	was	on	some	Slight
AAA	The	part	East	
Railway	WOOD	is	held	
East			AAA	

From_____
Place_____
Time_____

The above may be forwarded as now corrected. (Z)

Censor. Signature of Addresser or person authorised to telegraph in his name.

"A" Form. — MESSAGES AND SIGNALS. — Army Form C. 2121.

Prefix	Code	m.	Words	Charge	This message is on a/c of:	Recd. at	m.
Office of Origin and Service Instructions.			Sent			Date	
			At	m.	Service.	From	
			To				
			By		(Signature of "Franking Officer.")	By	

TO O.C. 9th R.B.

Sender's Number	Day of Month	In reply to Number	AAA
OR 2	21		

my night patrol he found
 _ _ _ _ _ _ _ _ _ _ _ _ _ _ movin bodies of Frenchmen
W of BOULEVARDE FARM _
past some strength

From	O.C. 1st Bucks L.I.		
Place			
Time	10 A.M.		

The above may be forwarded as now corrected. (Z)

5th Oxford & Bucks Lt Infantry Orders. No 2

(Appendix 5)

1. The Battalion will be relieved tonight in the trenches by the 6th Somerset Lt Infantry

2. The relief will be carried out as follows
   D Coy will be relieved first by C Coy from L.1
   then B "   —   —   —   —   B —   —
   then A —   —   —   —   —   A —   —

The hour of starting reliefs will be about 10 pm
O.C. Coys will have everything ready by 9.30 pm.
As soon as one Company is relieved an officer & a sergeant of that Coy should be sent to inform the O.C. the next Coy for relief.

Companies will leave the trenches on relief by platoons, & platoons will move independently down the Communication trench via the ECOLE - MENIN GATE - YPRES, to the cross roads at
H.12.C.1/7. where the leading platoon will halt & await the assembly of the whole Battalion.

Intervals of at least 100 yards must

be kept between platoons, and at halts all roads are to be kept clear.

3. OC Coys will prepare a list of their trench stores in duplicate. They will hand over all their stores to their reliefs, signing one himself which he will hand over to the Officer relieving him, and obtaining the relieving Officer's signature on the other which he will keep.

4. Absolute silence will be maintained during the relief & the march, and no smoking is allowed after relief has begun till orders are given.

42nd Inf. Bde.
14th Div.

Attached.
Appx. I to VI.

5th Ox & Bucks L.I.
July 1915.

CONFIDENTIAL

WAR DIARY

— OF —

2nd Cavalry Divisional Signal Company.

FROM 1st March TO 31st March 1918

VOLUME 28

Duplicate

Army Form C. 2118.

13

WAR DIARY
or
INTELLIGENCE SUMMARY

(Erase heading not required.)

Instructions regarding War Diaries and Intelligence Summaries are contained in F. S. Regs., Part II. and the Staff Manual respectively. Title pages will be prepared in manuscript.

Place	Date	Hour	Summary of Events and Information	Remarks and references to Appendices
Billets 3 miles W. of POPERINGHE	1.7.15		Coys went for route march independently.	19th
"	2.7.15		Draft of 96 N.C.Os & men arrived. Working party of 160 N.C.Os & men per Coy, each under an officer, the whole under Major WEBB went by motor-bus to YPRES — from there marched via LILLE gate to dig trenches on the salient. The Battalion is now up to strength except in officers. 7 short.	19th
"	3.7.15		Working party returned 4.30 A.M. No casualties. Coys practised attack on trenches in the afternoon.	19th
"	4.7.15		Divine Service 10 AM.	
"	5.7.15		Sgt. Majors drill for last draft. There are about 15 men of the draft, who are not fit for service, having been wounded + sent out again too soon. 2d Lt CARTER proceeded to BAILLEUL for dental treatment. Lecture by Sanitary Officer & INF BDE, a gas + live bomb thrown.	19th
"	6.7.15		Saw a working party of 4 officers + 274 O.R. to YPRES by motor bus to dig trenches in the salient.	19th
"	7.7.15		C.O. spent all day in trenches at RAILWAY WOOD arranging the taking over of them tomorrow night from 8th RIFLE BRIGADE.	19th
"	8.7.15		Advance party consisting of 1 officer per Coy, Signally Officer, M.G. Officer, will Supplies M. Gunners Bombers & 4 Snipers marched off for the trenches at 6.15 A.M. 2d party of 2 platoons per Coy paraded at 2.45 pm & marched off under Major WEBB this party halted –6 PM, 1 mile west of YPRES, where tea was served.	19th

Army Form C. 2118.

WAR DIARY
or
INTELLIGENCE SUMMARY

(Erase heading not required.)

Instructions regarding War Diaries and Intelligence Summaries are contained in F. S. Regs., Part II. and the Staff Manual respectively. Title pages will be prepared in manuscript.

Place	Date	Hour	Summary of Events and Information	Remarks and references to Appendices
RAILWAY WOOD Trenches	9.7.15		3rd party consisting of remainder of H.Q. and Coys paraded at 5.45 P.M. & were taken in motor buses (20) to road junction just West of YPRES, where 2nd party joined it: this point was the advanced starting point Batt's moved off at 6.30 pm. with ½ hour interval between Coys. Yearly Coy reached MENIN Gate at 9 pm, where guides from Batts in the trenches met them. Relief of trenches completed by 1.5 A.M. Casualties, 3.O.R. wounded by shrapnel — first party Heavy mist at dawn utilised for reconnaissance: all troops in trenches stood to arms till 7 am on account of the mist.	M.P.
"	10.7.15		Carrying parties from 5/ K.S.L.I. strength about 400 brought up all the stores to Batt's last night; there we have 2 Battns in the trenches & 2 in Reserve, the 2 latter do all the carrying for the 2 in the trenches. Casualties Killed O.R. 1. Wounded O.R. 3. Wounded at duty O.R. 1. Enemy bombarded our Railway Junctions at 7.30 am & knocked it down about 100 H.E. Shells were fired in all. It fair amount of about fire from both sides all day, also french howitzers. Casualties Wounded O.R. 7. Wounded at duty O.R. 1.	M.P.
"	11.7.15		Pair of carrier pigeons released this morning from CAMBRIDGE Road, flew to POPERINGHE with message for test: message will be on myself in front trench, when will be	Appx. I

Army Form C. 2118.

/5.

WAR DIARY
or
INTELLIGENCE SUMMARY.

(Erase heading not required.)

Instructions regarding War Diaries and Intelligence Summaries are contained in F.S. Regs., Part II. and the Staff Manual respectively. Title pages will be prepared in manuscript.

Place	Date	Hour	Summary of Events and Information	Remarks and references to Appendices
RAILWAY WOOD TRENCHES	12.7.15		Unable in a few days, thus holding up D 10 & D 12 fire trenches. Casualties Wounded O.R. 17 Wounded at duty O.R. 1.	
			Grenade exploded in one of C Coy bombing posts at 3 a.m. killing 1 & severely wounding 3 others, of whom 2 died. It was impossible to discover cause of accident; it probably being their rifle grenade into pit, which exploded one of our bombs. Casualties Killed O.R. 1 Wounded O.R. 13.	1/P.
"	13.7.15		Our own bombarded enemy barricade on railway, commencing at 9.45 A.M. Considerable damage done. Bombardment was to have lasted one hour, but at 10.50 a.m. a British aeroplane observing for the sh[oot] was shot down by aero-plane. After a shell had burst in front of it. Aero-plane fell about 800 yards behind the enemy lines, & bombardment ceased	Appx II & III
			Battalion relieved in trenches by 5/K.S.L.I., commencing at 9 P.M. from the MENIN GATE. Wire party arrived CAMBRIDGE Road at 10.45 P.M. Relief stopped for about half hour by order of 42d INF BDE on account of enemy attack to N. of YPRES. Relief completed by 1.15 A.M. without casualties. Casualties Killed O.R. 1, Wounded O.R. 13.	1/P. Appx IV

Army Form C. 2118.

16

WAR DIARY
INTELLIGENCE SUMMARY.

(Erase heading not required.)

Place	Date	Hour	Summary of Events and Information	Remarks and references to Appendices
YPRES	14.7.15		After being relieved in the trenches the Battalion went into dug-outs in the Ramparts of YPRES between the MENIN gate & SALLY PORT as Brigade Reserve. 1 Coy N of MENIN gate. Battalion provided a carrying party of 9 officers & 443 O.R. to take rations, water, & stores up to 5/7 KSLI in the trenches. Casualties: Killed O.R. 3. Wounded O.R. 7.	HP
"	15.7.15		Day spent in cleaning up, clearing roads of debris & building more dug-outs. Very wet night, & carrying party took 3½ hours to reach CAMBRIDGE Road, usually done in one. Strength of carrying party 8 officers & 411 O.R. Rations, water & stores for Batt⁵ in Ramparts are brought up nightly by Regt Transport & dumped inside the Ramparts, 2 wagons remaining till return of carrying parties to take back wounded men's kits & rifles, all salvage, & empty water cans. Rations etc. for Batt⁵ in the trenches are taken to a dump outside YPRES between the MENIN gate & L'ECOLE on the MENIN Road, & dumped there, & taken on by carrying party.	HP
"	16.7.15		Work on pulled down walls of ruined houses, & cleaning the streets of debris. Carrying party of 8 officers & 372 O.R. Very wet night.	HP

Army Form C. 2118.

WAR DIARY
INTELLIGENCE SUMMARY.
(Erase heading not required.)

Place	Date	Hour	Summary of Events and Information	Remarks and references to Appendices
YPRES	18.7.15		In addition to carrying party of 8 officers + 399. O.R. Battalion provided a working party of 2 officers + 100. O.R. for work on support + communication trenches at Y. wood.	11/1
"	19.7.15		Battalion relieved in YPRES by 10th D.L.I. at 10 p.m. Battalion marched there out by Coys independently via VLAMERTINGHE to dug-out shelters in a field at G.17.d Sheet 28 between VLAMERTINGHE & POPERINGHE 1 mile S. of the road.	11/1
Camp G.17.d Sheet 28.	19.7.15		Battalion arrived in Camp. Reserve at one hour's notice. Battalion rested in camp in the afternoon till about 1 am: 42nd Inf Bde is now in Corps Reserve. During the afternoon flew several times one hostile little aeroplane driven away by 3 British biplanes. Saw HOOGE Chateau blown up by our mine at 7 pm to the east of it, followed by barrage of Arti: fire. Battalion billeted by ½ Coys at POPERINGHE, & got a change of shirts + socks.	11/1
"	20.7.15		Battalion provided two working parties each of 2 officers + 100 O.R. one in the morning + the other in the afternoon to work on Redoubt 1½ miles W. of YPRES at H.17.a. "19 Sheet 28. Also working party of 4 officers + 200. O.R. to work on Redoubt East of ÉCOLE at I.9.d Sheet 28. Draft of 2 officers + 20.O.R. arrived to day	Appx Y
"	21.7.15			

LT. BIRD S.M. + LT NEWMAN L.S.M.

Army Form C. 2118.

WAR DIARY
or
INTELLIGENCE SUMMARY.
(Erase heading not required.)

Place	Date	Hour	Summary of Events and Information	Remarks and references to Appendices
CAMP G.17.d Sheet 28	22.7.15		Battn provided working party of 2 Officers & 100 O.R. on in the morning & the other in the afternoon to work on Redoubt H.17.a. 1/9 Sheet 28. 1 Officer & 2 N.C.Os attached to 6 C. M.M.G. Battery for M.G. Course. Wkg till 31/7/15. Total Casualties between 6/6/15 & 15/7/15:— Killed Officers 1. O.R. 27 Died of Wounds O.R. 8 Missing Officers 1 O.R. 1 Wounded Officers 6 O.R. 195	HP
"	23.7.15		Rained all night. Each Coy sent out a working party 2 Officers + 100 O.R. to work on 2 Redoubts west of YPRES in 2nd line of defence. Draft of 1 Officer (LT H.J.T.DAY) + 60 O.R. arrived.	Appx VI BP
"	24.7.15		Each Coy sent out working parties of 2 Officers + 100 O.R. for work on Redoubts at H.17.a. 1/9 Sheet 28, + one of the ECOLE at I.9.d, & also laying cable underground from YPRES to trenches.	
"	25.7.15		Working party of 4 Officers + 200 O.R. sent to work Redoubts H.17.a.1/9 Sheet 28.	

WAR DIARY or INTELLIGENCE SUMMARY

Army Form C. 2118

Place	Date	Hour	Summary of Events and Information	Remarks and references to Appendices
Near POPERINGHE	26.7.15		Advance party of Maxim Gun, Signallers & Bombers started at 7 am for trenches, to relieve those of 10th DLI & 10th DCLI of 43rd Brigade, when we relieve tonight. Still made behind sprayer in the afternoon. Coy parades independently as follows to proceed to the trenches TB 6.30, A 6.45, B 6.30, C & Hd Qrs 7.15 PM. & marched via VLAMERTINGHE to YPRES. Firing Coy left MENIN gate at 9 PM, others at ½ hour interval, led by own guides, & also guides from 10th DLI & 10th DCLI. The 43rd Bde have 3 Coys in firing line & 1 in support, where as 4.2 Bde have 2 & 2. This makes relieving more difficult & complicated that if both Bdes had the same. Relief completed 12.30 am. Communication trenches very muddy after the rain. Casualties Killed OR.1, Wounded at duty OR.1	P/P
RAILWAY WOOD I.11.b. Sect. J.5.	27.7.15		Quiet Day. Enemy did a lot of whizz-banging, to which our 18 pdrs replied. Enemy have strengthened their position, have devised a good move known to our trenches than they used to do. We do the same. Casualties Killed OR.3, Wounded at duty OR.1	P.M.
	28.7.15		Lot of shooting from both sides into mortars, rifle grenades & bombs, also with field guns. We have now got two catapults with which we lob bombs with great success into enemy trenches, which are out of reach of hand thrown ones. Casualties Killed OR.2, Wounded Capt R.O. LOGAN, O.R.8, Sent OR.1, Wounded at duty OR.1	

WAR DIARY
INTELLIGENCE SUMMARY

Army Form C. 2118.

Place	Date	Hour	Summary of Events and Information	Remarks and references to Appendices
ZILLEBEKE 29/7/15 RAILWAY WOOD	29.7.15		Enemy manoeuvres threw large mortar in CAMBRIDGE Road at 6.45 A.M. Bomb exits to own enemy, & looked like large polished metal bottle. It did not turn here & over in flight, but wobbled a good deal. It burst with tremendous violence, almost immediately after landing. This is the first burst of this mortar had here: probably gun brought from HOOGE. Otherwise quiet day. Our 3" Howitzer Battery reported or brought opposite sudden burst from which ammunition believed to have fired burst but might, put in H.E. Shell in with good effect. We sniped 5 enemy as they retired out of Redoubt. Working party of 150 men of 5/ K.S.L.I. came up to surpose work on communication trenches & Support points. Casualties killed O.R. 1. Wounded O.R. 7.	AP
"	30.7.15	3.15 AM	Enemy type another large bomb into RAILWAY wood last night about 3.15 AM. Nature bombardment stated by E.O.T. to which replied. Lasted for 1 hour, & the enemies fire violently till 7 a.m. LT BLEECK reported seeing stream of liquid fire through our own trenches near HOOGE. Sent wire back to Battalion Hd Qrs from O.P. were our account as soon as bombardment started. Also was own line to Brigade H.Q. Or shortly afterwards, just had time to get DX - 1 Message through. Sent away by Runner at 4 AM, a by hand at 4.30 AM. Brandt

Army Form C. 2118.

WAR DIARY
or
INTELLIGENCE SUMMARY.
(Erase heading not required.)

Place	Date	Hour	Summary of Events and Information	Remarks and references to Appendices
RAILWAY WOOD	30.7.15		Communication in action of the hill by battalion was good with left of 4th R.B. between Coy's & with W. Yorks & Enemy Artly was specially heavy on SUNK ROAD SW of RAILWAY WOOD WITTE POORT farm & from there to railway W of CAMBRIDGE road. Some matters were also not awar. Information received that enemy, after repeated trenches held by 41st B'de near HOOGE Chateau had captured them & the 41st Brigade retiring to ZOUAVE & SANCTUARY WOODS. Fairly quiet beside RAILWAY WOOD	
		2 P.M.	Reports. On W. front, preparation to counter-attack on HOOGE. Enemy shelled heavily in return. Specially Y wood, WITTE POORT, blown west of F. 12 Reserve trenches, 9th K.R.R.C. recaptured C 10 trench, 41st B'de held up. Three H.E. shells fell in CAMBRIDGE road, a good many on the Reserve trenches but no damage done. H.E. shells were in most cases followed by shrapnel – many hundreds every five a large numbers of their mortars on H 20 + H. 21 blown in some dug-outs & parapets. From observation of shelling it is evident that W. communication trench should be connected direct with C.T. leading to H. 17 + H. 18, as the Sunken road is very heavily shelled. Communication with left of 9th R.B., W. YORKS, & behind Coys with 6th Dur L.R.F.A. & supporting Batteries maintained throughout.	
		11 P.M.	Our own Command shelling again. Not much reply on RAILWAY wood. Trench mortars were however very active again & caused some damage in H 21, H 27	

Army Form C. 2118.

WAR DIARY
INTELLIGENCE SUMMARY.
(Erase heading not required.)

22

Place	Date	Hour	Summary of Events and Information	Remarks and references to Appendices
RAILWAY WOOD	30.7.15 (cont)		Casualties killed O.R. 3. Wounded Lt C.T. JURY, 27 O.R. Shrame O.R. 2. Ratliffs, which Mould have taken place to-night are cancelled	
"	31.7.15		Situation; 3 Batts 43 rd Bde relieved 41 st & 42 nd Bde last night about 2 am.	
		2 AM	Enemy made heavy attack on strongly protected ZOUAVE WOOD. Our det- appear to have beaten off great pow of attack, + a counter-attack by 6th D.C.L.I. recaptured N edge of ZOUAVE wood. Position we now hold is as follows:— 9th K.R.R.C. G.10 west of HOOGE to Mr house on MENIN Road, thence 43rd Inf Bde E. N. edge ZOUAVE + SANCTUARY wood. Quiet all the morning except for rifle grenades + mortars. Enemy seem to have very large supply of Amm.n for latter.	M.P.
		5.15 PM	Enemy opened very heavy shell-fire on our support trenches, on ridge S of Junction of MENIN road + Railway. Reported that 9th K.R.R.C. had repulsed two attacks.	
		9 PM	Enemy opened rapid fire on our trenches + 9th R.B. also heard rapid work the front of 9th K.R.R.C. charge masses of enemy reported moving up to Lt BELLE- VAARDE farm. No attack. Our 9.2 Howitzers shelled the farm. Otherwise all quiet	

"A" Form.
MESSAGES AND SIGNALS. Army Form C. 2121.

Prefix	Code	m.	Words	Charge	This message is on a/c of:	Recd. at	m.
Office of Origin and Service Instructions.			Sent		Service.	Date	
Secret			At	m.		From	
			To				
			By		(Signature of "Franking Officer.")	By	

TO 5th Oxf't Bucks L.I.

Sender's Number.	Day of Month	In reply to Number	AAA
* Bu 249	12		

14th Div have arranged with 6th Div to bombard enemy redoubt I 11 b 9 8 from 9.45 am – 10.45 am tomorrow AAA 4.5" + 6" Howitzers will engage redoubt & 18 pdrs will cover ground to East. AAA Withdraw all troops in vicinity of barrier so that no men are within 100x of redoubt which is to be bombarded AAA You should cover approaches to railway barricade by Machine Gun from North corner of D 10 during above period AAA Artillery will also fire a few shots into Sap from I 11 b 9 8 to railway barricade. AAA acknowledge by wire

From	42nd Inf Bde
Place	
Time	9 P.m.

Appx I Bn 7/131

5th Oxf + Bucks L.I.

With reference to my conversation with you on the telephone about 11.15 a.m. The 14th Div. feel the greatest importance on completing the French Trench ready for occupation at once.

The B.G.C. wishes you to commence work as under immediately on receipt of this message.

1. All filled Sandbags with the Sap at D.9. will be carried to the North end of D.10 & dumped ready for use tonight.

2. Further Sandbags will be filled in rear of the Barricade at Sunken Road & be kept there in readiness for carrying up to North end of D.10 as soon as those in 1 are carried out.

3. A working party will occupy as much of the trench as possible & continue to fill Sandbags in the bottom of the trench ready for use tonight.

4. The details for a working party for tonight will be settled by you in consultation with the B[attalio]n Major who will be at your H.Q. at 2.45 p.m.

Acknowledge by wire

Dwora[k] Maj[or]
B[riga]de Major

"C" Form (Original). Army Form C. 2123.
MESSAGES AND SIGNALS. No. of Message..........

Prefix	Code H/ Words	Received From A7	Sent, or sent out At .... m.	Office Stamp. OC1
Charges to collect £ s. d.		By Sgt Tom	To........	13/7/15
Service Instructions. A7 III			By.......	

Handed in at................ Office..... m. Received..... m.

TO **Aaj**

*Sender's Number | Day of Month | In reply to Number | AAA

Aeroplane observed falling over enemy's lines at 10.30 this morning AAA Believed British AAA Distance 1200 – 1300 yards

FROM Lt Clark 1½ Trench
PLACE & TIME 11.40 am

"A" Form.
MESSAGES AND SIGNALS.

Army Form C. 2121.

Prefix	Code	m.	Words	Charge	This message is on a/c of:	Recd. at	m.
Office of Origin and Service Instructions.			Sent			Date	
			At	m.	Service.	From	
			To		IV		
			By		(Signature of "Franking Officer.")		

TO .... 5th Oxf + Bucks L.I.

Sender's Number.	Day of Month	In reply to Number	AAA
* Bn 275	13th		

Relief	will	stand	by	until
further	orders	AAA	our	line
to	you	in	an	.....
D.18	AAA	the	first	news
you	will	probably	the	will
be	the	arrival	of	Shop
L1	AAA	the	relief	can
then	proceed			

From 42nd Inf Bde
Place
Time 8-45 pm

The above may be forwarded as now corrected. (Z)
Censor. Signature of Addressor or person authorised to telegraph in his name.
* This line should be erased if not required.

(T1809) Wt. 14142—641. 45000 pads. 4/15. Sir J. C. & S.

App x V

5th Oxf & Bucks L.I.

Please detail the following working party daily until further orders.
1st Relief. 2 officers + 100 men.   Time 7 a.m - 11 a.m. B
2nd Relief. 2 "   " 100 "   "   12 noon - 4 p.m. C
Site of Redoubt on which the party will work is
Ref. Sheet 28   H.17.a.1.9

Tools and stores are provided at the redoubt.
One officer will arrive at the redoubt half an hour ahead of the party in order to learn from R.E. what work has to be done and to allot the work accordingly before the arrival of his men.
The time laid down above are the times at which the parties will arrive at the redoubt.

Please acknowledge.

Wood
Major
Bde Major
42nd Inf Bde.

19th July 1915.

Coys will find a working party of 2 officers & 100 men for work on Redoubt at H.17.a.1/9 sheet 28 as follows

5th Oxf + Bucks L.I.
5th Shrop LI
9th KRRifC
9th Rif Brig

App. VI
BM 7/91
23-7-15.

Please detail the following working party for tomorrow night
Strength 100.   No tools required.

2500 Sandbags will be drawn by you from the R.E. Park VLAMERTINGHE and conveyed by you to YPRES where they will be dumped, divided into bundles of 25 and await the arrival of the party. 20 motor busses will be at road junction G.18.a at 7.P.M. Four of these busses are allotted to your party, and will convey them to YPRES where they will pick up the 25 sandbags per man & proceed to road junction I.9.d-8-5 ready to commence work at 9.P.M.

Major G.J. DAVIS. 9th Rif Brig will Command the whole working party (100 from each Battⁿ)

Major DAVIS and one officer from 5th Oxf + Bucks L.I. one officer from 5th Shrop LI, + one officer from 9th K.R.Rif.C. will report at Div. H.Q. at 7 P.M. + will be conveyed by motor car to YPRES + will report to R.E. Officer at I.9.d-8-5 at 8-15 P.M for instructions.

The busses will bring the parties back.
Please acknowledge by wire.

D Wood Major
B.M.

"C" Form (Duplicate). Army Form C. 2123.
MESSAGES AND SIGNALS. No. of Message _____

			Charges to Pay.	Office Stamp.
SM 1/m 37	ZDB 9? Thorne F.		£ s. d.	

Service Instructions. ZDB

Handed in at _____ Office 9 ___ m. Received 9.25 ___ m.

TO 5th OXF & BUCKS L.I.

Sender's Number	Day of Month	In reply to Number	AAA
BM 295	9th		

Aircraft report for last few days show considerable activity on railways and roads east of our front aaa Actual direction uncertain but everything much above normal

FROM PLACE & TIME   42nd INF BDE 9 pm

"C" Form (Duplicate). Army Form C. 2123.
MESSAGES AND SIGNALS. No. of Message_____

| Service Instructions: SM BLPM 61 ZDA ZDB D/13 | Charges to Pay. £ s. d. | Office Stamp. OLI 9/7/15 |

Handed in at 42nd Bde Office 2/55 p.m. Received 3/15 p.m.

TO O/5th OXFORDS

Sender's Number: BM 287   Day of Month: 9th   In reply to Number: AAA

Please consider the possibility of constructing a supporting point in railway wood or have an alternative position just south of sunken road AAA Will discuss this with you tomorrow morning AAA First thing to be done is to wire the fire trenches AAA Supporting point comes next in order of importance AAA

FROM
PLACE & TIME 42nd BDE
2.50 PM

"C" Form (Duplicate).
MESSAGES AND SIGNALS.

Army Form C. 2123.

No. of Message.

SM ABRM 46.   ZDB
ZDB   SB

Charges to Pay. £ s. d.

Office Stamp. OLi 10/7/15

Handed in at 42nd Bde   Office 1/10 p.m.   Received 1/23 p.m.

TO 5th OXFORDS

Sender's Number: BM 303
Day of Month: 10th
In reply to Number:
AAA

It has been decided to construct two strong posts at the RAILWAY WOOD on the sites inspected this morning AAA Capt CHESNEY 61st Coy RE will reach your HQ about 2.30 PM today to advise regarding them AAA

FROM PLACE & TIME: 42nd BDE 1.5 PM

42/14

121/6607

14ᵗʰ/15 Burovin

5. O.K.: 1ᵗᵉ Buchs: L.J.
Vol: IV
from 1 - 31. 8. 15

J.D. H.25.
11 sheet

WAR DIARY / INTELLIGENCE SUMMARY

Army Form C. 2118.

Place	Date	Hour	Summary of Events and Information	Remarks and references to Appendices
RAILWAY WOOD YPRES.	1/8/15		Fairly quiet day. Usual large numbers of mortars & grenades sent over by enemy. Communication between Battalion HQrs in the trenches & supporting Batteries needs improvement too slow at present. Also we are still to short of gun ammunition to be able to give the enemy anything like the amount of damage they give us with their H.E. Rifle & gun shells. We retaliated with friends mortars & bomb Catapults. Enemy appear to have evacuated most of their front line trenches opposite us, & judging by their flares, which seem to come from their second line. We are holding our front line lightly in case of bombardment. Casualties killed O.R. 2. Wounded 2ᵈ Lt FENWICK O.R. 17.	12P
"	2/8/15		Enemy working party of about 30 seen just S. of Railway — afternoon & dispersed by our Art. Enemy have been worked on their Communication trenches with great vigour during the last week. Enemy artillery spent being fire to an immediate right Spa about to have Signal was 2 green light followed by Red one. These signals seem to change very frequently. Casualties killed O.R. 2. Wounded L⁺ BIRCH O.R. 5. 9.5% of our casualties are caused by injury 3 in. H.E. shell. Commonly called the "whizz-bang", and by fire people, and shrapnel Guns, to be handled more or less not not not not no from an experience here. Enemy have improved their communication between ECLUSETTE & HOOGE & Chwst be easily sniped by us from H.17 down. Field gun Battery of enemy N. of Railway is England notified the ability of its position, but every Guns have not yet the silenced. We fire frequently upon the morning & a few rounds in it. from 4-5 am & 8-30-10.30 pm.	AP NP

Army Form C. 2118.

WAR DIARY
INTELLIGENCE SUMMARY
(Erase heading not required.)

Place	Date	Hour	Summary of Events and Information	Remarks and references to Appendices
	4/8/15		Morning. Mining effort to be in operation by the enemy in front of Railway barrier. R.E.I. reported to supervise construction of listening gallery. Casualty Wounded O.R. 4. Enemy observed working on new communication trench. Enemy gunners seen many times. Field gun Battery: 10 minuten later shell began to arrive in our trenches. Several of these Batteries have been located by our sniping lately & exact locality reported to artillery. More reports of enemy being opposite Railway.	BP
		3 PM	Barrier. Enemy opened fire with crumps & whizz-bangs on our trenches; our field guns covering this sector of trenches & replied as far as limited supply of ammunition allowed. Change number of mortars & rifles grenades fired at it. K.2.1 by enemy, to which we duly replied in sort. Our two novel spectacle rifle tubes which have a loop-hole glass appearance were seen from H.17. They can pivot, & at times disappear. They may be heard - light on some means of observation. They overlook HOOGE & valley west of it. They are an enemy parapet. Casualties Killed O.R. 2. Wounded O.R. 9.	PP.
	5/8/15		Enemy replying to our dart bombardment of HOOGE was to direct heavy field gun fire onto our trenches & some big shell. Enemy mortars active. Our also at work. Situation to-day more lively than usual, every thing moving vigorously. Mr H.E. 3" Shells into our trenches. Enemy aerial gun Torpedo gun located 9.2. Mounition fired at it. If that direct hit on thing near it. No more aerial torpedoes. Casualties Killed O.R. 2. Wounded O.R. 5	

Army Form C.2118.

25.

WAR DIARY
or
INTELLIGENCE SUMMARY.
(Erase heading not required.)

Place	Date	Hour	Summary of Events and Information	Remarks and references to Appendices
---	6/8/15	5 A.M.	Situation very lively at times to-day. Soon after 5 A.M., 13 Minenwerfer put into H.21. & RAILWAY WOOD. We replied with field guns, which stopped Minenwerfer fire for a time but they soon began again. Howitzers pitched on which effectually stopped the enemy fire. Enemy fired very heavy fire on our	
		12.30 P.M.	trenches with field guns at 12.30 P.M., enfilading our trenches in RAILWAY WOOD from the N. Our Arty replied; many fired entered fr. to hour & then ceased. Good deal of damage done to our trenches. Battalion relieved by 5/ K.S.L.I. to-night. We took up positions in reserve as follows: 1 Coy in cellars – YPRES, 2 Coys in dug-outs just W of function of MENIN Road & Railway, 1 Coy @ H.Q. Area. Relief completed. Casualties Killed `O.R. 7` Wounded LT. BIRD `O.R. 17`	P.P.
In Reserve	7/8/15	12 M.N.	Very little to Report. Have to be very careful not to be seen by enemy aeroplanes always on duty for this purpose. Sent a carrying party the usual hour for rations & water for 5/ K.S.L.I. LT-COL COBB Commanding the Battalion remained in the trenches as O.C. left Sector. Casualties Killed `O.R. 1`	P.P.
---	8/8/15		Quiet day except fr our bombardment of HOOGE which has taken place daily between 1 am & 3 am for the last 5 days. Usual ruts went to hour. Sent carrying party same as last night. 6th Division made successful attack on HOOGE & recaptured all the	P.P.
---	9/8/15		lost trenches & enemy rebuilt also very heavy bombardment prior to attack. Bombardment all day. Sent 1 Coy to relieve 9 R.B. in	

WAR DIARY

INTELLIGENCE SUMMARY

Army Form C. 2118.

Place	Date	Hour	Summary of Events and Information	Remarks and references to Appendices
	10/8/15		in Trenches S. of RAILWAY WOOD. We remained in Reserve less 1 Coy. 1 Coy moved up into X trench to be nearer RAILWAY WOOD, if required to support. Casualties Killed O.R. 1. Wounded O.R. 3.	PP.
Reserve			Quiet day by comparison. 10th DURHAM L.I. relieved us in Reserve to-night. Coys marched back independently through YPRES, & went into bivouac in a field 1 mile W. of VLAMERTINGHE. Should have thought that better arrangements & shelter could have been provided for Battalion after a fortnight in the trenches at YPRES! Battalion after all the shelter provided for a Battalion & all 4 & 6 large sheds are all crowded under the trees none the less at the field, to escape observation of enemy aeroplanes. Casualties Wounded O.R. 6. Enemy shelled VLAMERTINGHE in the morning & evening with heavy shells. Battalion intact.	PP.
VLAMER-TINGHE	11/8/15		Lt. Col. COBB took over command of the 42nd Inf. Bde. fm. Brigadier General MARKHAM invalided. Found working party of 1 officer & 50 men for rebuilt E. of YPRES near Junction of MENIN road & railway. This is a daily fatigue till further orders. Draft of 30 N.C.Os & men arrived. Major W. F. R. WEBB took over command of Battalion.	PP.
	13/8/15		Found working party of 2 officers & 100 men for work a Redoubt W. of YPRES, between that place & VLAMERTINGHE & a party of 1 N.C.O. & 30 men for road Ypres — Camp Thope. Parties are found every other day till further orders. Military while Battalion is not baths a change of shirts in POPERINGHE nearly all day.	PP.

Army Form C. 2118.

WAR DIARY
INTELLIGENCE SUMMARY.
(Erase heading not required.)

Place	Date	Hour	Summary of Events and Information	Remarks and references to Appendices
VLAMER-TINGHE	14/8/15		Two men sent to Course of instruction in care of enemy pigeons at 2nd Army Corps pigeon loft WATOU. Our officers, N.C.O. & 5 men sent for Course of instruction in TOBY mortar at LA LOVIE chateau near POPERINGHE.	BP.
—	15/8/15		Church Parade 10 a.m. Working parties as usual during last few in the trenches. Total Casualties — Officers W. 5. O.R. K. 27 W. 159 } 189. Total casualties since Battalion landed on 20th May 1915. Officers K. 1 Missing 1 W. 11 Invalided 1 } 434 O.R. K. 62 Missing 2 W. 345 Invalided 11 }	BP.
— " —	16/8/15		Coy did drill, extended order drill, rifle exercises, fire direction & control & rapid mapping. This will be done daily while Batt's in rest area. Lt-Col COBB resumed command of the Battalion. Brigadier General DUDGEON C.B. (having taken over command of the 42nd Inf. Bde.) inspected our heavy guns (15") and 3 rounds this evening, & stirred up a good deal of late Walking parties. Coml. rut- proceed along the Road to	BP.
— " —	17/8/15		YPRES on account of gas shells. Brigadier General DUDGEON C.B. inspected Coy at work in the morning. Major General Sir J. KEIR, Commanding VI Corps, inspected Battalion in the afternoon & expressed to all ranks his approval of the good work always done by the Battalion in the face of the enemy & their present smart appearance. 5 men sent on new 2 Supply Course.	BP.
	18/8/15			

WAR DIARY
INTELLIGENCE SUMMARY.
(Erase heading not required.)

Place	Date	Hour	Summary of Events and Information	Remarks and references to Appendices
VLAMER-TINGHE	19/8/15		3 Officers sent up to the trenches by WYE WOOD to see the trenches which we take over to-morrow night with 2 Coy. Received 500 high velocity sporting rifle with which to shoot at the German armoured aeroplane. Commonly known as "Coffin-lidded Fritz", which so often sails low over our trenches.	B.P.
	20/9/15		Draft of 88 N.C.Os & men arrive. Only 18 Officers left for duty. 2 the Coy Signallers, Machine Gunners & Bombers went to the trenches to relieve by Officer Companies paraded & marched off independently at 10 minute intervals commencing at 7 P.M. an ultimatum route had been reconnoitred — the enemy in case the men need to YPRES was being shelled, but it was quite quiet, so Companies marched by the main road to the prison at YPRES, then to the DIXMUDE gate on the N. side of the city. Here guides from the 6th K.O.Y.L.I. were to meet each Company, but none could be found, so moved on up the MENIN road + guides were picked up at the ECOLE Battalion distributed in the trenches as follows:— 2 Coys H13-H17 (WYE wood) to be under the Command of O.C. LEFT SECTOR. 1 Coy. of R.B., 1 Coy F.13, which is a Reserve trench recently constructed about 800 yds W. of RAILWAY wood, + 1 Coy G.H.Q. Relief completed 11.20 P.M. No Casualties. Very quiet night. Batt = Hd Qrs in dug-out on the Railway 200 yds E. of junction of MENIN road + Railway. No fires allowed in F.13 & G.H.Q. for fear of observation by hostile aeroplanes, or observation balloon. 2d LT J N G MITCHELL joined Batt for duty	B.P.

(T.F.)

WAR DIARY
INTELLIGENCE SUMMARY.

Army Form C. 2118.

Place	Date	Hour	Summary of Events and Information	Remarks and references to Appendices
Trenches E. of YPRES	21/8/15		Heavy Rain in the morning. Some 3" H.E. shells fell & exploded near Hd. Qr. dug-out 3 - 3.30 p.m, also some on C.T. Heavy shells into CHATEAU went on MENIN Road. Batt's found working parties of 3 Officers & 150 O.R. from A + B Coys to night — the trenches H 13 - H 22. Pack horses carry Rations for Coys in the firing line & dumps at foot of hill just W of RAILWAY Wood. Cap L-F.13 & G.H.Q. carry their own Ration & water from dump on the MENIN Road to which front Rations & water are brought by Reg. Transport from camp. Water for Coy in the firing line is carried up by hand from the SALLY Port. Dug out men carries 2 Pantongs contains 16 mess Rations + pad. One pack pony carries Rations + pad for V.64. Men J is trolley is being here experimented with to run from VLAMERTINGHE to CAMBRIDGE Road, a mile. Using it as far as YPRES, whence it is man-handled. Wheels carried with leather to Prevent noise. No casualties to-day. Extra-ordinarily quiet on our front. While Coy. walk out in front at night, wiring & strengthening parapet, mended stiles. By day the enemy fire a good many trench mortars & 3" H.E. shells, but nothing like the minimum they fired a week ago. Enemy aircraft very active to day one spying over Trenches. Lieut Mullin sheared by the enemy. A + B Coys from G.H.Q. & F.13 respectively relieved C + D Coys in the Trenches. Capitaines Syphilles, Boutin, a Machine Gunner relieved by day. No Casualties. 3 Officers + 3 O.R. sick. Obtained valuable information of enemy trenches in our front from Reconnaissance carried out by	App
	22/8/15		Lieut to HOOGE Trenches for the purpose	App

WAR DIARY
INTELLIGENCE SUMMARY

Army Form C. 2118.
30

Place	Date	Hour	Summary of Events and Information	Remarks and references to Appendices
YPRES Salient	23/8/15		Good deal of field gun fire by both sides in the morning. Officers of 5/KSLI came to arrange relief to be by held to-night. Relief completed 11 PM. Coys marched back independently as soon as relieved to huts just W. of YLAMERTINGHE. Enemy have put a few mortars over on the last two days. These have burst in the air & emitted a brown fluid which hangs about & then they also emit dense cloud of smoke. Casualties Wounded LT Bleach (Drum of ear broken by burst of trench mortar O.R. 2 (shock).	AP
YLAMERT- INGHE	24/8/15		Battalion found 400 men for working & carrying parties E. of YPRES. 2 LT BECKINGHAM + 50 O.R. sent to YPRES to entrain dig-outs in the Ramparts will probably be away 3-4 weeks. Battalion provided carrying parties to the trenches to-night of 4 officers + 380 O.R.	AP
"	25/8/15		Great deal of aerial activity to-day. Lily & 9 an anti-aircraft shelly fell in Camp. Battalion front carrying parties to the trenches to-night 5 officers, 420 O.R. Casualties 3 killed & wounded by 3" H.E. Shell in CAMBRIDGE Road last night.	AP
"	26/8/15		Carrying parties of 4 officers + 426 O.R. to-night. Have now had no real rest since 7/7/15; very much needed now for Re-Organisation, training of Young Officers + N.C.O.s - Drafts. Cannot do much when all available Men are taken nightly for carrying to the trenches. All such things as M.G. Section + Signallers have for exceeded the numbers laid down in War Establishment e.g. We require 6 M.G. teams from the Battalion	AP
"	27/8/15		

Army Form C. 2118.
31.

WAR DIARY
~~INTELLIGENCE SUMMARY~~

(Erase heading not required.)

Instructions regarding War Diaries and Intelligence Summaries are contained in F.S. Regs., Part II. and the Staff Manual respectively. Title pages will be prepared in manuscript.

Place	Date	Hour	Summary of Events and Information	Remarks and references to Appendices
VLAMERTINGHE	28/8/15		When in the trenches each team consists of 1 N.C.O. & 6 men, a total of 6 N.C.O. + 48 men in the Battalion as trained machine gunners. So that there are now about 350 Specialists & supply in the Battalion leaving only 350-400 available for working & carrying parties. C.O. C.H. C.O. & 13 provided a party to the trenches to augment & officers 385 O.R.	App.
"	29/8/15		Draft of 3 men joined Battalion. 4 2nd Lt Bee returned by 43rd Bt Bee in the trenches to-night. Battn in charge of Mints & orderly room schedule for all the Battalion at POPERINGHE.	App.
"	30/8/15		2 Lt L.E. MESSURIER rec-rmd, recommended Base Employment Battalion front working party of 4 officers + 250 O.R. tonight for defence of WHITE CHATEAU east of YPRES. 2 N.C.O.'s + 12 men sent as garrison of french dug-outs just W of the asylum YPRES: 1 Officer & N.C.O.s sent for Course of Instruction to Brigade Grenade School.	App.
"	31/8/15			App.

J.B. Payne Capt & Adjt
51 Oxf & Bucks L.I. (?)

121/7050

14th Division

5th O.K. and Rucks
Vol. 5
Sept. 15

Operations
22nd Sept/1915

5. I.J.
35 sheet

Army Form C. 2118

WAR DIARY
INTELLIGENCE SUMMARY
(Erase heading not required.)

Place	Date	Hour	Summary of Events and Information	Remarks and references to Appendices
Camp near VLAMERTINGHE	1/9/15		Nothing of interest to record. Attached to War Diary is a schedule showing numbers admitted to Hospital or field ambulance daily, account of sickness – also made Batt⁵ ladies – France 20/5/15. This will be attached monthly in future	PP
	4/9/15		Rec'd all the morning. Draft of 30 W.C. Os & two arrived. Batt⁵ paraded working parties of 4 Officers & 300 O.R.	PP
	5/9/15		The day for a Ch. Hd. was cancelled. Cap't. practical organisation & execution of attack on enemy trenches. This requires a great deal of very careful organisation & rehearsal & much can be done by digging skeleton plans (actual trench) of the trenches to be met & enemy in rear camps from aeroplane photos. This is easily done & very instructive & instructive. Taught will be done by troops training in England.	PP
	6/9/15		Batt⁵ paraded working parties to number of 2 Officers & 200 O.R. for work on Redoubts between VLAMERTINGHE & YPRES.	
	7/9/15		Received orders to proceed to the trenches tomorrow night. O.C. Cap't & C.S.M. Signallers, Machine Gunners & Bombers went up in advance by day. Cap't Mardell off at 10 minutes interval commencing at 6 P.M. Very quiet night. Went via YPRES & MENIN Rd. PRES. HELL FIRE Corner to trenches H.13 to H.19 – front of Y wood. One Coy in support – F.2. Relief completed 11 P.M. without one hitch.	PP

WAR DIARY / INTELLIGENCE SUMMARY

Army Form C. 211

Place	Date	Hour	Summary of Events and Information	Remarks and references to Appendices
TRENCHES Y WOOD N. & HOOGE	8.9.15		1 Officer + 2 N.C.Os + 1 man proceeded on 6 days leave to England. C.O. went round Trenches & reported on them as follows to Brigade:— Trenches taken over last night are in very dilapidated condition after recent heavy rain. MUD has the chief means of communication with the setts by day "badly". We are knee deep in water in many places, & require cleaning & draining badly. No Casualties.	RR
	9.9.15		Quiet day. No casualties.	RR
	10.9.15		Intelligence Report:— (1) During morning enemy appeared to be working on E. edge of BELLEVAARDE ETANG, & what appeared to be band of gun was noticed. Working party fired on with rifles & dispersed. (2) Between 11–12 noon enemy trench mortars active. (3) Enemy dropped heavy shell on H16–H19, & S.16–H.19 C.T. S21 + Small Rd. There are unusual localities, except last named. No material damage done. (4) Enemy displayed flags on front trenches from front of BELLEVAARDE to Pt 67 (see official trench map) 4 that flag placed at regular intervals, 3 of which were white with black crosses, + 1 yellow with black inside eagle. These were flying at dawn & remained up all day. (5) Enemy train had apparently been due E. of CHARING X from triangle of H.13. Engine + trucks could be heard appeared to be given heave at same point immediately afterwards. Time 6:30 PM. Close to BELLEVAARDE Lake.	RR

Army Form C. 2118

WAR DIARY
— or —
INTELLIGENCE SUMMARY. /M.

34

Place	Date	Hour	Summary of Events and Information	Remarks and references to Appendices
TRENCHES Y Wood N. of HOOGE	11/9/15		2/Lt A.W. WOOD joined yesterday from 3rd (Res) Batt: C.O. visits the CRATER & Q2.0 at HOOGE, & obtained an excellent view of enemy trenches in front of Y wood & valuable information of various points, a condition of wire noted. Several M.G. em- placements being spotted, a large part of German may have been in the day out weakly held, but a large part of German may have been in the day out. The only time to do really effective reconnaissance of enemy trenches from our trenches is 4.30 AM to 5.30 AM. at this time it is possible to do a large amount of direct observation with field glasses, if due precaution is taken. There is always shelling in the afternoon now.	
		6-7 AM	Some trench mortars by enemy, to which our trench mortars replied effectively	
		1 PM	12 heavy shells fell in Y Wood. Enemy shelling rather more active to-day, but not nearly so active as a month ago.	
			Batt: relieved to-night by 5/K.S.L.I. — the firing line 1 Coy at Hd Qrs at L farm 1 Q.d.8/5 (Sheet 28), 1 Coy. G.H.Q. line N. of MENIN road 1 & 1 Coy in F.13 (not E. of G.H.Q. White Batt: to fire trenches. Ration, water, & RE stores brought up MENIN road last night in Batt: Transport & dumped at I=2: each by rest its own ration party to the dump for its rations + water & the Coy. in support at F.2 carried up RE stores to the other 3 Coys in firing line	M/P.

WAR DIARY
INTELLIGENCE SUMMARY

Army Form C. 2118

Place	Date	Hour	Summary of Events and Information	Remarks and references to Appendices
G.H.Q. Line Reserve	12/9/15		Whole Battⁿ: Reserve at L. Farm, G.H.Q, & F.13, Return & water brought up each night to trolly along the railway from VLAMERTINGHE, trolley drawn by two mules. Casualties, wounded O.R. 2: Accidentally wounded by bayonet O.R. 1 Officer, 2 N.C.Os, & 5.O.R. proceeded on 6 days leave to England. Battⁿ Adm. found working parties at night of 4 officers & 400 O.R. digging sanitary	P.P
"	13/9/15		trenches & preparing to the camp attack on BELLEVAARDE. Working parties same as last night. Stalin quiet	B.P
"	14/9/15		Working parties same as last night. Casualties Wounded by French mortar S.O.R. All ranks have worked ex- ceedingly well during this tour in the trenches, & the result is that we have	M.P
"	15/9/15		dug all our an assembly trenches on the front H.16 - H.18 belt inches and made necessary dug-outs & bomb stores. Battⁿ relieved by 6ᵗʰ Somerset Q⁴ 4/9/151, 43ᴹ of 5⁴ᵉ fallen back by to WEL F.27 a Battⁿ: has not been to rest W. of POPERINGHE train from ASYLUM of YPRES to POPERINGHE: thence by rest brand since 7/7/15.	P.P
POPERINGHE	16/9/15		6ᵗʰ Corps Commander inspected the Transport of the Battⁿ: & expressed his entire satisfaction with it, & his appreciation of its good work in carrying rations up every night through YPRES, while Battⁿ: in the trenches. Draft of 24 N.C. Os & men arrived	P.P

Army Form C. 2118
36

WAR DIARY
—or—
INTELLIGENCE SUMMARY
(Erase heading not required.)

Instructions regarding War Diaries and Intelligence Summaries are contained in F. S. Regs., Part II. and the Staff Manual respectively. Title pages will be prepared in manuscript.

Place	Date	Hour	Summary of Events and Information	Remarks and references to Appendices
POPERINGHE	17/9/15		All Officers & N.C.Os visited spot-locked plan of our trenches & enemy trenches near BELLEVAARDE farm, which have been laid out to correct map from airplane photos. Physical drill & dentry before breakfast. Rifle exercises, musketry, bayonet fighting both in squads & at dummies after breakfast. The 2nd Army Commander inspected Battalion on parade at 5 p.m. M.G. Officer studied diary M.G. Course at WISQUES	M
	18/9/15		All Coys worked at digging out spot-locked plan of trenches, making them 2' wide 1' deep, each Coy doing its own bit of our line, & the lot of trench here it will attack. Bayonet fighting, musketry, & drill in the afternoon. Bombers & M.G. received special instruction, also stretcher bearers & Orderlies	1P
	19/9/15	7.30–8 AM	Physical drill	
		11.30 AM	Lt. Col. Batty led Lt Matters & Change of Mounts at POPERINGHE. Parade for Divine Service. The officers went up to the trenches to know that all necessary work had been satisfactorily carried out, & arrange for any more which might be necessary	1P
	20/9/15	6.30 AM	Battn. Practice attack on Meltton trenches — the afternoon Parades as strong as possible. Signallers, M. Gunners, Bombers, Stretcher bearers & W.L. Os, Orderlies as such. March to Brigade Grenade School	

1577 Wt.W10791/1773 500,000 1/15 D.D.&L. A.D.S.S./Forms/C. 2118.

WAR DIARY
INTELLIGENCE SUMMARY
(Erase heading not required.)

Army Form C. 2118

37

Place	Date	Hour	Summary of Events and Information	Remarks and references to Appendices
POPERINGHE			when Lewis Gun Teams are & practised assembly & attack; first the Batt. by itself & then in conjunction with 9 Rifle Brigade on our left. Signallers practised running out telephone line, & did so in 35 seconds. Trench blocking parties also practised. 6 N.C.Os & men as Scout Blocking party. 16 N.C.Os & men as dog-out construction party are trained daily by R.E. at Bomb School	AP
	21/9/16	7am	Physical drill & doubling M. Gunners carry their loads	
		8.45 AM	Batt: handed over so that an possible. Marched to Bomb School; carried out another attack on Militia Trenches: well done. Carrying Parties & details practised their special duties. Bayonet Fighting in the afternoon will now carry out Night Shoulder wire cutting pickets wear white straps of cloth on the right shoulder. An excellent panorama photo of enemy line N.T.S. of BELLEVARDE Farm received to-day, taken by 6c Corps Photographic Sec. These aeroplane photos are of great value to units, & should be used to them at freq. intervals	Q
	22/9/16	7 AM	Physical drill & dentally before Breakfast.	
		11 AM	Batt: handed same as yesterday field kitchens front kitchens worked	AP
		6.30 pm	Another attack practised on Militia Trenches in the dark	AP

Army Form C. 2118

35

WAR DIARY
or
INTELLIGENCE SUMMARY.
(Erase heading not required.)

Place	Date	Hour	Summary of Events and Information	Remarks and references to Appendices
POPERINGHE	23.9.15		Officers + Staff Sergts began proceeded to the Trenches to take over special stores & take over water, rations &c. Bombing & Signalling proceeded to the trenches in the morning. Batt. proceeded to the trenches — Signalling proceeded to the trenches in the morning. Very quiet night. Contrary to expectations. Began to dump at 6 P.M.	A.1
L. Farm Trenches	24.9.15	3.30 AM	L Farm (1.15 U/S & S.HW20) shelled with 4.25" shellfire during the night, all "duds". Intense Bombardment by our Art. lasting for 1 hour. Our own "Battering" 6" (How & Seige) hit 14 Mills hut in own trenches H.17, H.16, & H.16S. Three guns appeared to fire enfilly & 4.5" gun was persistently short. There always seems to be one gun short in the Battery. About 21 of our men were killed + wounded & about 15% of 5/KSLI by these Shells, & some damage done to our trenches.	1st
		7.30 PM	C.O. + Adjt. proceeded to 2nd Lt's H. Qrs in H.17, see attached sketch	7
		10.30 PM	Capt. Farm L Farm + H.Q. O? Coy proceeded to the trenches arriving there by 11.45 P.M. the Battalion dg Capt Mann for assault see attached sketch	6
			for operation Orders for attack see appendix 2 attached	2
	24.9.15		Adjutant proceeded to H.Q. of 9th RB + 9th KRR — train guards dug-in RAILWAY WOOD to rendezvous with Corps troops.	
		12 MN	On account of the part played by the Battalion — the attack + subsequent retirement & an anyway himself see appendix 3 + Sketch 7 attached. For Special report by O.C. right column see appendix 4 attached. For message sent & received see appendix 5 attached. The Right Colm gained its objective comparatively easily i.e. the 2nd German line & consolidated there. The failure to kill the perilin guard was	3 + 7 4 5

WAR DIARY
INTELLIGENCE SUMMARY

Army Form C. 2118

39

due to two causes:—

1. Our left Column, consisting of 'A' Coy & party of bombers under Lt ESCOTT was practically destroyed by shell fire & M.G. fire before assault took place. Of the 6 Officers with the Coln 4 were killed & 2 wounded. Only 2 N.C.Os & 20 men managed to make the charge & they went on, but too much to their left, keeping touch with the 9 R.B. who lost direction, & from all accounts of the survivors of our left column, never penetrated German 1st line between pts 24 & 72 (see attached sketch 7), but went far too much to the left & only entered the German line between 8 & 24; 3 of our bombers being on the extreme right flank, & who gave very clear & accurate description to prove this.

2. The 2nd reason was the failure of 9th R.B. Column to keep direction. It was through the gap so made that the German Counter attack penetrated.

The Counter attack developed very quickly. Several small parties of our right Colm being cut off in the "German 2nd" had the M.G, when we succeeded — coming to this line was unfortunately but no of action shortly before the counter attack took place by

WAR DIARY
INTELLIGENCE SUMMARY.
(Erase heading not required.)

Army Form C. 2118

40

Place	Date	Hour	Summary of Events and Information	Remarks and references to Appendices

the grapple cup being smashed by the fragment of a shell. The gun next up to replace this arrived too late, & the gunner was killed before he could attempt to carry on the attack beyond the original front line. We had only 2 officers, 160 other ranks (which includes runners, orderlies, signallers etc.) to stop them but they came on.

The counter attack was made in great strength though it is difficult to estimate the strength, but it has never held its strong & front tonight.

In the attack we captured 13 prisoners & 3 M.G.s, the latter however were lost again.

Apparently every man in the enemy counter attack carried bombs. The Germans seem now to have only one type of bomb, as we only found and had among the hundreds we captured & used in the attack. This is a great assistance to training, to have only one bomb to teach that a very simple one like the new pattern. This bomb has many effective actions, water proof, large, light, & detonates it is an easy one to throw. See sketch.

Detonator fitted into top of handle, which screws into bomb case. Safety pin — handle — stays — use = 5½ sec.

operated by left of hand rod of handle loop

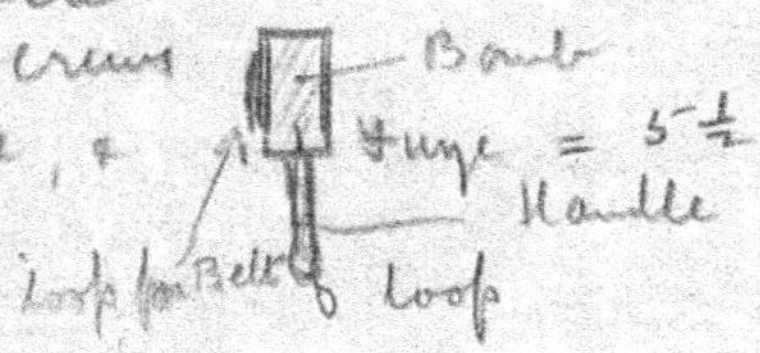

[sketch of bomb with labels: Bomb, Handle, loop]

WAR DIARY

INTELLIGENCE SUMMARY

(Erase heading not required.)

Army Form C. 2118

4/1

Place	Date	Hour	Summary of Events and Information	Remarks and references to Appendices

That such men should carry on be able to use knives in a counter attack is a great help to secure a wall nearly. But to be able to turn their fire upon an enemy type of rifle bomb. Another known brand was the necessity for funky found several M.G. at our posts the Captain knew to stop counter attack. M.G. should he walked — parts, to work rule of that failure of fire Batt[n]s returned by 10th D.L.I. the 43rd Inf. Bde that bought relief. We got in as huge wounded as possible from our front before day-light had rifle fire of many an started difficult & dangerous by his left afternoon as far as we would at between the morning trenches crawled out the heavy barrage, where he was killed instantly Mch— cold blood.

Casualties as follows.

Killed Capt. E.F.K. CARFRAE, LT. A.W. WOOD + O.R. 51

Missing believed killed LT L.W. SWEET-ESCOTT, LT. H.F. CLARKE,
LT. J.N.G. MITCHELL, + O.R. missing 214

Wounded CAPT. N.F. BARWELL, CAPT. H.H. COBB, LT. E.W. MAUDE,
LT. L.S. M. NEWMAN, LT. L.S. LEE, 2/LT W.T. BECKINGHAM, 2/LT F.H. FREMANTLE
2/LT C.H. WALTER, + O.R. 176

WAR DIARY

INTELLIGENCE SUMMARY

Army Form C. 2118.

42

Place	Date	Hour	Summary of Events and Information	Remarks and references to Appendices
POPERINGHE	26.9.15		Total Casualties 13 out of 15 Officers & 441 O.R. Battalion returned to POPERINGHE by train from LA LOVIE Station's which joined Batt'n & duty all 2. LT's Day spent in cleaning up & sorting kit. N.C.O. sent round to neighbouring field ambulances to search for missing men. Draft of 60 N.C.os & men arrived	MP
"	27.9.15		Organised the Coy's & posted new officers allotted at Bde Bomb School for instruction. 5" Corps Commander addressed Batt's in the afternoon & emphasised them on their gallant attack. He said that never before had troops been so be excited by their M.G. fire & yet continued to advance. C.O. inspected kit of Batt's. Coy drill. 1 officer + 2 N.C.Os attended M.G. Course	MP
"	28.9.15		Rained all day, men all — tents lecture by C.O. to all Officers & N.C.O.s on trench duties	MP
"	29.9.15		6" Corps Commander addressed Batt's on parade this afternoon & congratulated the Batt's on it gallant attack on BELLEVARDE. He said had all done well. He thanks Batt's especially for that 42d INF BDE Corrected Casualties as follows	MP

24/9/15. LT. & S.M. NEWMAN Wounded O.R - K 4 - W 13.
25/9/15 Capt C F K CARFRAE Killed (previously reported missing) Officers - W 7 - M 3
died of wounds 1 - O.R - K 46 - W 249 - M 111 died of wounds 6
136

Army Form C. 2118

WAR DIARY
or
INTELLIGENCE SUMMARY.

(Erase heading not required.)

Instructions regarding War Diaries and Intelligence Summaries are contained in F. S. Regs., Part II. and the Staff Manual respectively. Title pages will be prepared in manuscript.

43

Place	Date	Hour	Summary of Events and Information	Remarks and references to Appendices
POPERINGHE	30.9.15		Parades, musketry, drill, extended order drill, Bayonet fighting. Classes of instruction for Bombers, M. Gunners, & Signallers.	PP.

B Sayer Capt + Adjt
51 Oxf + Bucks L.I. + H.I.

K. killed W. Wounded. S. Sick admitted to Hosps. M missing
DW. Died of wounds

Date	K	W	S	Date	K	W	S	
15.8.15	-	-	-	12.9.15	-	-	5	Capt. C.F.K. CAREFRAE K
16	-	1	6	13	-	-	3	Capt. N.F. BARWELL W
17	-	-	2	14	-	-	5	" H.H. COBB W
18	-	-	5	15	-	-	-	Lieut E.W. MAUDE W
19	-	-	4	16	-	-	-	" L.W. S-ESCOTT M
20	-	-	7	17	-	-	-	" L.S.M. NEWMAN W
21	-	-	-	18	-	-	8	" H.F. CLARKE M
22	-	-	-	19	-	-	-	Lieut W.T. BECKINGHAM W
23	-	1	3	20	-	-	-	" L S LEE W
24	-	-	-	21	-	-	1	" T.F.H. FREMANTLE W
25	-	-	7	22	-	-	2	" A.W. WOOD DW
26	-	3	5	23	-	-	5	" C.H. WALTER W
27	-	-	7	24	4	13	-	" J.M.G. MITCHELL M
28	-	1	1	25				missing
29	-	-	2	25				missing
30	-	-	2	26	-	-	-	25/9/15 Officers killed
31	-	-	1	27	-	-	-	one, wounded 8, missing
1.9.15	-	-	5	28	-	-	1	3. died of wounds on
2	-	-	-	29	-	-	1	Other ranks killed 46
3	-	-	-	30	-	-	2	wounded 249, missing
4	-	-	6					136 died of wounds 6.
5	-	-	2					Total 12 Officers 437
6	-	-	1					other ranks.
7	-	-	-					
8	-	-	-					
9	-	-	-					
10	-	-	4					
11	-	-	3					

K. Killed. W. Wounded. S. Admitted to Hospital

Date	K	W	S	Date	K	W	S	Date	K	W	S	
20.5.15	-	-	-	18.6.15	-	-	2	17.7.15	-	2	-	Officers K
21	-	-	-	19	-	1	3	18	-	-	-	Lt Berlein 15/6/15
22	-	-	-	20	-	6	25	19	-	-	31	
23	-	-	-	21	-	2	3	20	-	-	1	W
24	-	-	-	22	-	5	53	21	-	-	-	Capt Canfrae 16/6/15
25	-	-	1	23	-	2	2	22	-	-	-	" Logan 24/7/15
26	-	-	1	24	-	1	6	23	-	-	5	Lt Birch 2/8/15
27	-	-	1	25	-	-	-	24	-	1	2	" Crawford 19/6/15
28	-	-	-	26	-	1	4	25	-	-	4	" S Escott 10/7/15
29	-	-	1	27	-	-	5	26	-	-	22	" Jackson 22/6/15
30	-	-	-	28	-	-	-	27	-	2	4	" Curry 16/8/15
31	-	-	-	29	-	-	7	28	-	1	8	" Fenwick 1/8/15
1.6.15	-	-	2	30	-	-	5	29	-	2	3	" Jury 30/7/15
2	-	-	1	1.7.15	-	-	-	30	-	3	25	" Bird 6/8/15
3	-	-	1	2	-	-	-	31	-	1	15	" Clarke 19/6/15
4	-	-	4	3	-	-	-	1.8.15	2	17	6	S
5	-	-	-	4	-	-	7	2	-	1	15	Col Cobb 24/7/15
6	-	2	4	5	-	-	3	3	-	-	4	Capt Sanderson 11/8/15
7	-	-	2	6	-	-	1	4	-	2	9	" R Jones 18/8/15
8	-	1	-	7	-	2	11	5	-	2	5	" Lee 17-8-15
9	-	-	-	8	-	3	9	6	-	7	17	Le Messurier 4/8/15
10	-	2	1	9	1	19	9	7	-	1	1	A.C Walker 19/8/15
11	-	-	-	10	-	22	7	8	-	-	2	K.V Carter 3/8/15
12	-	-	-	11	1	16	6	9	-	1	3	Missing believed K
13	-	-	2	12	4	9	7	10	-	-	6	Lt Davis 22/6/15
14	-	-	2	13	-	4	5	11	-	-	1	
15	-	-	-	14	-	-	-	12	-	-	1	
16	-	1	28	15	-	8	2	13	-	-	1	
17	-	-	1	16	1	-	-	14	-	-	-	

MESSAGES AND SIGNALS.

TO 9' KRRC

Sender's Number: 437
Day of Month: 24

Please twenty bombers with bombs
AAA have only seven
left

We have no
bombers left that we can spare
O.C. 9" KRRC

14/9/15   25/9/15

From: 5' Ox & Bucks L.I.
Time: 8.45 a.m.

D.A.Q.
 3rd Echelon

Will you kindly attach report on operations by Capt. N.F. Barwell to my War Diary, sent you yesterday

2/10/15.

B Pagan
Capt.
Commanding 8th Service Btn.
Oxford & Bucks. L.I.

Special Report on Operations of 25th Sept. 1915.
by O.C. Commanding D.Coy. (Lt.Col).

The following observations concerning the condition, design & equipment of enemy trenches on the morning of the 25th Sept., were made by me and are forwarded for information.

Reference:- Trench map Bellevarde Farm, and trenches to South & East of it.

Wire:

The primary and secondary wire entanglements were almost wholly destroyed except at head of sap, and offered no obstacles. A third stretch of wire was observed by its remains to have been erected along the line of the farm road running N. & S., and passing through the middle of the position (this is not to be confused with the further and larger road which formed the termination of the left column's objective.)

Fire Trench:

The front line trench seems only to have been partially sandbagged and to have been deepest at its junctions with the sap heads. At the "International Trench" end it was over 8 ft. high, and very little damaged by shell fire. The middle portions of the trench were much blown in. There was no sign of any trench mortars, large periscopes, search-lights, or other unusual equipment, long suspected in this trench.

Dug-Outs:

Were all much below level of the ground, and, though protective mounds of earth had been mostly blown away, many of these dug-outs were habitable, and we killed between 12 and 20 of the enemy in their endeavour to take refuge there. One large dug-out in the ruins of Bellevarde Farm, covered with rubble, facing South, was intact, and enemy were killed there.

Support Trenches:

Defence of Bellevarde Farm seems to have been designed against attack from N.W. & S.W. Frontal attack does not seem to have been considered likely. The network of trenches running from the oval system of dug-outs towards the lake were all prepared as fire trenches with fire steps, planks nailed onto short fir stumps. Here too were several cross-bows made of 1/2" iron about 3 ft. long.(vide sketch) Each trench seems also to possess a long green case for bombs, labelled "handgrenaden". I had time to look at two of them: they were empty.

Special Report by O.C. D Co. (Cont'd)   (2)

These trenches were partially occupied when I with second line of attack passed over them. Here we took a few prisoners and met with no serious opposition. These trenches were not sandbagged and were about 10 ft. deep, and but little damaged by direct shell fire.

Communication Trenches.

The C.T's running directly E. & W. were a good deal blown in. All had small dug-outs leading out of them in places; which dug-outs were mostly intact. The Main Communication Trench is, however, designed for lateral communication & formed the line of our objective. It is of extraordinary depth. I estimated it at from 12 to 15 ft. sides absolutely vertical, and it is not sandbagged. It was fairly dry but I saw no arrangements for draining it. Several spades about 9 ft. in length were in this trench, evidently used for building these deep trenches. Latrines lead out of this in an easterly direction; were well designed and in a sanitary condition, and could accomodate from 12 to 15 men at a time. I saw no Minnenwerfer in any part of the work.

Machine Guns.

From the second line attack which I was personally leading, I only saw one enemy gun in action. This was in point 67, and was firing E. & N.E. I brought rifle fire to bear on it from a shell hole about 20 yards away, and ordered bombs to be thrown at it. This instantly silenced it and the gun and its detachment fell into the hands of my own machine gun detachment which was following in my right rear. I saw no signs of any other enemy guns. None were in action on S. side of the ruins.

Garrisons.

The fire trench seems not to have been garrisoned at time of assault as far as I could see, but an advanced sap running parallel to and 10 yards S. of International Trench was held as late as 6.40 a.m. though how I do not know. Three or four of the enemy fired at me from it as I was being dragged over a portion of the International Trench, wounded.

The Support Trenches seems to have been fairly strongly manned. The greater part of the garrisons falling to the bombers of our second line. A great many men were distibuted in the dug-outs throughout the sector. Of the two officers whom I encountered, each emerged from a dug-out, neither wore any equipment & one only was armed (pistol). Garrison was formed of 242nd Reserve Regiment, and almost all were

Special Report by O.C. D.Coy. (Contd)   (3)

fatigue uniform. A party of 8 men whom I now suspect to have been an advanced patrol of the counter-attacking force all wore helmets, equipment with packs, and had fixed bayonets. This party gave me my second round, and they appeared at the point where I expected to join hands with Capt. CARFRAE'S Column. Two of them escaped along the trench in a northerly direction. I saw only one other man so equipped and he was dead and wore an infantry bugle strapped over his pack.

(Sd) N. Barwell Capt. Comdg. Rt. Column of attack.

5th Bn. Oxf. & Bucks. Light Infty.

OPERATION ORDERS: 22/9/15.

The Battalion will proceed to the trenches as follows tomorrow the 23rd inst.

1. Bombers under Sgt. Adams, for the four posts, as detailed by Lieut. Escott. Lieut. Clarke, and the Regl. Sgt. Major will proceed by Motor Lorry from L.3. Central sheet 27, at 9 am. Lieut. Clarke & Regl. Sgt. Major to take over all special stores in the trenches in accordance with instructions received.

2. Signallers as detailed by Capt. Cobb will proceed to the trenches in accordance with his orders. O.C. 14th Signal Coy. will arrange for conveyance of those who go in advance of Battalion.

3. A. & C. Companies under the command of Lieut. Newman, will proceed by train leaving Poperinghe at 6 pm. They will leave the Menin Gate at 7.40 pm. with 5 minutes interval between companies, and proceed via Menin Road, and Cambridge Road, to occupy trenches as follows:-
   A.Coy. H18A, 18, 18S & half H17A, 17, 17S.
   C.Coy. New trench 17 (d) & half H17A, 17 & 17S.
   Sgt. Culwick will go with A.Coy. and report to Regl. Sgt. Major in the trenches.
   Hd.Qr.Coy. consisting of Signallers & Bombers not already detailed, Machine Gunners, Hd.Qr. Orderlies, Stretcher bearers, Pioneers, and B. & D.Coys. will parade in camp at 6.15 pm. and proceed from Poperinghe by train leaving at 8 pm.
   B.Coy. will occupy dug-outs in the Ramparts of YPRES; remainder will leave Menin Gate at 10 pm. and proceed to dug-outs at L.Farm.
   Companies will proceed to their trenches and positions as soon as possible after detrainment.
   Signallers, Bombers, and Stretcher bearers detailed to companies will parade and go to the trenches with those companies.

4. Bomb-throwers and Carriers will be required as follows:-
   (a) Throwers, no rifles or entrenching tools, but armed with cudgels.
   (b) Carriers, no entrenching tools, or ammunition in the pouches, but armed with rifles & bayonets, 10 rounds in the magazine.

5. All N.C.O's and men will carry great-coats rolled. No packs or waterproof sheets will be taken to the trenches. All spare kits will be packed in the packs, and stacked by companies outside the Q.M.Stores by 4 pm. tomorrow. Officers' valises and spare kit stacked separately by the same hour.

Operation Orders, (Contd). (2)

6. Machine Guns of Battalion will be taken in limbered G.S. wagons to L.Farm tomorrow night, arriving there about 10.30 pm. and these wagons will take back from there 16 boxes SAA and 100 shovels to B.Coy. in YPRES Ramparts. O.C. B.Coy. will arrange dump for these, and detail a N.C.O. to meet Transport on its return to Ypres, and show N.C.O. in charge the position of the dump.
Machine Guns and Rifle Batteries of 43rd Inf. Bde. will not be relieved.

7. All Ammunition, Trench Stores, Tools and Bombs will be taken over from companies relieved, and lists of stores, etc. taken over will be sent to the Adjutant as soon as possible after relief.

8. The rifles and ammunition of bomb-throwers, and the entrenching tools and ammunition, less 10 rounds, of bomb carriers will be returned to the Q.M. Stores tomorrow morning.

9. The 18 N.C.O's and men of C.Coy. Wiring party will parade with B.Coy. and will remain with that company until 24th September. On that date they will report at 10 pm. to O.C. 62 Coy. R.E. at the road junction 1.8.a.9/3.

10. Roll of N.C.O's and men not accompanying Battalion to the trenches will be issued to O.C. Companies tomorrow.

11. Reserve Stretcher bearers under Sgt. Hiorns will be in a dug-out in the centre bay of H.18 on the night of 24-25.

(Sd) B.C.T. Paget, Capt & Adjt.
5th Bn. Oxf. & Bucks. Lt. Infty.

5th Bn. Oxf. & Bucks. Light Infy.

Sept. 24th, 1915.

OPERATION ORDERS.

1. 42nd Inf. Bde. will seize the BELLEVARDE FARM position.
2. The Regt. will form the centre Battalion in the attack - 5th K.S.L.I. on the right, and 9th R.Bde. on the left.
3. Distribution as under:-

   Left Column, under Capt. Carfrae.

B.Coy.	)	Objective- 12A72 exclusive to 12A71 inclusive in
1 Platoon A.Coy.	)	2nd German line.
1 Machine Gun	)	12A42 exclusive to 12A40 inclusive in 1st German
	)	line.

   Right Column.

D.Coy.	)	Objective- 12A71 exclusive to 12A80 inclusive in
2 Platoons A.Coy.	)	2nd German line- 12A40 exclusive to 12C58 inclu-
1 Machine Gun	)	sive in 1st German line.
	)	12C68 & 12C79 are in this column area.

   Reserve.

   1 Platoon A.Coy.
         C.Coy.

4. Distribution before Assembly.
   Left Column in depth -H18A, H18, H18S, Part of H17S North-
   Right Column- H17A, H17, H17S, Patrol trench if required.
   Reserve -A.Coy. Platoon- H17S (North)
         C.Coy. New trench behind H17S, H16D, to Mud Lane.

5. Distribution in Assembly.
   Left Column- 2 Platoons of B.Coy. front line.
         Remainder in Coy. Column.

   At the commencement of bombardment get out through gaps in H19 into field North of H19- first line level with Bomb post H18A lie down.

   Right Column.- Half-a-hour before bombardment starts assemble in Assembly trenches H17A & H18A.

   Reserve, move to H17 & H18 & S. end of H17A, Platoon of A.Coy. on left

6. Action.

   The first line of both columns will sweep forward to the German 2nd line. One platoon, left column, will swing into BELLEVARDE FARM and search for machine guns. One platoon, left column, will arrange to

Operation Orders, (Contd)   (2)

enter BELLEVARDE from the South, and arrange fire to keep down machine guns if necessary. Machine Gun with left column will also pay special attention to the ruins of the farm.

Reserve Platoon A.Coy. will dig out C.T. along Hedge Sap. C.Coy. will dig out International trench and furnish carrying parties under Regl. Sgt. Major to carry up stores in following order:-
1. Bombs & tools.
2. Water.
3. Ammunition.
4. Sandbags.
5. Rations.

2 Machine Guns will be on the alert to counter enemy machine guns and will take position in German 2nd line.

All trenches leading to front & flank will be blocked by bombers & blocking parties till communication established.

Special Bombing Parties.

Lieut. Escott & 10 men down Hedge Sap. Cpl. Stent & 9 men down International trench.

3rd lines of columns will remain in German first line unless required for reinforcement.

7. Position won will be immediately consolidated and communication established between the two enemy lines, by platoons detailed by O'Cs Columns.

8. Mine at O4 will be exploded at 4.19 am.

Assault will be launched at 4.20 am. regardless of mine or artillery. Artillery bombardment will commence at 3.50 am. At 4.20 am. it will lift for one minute to midway between lines. At 4.20 it will lift for 2 minutes on to 2nd enemy line, and thence at 4.23 to enemy third line and form a barrage. Trench Mortars will fire smoke balls to cover consolidation.

9. Every man except bombers and stretcher bearers to carry 220 rounds SAA, 4 sandbags, Iron ration. Front line, every third man a shovel. Half second line and third line every man carry a shovel.

10. German Arty. screens are not to be removed. Bombers' progress will be indicated by their flags.

11. Occupation of captured line.
Unless heavy casualties render other dispositions necessary, captured

Operation Orders, (Contd)   (3)

line will be held as follows:-

B.Coy. in depth on front 72 to 71 & 42,40 in first enemy line.
D.Coy. 71 to 80 inclusive, 68 & 59 to 58 in first enemy line.
1 - Platoon, A.Coy.- 40 to 59. Remainder A.Coy. will occupy H18A, H18, H18S.
C.Coy. will occupy H17A, H17, H17S. Men should be distributed in C7S, also in captured position in order to avoid loss by shell fire.

12. Constant reports by telephone or messenger or semaphore to H.Q. in H17A.

13. Prisoners to be evacuated by A.Coy. via Mud Lane to G.H.Q. and handed over to Reserve Cavalry Division. Receipts to be taken.

14. Medical Aid Post at BIRR CROSS-ROADS - All walking cases to be evacuated by Mud Lane & Castle Street to YPRES, ASYLUM, as far as possible. Stretcher cases to be collected in H18, and evacuated by Cambridge Road to BIRR CROSS ROADS, by night.

15. Brigade Hd.Qrs. at 1.10.a& 8.6. from 6 pm. 24th Sept.
Battn. Hd.Qrs. H.17A.

16. Special precautions to be taken against counter attack with gas.

17. Red & Green rockets will be issued to each Battalion Hd.Qrs., and when up simultaneously indicate S.O.S.

18. Watches of O.C. Companies will be synchronised with the Adjutant at 12 M.N.

(Sd) W.F.R. Webb, Major,
Comdg. 5th Bn. Oxf. & Bucks. Lt. Infty.

5th Bn. Oxf. & Bucks. Light Infty.

Report on Action of 25th September, 1915.   3

The Regiment was ordered to attack BELLEVARDE FARM at 4.20 am. on the 25th September.

The Right Column under Capt. Barwell occupied its assembly trenches in H17A & H18A before the bombardment started. These trenches were not much shelled. The first line penetrated about point 12C58 followed by the second line. A Machine Gun opened from German Sap Head running from 12C58 to H16 but was quickly bombed out of action. The wire was successfully destroyed by the Artillery. This column secured the objective allotted to them, viz:- 12A71 & 80, also 12C69 & 68. There were only a few Germans left in the first line who were despatched. Capt. Barwell himself with some bombers cleared the ruins of BELLEVARDE where a Machine Gun was found facing South. He also cleared some dug-outs in the region of point 12A71.

By 5.20 am. the line was fairly established on this front and communication established with the 5th K.S.L.I. on the right, but I received no report till 6 am. by runner that enemy first line was captured, and works South of BELLEVARDE. At 6.25 am. I had a report that second line was secured. An attempt was made to push up bombs and ammunition by the C.T. from H16 to 58, but at 7 am. it was reported that German snipers were very active from direction of 12C67. These were some men evidently left behind by the K.S.L.I. attack in advanced sap or come up from ECLUSETTE. I asked K.S.L.I. to have these men bombed out.

I received a message from Lieut. Maude timed 7 am. that our men were holding German 2nd line and had dug in, and that three machine guns had been captured, but that communication was not established on the left. He asked for a machine gun to be sent. The sniping on the communication trench from the South was not at this time. I sent a message telling Lieut. Maude to establish connection with my left column and told him to look out for his left as I had heard that 9th R.B. had lost the second line again.

At 7.15 I sent a message through 9th K.R.R.C. at French Dug-Out to inform Brigade of situation as I had no direct communication. I had previous to this sent a message by runner to the culvert post. Communication was very slow and much interrupted. I sent up another machine gun at this time as it appeared that it was urgently required., and this gun was got up in spite of the snipers on the Communications. The gunner was shot when setting up the gun

Report on Action (Contd).   (2)

and it did not go into action.

At 7.45 I heard by runner that Germans were advancing on right and left fronts and asked for S.O.S. to F.O.O. & through French Dug-out F.O.O. tried to flag it, and Signal Officer also lamped it. The guns opened a few minutes later but it was too late. At 7.45 a.m. I asked for two platoons from 9th K.R.R.C., and some bombers.
I received report timed 7.50, that we were having to retire on our right as Germans were developing strong attack, and that enemy were also advancing from BELLEVARDE FARM.

Lieut. Maude came in about 8 am. being wounded.

The German attack developed rapidly. Enemy advanced from North of BELLEVARDE, and from wood East of the line (Dead Man's Bottom) along the North side of the Etang. The 5th K.S.L.I. and our men were forced to retire and only just avoided being cut off by enemy from BELLEVARDE who advanced in the open in front of H17A, their right appearing for a minute or two on the crest of the hill. Fire was opened at once by all the spare men in the trench (orderlies, etc.) and the enemy got into his front line trench again I saw about 50 Germans at this point. Our men suffered heavily in the retirement. I reported to Brigade by telephone through French Dug-out and runner that I was holding original line with about 200 men. Two platoons of 9th K.R.R.C. came into H17 & H18. I reorganised defence as soon as shelling got less, and it became evident that enemy did not purpose a further advance. According to report our men accounted for 60 or 70 Germans in the attack and dropped many more with rifle fire in the counter attack.

The Left Column was to move out at the start of the bombardment and lie down in a field to the North of the Hedge Sap in an old trench and a hollow. It appears that they were spotted moving out, or that the Germans had reason to be suspicious of this piece of ground, for it was heavily shelled. The enemy sent up flares just after they began to move out. At all events this column suffered very heavy casualties from shell fire and were also shaken by the explosion of the mine, the debris of which fell amongst them. When they did advance according to men who returned a machine gun opened fire on them and only 8 men of the first line reached the German lines with some of the 9th R.B's. They mistook their directions also and went more towards the line O4-24 than 41 which was their objective. Only about 7 men of the 2nd line reached the German trench but were unable to get in, and took cover in shell holes outside. The third was almost destroyed A few men went with the 9th R.B. column. These facts account for

Report on Action (Contd).

the gap in the line in the N. of BELLEVARDE, and the absence of news. Orderlies I sent returned saying they could not get through. A Bombing party which went up the Hedge Sap has not been heard of: the above Orderlies state there were many dead in the trench. Carrying parties with bombs started up this way also and were apparently wiped out. These parties never got anyone back to let me know the state of things on that side. From reports of the men who went with the 9th R.B. it appears that they went into the line 04-24, and worked down to a Redoubt in the 2nd German 2nd line. It does not appear that anyone went to the line 40-42 or beyond, as the men say there was no one on their right, but they that bombed along the trench for some distance. They returned by the Crater having to bomb their way back. Men working in the C.T. up the Hedge Sap said that the sniping was very hot from the C.T. from 41 to the 2nd German line, and that it was from there the carrying parties were hit. The German counter attack from the left evidently came by this trench and reoccupied BELLEVARDE after it was cleared by Capt. Barwell. From reports of men our shell fire had considerably damaged German first line and dug-outs in 2nd line, especially South of BELLEVARDE and about point 71. A derelict machine gun and two gunners were seen on the parapet near the farm. A party of 40 or 50 who had been working between their lines had been caught by the bombardment and totally destroyed. Thirteen prisoners including an officer were captured by the Right Column, but I understand some were killed in the Sunken Road on the way down.

(Sd) W.F.R. Webb, Major,
5th Bn. Oxf. & Bucks. Light Infty.

5th Bn. Oxf. & Bucks. Light Infty.

Report on Operation by Capt. Barwell, D.2. 25th Sept.15.

Attack launched at 4.20 precisely: first line got away well in right direction. I personally moved with centre of second line which broke more into groups from the first. No obstacles were encountered and no trouble from artillery fire. The first few casualties seemed to be from rifle fire. A M.G. somewhere in enemy's first line close to junction of International trench was firing at short range as our line approached. I think it had only just come into action. I opened fire with three rifles from the nearest shell hole and one bomb was thrown at it. This put it out of action and killed a greater part of its detachment. On reaching front line trench I found it unoccupied. In the triangle to my right front three Germans surrendered and one officer severely wounded. In the largest group of dug-outs which were much destroyed a number of the enemy were seen taking cover. I directed bombs to be thrown into them at close range and killed them. 10 yards further up the trench going East two Germans made a show of resistance and were shot. At this point a number of Shropshires made their way into the trenches from the right but they were an isolated group and had no information. The light was still too bad at 5.30 to see developement of attack on my right, nor on reaching my final position could I or Sgt. Godfrey, who then joined me with 8 or 10 rifles see anything of B.Coy. 8 or 10 men of enemy were encountered going up these trenches: they were either shot or captured. By 5.45 I had occupied the required ground and had taken one M.G. and 11 prisoners. I last saw enemy retreating N.E. down a short communication trench along which I had expected to find B.Coy. working. I was shot by one of these men. I placed Sgt. Godfrey in charge of the further line directing one squad to face half right until K.S.L.I. made good and joined hands. I reinforced Sgt. Godfrey from the trenches behind and placed the second defence line in position. I sent a M.G. which I found at the top of the International Trench into Sgt. Godfrey's line with orders to sweep the right front. When I left with a number of prisoners and other wounded some enemy still lurked in the right International Trench. I had no report from Mr. Lee, but it is understood that Mr. Mitchell commands.

(Sd) Capt. Barwell.

5th Bn. Oxf. & Bucks. Light Infty.

Messages re Operations.

To Sgt.Mjr. Smith. from the Adjutant. 5.30 am. Ox.24, 24/9/15.

You must make great effort to get bombs up to B.Coy. along hedge sap trench. Report progress.

From Sgt.Major to O.C. 6 am.

The whole of carrying party left with bombs & entrenching tools. None except wounded yet returned. When they do I will send more bombs and ammunition. The wounded man who returned reports that he got some bombs into the second line and was then wounded and returned.

From Capt. Barwell, to C.O. 6.15 am. D/1. 25/9/15.

We occupy the position and are in trench with part of K.S.L.I. B.Cos. platoon was not through Bellevarde at 5.45, but we cleared the ruins. Enemy is still in one or two saps in front of part of K.S.L.I. Am wounded in one or two places) will get properly bandaged & get back. I have taken 11 prisoners. A few more bombs needed.

From Lieut. Maude, to O.C. 7 am. 25/9/15.

We want bombs. The front line seems alright. We have not got communication with B.Coy. on the left yet. The K.S.L.I. & ourselves are holding a portion of front line. I have been hit. We are bombing to the left to try and get in touch with B.Coy. We hold between us front of about 200 yds. We have got the front of Bellevarde Farm and captured three machine guns. We also want more sandbags. The front line says they could do with some more men.

From O.C., to Lieut. Maude. 7.30 am. Ox.33.24/9/15.

You must establish connection with B.Coy. on your left. Hold first line at all costs. Impossible to send machine gun up at present. Get reinforcements from platoons in rear if necessary, but do not overcrowd front line. Bombs will be sent up in driblets. Look out for your left. Believe Germans bombing from that direction.

From Lieut Maude, to O.C. 7.50 am.

We want a machine gun up in the front line. Can you send a wire up the trench to us. D.Coy. on the right have had to retire. The Germans are advancing on the left of Bellevarde Farm. We want more men up here. Can't find anything of B.Coy., they don't seem to have advanced at all. We want more bombs.

Messages re Operations. (Cont'd)   (2)

From O.C. to 9th K.R.R.C. OK.37, 24/9/15. 8.45.
   Please send 20 bombers with bombs. I have only 7 left.

From O.C. 9th K.R.R.C. to O.C. 5/Ox.& Bucks. L.I.
   We have no bombers left that we can spare.

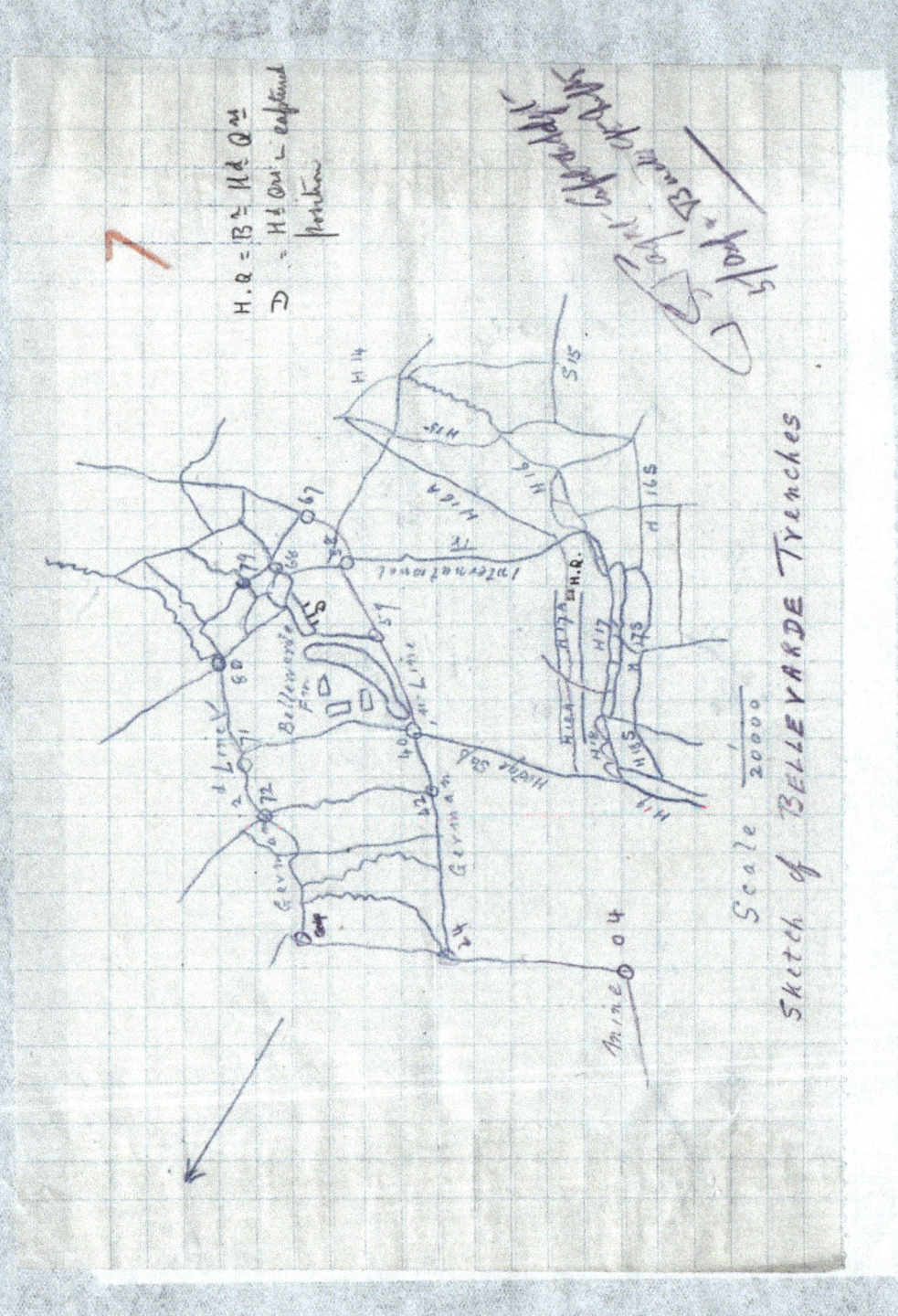

Dispositions prior to assault at
4.15 am. 25th Sept.

21/75/5

14th Division

5th OR: Anello:
vol 6

Oct 15

L. Cabral
6.T.J.
11 sheets

WAR DIARY
INTELLIGENCE SUMMARY.
(Erase heading not required.)

Army Form C.
2118

Place	Date	Hour	Summary of Events and Information	Remarks and references to Appendices
Hutts Camp near POPERINGHE	1/10/15		Coys did Musketry, Bayonet fighting & Sgt-Majors drill. Corrected Casualty return for 25th Sept:— Officer killed 1, died of wounds 2, wounded 5, missing 4 (believed killed) O.R. " 46, " " " 6, " 249 " 136	App.
"	2/10/15		2 Officers joined Battn to-day for duty. 3 Prels Representating ninth Battn for acct of an attack on 25th Sept. Notified by 14th Div that Captn C.F.K. CARFRAE would have received Military Cross for his work as observer to the Div during the 6th Divs attack on HOOGE 9th August, had he lived. This Officer was killed — action 25/9/15	BP
"	3/10/15	10 AM	Church Parade. Draft of 200 N.C.Os & men arrived from 9th Battn. Very good looking lot of men.	PP
"	4/10/15		Rough march — the morning drill in the afternoon 3 Officers joined Battn for duty. No Captain or Senior Officer	PP
"	5/10/15		Rained all day. Most of huts & wattle huts drying now. Recreation Room & Canteen Latrines & wash places proceed rapidly. Capt R.O. LOGAN & Major K.F. WORTH joined Battn for duty. Starts to hold 100yd Range. One of these 25 Yd Range should be constructed in every Camp, Drafts now require plenty of practice rapid loading & firing. 2000 dummies per Battn also required	PP

1577 Wt. W10791/1773 500,000 1/15 D. D. & L. A.D.S.S./Forms/C. 2118.

WAR DIARY
INTELLIGENCE SUMMARY

Army Form C.2

Place	Date	Hour	Summary of Events and Information	Remarks and references to Appendices
Camp near POPERINGHE	7.10.15 8.10.15		LT QUINN and Batt'n took duty. 2 Coys practised relief of trenches & movement under cover. Trenches dug by the Batt'n & from the aeroplane photo to practise of the attack on 25th Sept.	
—	9.10.15		Church Parade. Draft of 3 officers & 134 O.R. arrived.	
—	10.10.15		2 Coys practised trench duties in skeleton trenches, & were then relieved by the other 2 Coys. Lecture by C.O. to all officers & N.C.Os on trench duties. No 10640 Sgt SEYMOUR (since killed in action) & No 10696 Sgt GRAUBNER (since wounded) were awarded cards for "Gallant & meritorious service".	
—	11.10.15		Battalion officers & recent draft went up to the trenches for instruction. Coys did Musketry drill, Bayonet fighting, Fire Control in the trenches, Practice in putting in smoke helmets, also firing at aeroplanes & preparation for proceeding to the trenches to-morrow.	
—	12.10.15		Lecture by C.O. to all officers. Battalion proceeded to the trenches, & relieved the 8 K.R.R.C. of 43rd Inf Bde in the RAILWAY WOOD sector. Machine Gun section went up last night. Squadron & Grenadiers relieved to-day. O.C. Coys & N.C.Os per Coy proceeded to the trenches by day.	
—	13.10.15		Batt'n paraded 4.15 P.M. & marched to POPERINGHE, thence by train to the ASYLUM at YPRES, arriving 6.30 P.M.	

Army Form C. 2118.

WAR DIARY
or
INTELLIGENCE SUMMARY
(Erase heading not required.)

Place	Date	Hour	Summary of Events and Information	Remarks and references to Appendices
RAILWAY Wood Trenches			YPRES & the approaches to it were being heavily shelled till 7.30 P.M. & then moved off. But shelling was still very heavy & Batt. waited under cover of Canal bank W. of YPRES till 9 P.M. As shelling still continued, C.O. decided to push on, via the DIXMUDE gate & MENIN road. Shelly eased about 11.30 P.M. Relief completed 2.30 A.M. Only 1 O.R. wounded.	M
"	14.10.15		Situation quiet except for enemy snipers, & trench mortars, which latter were particularly on A.1. just N. of Railway. Our trench mortars fired 6 heavy shell into enemy centre by way of retaliation. We bagged one enemy sniper.	M
"	15.10.15	3.20 AM	Batt. having & knowing enemy tried to bomb K.21, but never succeeded in throwing far enough. Quiet night.	
			Enemy fired 2 red & green rocket over H.1.9. Morning very foggy till about 9 A.M. but sides took advantage of fog to work. but sharp look out kept for fog lifting, which it did very rapidly, & snipers told off to watch for targets. Good deal of trench mortar by both sides. Enemy sent over some large aerial torpedoes, which blew in A.1. in several places.	
		3 PM	Enemy fired about 30 H.E. shell into RAILWAY wood, quite 50% failed to explode. Our 4.5" Howitzers retaliated on	

WAR DIARY
INTELLIGENCE SUMMARY

Army Form C. 2118.

Place	Date	Hour	Summary of Events and Information	Remarks and references to Appendices
RAILWAY WOOD / Menin	16.10.15		Enemy 2ⁿᵈ line with effect. Casualties O.R. killed one. Quiet morning. Heavy fog early. Unfortunately party of 5 men carrying knife rests down the railway were caught by fog lifting, 2 were killed & 2 wounded. Enemy fired crumps & whizz-bangs into RAILWAY WOOD in the afternoon, & our guns retaliated. Every available man — the Battⁿˢ would all night, as there is a great deal of repairing & draining to be done. Casualties Killed O.R. 2, Wounded O.R. 6.	1ˢᵗ
	17.10.15	5.15 AM	Enemy exploded mine under the junction of H.20 & H.21. Our mine shaft in H.20 was blown up. It appears to have been a defensive measure only as no attack was made, & no attack made till later. The fire trench at the junction of H.20 & H.21 was destroyed for about 4 bays on either side of the junction. The earth was very much thrown up round the lip of the crater & runs in a long ridge to the Enemy Crater of the 2.5 Regt of Crater about 40 Yds — diameter and 30-40 ft. deep	1ˢᵗ
		7 AM	About 7 a.m. the enemy made 2 bomb attacks, one directed against the Crater, & the other against the SUNKEN ROAD. Both were briskly	

WAR DIARY / INTELLIGENCE SUMMARY

Army Form C. 48

Place	Date	Hour	Summary of Events and Information	Remarks and references to Appendices
RAILWAY Wood trenches			Repulsed by our bombers & by rifle fire. The behaviour of the men was excellent throughout, though the great majority of Officers, N.C.Os & men. it was their first experience of the trenches. There being only 3 Officers in - cluding the Col. & Adjt., who had been in the trenches before. Immed- iately after the mine went up, the survivors in H20 N & in H20 S opened a very steady rifle fire, to which there was hardly any reply; 2 platoons started work at once under 2nd Lt RODOCANACHI to dig out the men buried in H20, & they succeeded in getting several out alive. They continued the work through the hole attack & — spite of severe enemy fire by the enemy. Work was also started on wiring between H20 & S20 & digging a trench from the Crater. The wiring was completed that night, & also a trench encircling half the Crater, with a front post & loophole at each end: S20 was also continued towards H21 to join up up N. of Crater. 200 bombs were sent up by the Brigade during the day, also 1 Coy 5/KSLI, & 1/6 of their bombers. Bn 2nd. Lt? Wood to arms all higher. Casualties killed Capt. R.O. LOGAN. 2nd LT A.D.J. MELLISS, 13 O.R. Missing, believed killed - then valley — the mine. O.R. 22. Wounded O.R. 31	AP.

1577 Wt.W10791/1773 500,000 1/15 D.D.&L. A.D.S.S./Forms/C. 2118.

WAR DIARY
INTELLIGENCE SUMMARY

Army Form C. 2118.

49.

Place	Date	Hour	Summary of Events and Information	Remarks and references to Appendices
RAILWAY WOOD Trenches	18.10.15		Situation quiet except for a lot of trench mortars & snipers. During last night an enemy M.G. made of the railway continually swept our trenches with fire, especially there in RAILWAY WOOD.	MP.
	19.10.15		Sentry on A¹ bagged an enemy sniper. Got of trench mortars a lot richer & snipers hardly by enemy. But we are getting our snipers organised, & soon shall be able to give better than we get. Message received from B.G.C. re behaviour of the Battalion, when the enemy exploded a mine under our trenches on the 7ᵗʰ. "I was may — informed, no troops could have shewn a bolder front than the Borders & A Coy (holding H 20) after the mine was exploded. Battⁿ relieved to-night in the trenches by 7ᵗʰ R.B. of 4ᵗʰ 1ˢᵗ Bde. except the 4 M.G. teams who were relieved the next night 21/22. Battalion went back as follows Hd Qrs & 2 Coys L. to SEMINAIRE Relaeté on the YPRES – VLAMERTINGHE Road, 2 Coys n° BRIELEN Houses.	MP.
L.4. SEMINAIRE W YPRES	20.10.15		Inspection of arms & kit. Officers reconnoitred routes through YPRES Batt⁻ provided carrying parties of 400 to-night to the trenches.	

WAR DIARY
INTELLIGENCE SUMMARY

Place	Date	Hour	Summary of Events and Information	Remarks and references to Appendices
L.4. SEMINARE nr. YPRES	22.10.15		Officers reconnoitred YPRES' front north. — Case of shelling Batt'y. Provided carrying parties of 400 to the trenches at night. Batt'y shed tp halt by tram to POPERINGHE.	AAA
	22.10.15		In AIRE at 7.20 P.M. Arriving (POPERINGHE 8.10 P.M.) Thence by route march to HERZEELE (10 mins). No men fell out. Coys very pleased — killets in farms. Got to billets about 12.30 A.M.	AAA
HERZEELE	23.10.15		Following message received from 14th Div'n to 42nd Inf Bde:— The G.O.C. desires to express to you & to the troops under your command his high appreciation of the work done on the defences (front & support line particularly — RAILWAY WOOD (held by the Batt's) during the past week. The condition in which the defences were handed over to the Relieving Div'n reflects great credit on all concerned. From G.O.C. 42nd Inf Bde to O.C. Batt'y "The B.G.C. is very pleased to have received this report & congratulates the Batt'y which held the front line on the good work done. These Batt'ns were the 5/ Oxf + Bucks L.I, 5th Shrops L.I, & 9th K.R.R.C.	

WAR DIARY
or
INTELLIGENCE SUMMARY.

(Erase heading not required.)

Army Form C. 2118

Instructions regarding War Diaries and Intelligence Summaries are contained in F. S. Regs., Part II. and the Staff Manual respectively. Title pages will be prepared in manuscript.

Place	Date	Hour	Summary of Events and Information	Remarks and references to Appendices
ReBELLE	23.10.15		Made out Programme of Training for Batt. while in Rest Area	
"	24.10.15	11.30 a.m.	Church Parade. 11.30 a.m.	
"	25.10.15		Rained all day. 2 officers & 6 N.C.O.s attend class of instruction under M.R.E. at LMOUF & R.Q.M.S. in making dug-outs & loopholes, building parapets, draining tren ches etc. Class to last 1 week. 1 officer to 1st Army General School for Course, 2 N.C.O.s to 2nd Army School for N.C.O.s	
"	26.10.15		Army C.O. inspected lot 96 Coys at work in the morning. Coys old musketry drills, extended order drill, stiff my tumbler, bayonet fighting & gas curtain. Bombers practised, also M.G. Section.	
"	27.10.15		Rained all the morning. Carts sent to Review detachments of all units in 2nd Army & reviewed by H.M. the KING & the Prince of Wales.	
"	28.10.15		Coys Co. inspected Grenadiers & 2 Coys at work. C.O. received orders to reorganise Grenadier Section & N.C.O. to M.G. N.C.O. recently returned from 2nd Army N.C.O. School.	
"	29.10.15		Recreation Room opened at village school.	
"	30.10.15		Batt. was part of at POPERINGHE. Had parade as usual and for Pulley fund etc. Route march in morning, weather pleasant. Men marched & well wearing smocks	
"	31.10.15		helmets. 3 N.C.O.s & Machine gun class at M.T.M.C.E. 2 officers return making total of officers absent during month 17. Church Parade.	

5th (S) Bn Oxford & Bucks Lt Infty

Return of Officers NCO's & men Killed, wounded, missing & sick during Oct 1915

Date	Other ranks				Officers
	Killed	Wounded	Missing	Sick	
1.10.15					
2.10.15					
3.10.15					
4.10.15				1	
5.10.15					
6.10.15				1	
7.10.15				3	
8.10.15				1	
9.10.15				2	
10.10.15				3	
11.10.15					
12.10.15				2	
13.10.15				4	
14.10.15					
15.10.15	4	13		2	
16.10.15	9				1 Officer Died of Wounds, Capt. R.O. Logan
17.10.15	5	33	28		1 Officer Killed in Action, Lieut. A.J.D. Melliss
18.10.15				6	
19.10.15					
20.10.15				1	
21.10.15				1	
22.10.15					
23.10.15				7	
24.10.15					1 Officer Hospital :- Lt. Farrer
25.10.15				1	
26.10.15				3	
27.10.15				4	
28.10.15				1	
29.10.15				2	
30.10.15				3	
31.10.15					

5th Ox: Othello d/.
Vol: 7

131/7693

M D.
7.75
6 sheet

14th K warm

Nov 15

K

WAR DIARY or INTELLIGENCE SUMMARY

Army Form C. 2118

Place	Date	Hour	Summary of Events and Information	Remarks and references to Appendices
HERZEELE	1/11/15		Coys work on Coy programme. Weather very bad. A new class of 2 N.C.Os & 2 M.G.s detailed for instruction R.E. work.	AP
-	2/11/15		Weather too bad for out door work, programme used/not availing by Bn. Farmer aged 46 died of wounds (28.10.15)	AP
-	3/11/15		Cpl's R.C.T. PAGET & L-Cpl T. ROOD CAMACHI awarded Military Cross Bt. 2nd Bn. Weather fine	AP
-	4/11/15		Work by Coys. on Coy programme. The B.G.C. inspects "C" Coy at work (range) and - A Coy (attack in trenches). Special Order of the Day by F.M. French	AP
-	5/11/15		Brigade Route March. First line Transport accompanies Bn. Parade state 19 officers 639 O.R.	AP
-	6/11/15		Work by Coy on Coy Programme. Battn. Horse Show during afternoon.	AP
-	7/11/15		Church Parade. Weather fine.	AP
-	8/11/15		Work on Coy programme. Sgt Major class started for backward officers & N.C.O. 24 officers are selected from coys. An R: & L" rifle grenades. G.O.C. 14 (Lt. Div) inspects Guards for Gallantry & Meritorious Service to 7 N.C.Os & privates. 15 cards were awarded to B: (L/C being next on list 12.) Presentation took place at MOOTHERQUE.	AP
-	9/11/15		2 Coys - 6 N.C.O. & 2 M.G. sent to new R.E. class. D.M.S. inspects all drafts/miscellaneous Coys. 6 Lenchr. (nearly 400)	AP
-	10/11/15		Bn Route March. Weather cold but fine.	AP
-	11/11/15		B.G.C inspects "B" Coy at drill, also all platoon cdrs., one platoon at R.E. work, 2 platoons 20 each at drill in light attack trench.	AP
-	12/11/15		Brigade Route March cancelled on account of weather.	AP
-	13/11/15		Class Parades as follows - Control, rapid fire with Mindles, use of wind-gauges, fire direction & control, rapid fire with Mindle blanks on a 30ft range, drill + musketry, Bayonet fighting	AP

WAR DIARY
INTELLIGENCE SUMMARY

(Erase heading not required.)

Army Form C. 2118

5-3

Place	Date	Hour	Summary of Events and Information	Remarks and references to Appendices
HERZEELE	14/11/15		All men went to usual Church Parade or later under canvas.	AP
		11 A.M.	Officers & NCOs to Class of instruction in Lewis Gun at WATOU to last 1 week. Sharp frost to-night.	
	15/11/15		Work as on Sat. 13/11/15. Coys on week on parade, because there is so much speculation in this war.	AP
	16/11/15		Lecture by staff to all Officers & NCOs on use of Snipers. Parades as usual in the morning. Battalion conducted a headshake of 14th Divs pattern 5-7 P.M. Did not nearly complete it. Parade as usual. Weather fine & cold.	AP
	17/11/15		All Battrys of the Brigade except this Batt.'s proceeded to the trenches to-night	AP
	18/11/15			AP
	19/11/15	11.45 A.M.	Paraded 11.45 A.M., marched off 11.55 A.M. vis WATOU & POPERINGHE to B huts (G.6.d. sheet 2.6). Distance 12 miles. Arrived 4 P.M. No man fell out. Camp very not-ruity.	AP
B huts G.6.d Abeele	20/11/15		C.O. & Coy commdrs. proceeded to the trenches to-day to inspect the line before taking over them on morrow. No communication possible by day between Snipers & front line on account of Flanders centers, Shroders & active Snipers	AP

1577 Wt.W10791/1773 500,000 1/15 D.B.&L. A.D.S.S./Forms/C. 2118.

WAR DIARY
INTELLIGENCE SUMMARY

Place	Date	Hour	Summary of Events and Information	Remarks and references to Appendices
YPRES	21.11.15		Battalion relieved 5/K.S.L.I. trenches A3 & A5h. 9 x 2 & 3 Balls fell Out in POTIJZE Wood. Relief completed 8.16 PM. 51st Brigade A.1.E Air 5 an on our Major. 43rd Brigade runner 9th R.D. on our left. Good deal of enemy M.G. fire during the night sweeping our front. Trenches are in very bad state full of mud & water & fallen in in many places. Through neglect of drainage required water independent of R.E. 2 LT GRAF wounded.	P.P.
	22.11.15		Quiet all day. 2 enemy barraged by our snipers. Patrols reported the MOUND unoccupied. Patrol of 2 men arrived at MILEPOST 4 returned later. 2 LT DOWNTN went out at 11.30 PM towards MOUND. This patrol have returned. Work carried on day & night drawing, revetting, refilling.	P.P.
	23.11.15		Three Rumoured attack by enemy on Salient infantry reported by 2nd Army. 1 O.R. Casualties. 1 O.R. wounded.	B.M.
	24.11.14		Batt. relieved by 5/K.S.L.I & relieved K.B. Hut & G.d.(Wooden) Huts. Heavy fall of snow throughout in by Col.	P.P.
	25.11.15		Captain PAGET attended Brigade HQrs. 14 & Rifle Bde. handed over	P.P.
	26.11.15		Entries by 2nd LT SEBASTIAN	

Army Form C. 2118

WAR DIARY
or
INTELLIGENCE SUMMARY.

(Erase heading not required.)

Place	Date	Hour	Summary of Events and Information	Remarks and references to Appendices
G.G.d	27.11.15		Battalion relieved 5/KSLI. Train to Asylum + thence marched	
Shn28	28.11.15	15	Considerable artillery activity on both sides. Wood + Village of POTIJZE shelled. 5/KRRifles slightly wounded one casualty.	
POTIJZE	29.11	15	Artillery duel all day. A's whiz bangs came as usual went alled intermittently. No casualties.	
I4(abcd)	30.11	15	Wood + village shelled slightly morning. Heavier later afternoon. Evening when relief by 5/KSLI — hand hand grenade of wood and X Roads. No casualties. But relief delayed. Owing to KAAIE SALIENT, pp3	
			relieved 5/KSLI (about 2p) + began — POTIJZE DEFENCES C1a2 (above2p) + relieved all salient sections. He was uncomfortable. Draft extending men as 5th	
KAAIE	1.12	15	impetuous numbers. Relief of KSLI left both the counted same. On return to Camp for holiday	
	2.12	15	Ewkef implement work.	

S.R. Ox / Bucks
Vol: 8
27 Nov - 31st Nov
Dec.

14:

8. EJ
6 sheet

WAR DIARY or INTELLIGENCE SUMMARY

Army Form C. 2118

Place	Date	Hour	Summary of Events and Information	Remarks and references to Appendices
BRANDHOEK	27.11.15	—	Bn. at "B" Huts – Paraded by train at 6.30 pm to Asylum sidings & marched to trenches A3–A5, X2, X3 Potijze by Kents Trench. – Trenches very wet – cold on the occasion.	
POTIJZE	28.11.15	—	In trenches – Enemy shelled POTIJZE Wood & village – Canr. G. Dun working parties moving up & down road fm dump. One R.S. shelled enemy lines lines – Pty moved heavily bombarded by enemy. Lt ROBINSON and 1 O.R. slightly wounded shellfire	
POTIJZE	29.11.15	—	Artillery duel – Snow & shelling on front lines – POTIJZE WOOD shelled intermittently. Pty wood bon parties – One O.R. wounded (bullet)	
POTIJZE	30.11.15	—	Enemy shelled dump & wood – Heavy gun staff by Corps Arty on BELLEVARDE RIDGE in retaliation for shelling Pty Wood – Enemy did not reply – Relieved by 5th K.S.L.I. – Enemy shelled road village very heavily – Relief much delayed – Trench filled very badly – No casualties in Bn. Rest Units same in working parties. Julian Corps. – Tns. had heaviest shelling of communication trench since June July – handed to KAAIE SALIENT – YPRES on relief arriving 4.30 am	
KAAIE	1.12.15	—	Inspection – Afternoon fatigues on dug outs – Dug outs all wet & muddy on arrival trench	
KAAIE	2.12.15	—	KAAIE Salient defence in state of eclipse – Work on trenches – 11.0 pm paraded to relieve 5th K.S.L.I. at POTIJZE – Quiet relief but late owing to state of trenches	
POTIJZE	3.12.15	—	Relief completed 5.0 am Recon – hope taken to trenches – work by working parties not apparent – Wood & Village shelled as usual –	

WAR DIARY
or
INTELLIGENCE SUMMARY.
(Erase heading not required.)

Army Form C. 21

Instructions regarding War Diaries and Intelligence Summaries are contained in F. S. Regs., Part II. and the Staff Manual respectively. Title pages will be prepared in manuscript.

Place	Date	Hour	Summary of Events and Information	Remarks and references to Appendices
POTIJZE	4/12/15		Quiet day - Rain - Defences seen enemy grenades - Patrol under Sgt O'Grady investigated	
POTIJZE	5/12/15		Second in front of A3 FAS located sniper pit. Quiet day - Incessant work draining but fine again - Relieved by 5th KSLI. Returned to KAAIE SALIENT	
KAAIE	6/12/15		Disposition - 1/2 Coy Canal Bank, 1/2 Coy POTIJZE defences, 1 Coy KAAIE defences, 1 Coy Brewery. Belgian deserts - POTIJZE defences shelled - 2 wounded by shell fire - Work on dug outs & KAAIE defences & burying shells -	
KAAIE	7/12/15		Fine day - Work on defences - 6-17 "shells fell into YPRES	
KAAIE	8/12/15		Work on KAAIE defences - return onto - June - Relieved 5th KSLI. in A3 FAS	
POTIJZE	9/12/15		German heavy Artillery bombarded Ypres & roads from 5.0 am to 6.15 am - Working party was sec. at EITEL FRITZ FARM and Artillery intd fwd - Duty disposed to fill gaps - Wet night - Some shelling in POTIJZE Rd.	A3 & A5 trenches all night seen - 9th R.B. & 9th KRRC alternated in hip trench. On night 9/10 dark little Rifle week
POTIJZE	10/12/15		Some - Coy in front line were relieved at 11.0 pm - Some shelling in POTIJZE rd. dump. Heavy shelling enemy communication by our Arty	
POTIJZE	11/12/15		Quiet day - Lieuts McMILLAN & SHAW joined from Artists Rifles	
POTIJZE	12/12/15		Brewery Farm & track of A3 shelled - Fine - Relieved by 5th KSLI. at 11.15pm.	

Army Form C. 2118

WAR DIARY
or
INTELLIGENCE SUMMARY.
(Erase heading not required.)

Instructions regarding War Diaries and Intelligence Summaries are contained in F. S. Regs., Part II. and the Staff Manual respectively. Title pages will be prepared in manuscript.

Place	Date	Hour	Summary of Events and Information	Remarks and references to Appendices
Sheet 28				
B Camp (F22)	13.12.15		By march route from POTIJZE to ASYLUM – YPRES – Vlamertinghe to POPERINGHE – thence by march to B Camp arriving 4.0 am. – Camp a likes of mud – Transport stuck all day.	
			Light Trophies & cleaning up james etc. –	
B Camp	14.12.15		Inspection of Kit. – Baths at Poperinghe – Order to march back to HERZEELE	
HERZEELE	15.12.15		Marched at 10.0 am arriving HERZEELE 1.30 pm. Westoutre billets – Roads good w/f	
			Poperinghe – less mud in farms –	
HERZEELE	16.12.15		Refitting – Inspections – Remands of Bde unusual HOUTKERQUE	
HERZEELE	17.12.15		Refitting – Drill –	
HERZEELE	18.12.15		C.O.s inspections – Night alarm – expected German for attack	
HERZEELE	19.12.15		German gas attack at 5.15 am. News received at 6.10 am – Regt stand by ready to move – stood down at 8.30 am.	
			Gas attack not being followed by infantry attack – Church service at 3.45 pm	
HERZEELE	20.12.15		Distribution of prizes by Army Cmdr before Cmpets for Brigade – Rents branch –	
HERZEELE	21.12.15		Training	
HERZEELE	22.12.15		Training	
HERZEELE	23.12.15		Training	
HERZEELE	24.12.15		Rents March	

Army Form C. 2

WAR DIARY
or
INTELLIGENCE SUMMARY.

(Erase heading not required.)

Instructions regarding War Diaries and Intelligence Summaries are contained in F. S. Regs., Part II. and the Staff Manual respectively. Title pages will be prepared in manuscript.

Place	Date	Hour	Summary of Events and Information	Remarks and references to Appendices
HERZEELE	25-12-15		Rest	
"	26-12-15		Coy Inspections. - Orders to relieve 4/9th Durn.	
"	27-12-15		Training	
"	28-12-15		Training	
"	29-12-15		Battn. conveyed in buses to 'B' Huts C.12.c sheet 28	
"B" HUTS	30-12-15		Battn. relieved 5+6 W.R.R. 147 Bde. 49th Durn. in tr. from sect. of Salient B.12. 18.c. 7+13. Trenches very bad. 2 cos. wre. to battn. EAST CANAL and 2 west in PELISSIER B.21.a.2.1 MALAKOFF B.22.b.10.4 HULL B.18.c.10.2 SARAGOSSA B.24.a.1.5 and MODDER B.17.b.9.5. On our left trench on our right 41st.Bde. 8th R.B. 2/Lt. S.E.BURROWS and 2 other ranks killed.	
ST. JEAN	31-12-15		Last day. - Barnsley Rd. slightly shelled. 1 other rank killed. 2 other ranks wounded.	

T.J.134. Wt. W708-776. 500 000. 4/15. Sir J. C. & S.

5th Ox: Buckle d.
Vol. 9

9. T.5.
5 sheet

42 Bde

Army Form C.

WAR DIARY
or
INTELLIGENCE SUMMARY.
(Erase heading not required.)

Instructions regarding War Diaries and Intelligence Summaries are contained in F. S. Regs., Part II. and the Staff Manual respectively. Title pages will be prepared in manuscript.

Place	Date	Hour	Summary of Events and Information	Remarks and references to Appendices
St Jean	1.1.16		Quiet day. 2 batt. in trenches relieved by 2 batt. in farm, back in trenches next day. 3 OR killed 5 wounded	
"	2.1.16		Quiet day. Back in trenches. 4 OR wounded	
"	3.1.16		Colne Valley (C.13.b.0.3 about 28 trees) bombarded with H.E. & Shrapnel. Retaliation with Field Guns, 4.5, 4.7 and French 75 and heavier very effective. Sixth Corps Commander visited B.H.Q. 10 OR wounded. 1 Farm occupied. 20. Relieved by 2 R.B. & went to A Comp A30 d. 8.5 -	
A30	4.1.16		Fine day - in festoon 1 OR killed	
"	5.1.16		Fine day - festoon. Lectures - wiring by Capt. Fowler.	
A.16.c.	6.1.16		Fine day. Batt. moved to Camp A.16.c. very dirty with mud	
"	7.1.16		Fine day - Inspections - Training - 2 Batt. baths	
"	8.1.16		Fine day - Training - 2 Batt. baths - Batt. went to ELVERDINGHE - H.Q. + C. Coy at Chateau - A. Coy at farm B.13.b.4.4. - B. Coy at Farm B.19.a.0.11.	
ELVERDINGHE	9.1.16		Fine day - Inspections - taking jobs for Bde. - Garden Platoon cancelled - 1 OR wounded	
"	10.1.16		Fine day - Rest working parties for Bde.	
"	11.1.16		Batt. Relieved 9th K.R.R. in St Jean salient - French on left - 5th K.S.L.I. on right - C + D Coys in front line - A + B Coys in support. B in farm.	

Army Form C. 2118

WAR DIARY
or
INTELLIGENCE SUMMARY.
(Erase heading not required.)

Instructions regarding War Diaries and Intelligence Summaries are contained in F. S. Regs., Part II. and the Staff Manual respectively. Title pages will be prepared in manuscript.

Place	Date	Hour	Summary of Events and Information	Remarks and references to Appendices
St. Jean	12-1-16		Enemy shelling enemy retaliated with trawes on Colne Valley & canal Bank. – our trawes retaliated	
"	13-1-16		Bridge 6D shelled. Periscope observed C7a04 when shot at machine gun opened. 1OR killed 2 wounded.	
"		5am	Germans field guns in taches just West of Canal – Enemy registered F31 and shrapnelled Bridge 6D. 1OR died of Wounds	
"	14-1-16		Artillery activity both sides. FARGATE, BARNSLEY and COLNE VALLEY shelled, relieved by 9th R.B.	
"B" Huts	15-1-16		Returned to 'B' Huts. 2OR killed and 1OR wounded.	
"	16-1-16		Inspections and Baths, 1OR died of wounds.	
"	17-1-16		Training	
"	18-1-16		Training	
"	19-1-16		Battn. moved to ELVERDINGHE. A Coy at same farm. B Coy in Chateau. Capt Forbe appointed 2nd in command.	
"			night working parties	
ELVERDINGHE	20-1-16		"	
"	21-1-16		"	
"	22-1-16		Relieved 5th KSLI in left sector COLNE VALLEY handed to right sector – platoon tech on Canal. A Coy	
"	23-1-16		left B Coy on right C Coy at PELISSIER D Coy at MALAKOFF. F31 heavily shelled no casualties no damage	

T2134. Wt. W708–770. 50(000). 4/15. Sir J.C. & S.

Army Form C. 2118.

WAR DIARY
or
INTELLIGENCE SUMMARY.
(Erase heading not required.)

Instructions regarding War Diaries and Intelligence Summaries are contained in F. S. Regs., Part II. and the Staff Manual respectively. Title pages will be prepared in manuscript.

Place	Date	Hour	Summary of Events and Information	Remarks and references to Appendices
ST JEAN	24.1.16		Heavy Trench mortaring and bombardment of French installation to their shelling. Some mortars on Canal Bank N. of Bridge 7Z. E28 Heavily bombarded. Enemy M.G. rifle fire attacked & his trenches. M.G. rifle fire against our aeroplanes - no results. Our own front at rifle M.G. + aeroplanes active at night.	
	25.1.16		Germans trenches in B12 + C7 and opposite E28 bombarded by French & our Heavy retaliation. M.G. rifles more active at night. E35, 34, 33, + E28 encountered at daylight were received at night without incident.	
	26.1.16		Further bombardment of French & hostile E28. Practically no retaliation. M.G. rifles quiet at night. Known hostile attacks & aeroplanes detected by G.H.Q. - nothing happened. Shelling of Canal Bank - little damage - relieved by 9 K.R.R. + went to 73 huts.	
B. Huts	27.1.16		Rest	
	28.1.16		Inspection - musketry - bombing	
"	29.1.16			
	30.1.16		Church services	
	31.1.16		March to ELVERDINGHE	

5 d/ Cox & Backs
Vol 10.
14 & D3

g.D. 10. TJ
6 sheet

Army Form C. 2118.

WAR DIARY
or
INTELLIGENCE SUMMARY.
(Erase heading not required.)

Instructions regarding War Diaries and Intelligence Summaries are contained in F. S. Regs., Part II. and the Staff Manual respectively. Title pages will be prepared in manuscript.

Place	Date	Hour	Summary of Events and Information	Remarks and references to Appendices
	1-2-16		Relieved 9th R.B. in night sector E28, F30, C7 & d, COLNE VALLEY, WEST CANAL BANK, BRIELEN, C Coy in trenches, D Coy ½ COLNE VALLEY, ½ CANAL BANK, A Coy CANAL BANK, B Coy BRIELEN. Relief without incident and quiet night. Works	
	2-2-16		Quiet day and quiet night.	
	3-2-16		Quiet day and quiet night. D Coy relieved C Coy.	
	4-2-16		Patrol under Lt. FARMER inspected open ground before F30, heard work but saw nothing. Canal Bank shelled. Bridges C,D & W broken in places. - in afternoon F30 trench mortared 5 men hurt but only slightly - bivouacs shelled in evening. Night quiet.	
	5-2-16		A Coy relieved D Coy. B Coy relieved C Coy. Quiet day.	
	6-2-16		Our heavies on 91-5.6, enemy retaliated on F30 and E28 with field guns. Bomb store in COLNE VALLEY blown up. Road behind canal crumped with 5.9. - 6 Wagons shelled.	
	7-2-16		B Coy relieved A Coy. - night quiet - HQ shelled with 5.9 in dugouts - boarding at back saved C.O. who was asleep - later further shelling with field guns. No casualties.	
	8-2-16		Quiet day.	
	9-2-16		German patrol of 6 found outside wire in front of F30, but were bombed away, second patrol came but driven off by rifle fire. Two Germans wounded & own in shell hole. F30 heavily shelled.	

T2134. Wt. W741–776. 60C090. 4/15. Sir J. C. & S.

Army Form C. 2118.

WAR DIARY
or
INTELLIGENCE SUMMARY.
(Erase heading not required.)

Instructions regarding War Diaries and Intelligence Summaries are contained in F. S. Regs., Part II. and the Staff Manual respectively. Title pages will be prepared in manuscript.

Place	Date	Hour	Summary of Events and Information	Remarks and references to Appendices
	9-2-16 (CONTD)		12noon - 3.30 Heavy stuff & Whizzbangs at H.Q. 4.40pm. Relieved by 6/4 K.S.L.I. in E.28 9th K.R.R.C in F.30 & went to ELVERDINGHE.	
	10-2-16		Relieved by 6th OX. & BUCKS 20th Divn. & marched to HOUTKERQUE	
WORMHOUDT	11-2-16		Marched to rest billets at WORMHOUDT.	
	12-2-16		Rest.	
	13-2-16		Church service & inspection	
	14-2-16		Training	
	15-2-16		Training	
	16-2-16		Training	
	17-2-16		C-in-C inspection	
	18-2-16		Route March	
	19-2-16		Training	
	20-2-16		Marched ESQUELNEC & entrained	
LONGAEAU	21-2-16		Detrained LONGAEAU, marched to BERTEAUCOURT (LENS to where C.6)	
BERTEAUCOURT	22-2-16		Rest	
	23-2-16		Training	

Army Form C. 2118.

WAR DIARY
or
~~INTELLIGENCE SUMMARY~~.
(Erase heading not required.)

Instructions regarding War Diaries and Intelligence Summaries are contained in F. S. Regs., Part II. and the Staff Manual respectively. Title pages will be prepared in manuscript.

Place	Date	Hour	Summary of Events and Information	Remarks and references to Appendices
GEZAINCOURT	24-2-16		Marched GEZAINCOURT (D5)	
RULLECOURT	25-2-16		Marched GRAND RULLECOURT (F3)	
	26-2-16		Rest	
	27-2-16		Rest	
	28-2-16		Training	
	29-2-16		Marched SIMENCOURT (H3)	

Army Form C. 2118.

WAR DIARY

5th S[?] Bn Batt[?] of [?]
INTELLIGENCE SUMMARY.
(Erase heading not required.)

Place	Date	Hour	Summary of Events and Information	Remarks and references to Appendices
SIMENCOURT	1.3.16		Marched ARRAS relieved batt[?] of 33rd French regiment - one coy in SCARPE + one coy in RLY DEFENCES	
ARRAS	2.3.16		Quiet	
"	3.3.16		Quiet	
"	4.3.16		Quiet	
"	5.3.16		Relieved 7th R.B. & H sector front line + 8th R.B. in RONVILLE. 9th R.B. on right. 8th R.B. on left.	
RONVILLE	6.3.16		Quiet	
	7.3.16		Quiet	
	8.3.16		Quiet	
	9.3.16		Quiet	
	10.3.16		Quiet Cafe Fouche 2nd in command wounded	
	11.3.16		Quiet	
	12.3.16		Quiet 1 OR wounded	
	13.3.16		Relieved by 9th KRRC marched SIMENCOURT	
	14.3.16		Rest	
Simencourt	15.3.16		Training	

Army Form C.

WAR DIARY
5th Ser. Bde. Duke of Cornwall's L.I.
INTELLIGENCE SUMMARY.
(Erase heading not required.)

Instructions regarding War Diaries and Intelligence Summaries are contained in F. S. Regs., Part II. and the Staff Manual respectively. Title pages will be prepared in manuscript.

Place	Date	Hour	Summary of Events and Information	Remarks and references to Appendices
Lenancourt	16-3-16		Training	
	17-3-16		"	
	18-3-16		"	
	19-3-16		"	
	20-3-16		"	
	21-3-16		Relieved R.I.R.B. in H. Sector, 8th R.B. left, 9th R.B. right.	
RONVILLE	22-3-16		Snow, quiet	
	23-3-16		Snow, quiet	
	24-3-16		Quiet, 1 OR wounded.	
	25-3-16		Quiet, 1 OR wounded.	
	26-3-16		Quiet	
	27-3-16		Quiet	
	28-3-16		Quiet.	
	29-3-16		Relieved by 5th R.I.B. Sp. proceeded to billets. A Coy ACHICOURT, B Coy RONVILLE C, D & HQ 25 HRRAS	
	30-3-16		Rested during day, working parties at night. A Coy shelled by whizz-bangs. 4 Woolly Bears. 3 casualties, 2 fatal.	
	31-3-16		Inspections and working parties	

Vol. 12   5th (S) Bn. Oxford & Bucks L.Infy.   12.T.J
Army Form C. 2118.   XIV   2 sheet

WAR DIARY
or
INTELLIGENCE SUMMARY.
(Erase heading not required.)

Instructions regarding War Diaries and Intelligence Summaries are contained in F. S. Regs., Part II. and the Staff Manual respectively. Title pages will be prepared in manuscript.

Place	Date	Hour	Summary of Events and Information	Remarks and references to Appendices
ARRAS	1-4-16		Inspection & night working parties	
"	2-4-16		"	
"	3-4-16		"	
"	4-4-16		"	
"	5-4-16		Relieved 9th KSLI in H sector. 9th RB on right 11th RB on left. A coy is sector C left	
"	6-4-16		Quiet	
"	7-4-16		Quiet	
"	8-4-16		Quiet	
"	9-4-16		4.5 hows dropped 7 shots behind H.35. D relieved C	
"	10-4-16		Quiet	
"	11-4-16		Went for a Ramble received 15 R wounded	
"	12-4-16		Quiet	
"	13-4-16		Relieved by 9th KSLI & marched Savonnet. 1 O.R. killed	
"	14-4-16		Rest	
"	15-4-16		Training & Fatigue	
"	16-4-16		Ditto	

Army Form C.

5th Batt. O.C. Mc L.H. Jeffy

WAR DIARY
or
INTELLIGENCE SUMMARY.
(Erase heading not required.)

Instructions regarding War Diaries and Intelligence Summaries are contained in F. S. Regs., Part II. and the Staff Manual respectively. Title pages will be prepared in manuscript.

Place	Date	Hour	Summary of Events and Information	Remarks and references to Appendices
	17-4-16		Muster Rolls & Coys training	
	18-4-16		Training & fatigues	
	19-4-16		ditto	
	20-4-16		ditto	
	21-4-16		ditto	
	22-4-16		Relieved 5th RSLI in 1 sector 2 Coys right centre S left A reserve	
	23-4-16		Quiet	
	24-4-16		Heavy shelling of right + centre coy. B + C Coy T-M trench very large	
	25-4-16		Quiet 2 OR wounded A relieved B	
	26-4-16		Quiet	
	27-4-16		Heavy shelling of right coy A. 5 OR killed 2 OR wounded	
	28-4-16		Quiet	
	29-4-16		Relieved by KSLI went to ARRAS billets JEUNES FILLES ARRAS, C Roeuille & billicout	
	30-4-16		Quiet	

From
    Officer Commndg
        5th (S) Bn Oxf & Bucks L. Infty

To
    Officer I/C
    D.A.G's Office
        3rd Echelon.

Herewith War Diary for the Battn under my command for month of May 1916

2/6/16

M. Setatain Capt.
Commanding 5th Service Btn.
Oxford & Bucks, Lt. Infy.

WAR DIARY
or
INTELLIGENCE SUMMARY.

XIV 5th Oct 15thh L.S. Vol 13

13.TJ
3 sheet
L. abbey

Army Form C. 2118.

Place	Date	Hour	Summary of Events and Information	Remarks and references to Appendices
Arras	1-5-16		Both alt. made in command during the forry absence of C.O.	
	2-5-16		"	
	3-5-16		" from measles.	
	4-5-16		"	
	5-5-16		" 1 OR killed	
	6-5-16		"	
	7-5-16		"	
	8-5-16		Relieved by 5th KSLI in left sector, sector one left of R.I. on right. C.A.A.D reserve	
Roeville	9-5-16		Quiet	
	10-5-16		Quiet	
	11-5-16		Quiet	
	12-5-16		Quiet	
	13-5-16		Quiet Lt Farmer accidentally wounded	
	14-5-16		Quiet	
Bomille	15-5-16		Quiet Relieved by 5th KSLI and proceeded to Berneville	
	16-5-16		Rest	

Army Form C. 2118.

WAR DIARY
or
INTELLIGENCE SUMMARY.

(Erase heading not required.)

5th Oxford & Bucks Infantry

Place	Date	Hour	Summary of Events and Information	Remarks and references to Appendices
Reninghelst	17-5-16	Training		
	18-5-16	"		
	19-5-16	"		
	20-5-16	"		
	21-5-16	"		
	22-5-16	"		
	23-5-16	Relieved 5th KSLI in left 4 metre 3rd Div interlaced in left of RA right. D.B.A.C. reserve		
	24-5-16	Quiet		
	25-5-16	Quiet 2 OR wounded		
	26-5-16	Quiet		
	27-5-16	Quiet		
	28-5-16	Quiet		
	29-5-16	6" & 4.5" fired on Godebi Msasq redoubt on X + Y maps on 4th centre. 1 OR wounded		
	30-5-16	Quiet		
	31-5-16	1-3 am German heavy shelling on 4 KSLI. Relieved by 5th KSLI to own Bat Renville A at A Camp		

From
  Officer Commdg
    5th (S) Bn. Oxf & Bucks Lt Infy

To
  Officer i/c
    D.A.G's office
      Base

Herewith War Diary for the Battn under my command for the month of June 1916.

In the field   H. Sebastian 2/Lt & Adjt for
1.7.16   Commanding 5th Service Btn.
                Oxford & Bucks. Lt. Infy.

42/14

WAR DIARY 5th (S) Bn. Oxford & Bucks L.I. Vol 14

INTELLIGENCE SUMMARY.

Army Form C. 2118.

XIV

Place	Date	Hour	Summary of Events and Information	Remarks and references to Appendices
Arras	1-6-16		Quiet 1 OR wounded	June
	2-6-16		Quiet	
	3-6-16		Infantry fire	
	4-6-16		Looking practice 1 OR wounded	
	5-6-16		Looking patrol	
	6-6-16		Infantry fire	
	7-6-16		W Wells killed 1 OR wounded 1 OR wounded – died	
RONVILLE	8-6-16		Relieved 5th KSLI slept 4 nights 9 RWF right st Brigde onto BCD A in Ronville	
	9-6-16		Quiet	
	10-6-16		Slight shelling of H.Q. lines. 2 OR slightly wounded	
	11-6-16		Quiet – Rain 1 OR wounded	
	12-6-16		ditto 2 OR wounded	
	13-6-16		" "	
	14-6-16		" "	
	15-6-16		" "	
	16-6-16		1 OR wounded 1 OR killed	

WAR DIARY
or
INTELLIGENCE SUMMARY.

Army Form C. 2118.

5th (S) Bn. Bedfords & Bucks L.I.

(Erase heading not required.)

Instructions regarding War Diaries and Intelligence Summaries are contained in F. S. Regs., Part II. and the Staff Manual respectively. Title pages will be prepared in manuscript.

Place	Date	Hour	Summary of Events and Information	Remarks and references to Appendices
	17-6-16		Gates fitted. 30ft ----- - 1 died. O.P truck wounded	
	18-6-16		all ... 1 OR wounded	
	19-6-16		Quiet	
	20-6-16		Quiet	
	21-6-16		Quiet	
	22-6-16		Quiet	
	23-6-16		Quiet	
	24-6-16		Relieved by 9th ----- billeted in O----- 1 OR -----	
	25-6-16		Quiet	
	26-6-16		Quiet	
	27-6-16		Bombardment	
	28-6-16		Heavy shelling over billets area. Raid. ------	
	30-6-16		Quiet	

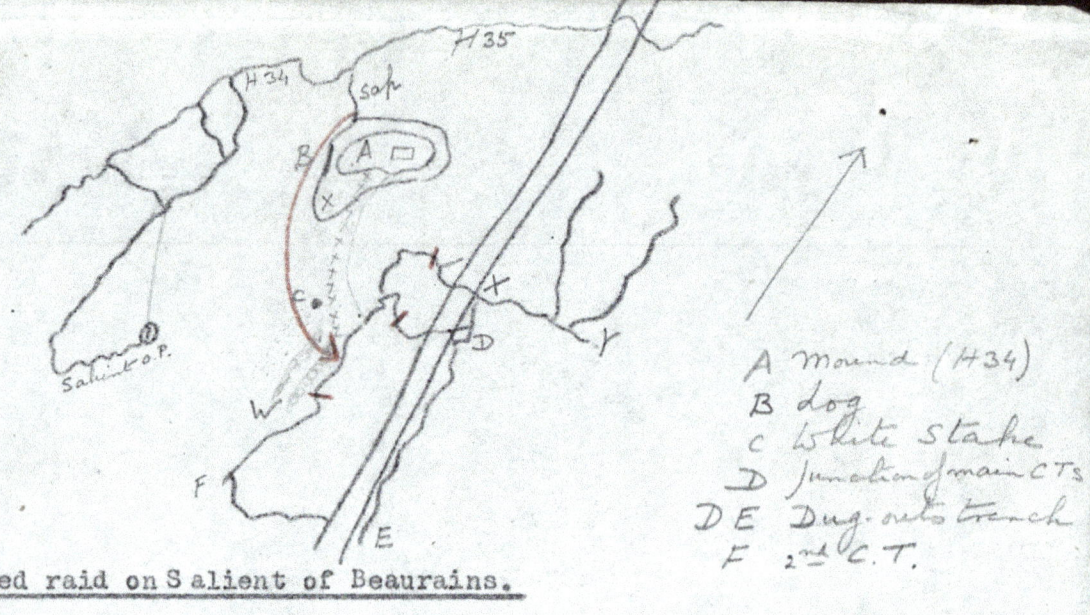

A Mound (H34)
B dog
C White stake
D Junction of main CTs
DE Dug-out trench
F 2nd C.T.

Proposed raid on Salient of Beaurains.

1. Strength of Party :-
   One Officer   - Lt. Weston-Webb)
   3 N.C.O's & 26 O.R.   ) 5th Bn. Oxf & Bucks. Lt.Infty.

2. Object :-
   To obtain prisoners
   To capture a suspected Machine Gun.
   To see if there is any mining in progress.

3. Party to be divided into 4 sections :-
   (a) One N.C.O. and 6 to clear trench to right.
   (b) One N.C.O. and 6 to clear trench to left.
   (c) One N.C.O. and 5 to clear C.T. and look for mine shaft.
   (d) One Lce Cpl. and ~~two~~ 3 men to remain on parapet to assist returning raiders out and mark spot where wire is cut.
   (a), (b) & (c) parties each leave one man with officer when trench is entered and will remain where C.T. leaves fire trench until withdrawal is ordered. They will be used as messengers to the groups to withdraw.
   An emergency signal to withdraw of three sharp whistle blasts will be arranged.

4. Parties will get out in column from sap behind mound, following course indicated by arrow.
   Each party - 2 bombers with bombs & knobkerries only.
                3 riflemen with bayonets and bombs.
                1 N.C.O.
   Except party (d) who will be all rifles.

5. ~~All to carry~~ 3 wire cutters per squad.
   NO superfluous equipment.
   Wounded to be brought in if possible.

6. **Wire Cutting by Artillery.**
   Direct view on spot marked by a white stake from Salient in H35.
   Wire is in 3 lines.
   (1) Outside - ordinary entanglement on screwpoles.
   (2) Double line of French wire.
   (3) Double line of French wire.
   There are lanes between rows and it appears there is a passage through the row now where white stake is.

7. Vickers Gun to fire in gap to prevent repairs from Salient.

8. **Covering Party.**
   A Lewis Gun protected by bombers on the mound A. These bombers will deal with sentry in sap should he become alarmed.

9. **Barrage Fire.** - By Artillery along XDE & WFE. Stokes Guns or Mortars at barricades X & D in Ronville Road. By Vickers Gun along trench North side of Ronville Road.

10. Patrol to reconnoitre effects of wire-cutting & route, night previous to raid.

11. O.C., Battn. to right coy H.Q. of centre sector.

12. **Date & time proposed.** 29th June - 12 midnight.

13. If darkness permits, raiders to crawl forward to wire and assault as first gun of Artillery fires. If night is light raiders to go forward at steady pace 2 minutes before time for barrage fire to commence.

(Sd) W.F.R. Webb, Lt. Col.
June 28th, 1916.   Comdg. 5th Bn. Oxf & Bucks. Lt. Infty.

S E C R E T.
                                                42nd Inf Bde
5th Oxf & Bucks L.I.   S 16/16 B.M.
5th Shrops L.I.
9th K.R.Rif.C.
9th Rif Brig.
Bde M.G.Coy.
Bde T.H.Bty
Y/14 Medium Trench Howitzers
46th Bde R.F.A.

The following minor enterprise will be carried out tonight :-

5th Oxf & Bucks L.I.

1. **Strength of party**

   1 officer (Lieut. WESTON-WEBB)
   3 N.C.O's and 10 men

2. **Object**

   To obtain prisoners and identifications
   To capture machine gun if found
   To see if any mining in progress.

3. **Time and barrage**

   Artillery barrage of 18 prs and 4.5" Howitzers to start at 12 Midnight, Signal time.
   Raiding party to be in position to enter enemy trenches as soon as possible after Barrage starts.
   Barrage to cease at 12.25 am. unless O.C. 5th Oxf & Bucks L.I. asks for it to cease before then.
   At the same time one Stokes gun will barrage M.4.b.6½.0 to M.4.d.7.9½., and will cease when the Artillery barrage ceases.
   Machine and Lewis guns to sweep enemy parapet on flanks of raiding party as arranged by O.C. 5th Oxf & Bucks L.I. with O.C. Bde Machine Gun Company.

4. **Reports.**

   Return of raiding party to be reported by wire to Bde H.Q. with brief statement of results.
   Detailed written report of operations to follow as soon as possible.

29th June, 1916.   (Sd) B. Paget,   Capt.
                              Bde Major, 42nd Inf. Bde.

To - 42nd Inf. Bde.

1. The following is an account of a raid carried out by a party of the Regiment under my command on the enemy trenches in front of BEAURAINS on the night of 29th - 30th.

2. Proposed plan of action was sent you on June 27th.

3. Up to 11.40 pm a Vickers gun ensured the gap in the wire being kept open.
At 11.45 a covering patrol got out on the mound (M.4.b.5/1) and the raiding party got out at the side of the sap and lay down in column.
At 11.50 pm. the party crawled forward and reached a point about 10 yards from the gap.
At 12 Midnight precisely the artillery opened fire, the Stokes guns barraged the barriers on the Ronville-Beaurains Road, and a Vickers Machine Gun swept the trench of the enemy second line running parallel to the road. The raiding party rushed into enemy trench with the first round of the guns. The wire had been well cut and proved no obstacle. The trench had been blown in and descent into it was easy.
Enemy were taken by surprise. There was no fire nor were any morethan the usual lights put up.

4. The party under Sgt. Bignell worked to the left encountering a small enemy working party 4 or 5 strong carrying sandbags, who bolted, and a post of 3 or 4 men, two of whom remained, the remainder bolted. These two were bayonetted and a third of the retreating enemy was caught and bayonetted. The remainder vanished down a dug-out steps and six bombs were thrown in on top of them. The party then came to a sandbag blockade in the trench and were unable to advance any further. After the first two enemy were killed unfortunately a short round from one of the supporting batteries fell on the parapet killing two of our men including the man who had bayonetted the first enemy met with. Two others were also wounded. Only two of the party reached the block which was of recent construction and placed in the trench between two entrances to a dugout. The party then came back to the point of entry to the trench and they say enemy threw two bombs from behind the barricade in the trench.

5. The right party went down the trench to the right finding it very much blown in. They found nobody there and after going along about 30 yards returned.

6. The centre party, who were to have searched a Communication trench, failed to discover it and got into a disused trench in which nothing was found and was very much knocked about. I think the C.T. they should have found was on the other side of the block in all probability.

7. After being 12 or 13 minutes in the trench Lieut. Weston-Webb commanding the party gave the signal to retire.

8. Some of the party lost their way for a time on the way back being confused by the proximity of the barrage and darkness of the night. As I could get no news of all being back I requested F.O.O. to continue barrage up to 30 minutes when I ordered him to stop.

9. The F.O.O. and Adjutant observing from MAISON ALLONGEE observed enemy fire two blind rockets which did not explode.
NO enemy machine gun fired and the only artillery action was a few 77 mm rounds on to HAVELOCK.
Enemy opened a very weak rifle fire of not more than 8 or 10 men when party were coming back.
Two men were hit by shell splinters on the way back.

10. A cap of the Bavarian Jaeger Regiment was brought back and has been sent to you. The return of it is requested.
It is regretted no other documents or prisoners were brought back but the few short rounds which occurred happened at the most unfortunate time and rather confused the only party which met with the enemy.

11. The work of the Artillery in wire cutting was excellent and the barrage put up by them with the exception of the few short rounds mentioned was very good.
The Stokes Mortar barrage on the RONVILLE-BEAURAINS Road was also excellent and the work of the Brigade Machine Guns in keeping the wire open and assisting the barrage was also very good. The two inch mortar fired a few rounds in the afternoon removing two knife rests blocking the gap.

12. The enemy trench was of the same type as ours about 8 ft. deep, hurdle revetted, wooden fire steps; considerably damaged by shell & mortar fire.
The sandbag barricade between two dug-out entrances has been met with before in raids. This one was evidently newly erected with a view to covering the gap in the wire and possible raid.

13. Enemy casualties:- 7 or 8 exclusive of casualties caused by barrages.
Our casualties :- 2 killed, 3 wounded.

14. Recommended for reward :-   2nd Lieut. Weston-Webb H.
                                  Sgt. Bignell C.
                                  Pte. Hall A.

June 30th, 16.   (Sd) W.F.R. Webb,   Lt. Col.

No. 1 Squad.
2nd Lieut. Weston-Webb.

7570	Sgt.	Bignell C.	D.	Coy.	
20994	L/C.	Ward R.	D	"	wounded
18758	Pte.	Mundy E.	D.	"	wounded
12516	"	Hassell S.	B	"	
10456	"	Hall A.	B	"	
17872	"	Fox E.	D	"	wounded
11193	"	Edkins W.	D	"	killed

No. 2 Squad.

9912	Sgt.	Wheeler W.	A	"	
19265	L/C.	Dennis F.	A	"	killed
11115	L/C.	Roote J.	A	"	
10088	"	Perkins P.	A	"	
18580	Pte.	Saunders J.	C	"	
18756	"	Goode T.	A	"	
16544	"	Rymer A.	D	"	

No. 3 Squad.

10464	Cpl.	Duester H.A.	B	"
18577	L/C.	Salter G.	C	"
8371	"	Lunnon G.	C	"
17271	"	Bradley W.	B	"
18676	Pte.	Webb A.	A	"
10774	"	Carvell W.	C	"

No. 4 Squad.

10703	L/C.	Jenkins E.	C	"
17757	Pte.	Goodman T.	C	"
20851	"	Woolridge W.	C	"
14678	"	Zimmerman S.	B	"

Lewis Gunners.
2nd Lieut. Tompkins.

10903	Sgt.	Sabin S.G.	D	"
10715	L/C.	Cox R.G.	C	"
10663	Pte.	Prentice A.	C	"

14th Divn. G.S. 2371.

Lt. Col. W.F.R. WEBB,
    Commanding
        5th Battn. Oxford & Bucks Light Infantry.

    Please convey to the Officers, N.C.O's and men of the raiding party the G.O.C's congratulations on the very successful operation carried out by them last night.
    The success of the raid reflects great credit on the Battalion, on the arrangements made and on the soldierly qualities of the Officers, N.C.O's and men who actually took part in it.

               (Sd) G.D. Bruce, Lt.Col.,
30.6.16.   General Staff, 14th (Light) Division.

Message from 9th K.R.R.C.

  Officers, N.C.O's and men send hearty congratulations on your fine show last night.
               9/60.   30.6.16.

Message from Corps Commander: through Bde.

  Corps Commander wishes you to convey to 5th Oxf & Bucks. L.I. his congratulations on their successful raid last night.

    30.6.16.

Confidential

Memorandum
of
Oxford Buck Ltd.
from July 1 to 31st 1918

From

Officer Commdg.
5th (S) Bn. Oxf & Bucks Lt. Infy

To

Head Qrs
14th (L) Divn

Herewith War Diary for the Battn. under my command for the month of July 1916

1/8/16

S M Selater Lieut & Adjt
.... Lt. Col.
Commanding 5th Service Btn.
Oxford & Bucks. Lt. Infy.

Army Form C. 2118.

WAR DIARY
or
INTELLIGENCE SUMMARY.
(Erase heading not required.)

5th Bn of March 2 J

Instructions regarding War Diaries and Intelligence Summaries are contained in F. S. Regs., Part II. and the Staff Manual respectively. Title pages will be prepared in manuscript.

Place	Date	Hour	Summary of Events and Information	Remarks and references to Appendices
MRAS	1-7-16		Relieved 9th KRRC in right sector trenches H25-34. Relief complete just before we started to relieve them. Mother sent mule with 2 stretcher cases.	
	2-7-16		Knocked out. 7 OR wounded. A night so on the left sector.	
	3-7-16		Rain + fairly quiet	
	4-7-16		Rain. Quiet	
	5-7-16		Rain. Quiet 1 OR killed + 1 wounded	
	6-7-16		Rain. Quiet	
	7-7-16		15D 5c 9 - C Sect	
	8-7-16		SD 5 9 - C+D. Major Bruny (O of g) 8 KRRC (was ordered in command)	
	9-7-16		Heavy shelling f.c. mel. 2 OR killed 2 wounded	
	10-7-16		Heavy shelling of C+D	
			2 OR wounded	
	11-7-16		Carried a part interview got result 2 OR wounded	
	12-7-16		ditto got good results relieved by 9th KRC proceeded to Rud	
			9 KRRC to Franvillers.	
	13-7-16		Rest 2 OR sick and + 7 OR wd - 2 mice died	

Army Form C. 2118.

5th Oxf & Bucks L.I.

WAR DIARY
or
INTELLIGENCE SUMMARY.

(Erase heading not required.)

Instructions regarding War Diaries and Intelligence Summaries are contained in F. S. Regs., Part II. and the Staff Manual respectively. Title pages will be prepared in manuscript.

Place	Date	Hour	Summary of Events and Information	Remarks and references to Appendices
	10-7-16		Training hath	
	30-7-16		Marched BERNEUIL - 3 hrs march fell out	

5th Bgd Machine Gun Coy

Army Form C. 2118.

WAR DIARY
or
INTELLIGENCE SUMMARY.
(Erase heading not required.)

Instructions regarding War Diaries and Intelligence Summaries are contained in F. S. Regs., Part II. and the Staff Manual respectively. Title pages will be prepared in manuscript.

Place	Date	Hour	Summary of Events and Information	Remarks and references to Appendices
	14-7-16		Rest	
RONVILLE	15-7-16		Relieved 9th KRRC in subsector H3-L2. A.S. & C in reserve	
	16-7-16		Heavily shelled. 4 officers 33 OR killed. 15 OR wounded. Enemy attacked frontline by 2 coys	
	17-7-16		Quiet	
	18-7-16		Showers returned. Capt. [?] Lewis Gun [?] Die train attached for 2 days	
	19-7-16		Quiet	
	20-7-16		Quiet. 1 OR wounded	
	21-7-16		Quiet	
AGNEZ	22-7-16		Relieved by 1st Division. Proceeded AGNEZ-LEZ-DUISANS	
	23-7-16		Rest	
	24-7-16		Route March	
	25-7-16		Rest Training	
	26-7-16		Training	
	27-7-16		Marched SUS-ST-LEGER complete 57 follow	
	28-7-16		Rest & Training	
	29-7-16		Marched MÉZEROLLES — 69 follow	

42nd Brigade.
14th Division.

1/5th BATTALION

OXFORDSHIRE & BUCKINGHAMSHIRE L. I.

AUGUST 1 9 1 6

Attached:- Report on Operations 25th August

CONFIDENTIAL WAR DIARY

of

5TH. OXF. & BUCKS L.I.

1st – 31st AUG 1916.

Army Form C. 2118

5th O of Munster J

WAR DIARY
or
INTELLIGENCE SUMMARY.
(Erase heading not required.)

Instructions regarding War Diaries and Intelligence Summaries are contained in F. S. Regs., Part II. and the Staff Manual respectively. Title pages will be prepared in manuscript.

Place	Date	Hour	Summary of Events and Information	Remarks and references to Appendices
BERNEUIL	1/8/16		Training	
"	2		"	
"	3		"	
"	4		" advance thro' woods	
"	5		"	
"	6		Transport marched CARBONNETTE/AMIENS I.F. 70000	
"	7		Batt.n marched at 4.30am to FERNVILLERS entrained 7.30 in tactical train, thence via FLIXECOURT + AMIENS to BUIRE-SUR-L'ANCRE (I.H.) detraining at RIBEMONT-SUR-L'ANCRE. Arrived BUIRE 6pm. Transport arrived 2-3pm about after Batt.n march on Division.	
BUIRE	8		Training	
	9		Training	
	10		Training	
	11		Training	
	12		Marched to ERICOURT at 5.30am. arrived bivouack in valley F 8 d 5.0 7.30am. relieved 7th S. Staff Regt of 17th Div. Transport at ALBERT E 4 r 33	62 D NE 1/20000

Army Form C. 2118.

5th Bn of Bucks L.I.

WAR DIARY
or
INTELLIGENCE SUMMARY.
(Erase heading not required.)

Instructions regarding War Diaries and Intelligence Summaries are contained in F. S. Regs., Part II. and the Staff Manual respectively. Title pages will be prepared in manuscript.

Place	Date	Hour	Summary of Events and Information	Remarks and references to Appendices
FRICOURT	13		Rest	
	14		Rest	
	15		Rest	
	16		Rest	
	17		Rest	
	18		Orders to move at short notice	
	19		Moved to MONTAUBAN (57°SW 1/20000) and occupied North + North West defences	
	20		Slight shelling. 3 OR wounded. Digging fast	
	21		ditto 2/Lt STYLES wounded. Digging + camping	
	22		ditto 7 OR wounded ditto	
	23		Occupied in Delville Wood. Trenches occupied + vacated by 5th KSLI (see reference orders)	
	24		Assaulted + took former trenches in Delville wood allotted to Bn II. line finally established from point west to Worcester Regt 100th Bde 33rd Div on FLERS Rd S12 a 54 through S12 c 99 to S12 c 84 where 5th KSLI joined. 5th KSLI deploying from inner French to edge of wood. Casualties 2/Lt BRADLEY + WESTON WEBB killed. Capt CRAWFORD	

Army Form C. 2118.

5th Bn of Bucks L.I.

WAR DIARY
or
INTELLIGENCE SUMMARY.
(Erase heading not required.)

Place	Date	Hour	Summary of Events and Information	Remarks and references to Appendices
	25		Lt FORSHEW 2Lt CLUTSOM, ROBINSON, DE PASS, & THOMAS wounded. 2Lt TALBOT & 3 killed, 115 wounded, 9 missing. On m.g. captured with 100 prisoners including 5 officers. Estimated enemy killed and wounded 150-200	
	26		Relieved by KOYLI and returned to camp at F'8 d 5.0	
	27		Rest	
	28		Occupied POMMIERS TRENCH trenches WEST of MONTAUBAN	
	29		Relieved by 4th RB & returned camp	
	30		Rest	
	31		Marched to DERNANCOURT into billets	
			A+B Coys with Lewis gunners and HQ marched ALBERT and entrained for AIRAINES (DIEPPE toward N.E. corner). Marched EPAUMESNIL 6 miles.	
			C+D coy followed 4 hrs later.	

Narrative of Operations of attack on DELVILLE WOOD August 2th 1916.

----

1. Regimental Orders for operations are attached herewith. These Orders were given verbally to Coy. Commanders and subsequently confirmed in writing.

2. Preparations for attack were as follows — On the 23rd inst. I was informed that withdrawal from front line would be necessary for the bombardment, and that it could not be used as an assembly trench. I therefore requested that a line should be dug during the night from S 11 D 6.1 to S 18 A 0.85 which work was excellently carried out by the 11th Kings Liverpools. A party of the Regiment also dug and improved a trench from S 17 D 6.8 to S 17 D 7.7. LEES TRENCH from S 18 A 1.7 to LONGUEVAL ALLEY was also improved and the Regiment was enabled to assemble in these and existing trenches in order of assault. Battalion Headquarters was in CRUCIFIX ALLEY near LONGUEVAL CHURCH at about S 17 B 85.40. Telephone communication was established with Brigade Headquarters and visual station in LONGUEVAL, and an earth buzzer was installed. Dumps of ammunition, bombs, water, etc., were established in original front line, and in CRUCIFIX ALLEY in vicinity of Battalion Headquarters. Medical Aid Post was in a trench at the shrine on CRUCIFIX ALLEY S 17 D 1.0. Tapes showing direction of assault were put out by first two lines during night 23/4th August.

3. At 3.45 p.m. the bombardment of German lines in DELVILLE WOOD commenced by the heavy artillery and from observation appeared most effective. At 5.45 p.m. the leading line of the assault left their trenches and were followed by the second and third lines as directed in Regimental Orders. The first line was enabled to get closer up behind the barrage before it lifted and at the lift advanced and carried the enemy first line (INNER TRENCH), and passed on behind the barrage to the edge of the wood. The second line dropping the bombing squads previously detailed followed, and merged into the first line outside the edge of the wood. Under cover of the artillery barrage these lines reformed and awaited the lift of the artillery. Some casualties occurred during the advance. A heavy shell on the extreme left of the line caused some casualties amongst the bombers and some others occurred from splinters or from the enemy barrage which opened at 5.35 p.m. as soon as our intense barrage commenced. Enemy appear to have barraged in two lines, on our original front line and also on the assembly trenches in rear but it was not in sufficient density to stop the succeeding waves which advanced in good order in spite of some casualties. Enemy barrage was heavier on right of attack than on the left which was comparatively free from shell fire. Enemy were holding INNER TRENCH in force but were much demoralised by our bombardment and surrendered to the first lines without much difficulty with the exception of about 50 men with a machine gun who commenced to fight after third line had passed. These men commenced to fire at the leading lines from the rear and at the fourth line but were speedily put out of action and captured by a part of the fourth line under Lieut. ANDERSON (B Coy) and a section of the Brigade Machine Gunners. The company forming the right of the first and second lines (A Coy) suffered a good many casualties in this first advance and all their officers were put out of action. The company forming the left of the line (C Coy) with the exception of casualties to the bombers who were on their left, by the shell mentioned, advanced without much difficulty taking prisoners on the way and reached the edge of the wood (6.5 p.m.). They were then some little distance from the FLERS ROAD. A small party of the enemy was left in the

gap caused by the casualties to the bombers and caused some annoyance till cleared up by C.S.M. HILL and a few men. The third line (D Coy) followed the second line at about 100 yards and not finding any enemy trench on the edge of the wood commenced to consolidate INNER TRENCH. One platoon of this company lost direction slightly and met some men of the 9th K.R.R.C who had come too far to the left but subsequently rejoined their company. Five officers and about 200 prisoners were taken in INNER TRENCH and one machine gun. The fourth line (B Coy) moved as directed in orders and occupied S 12 C central and commenced consolidation and construction of C.T. to old front line. Stokes Mortars and carrying party for bombs were somewhat disorganised by enemy party cleared by Lieut. ANDERSON and did not come into action. The first and second lines reorganised meantime outside the wood in one line in the most perfect order, the conduct of the N.C.O's of A Coy. (particularly SGT. LEWENDON) being most noticeable in this respect and on the barrage lifting at 6.45 p.m. advanced and seized the final objective (7.5 p.m.) establishing communication with the 100th Brigade on the left and the 5th K.S.L.I on the right and commenced to dig in about 200 yards outside the edge of the wood. At this period the 5th K.S.L.I finding the attack of the 9th K.R.R.C had failed and their right flank was exposed were ordered to retire to the edge of the wood. This movement was carried out in good order but left the right flank of my Battalion in the air. The Officer Commanding the first line (Lieut. RODOCANACHI) seeing this sent an officer to find out what had happened. This officer Lieut. JACKS restored the line by forming a defensive flank with some of the 5th. K.S.L.I. aided by a platoon of D Coy from S 12 central southward to INNER TRENCH and consolidated this line. The conduct of Lieut. ASHMAN in reorganising his company and part of the 5th K.S.L.I on this new front was also very noticeable. Meanwhile B & D Coys consolidated INNER TRENCH in spite of barrage fire which was considerable and especially heavy on the northern angle of the wood. The Vickers Gun of the Brigade Machine Gun Coy. advanced as ordered and was established in S 12 C central, the other gun suffered casualties and was unaccounted for for some time and I sent forward the reserve gun to take its place which was established in INNER TRENCH and subsequently all three guns were installed there. Telephone communication broke down between Battalion Headquarters and Brigade as soon as enemy barrage commenced.- a heavy barrage was put up on the line LONGUEVAL CHURCH south edge of DELVILLE WOOD. The special earth buzzer was read at the visual station for some time but subsequently ceased to act, all communication was by runner. The visual station could NOT be reached or worked owing to barrage on LONGUEVAL. Information from front line though somewhat delayed was good, and a good idea of the situation was obtained from wounded officers passing through and from an officer sent down by Lieut. RODOCANACHI to explain the situation with regard to the 5th K.S.L.I. The Adjutant, Lieut. Sebastian made an excellent reconnaisance at about 2.30 a.m. and confirmed reports previously received as to situation of the line. The front entrenched by the first line was extensive, and valuable assistance was afforded by an R.E. Coy. of the 33rd Division lent by a Battalion of Worcester Regiment on the FLERS ROAD, A platoon of the 100th Brigade held a portion of the trench on the road. During the morning of the 25th enemy registered the new line and about 6.30 p.m. in the evening evidently fearing an attack, he opened a heavy barrage fire from guns of various calibre on our new front and on the old front line. Prisoners captured were of 119th and 121st Regiments. When final objective was reached many enemy were seen retiring in the open north west of FLERS ROAD and fired upon. Our artillery barrage, Lewis Guns and snipers inflicted heavy casualties on these parties. During the morning of the 25th enemy were seen entrenched to N.W. of FLERS ROAD, probably TEA SUPPORT and attack was at one time thought imminent. He appeared subsequently to be working on the trench. Good visibility is now possible on the Switch line trenches and FLERS VILLAGE. Trenches at S 12 A 9.2 appear old gun emplacements as shells in baskets could be seen standing in the vicinity. Casualties in the Battalion are estimated at Officers: 2 killed, 1 missing and 6 wounded, and 160 O.R. killed, wounded and missing – some of these occurred on the 25th inst.

Aug 27²   *[signature]*

Lt. Col.,
Comdg. 5th (S) Bn. Oxf. & Bucks Lt. Infty.

OPERATION ORDERS.

1. 42nd. Infantry Brigade in conjunction with 33rd Division on the left and 20th Division on right and more extensive operations by the French will attack and clear DELVILLE WOOD and secure a line outside the edge of the wood from junction of ALE ALLEY and BEER TRENCH to FLERS ROAD at S 12 a 55.

2. Regiment will attack on left of Brigade front and secure from S 12 central to FLERS ROAD -- 5th K.S.L.I are attacking on our right and 100 Brigade on the left.

3. Regiment will attack in 3 lines. A & C Coys in first two lines, each on a two platoon front. D Coy. will form the third line. B Coy. will form fourth line as reserve.

4. OBJECTIVES.

First line will take edge of DELVILLE WOOD leaving a party of Battalion Grenadiers in INNER TRENCH to deal with enemy left. Second line will follow at 100 yards distance ensuring that no enemy capable of resistance are left in INNER TRENCH. It will pass on to edge of wood where squads of Battalion Grenadiers with this line and assisted by third line will clear out dugouts.

Third line will follow to edge of DELVILLE WOOD and secure it paying special attention to the left flank on the N.W. corner of the wood. They will consolidate this portion of the wood and will not reinforce the first two lines unless absolutely necessary, and in any case two platoons will remain and hold wood with two Lewis Guns. The barrage will not lift for some time as notified herein from a line in front of the wood. During this time first two lines of A & C Coys will reform in one or two lines at discretion of Company Commanders. At lift they will advance and take final objective 200 yards outside edge of wood.

5. B Coy in reserve will move via CRUCIFIX ALLEY as soon as third line has moved forward to our front line..

The O.C. Coy will detail one platoon to occupy and consolidate strong point at S 12 Central and one platoon to dig Communication Trench to it from front line. One platoon will be placed at O.C. Stokes's disposal and carry bombs. O.C. Coy will establish his Lewis Gun in INNER TRENCH, one to be at S 12 C central. He will carry forward bombs and ammunition if required by front line. Rifle grenades and bombs will be sent forward to strong point S 12 C central as soon as possible. He will supply carrying parties for

A & C Coys at dusk to carry Ammunition, bombs and rifle grenades – also water.

O.C. B Coy. is charged with defence of strong point S 12 C central and original front line. 4 Vickers guns will be in original front line.

6. Every effort is to be made to obtain the final objective but at all cost edge of DELVILLE WOOD and INNER TRENCH are to be held. Touch must be obtained on the flanks in between Coys.

7. As a means of communication runners are to be employed and flares are to be lit as under:-
   1. On reaching edge of DELVILLE WOOD.
   2. On obtaining final objective.
   3. At 7.30 p.m. on 24th Aug (today).
   4. At 6.0 a.m. on 25th Aug (tomorrow).

8. Barrage will consist of Heavy Artillery and mortars in the wood starting 2 hours before zero. Artillery will concentrate on INNER TRENCH 10 minutes before zero.
   At zero 1st. line of assult will leave trenches and advance as close to barrage as possible. Barrage lifts at 0.5 by 25 yards at a time. Subsequent lines will follow at 100 & 100 yards distance respectively. (5 minutes per 100 yards being allowed if lines are not already distanced).
   Barrage will be maintained for one hour after zero outside edge of wood at which time advance will be continued. This barrage is a field gun barrage and is to be followed closely.

9. Stokes gun will move to position at zero by CRUCIFIX ALLEY at S 12 ∅ 4.4 and will cover advance if necessary. They will subsequently move to N.W. face of wood S 12 C 3.8.

10. Vickers guns. One will be established in strong point S 12 C central as soon as possible and the second on N.W. face of wood S 12 C 2½ 8 as soon as D Coy. has secured that objective.

11. Zero will be at 5.45 p.m. and should zero be subsequently altered all action will be taken as already detailed from the new zero hour.

12. Artillery boards will be subsequently sent up and put on furthest lines reached and must be under cover from enemy view.

13. S.O.S signal is one golden rain rocket.

Aug 24 1916

Cmdg 5 Oxf & Bucks L.I.

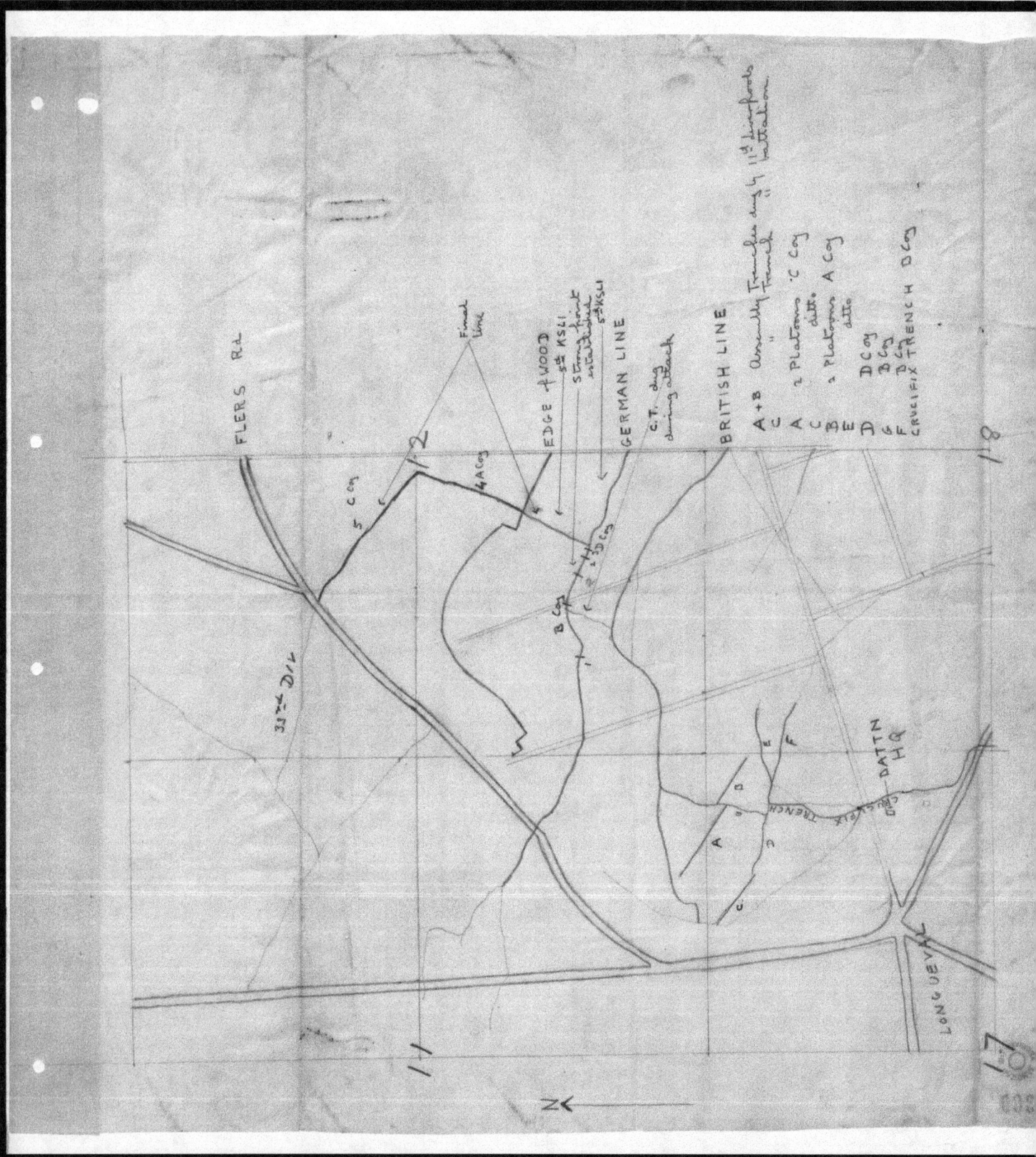

14

S Bacon Back
Vol 11

C O N F I D E N T I A L.

W A R   D I A R Y

of

5th Bn. Oxfordshire & Buckinghamshire L.I.

From September 1st to September 30th, 1916.

Army Form C. 2118

WAR DIARY
or
INTELLIGENCE SUMMARY.

(Erase heading not required.)

Instructions regarding War Diaries and Intelligence Summaries are contained in F.S. Regs., Part II. and the Staff Manual respectively. Title pages will be prepared in manuscript.

Place	Date	Hour	Summary of Events and Information	Remarks and references to Appendices
EPAUMESNIL	Sept 1		Rest	
	2		Training	
	3		Church Parade. Draft of 25 from OXFORD & BUCKS L.Infantry arrived	
	4		Training	
	5		" draft of 55 Oxf & Bucks + R.S.M. ARLETT	
	6		" Lt/Col ISO 2/5 E Lancs.	
	7		"	
	8		" draft of 87 R.F.A. from Oxf & Bucks 3rd	
	9		" won 1 da relay race	
	10		Church Parade. Transfer moved to AILLY-SUR-SOMME	
ALBERT	11		marched to AIRAINES and trained to MÉRICOURT. Bivouaced field D 9	
MEAULTE	12		conf at F 13 c. Lt/Col rejoined Capt KNIGHTON, 2/Lt ROSE Sigs. Offr, 2/Lt BRINDLEY	
			HUTCHISON + ROOKE "A" Coy 2/Lts SCOTT, ATKINS, BECCOMBE, C Coy 2/Lts HOLIDAY + HARPER +	
			2/Lt ROWE & Coy 2/Lts CLIFTON, VIDAL + LESTER-SMITH.	
	13		Training. 2/Lt HUNTLY joined	
	14		Moved MONTAUBAN alleys off in trenches near MAMETZ and arrived between 11.30 P.M. + 1 am	
			in orchard west of MONTAUBAN N X 27c	

WAR DIARY or INTELLIGENCE SUMMARY

Army Form C. 2118

Place	Date	Hour	Summary of Events and Information	Remarks and references to Appendices
	15	4.00 am	Reveille	
		5.00	Moved to South of YORK ALLEY, south of DELVILLE and formed up in Artillery formation of Platoons file with 2nd WSLR in front - 6th KRRc on right. Order B on left D on right, C behind B, A behind D. Trench mortars + HQ behind C. Vickers + S.Bearers behind D. It [?] all wounded in afternoon.	
		6.20	ZERO moved forward though much oppo[sition]. [?] + finished firmly a Buller Rd when fn [?] consolidated.	
		11.00		
		1.30	It [?] all again wounded + [?] away by [?] [?] Major DRURY assumed command	
MONTAUBAN	16	3.40 am	relieved 4.33 the went to MONTAUBAN + then of Graham took 1 [?] machine gun + 8 field guns. Casualties counted at CAVE [?] wall. Officers wounded, 2/Lt Beane Turner Brooke and Atkins, on duty Left f[?] the R.A.M.C. + R. ROWE. OR killed 119 wd 23. (All Refns [?] consolidated [?] attacked separately)	

WAR DIARY or INTELLIGENCE SUMMARY

Army Form C. 2118

Place	Date	Hour	Summary of Events and Information	Remarks and references to Appendices
	16.9.16	3.30 p.m.	Received from the Division the following order "Under orders received from XV Corps the 5th OLI & 5th KSLI are placed at disposal of 43rd Bgde. Then 2 battalions will prepare to move forthwith and inform this office when ready to do so."	
		3.45	Before the "Attack on GIRD TRENCH and GUEUDECOURT" will recommence this evening the creeping barrage lifts off GIRD TRENCH at 6.55 p.m. and off GUEUDECOURT at 7.35 p.m. The MA 4/3rd Bgde is to co-operate in attack. 5th OLI and 5th KSLI are placed at disposal of 43rd Bgde. Two Coys at a time will probably be taken one side of another to reinforce front line from the 5th OLI and 5th KSLI. MA will move from present positions.	
		4.30	Orders issued for the support of attack if necessary MA are at 4.30 p.m. and relieve 4th & 5th Wilts. SWITCH TRENCH MA stand by. RB on right. MA Coys must take relief, and plan was that RB should relieve outside. Right Batt. HQ to 7.7. MA on move from present position. A.A. will carry under orders of G.O.C. 4/3rd Bgde Battn moved up and formed in Artillery formation just	

WAR DIARY or INTELLIGENCE SUMMARY

Army Form C. 2118

Place	Date	Hour	Summary of Events and Information	Remarks and references to Appendices
South of YORK Allen		5.45	Orders for 2nd Bde for attack "4.17" to take FIRD SUPPORT & mop up & hold FIRD TRENCH & consolidate. 5th B. & 1st KRR team at attack on GUEUDE court, they will move up from SWITCH TRENCH armed as bombers. As soon as the FIRD Coy at 7.25pm take barrage a GUEUDE COURT will lift & be launched. Officer patrols will be pushed ahead & later ascertain if FIRD SUPPORT taken. If not taken they will consolidate on BULL Rd.	
		6.0	Orders from 1.3rd Bde. Attack on GUEUDE COURT cancelled. 4.3rd Bde attack on FIRD SUPPORT. 5th B. & 1st KRR SWITCH TRENCH + HQ at 2 coys in GAP TRENCH. 1 coy in SWITCH TRENCH. 1 coy in reserve. 2nd in command will lead forward officer patrols to get in touch with 4.3rd Bde & reconnoitre situation. 1st D. of Rifle Bde will fall in 5th B. 1st Comdt left flank 2nd D at junction trench will swing left & in conjunct. 1st AAA 52/ASH to move up till AAA 52/ASH of Green Vickers of AP AAA 4.3rd Bde successful Vickers to move forward. Bde reserve if unsuccessful cross Bull Rd.	

WAR DIARY or INTELLIGENCE SUMMARY

Army Form C. 2118

Place	Date	Hour	Summary of Events and Information	Remarks and references to Appendices
			Battⁿ received orders. Officers Patrols sent to establish + hold in	
			GAP + SWITCH TRENCHES	
	16	10.30	Officers patrols returned & reported for the GIRD TRENCH, but NOT GIRD SUPPORT that flank of trench were in DULL Rd. (didn't advance) Reference XX made night (objects were not clear to us) Right not confirmed that we were in effect	
	17	1.30	Recd orders for 4 1/2 bns to come into line of place on Right. A Coy advanced to extract forward Platoon to make strong point on Gas Alley; also orders for relief	
		2.25	Recd message from 1st D.L.I. that O.C. FLERS—DUGLOP attack likely at 2 a.m. and victorious ordered GAP Coy to Bull Rd. & D Coy from SWITCH trench & evacuated & instructed GAP Coy to be given from D.L.I if they were required	
		3.30	Recd message that GAP Coy no required & GAP Coy returned & D Coy also with drew	

WAR DIARY or INTELLIGENCE SUMMARY

Army Form C. 2118.

Place	Date	Hour	Summary of Events and Information	Remarks and references to Appendices
Camp	18th	5.0	Aey. Pat. relieved by 13th Northumberland Fusiliers	
		5.30	SWITCH Trench relieved by 13th W. Fusiliers	
		5.45	12th Leicestershire failed to relieve GAP and plans altered to 13th W.R. to withdraw GAP Coy	
	19th		Batt. bivouaced at POMMIERS Redoubt for ready to rest	ALBERT
	20th	2.0	Marched camp at FISH	
			Heavy rain — marched camp DIEU	
	21st		Rest	
			Training, reorganisation	
Bradfullecourt	22nd		Transport moved to TALMAS	
	23rd		March French lines to GRAND RULLECOURT	
	24th		Training	
			Church Parade	
Dainville	25th		Bus to RAJUICHE between WANQUETIN & WARLUS and marched DAINVILLE	
	26th		Left DAINVILLE and relieved 11th Middlesex 3rd Bde 12 Div in right G sector. 9th KRRC on left, 8th KRRC 4/12 Middx on right. Relief completed 11.0 pm	

RIDER

At 2.50 pm a Brigadier-General of the 41st Division came to our H.Q. and asked if we would cooperate in an attack in FLERS which had been evacuated owing to the heavy shelling.

Two platoons were sent to support this attack as it meant the safeguarding of the left flank. When these platoons had advanced to HOGSHEAD, from which the 41st Division had previously retired, their attack went off in a North Westerly direction and our platoons remained to protect our flank.

Account of the Operations 15th September 1916.

At 6 a.m. the Battalion formed up in artillery formation at York Alley to advance through DELVILLE WOOD in accordance with Brigade Instructions. At the commencement of the advance LT.COL. WEBB was slightly wounded in the shoulder, but continued in command. The advance was maintained in the above named formation until the leading two companies arrived at SWITCH TRENCH where they extended entrenched the other two Companies continuing in Artillery Formation in Platoon Files.

The 9th K.R.R.C were on our right and the K.S.L.I in front of us.

During the advance through DELVILLE WOOD the Battalion only encountered a mild barrage.

On arrival at SWITCH TRENCH the Battalion came under Machine Gun fire from a position of the enemy half right. The advance continued passing through GAP TRENCH and then came under very heavy shell fire from BULLS ROAD.

At 9.30 a.m. the Battalion rallied about 200 yards S.W. of BULLS ROAD, two platoons of reserve company having reinforced the front line on the right in order to get touch with 9th K.R.R.C whose left rested on the GINCHY-GUEDECOURT ROAD, one Company K.S.L.I only being in front of us.

At 11.50 a.m. information was received that the K.S.L.I could advance no further, and our front line advanced to join up with them and immediately dug in. The line then lay across BULLS ROAD at 31 d 5 9½ to d 68 and thence in more or less a straight line to near junction of WATLING STREET and BULLS ROAD. On the Battalion's left a support trench was also dug by Platoons in support. The enemy artillery abandoned their guns losing gunners as they retired.

O.C. D Coy. (Lieut.WALTER) advanced to the guns to put them out of action but could not succeed and had to return to his line keeping the guns well under our fire.

Lieut.Col. WEBB was again wounded at 12.30 p.m. and I assumed Command.

At 2.30 p.m. a Brigadier General of the 41st Division arrived and instructed me to co-operate with his Brigade who were to re-occupy FLERS. I ordered C Coy. to advance in co-operation and shortly afterwards 41st Division troops were observed in front of FLERS. The position was then consolidated and remained so until our relief took place. It was observed the enemy moved heavy guns as our advance came over the rise at SWITCH TRENCH. About 2 p.m. large numbers of the enemy were observed moving out from GUEDECOURT and over the corn fields between GUEDECOURT and Les BOEUFS and occupying GIRD TRENCH. During the whole period up to night fall the enemy artillery shelled the position between SWITCH TRENCH and our front line.

At about 5.30 p.m. the enemy launched a counter attack against our right. This attempt was repulsed at once with considerable loss by rifle and Lewis Gun fire. The attack had no vigour in it.

At about 7.30 p.m. I was informed the Guards had withdrawn 400 yards on our right and I arranged with 9th K.R.R.C to hold on to the position we had consolidated.

The ground held by us was taken over by the relieving Brigade at 4.30 a.m. 16th. inst.

19.9.16.
G.V. DRURY, Major
Comdg. 5th.Bn. Oxf. & Bucks Lt. Infty.

OPERATION ORDERS.

1. **General Idea.** 2 Battalions 41st. Brigade capture Switch Line followed by 2 Battalions 41st. Inf. Bde to capture FLERS DEFENCES (Gap Trench) from T 2 d 2/5 to T 1 b 2/2.
Two Battalions of 42nd Inf. Bde to capture GIRD Trench and GIRD Support from N 33 C 4/5 to N 26 a 5/0 division of Battalions on GINCHY - GUEDECOURT Road. 2 Battalions 42nd. Inf. Bde to capture line N 33 Central N 27 a 6/0 - N 20 d 5/6 division of Battalions at N 27 a 6/0.
41st. Div. are responsible for capture of FLERS.

2. 5th. Bn. Oxf. & Bucks. Lt. Infty will capture GUEDECOURT and establish itself on the left sector of the final objective N 27 a 6/0 to N 20 d 5/6. The 9th. K.R.R.C. will seize the right final objective.

3. The Regt. will assemble in the MONTAUBAN DEFENCES prior to advance in order D, B, A, C, H.Q. from right to left. Coys. will be formed up and ready to move by platoon files, two platoons at a time at zero and move independently and take up Artillery formation South of York Trench

4. At   plus 1 hour the Regt. will advance in artillery formation in four lines two companies forming the first two lines and two the second lines, each Company on a two platoon front in platoon files at 100 paces interval and 100 paces distance between lines. B & D Coys. in front line, B on the left. C & A Coys. in second line, C on left. Bn. Bombers will form a separate file in centre of 3rd. Line. Remainder of H.Q. will form a separate file behind Battn.

5. The left will at first direct on CRUCIFIX ALLEY and enter DELVILLE WOOD about S 18 a 5/0 emerging with its left on COCOA Lane. A steady advance in this formation will be maintained till reaching GAP TRENCH when the right will direct on the GINCHY - GUEDECOURT Road. The interval will be increased to 150 yards from the right. The Regt. will pass through the 41st. Inf. Bde. in artillery formation and continue the advance to the line of BULLS Road but will not merge into the leading Battalions of the Bde. who will be on that line waiting for barrage to lift. The leading line will follow 5th. K.S.L.I. at 300 yards distance. Barrage lifts at   plus 4.55 hours. On arrival at GIRD Trench 1st and 2nd Lines will extend to the left and pass through the 5th. K.S.L.I. and also through the leading line of that Regt. in GIRD Support and on the barrage lifting at   plus 5.30 hours will carry the final objective GUEDECOURT. The 3rd and 4th lines will remain in platoon files unless forced by the situation to extend.

42nd Inf Bde

Report on Operations
of Sept 15th 1916

At 6 a.m. the battalion was formed up in platoon files on YORK ALLEY; 2 companies in front line; 2 companies in support; Vickers guns, Stokes guns, + HQ in reserve.

At 6.20 a.m. Lt Col W.F.R. Webb was wounded in the shoulder by shrapnel. He however continued to command the battalion until 12-45 pm when he was again wounded and had to be taken back on a stretcher.

At the time of assembly the 9th KRRC were on our right and 5th KSLI on our front.

At 6.20 a.m. in accordance with programme the battalion advanced. Whilst traversing Delville Wood and moving to SWITCH LINE which was done almost without a halt, slight barrage was encountered but this increased behind the battalion. As the rear was entering DELVILLE WOOD some 8in shells fell on the sunken road behind the WOOD.

At south edge of wood one man was shot dead by German prisoner with a British rifle. The German was killed.

On arrival at the SWITCH TRENCH the battalion came under machine gun fire from a crest half right and extended.

The advance in this formation was continued. When the GAP TRENCH was reached the battalion began to come under intense field gun fire particularly from battery on Bulls Rd.

9.30 The battalion halted about 200 yds south of Bulls Rd. At this time the battalion was still in the same formation save that 2 platoons of the rear right company had moved up to its right to make connection with the 9th KRRC whose left rested on the GINCHY-GUEUDECOURT Rd and held front between them and 5th KSLI of whom a company were in front of the battalion.

guns out of action.

Soon after this position was taken up the enemy were observed to advance in great numbers from the direction north and occupy GIRD TRENCHES RIDGE. At about 5pm the enemy ~~began an advance~~ counter-attacked against our right flank. This attempt was frustrated by our rifle and Lewis gun fire, the enemy retiring leaving considerable numbers on the ground.

During the whole time that the battalion was in front of GAP Trench the shelling from field guns & 4.2 guns was heavy with times of intense bombardment until the evening when things quieted down.

At about 8pm news was received that the Guards Division were dropping back on our right. The 9th KRRf & ourselves decided to hold on to the ground we had taken

A tank was just behind our line which was observed manoeuvring to deal with the aforesaid battery on Bulls Rd, but had had the worst of the encounter and been set on fire.

At about 11.50 on information that 5th KSLI were not going to advance to Bulls Rd the front line moved up on their left flank and the right rear company moved up on their right and dug in. The line then lay across Bulls Rd at 31 d 5 9½ to d 68 and thence in more or less straight line to near junction of WATLING ST and Bulls Rd. On the battalion left a support trench was also dug.

On the front line advancing the aforesaid battery ceased fire.

Shortly afterwards a white flag was observed from about HOG'S HEAD. The 4th Division then advanced + took some German prisoners from near that point.

An officer went to the battery and endeavoured to put the

and all the ground taken
was consolidated over in relief.

During these operations we disabled
2 French mitrailleuse & gained
control of 8 Field Guns — All
on Bulls Rd

Our casualties were
Lt Col Webb wd
Capt Maude wd
2/Lt Beaver wd
/Lt Turner wd
/Lt Atkin wd
/Lt Brooke wd

2/Lt Rowe + Capt Gillespie wd at duty.
OR 14 k, 119 wd, 23 m.

S R Shlad—
Lt & Adjt
5th Bn Buck L I

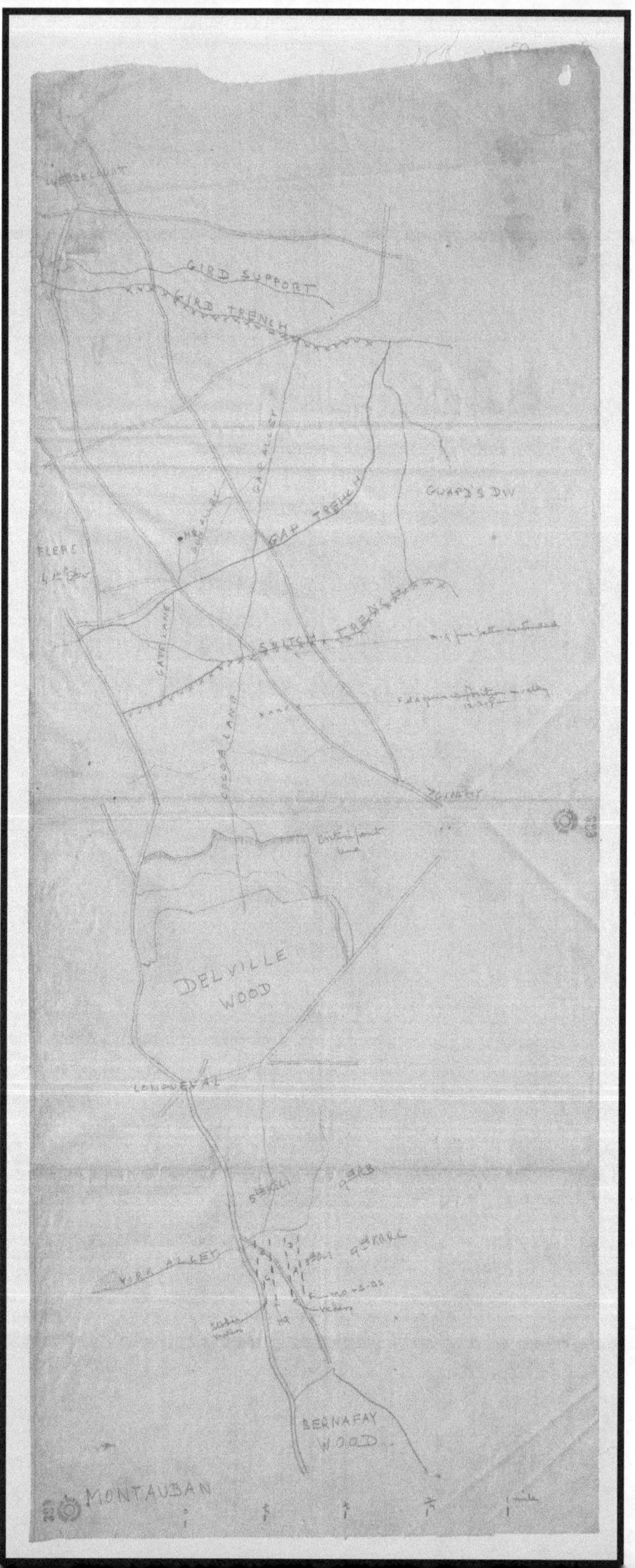

SECRET.
APPENDIX "C" to 42nd Inf Bde Operation Order No. 75.

TIME TABLE OF ATTACK.

ZERO 6.20 am.

- 0.53   Left Tank group starts.
- 0.30   ALE ALLEY Tank starts.
- 0.24   HOP ALLEY Tank starts.

0.00 (ZERO) Tank and Bombing attack on HOP ALLEY and ALE ALLEY starts.

0.00 " Infantry leave their trenches and advance close up to the barrage which will begin creeping back in front of them at - 0.0 minutes.
Creeping barrage will go back steadily at 50 yards per minute until it joins stationary barrage on first objective (green line).

0.25 minutes. Tanks reach positions on first objective EAST of FLERS Road.

(1) 0.20 min. (i) Barrage lifts from green line West of FLERS Road.
(ii). Barrage lifts from green line EAST of FLERS Road. Infantry capture first objective as the barrage lifts in each case. Creeping barrage halts 300 yards beyond green line.

1 hour 00 min. Infantry and Tanks advance together behind creeping barrage. Creeping barrage goes back 400 yards in three minutes, and on arrival at FLERS LINE joins stationary barrage.

1 hour 25 min. Barrage lifts from second objective, 41st Inf Bde capture brown line.

1 hour 45 min. Covering barrage goes back to allow Tanks to advance from brown line.

2 hours 00 min. Infantry advance and establish the blue line.

4 hours 15 min. Covering barrage taken off to allow Tanks to go forward.

(i) 4 hours 30 min.) Barrage lifts from ((1) Right boundary and
)   (Road N.32.b.38.
(ii) 4 hours 35 min.) GIRD TRENCH and   38.b.38 and
) GIRD   46.
(iii) 5 hours 00 min.) SUPPORT between   45 and

5 hours 30 min. Bombardment of GUEUDECOU... forward and Infantry compl... objective.

6. The attack on GUEDECOURT will be carried out by B. & D. Coys, first line moving through the village and second line being responsible for clearing it up. The platoons of each of the 3rd line Coys moving round the flanks of the village and acting as necessary. These flank platoons will come up into line on the final objective and must establish trench by posts with units on the right and left. The ffourth line will remain in reserve on the line of the road running through N 26 Central N.W. & S.E. Each Unit with front line will establish Platoon posts with local supports not more than 100 yards in rear. A continuous line will not be at first attempted.

7. Bombers and Lewis Gunners will be in the second line of Coys. Bn. Bombers will move as a separate platoon in the 3rd line under Lt. Jacks and will be specially used for the clearing of GUEDECOURT. The Bombers of the leading Coys must however be dropped in the village to clearing cellars etc. Bombers of the 4th line will be sent to assist if necessary but not until such necessity arises. After clearing village Bn. Bombers will patrol streets under orders of Lt. Jacks till village is proved clear of enemy.

8. Two stretcher bearers will accompany each company in the advance to tie up wounded.
M.O. and stretcher bearers will follow the Bn. and collect wounded on the well marked lines of trenches and after passing GAP Trench will remove them to the GINCHY - GUEDECOURT Road where they will be picked up. The M.O. will establish an AID POST on this road.

9. BN.H.Q. Trench Mortar carriers will move as a separate platoon file in rear of Battn. Bn. H.Q. will be established in a dugout in the GIRD Trench until the final objective is gained when it will move into GUEDECOURT.

10 Flares will be litc (1) When objective is reached
            (2) At 2 pm. and 5 pm. Z day.
            (3) At 7 am. day after Z day.
            (4) When called for contact planes.

11 S.O.S. signal is three blue rockets.

12. All ranks must make a resolute endeavour to attain final objective in this the final stage of the Battle of the Somme. The new land Dreadnoughts will assist in the operation and go with the leading line throughout providing effective covering fire and support. If operations are successful the cavalry will go through. Should the advance be held up the furthest objective possible should be gained and consolidated, and lines in rear will entrench. Troops are not to check because units on the flanks are held up. A resolute continued advance is the best way of assisting such failures. It may be necessary to detailunits for the assistance of units held

up on the flanks but this must only be done from the rear lines of the attack and if the results achieved would justify the weakening of the supporting lines. When the final objective is gained all units must work to the flanks until touch is obtained with units on the flanks. All ground gained must be immediately consolidated and held against counter attacks.

13 Signalling communication to be established by flag and lamp and by aeroplanes.
There will be a sign station on the N.E. side of DELVILLE WOOD in EDGE Trench.
Signalling communication is to be established with 41st Bde from GUEDECOURT if possible.

14 Stokes Mortars and Machine Guns attached will move in rear of Bn. in separate files in a fifth line and will act as ordered by Bn. Hq. Stokes Mortars if not used in the advance will take position in GIRD Support near N.26 d Central. Vickers Guns will move into position on front edge of GUEDECOURT as soon as village is clear and report to O.C. front line and BN. H.Qrs positions taken up.

15 All men are to be specially warned against enemy using British uniforms looting in dugouts and villages, taking letters and papers into action and that they must conform to the barrage and not TANKS.
(A Tank showing red flag is out of action)

14.9.16.
W.F.R.Webb, Lt. Col. Commdg.
5th. Bn. Oxford & Bucks. LT.Infty.

TIME TABLE OF ATTACK.

----0.53 Tank group starts.

----9.30 ALE ALLEY tank starts.
----9.24 HOP ALLEY tank starts.

ZERO   Attack on HOP and ALE ALLEY

ZERO   41st Inf. Bde attack 1st objective.

plus 1 hour   41st Inf. Bde. advance to 2nd objective.

plus 1.25 min. 2nd Objective carried.

plus 1.45 min. Tanks advance.

plus 2 hours.   42nd. Inf. Bde leading lines advance.

plus 4.15 hrs. Tanks go forward.

plus 4.30) Barrage lifts from) Right boundary and road W 32 b 38
plus 4.55) GIRD trench & GIRD) Road N 32 b 38 & track N 26 C 45.
plus 5. 0)   Support.   ) Track N 26 C 45 to left.

plus 5.39 Bombardment of **GUEDECOURT** and Inf. take village.

Approx. position of Regt.

ZERO – MONTAUBAN.

plus 1 hour   York Trench.

plus 2 hours   N. edge of DELVILLE WOOD.

plus 3½ hours   In front of FLERS defence line (GAP TRENCH)

plus 5.0   GIRD TRENCH.

plus 5.30   GUEDECOURT.

WAR DIARY

CONFIDENTIAL

5th Oxf & Bucks L.I.

From 1st Oct 1916. To 31st Oct 1916

VOLUME NO

WAR DIARY 8th Bedford? ? Army Form C. 2118
or
INTELLIGENCE SUMMARY.
(Erase heading not required.)

Place	Date	Hour	Summary of Events and Information	Remarks and references to Appendices
ARRAS	1.10.16		Quiet day	
	2/9/16		Relieved 9 KRR went to AGNY. Bn left reserve for R.B., 1 platoon A Coy at Mill Post	
	3		Bathing, Lectures on defence of AGNY	
	5		ditto, on how listed	
	6		ditto, holding ref from 6.17	
	7		Relieved 9 RB, 9 KRR left with Bde a right div reserve	
	8		A night, B centre, C left.	
	8		Quiet	
	9		Quiet	
	10		Quiet	
	11		Quiet	
	12		Quiet	
	13		Relieved by 9 RB went to DANVILLE	
	14		Training, working parties	

WAR DIARY 5th Oxford & Bucks L.I.
or
INTELLIGENCE SUMMARY.

Army Form C. 2118.

(Erase heading not required.)

Lieut & Adjt

Instructions regarding War Diaries and Intelligence Summaries are contained in F.S. Regs., Part II. and the Staff Manual respectively. Title pages will be prepared in manuscript.

Place	Date	Hour	Summary of Events and Information	Remarks and references to Appendices
	15		Training	
	16		Training	
	17		Training	
	18		Training	
	19		Relieved 9 R.B. in right C Sector - S.M.C. - left 4th in a night - GAS ALERT. A night is usual S left C reserve.	
	20		Received orders to take extra gas precautions, as complete evening.	
	21		Received message that our rides N of SCARPE had intercepted a message that gas was ready for liberation. Slight shelling of frontline - 2 OR wounded	
	22		Quiet	
	23		Quiet	
	24		Quiet	
	25		Quiet - Gas Alert cancelled - 1 OR Accidentally Killed	
	26		Relieved by 9th R.F. 12th Divn. and went to GOUY by motor lorry arrived there 5 am - 27th	
	27		Marched to DENIER, arrived 4.20pm. A-B-C Coys DENIER, D'Coy SARS-LES-BOIS	
	28		Rest - Usual inspections	
	29		Church Services	

Confidential

Vol 19

War Diary
of
5th Oxf & Bucks L.I.
*** *** *** ****

From 1st Nov 1916 to 30th Nov 1916.

(Volume 19)

Army Form C. 2118

5th Bn [illegible] 2[?]

WAR DIARY
or
INTELLIGENCE SUMMARY.

(Erase heading not required.)

Place	Date	Hour	Summary of Events and Information	Remarks and references to Appendices
DENIER	1-11-16		Training	[initials]
Sic Iq	2		ditto	[initials]
	3		"	[initials]
	4		"	[initials]
	5		"	[initials]
	6		"	[initials]
	7		"	[initials]
	8		"	[initials]
	9		"	[initials]
	10		"	[initials]
	11		"	[initials]
	12		"	[initials]
	13		"	[initials]
	14		"	[initials]
	15		"	[initials]
	16		"	[initials]

WAR DIARY
or
INTELLIGENCE SUMMARY.

5th (SERVICE) Bn. OXF. & BUCKS. LT. INFTY

Place	Date	Hour	Summary of Events and Information	Remarks and references to Appendices
	17		Training	
	18		ditto	
	19		"	
	20		"	
	21		"	
	22		"	
	23		Left at 10.0 a.m. marching as a battalion, halted I 34, J 34, K 31, K 28, then halted for dinner, collected packs at Vinquetrie K 28, where they had been dumped by lorries, halted with head of column at L 28 c, rest of battalion strung all over road by A.P.M. of 12th Division refusing to allow us to proceed except by halfs of 12 at one minute from ARRAS, reached ARRAS 6.10. A & C billetted in Faubourg d'Amiens. S.& H.Q. in same road as no 12th Battn. Trans. for left battalion marched to wells in AGNEZ-LEZ-DUISANS. One man fell out on the march, it carried in transport.	
	24		Received orders from 12th Division Div. that 2 coys were at disposal of 35th Bde.	

WAR DIARY
INTELLIGENCE SUMMARY

5th (SERVICE) Bn. OXF. & BUCKS. LT. INFY.

Place	Date	Hour	Summary of Events and Information	Remarks and references to Appendices
	25		In H.Sector under the 61st Field Coy R.E., and 2 Coys at disposal of 3.6th Bde. Up to H.Sector under 76th Field Coy R.E. Similar programmes were to be prepared & sent to us. No programme received from 36th Bde. Working parties degenerated into ordinary fatigue parties. Fatigue parties.	see
	26		"	see
	27		"	see
	28		"	see
	29		"	see
	30			

WAR DIARY.

CONFIDENTIAL.

UNIT, 5th Oxf & Bucks L.I.

PERIOD. From 1-12-16 to 31-12-16

VOLUME NO. 1

WAR DIARY
or
INTELLIGENCE SUMMARY

(Erase heading not required.)

5th D. of C. Bucks L. Infy

Army Form C. 2118.

Place	Date	Hour	Summary of Events and Information	Remarks and references to Appendices
ARRAS	1.12.16		Working parties	
	2		ditto	
	3		ditto	
	4		ditto	
	5		ditto 2 OR wd	
	6		ditto	
	7		March to DENIER + SARS-LE-BOIS. Same billets band instrument	
	8		Rest	
	9		"	
	10		"	
	11		"	
	12		" 1 officer + 14 ORs gone on leave (10-14 incl)	
	13		" 23 OR passage	
	14		Marched to DAINVILLE relieved 9th Royal Sussex at 13th Bde 12th Div 9hr	
	15		In full marching order no mans land	
	16		Relieved at R.F. Light Garden. A moore sniped one cliff	
	17		Quiet	
	18		"	
	19		"	
	20		"	
	21		Relieved by 9th RFs sanitation tresk — Agny — HQ. A+B Coy C+D sanitation	
	22		Quiet	
	23		" 1 OR wd	
	24		"	
	25		relieved 9 R. Suss right C. sector. A+B/D centre. C left D reserve	
	26			
	27			

Lt Col B.F.R. Webb reported

Army Form C. 2118.

WAR DIARY
or
INTELLIGENCE SUMMARY
(Erase heading not required.)

Instructions regarding War Diaries and Intelligence Summaries are contained in F. S. Regs., Part II. and the Staff Manual respectively. Title Pages will be prepared in manuscript.

Place	Date	Hour	Summary of Events and Information	Remarks and references to Appendices
Trenches	28		Quiet	
	29		Quiet 2/Lt V.b.Pearson reported for duty	
	30		"	
	31		" 1 OR killed	

WAR DIARY.

CONFIDENTIAL.

UNIT.   5th Oxf & Bucks L.I.

PERIOD.   From 1st Jan 1917   To 31st Jan 1917.

VOLUME NO.

Army Form C. 2118.

WAR DIARY
or
INTELLIGENCE SUMMARY

(Erase heading not required.)

5th Bty 1st Bde ?

Instructions regarding War Diaries and Intelligence Summaries are contained in F. S. Regs., Part II. and the Staff Manual respectively. Title Pages will be prepared in manuscript.

Place	Date	Hour	Summary of Events and Information	Remarks and references to Appendices
	1-1-17		Relieved by 9th R.F.A. went to Boisville. 2 Lt V.W. Bevan joined 2 Pooles Bty	
	2		Rest	
	3			
	4			
	5		Relieved by 9th R.F.A. a night a sect D left C reserve	
	6		Quiet	
	7		Quiet	
	8		2/Lt PALMER joined	
	9		Quiet	
	10		Quiet	
	11		Quiet	
	12		Relieved by 9 R.F.A. 11-12.30 pm	
	13		Quiet	
	14		Quiet 2/Lt BORMAN joined	
	15		Quiet 2/Lt PALMER joined	
	16		10.R.h. Relieved by 9 R.F.A. a night C centre N left D reserve	
	17		Quiet	
	18		2½ Foot rejoined	
	19		Quiet	
	20		Quiet	
	21		Quiet	
	22		Relieved by 9 R.F.A. mov-15 Boisville	
	23		Rest	
	24			
	25		Relieved 9 R.F.A. a night C centre D left A reserve	
	26		Quiet	
	27			
	28			
	29		Heavy shelling of B + C lrys 7-30 to 10-30 am	
	30		Quiet	
	31			

S. Roberton
Capt. A/Adjt.

WAR DIARY

CONFIDENTIAL

UNIT 5th Oxf & Bucks L.I.

DATE From 1-2-17 to 28-2-17

VOL NO

WAR DIARY
or
INTELLIGENCE SUMMARY

5th Bn. of March 19

Army Form C. 2118

Place	Date	Hour	Summary of Events and Information	Remarks and references to Appendices
	1-2-17		Quiet	
	2		Relieved 9th R B went to AGNY - A.R, HTR AGNY, C+D in Simla Rd	
	3		Quiet	
	4		Relieved 4, 9th K.L.R, Bg ttade, 36th Div went BARRAS, Schram Barracks	
	5		Relieved Coy 9 th S.L.I. (4,3rd Bde) RONVILLE. L&B battalion village	
	6		Relieved Coy of 8th S.L.I. the defences	
	7		A fatigue of men not taken for work	
	8		ditto	
	9		"	
	10		Relieved 9 th KRRC w left H Sector H 35-4 2. Trenches good but dirty	
	11		Quiet	
	12		Quiet	
	13		Quiet	
	14		Quiet	
	15		Relieved by 5 th KSLI went to DAINVILLE. Capt RODOCANACHI	
	16		Rejoined. Lt Battery + Jackson joined	
	17		Fatigue of 500 men on new railway. Rot on leave gun	
	18			
	19		Capt Lewis rejoined fr. R A Kgmed	
	20			

Army Form C. 2118.

WAR DIARY
or
INTELLIGENCE SUMMARY

5th Bat. Buck. L.J.

(Erase heading not required.)

Instructions regarding War Diaries and Intelligence Summaries are contained in F. S. Regs., Part II. and the Staff Manual respectively. Title Pages will be prepared in manuscript.

Place	Date	Hour	Summary of Events and Information	Remarks and references to Appendices
	21		Fatigues & training of dismounted men & bombers.	
	22		"	
	23		"	
	24		"	
	25		"	
	26		Relieved 9th R.B. in left H sector. A right D centre B left C reserve.	
	27		Quiet	
	28			

S.H. Marten
Lt Col
5th O.B.L.I.

WAR DIARY.

CONFIDENTIAL.

UNIT. 5th Oxf & Bucks L.I.

PERIOD. From 1-3-17 To 31-3-17

VOLUME NO.

WAR DIARY

of 5th Oxf Bucks Lt Infty
INTELLIGENCE SUMMARY

Army Form C. 2118

(Erase heading not required.)

Instructions regarding War Diaries and Intelligence Summaries are contained in F. S. Regs., Part II. and the Staff Manual respectively. Title Pages will be prepared in manuscript.

Place	Date	Hour	Summary of Events and Information	Remarks and references to Appendices
	1-3-17		Quiet 1 OR to hospital	SMJ
	2		Quiet 1 OR wnd	SMJ
	3		Quiet Right Coy relieved by 10th DLI. Withdrew. B + B in front A + C in Ronville	SMJ
	4		Quiet	SMJ
	5		Relieved by 1st KRRC. went to Ronville	SMJ
	6-10		Working parties	SMJ
	10th		Ronville heavily shelled. 5 OR wounded. Relieved by 5th KSLI. went to ARRAS	SMJ
	11th		Working parties	SMJ
	12th		Working parties	SMJ
	13th		marched out of ARRAS 4.30 am. reached FOSSEUX 9 am. Horses fell out	SMJ
	14th		FOSSEUX to SOMBRIN.	SMJ
	15th		Marched to SOMBRIN. went to billets for training. 2 OR rd ex Ronville. why l/pl for work	SMJ
	16th		Training	SMJ
	17th		Training – Major MOSSOP + 2/Lts Gwin & Haynes joined	SMJ
	18th		Lt Col W.F.R. Wall. White Hatter for medl. Lt Col P.J.S. N. SEBASTIAN 12th arr. to Jany. commanded of Battalion.	SMJ
	19th		Training	CBC
	20th		Training	CBC
	21st		Training	CBC
	22nd		Training	CBC
	23rd		Marched out of SOMBRIN 2.15 pm arrived FOSSEUX 4 pm	CBC
	24th		Rest	CBC

Army Form C. 2118.

WAR DIARY of 5th Oxf & Bucks Lt Infty
INTELLIGENCE SUMMARY
(Erase heading not required.)

Instructions regarding War Diaries and Intelligence Summaries are contained in F. S. Regs., Part II. and the Staff Manual respectively. Title Pages will be prepared in manuscript.

Place	Date	Hour	Summary of Events and Information	Remarks and references to Appendices
	25.3.17		Training	CBC
	26.3.17		Training	CBC
	27.3.17		Marched to SOMBRIN to carry out training for attack on 'flagged' positions.	CBC
	28.3.17		Ditto	CBC
	29.3.17		Battalion marched from FOSSEUX to ARRAS - where billets were taken over	CBC
	30.3.17		Major H.L. WOOD Oxf & Bucks Lt Infty joined & assumed command of Battalion. Training - 250 men for working parties	CBC
	31.3.17		Training at BAC du NORD - 250 O.R. working parties	CBC

CB. Crawford. Capt & a/Adjt
5th Oxf & Bucks. Lt. Infty

WAR DIARY of 5th Oxf & Bucks Lt Infty
INTELLIGENCE SUMMARY

Army Form C. 2118

Vol 24

Place	Date	Hour	Summary of Events and Information	Remarks and references to Appendices
In field	1.4.17		German aeroplane shot down by H.Q. Mess. Working parties dug assembly trenches at night were fired on by M.G. & shelled. 5 O.R. killed 23 wounded.	EBE
	2.4.17		Rest.	EBE
	3.4.17		Relieved 8th R.B. in H2 Sub Sector "A" on right "C" on left "B" Support "D" reserve	EBC
	4.4.17		Relieving 2nd R.B. Three officers Patrols sent out at night to reconnoitre HARP and vicinity. The Patrol of "B" Coy under 2Lt ANDERSON met a party of 10 or 12 Bosche who opened fire with a machine gun. Our Patrol lay down and the Bosche them (Probably frightened by proximity of Coy's Patrol in its near-rear across front of 2nd ANDERSON's party who hit 3 with a Lewis Gun (which jammed) they then were forward & captured the German Machine Gun and a rifle. Went to DUNEDIN CAVE.	EBC
	5.4.17		Working parties from caves.	EBE
	6.4.17		" " " "	EBE
	7.4.17		Moved to CHRISTCHURCH CAVES	EBC
	8.4.17		Took up final position in assembly trenches for the attack on TELEGRAPH REDOUBT 2nd portion of the HARP.	EBC
	9.4.17		Attacked TELEGRAPH REDOUBT at 7.30am. A certain amount of bunching was caused by Battalion on our right losing direction & K.S.L.I. who had to go through us - failing to wait for the lifts of the barrage thus finally missing up with the Battalion, leading wave. Three M.G. were knocked	EBC

2449 Wt. W14957/M99 750,000 1/16 J.B.C. & A. Forms/C.2118/12.

WAR DIARY 5th Oxf & Bucks Lt Infy CBC

or

INTELLIGENCE SUMMARY CBC

Army Form C. 2118

(Erase heading not required.)

Place	Date	Hour	Summary of Events and Information	Remarks and references to Appendices
~~Fampoux~~	9.4.17		Out lay L.G. fire & rifle grenades – about 150 prisoners taken. The objective was reached & consolidated. Casualties were as follows. Officers killed 5 wounded 8 OR killed 45 wounded 116 missing 11. Capt. HIGGINS, Lieuts STAMMERS, STEVENS, SCOTT & GRAY killed, Capts RADOCANACHI, GREENE, & WALTER, Lieuts ROBERTSON, STYLES, HALL, PARKER & VIDAL wounded. By 11 am the HARP was practically safe and men returned to dugouts there.	CBC
	10.4.17		Remained in captured position	CBC
	11.4.17		— do —	CBC
	12.4.17		Relieved by 6th Northumberland Fus. & marched to DAINVILLE where Bn billeted for night.	CBC
	13.4.17		Marched to LATTRE ST QUENTIN & billeted.	CBC
	14.4.17		Marched to LIENCOURT & billeted.	CBC
	15.4.17		Rest. Major N. BARWELL rejoined & took over duties of 2nd in command.	CBC
	16.4.17		Training & complimentary speech by G.O.C. Brigade. Capt F.W. MAUDE M.C. rejoined & took over 'B' from Major KNIGHTON who goes to 'C'. Capt J.L. SOUTHEY joined & took over "D" Coy. Lieut RICHARDS posted to "B" Coy. A draft of 205 OR joined Battalion.	CBC
	17.6.17.		Training. Very wet.	CBC
	18.4.17		Training. Very wet.	CBC
	19.4.17		Training. Commdg Officers Conference at Bde H.Q. 2 pm	CBC

WAR DIARY 5th Oxf & Bucks Lt Infty

Army Form C. 2118

INTELLIGENCE SUMMARY CBC

(Erase heading not required.)

Instructions regarding War Diaries and Intelligence Summaries are contained in F. S. Regs., Part II. and the Staff Manual respectively. Title Pages will be prepared in manuscript.

Place	Date	Hour	Summary of Events and Information	Remarks and references to Appendices
	20.4.17		Training as per Programme. Weather warm & dry.	CBC
	21.4.17		Training. Drafts lectured re Standing Orders and Out through Tear Gas. A draft of 30 OR. joined Batn. Ration Strength of Batn. 23 Officers 925 OR.	CBC
	22.4.17		Rest - Football Match v 9th KRRC.	CBC
	23.4.17		Marched to FOSSEUX & billeted in huts.	CBC
	24.4.17		Moved at 10 am. (½ hours notice) to BELLACOURT where Batn. stayed in huts until 5 pm - when marched to the HARP for night.	CBC
	25.4.17		Relieved 151st Bde in Trenches EAST of WANCOURT.	CBC
	26.4.17		In the line. 9th GORDONS on left, 9th R.B on right.	CBC
	27.4.17		In the line.	CBC
	28.4.17		In the line. Major KNIGHTON & Capt MAUDE wounded, relieved by 9th KRRC. and went to NEPAL Trench.	CBC
	29.4.17		Moved to HARP. Total casualties in Line. 2 Officers wounded, 3 OR killed 22 OR wounded.	CBC
	30.4.17		Rest. Working Party of 2 Officers 125 OR in line.	CBC

2449 Wt. W14957/Mg0 750,000 1/16 J.B.C. & A. Forms/C.2118/12.

Army Form C. 2118.

WAR DIARY
or
INTELLIGENCE SUMMARY.

5th Oxford & Bucks Lt Infty
Holman

(Erase heading not required.)

Instructions regarding War Diaries and Intelligence Summaries are contained in F. S. Regs., Part II. and the Staff Manual respectively. Title pages will be prepared in manuscript.

Place	Date	Hour	Summary of Events and Information	Remarks and references to Appendices
	30		Training - route march	
	31		Training	

CONFIDENTIAL

WAR DIARY

5th Oxf & Bucks L.I.

1. May — 31 May 1917

Army Form C. 211

WAR DIARY
of 5th Oxf. Bucks. Lt. Infty
INTELLIGENCE SUMMARY

(Erase heading not required.)

Instructions regarding War Diaries and Intelligence Summaries are contained in F. S. Regs., Part II. and the Staff Manual respectively. Title Pages will be prepared in manuscript.

Place	Date	Hour	Summary of Events and Information	Remarks and references to Appendices
	1.5.17		Rest. 1 O.R. killed by 4.2" shell. Shelled spasmodically at dusk.	EBC
	2.5.17		Enys. equipped with 'Battle order' in morning. Proceeded to assembly trenches in D19a and b (51b S.W.2) at 8pm. Order C-A-B-D-H.Q. No casualties. Runners + hot tea on arrival in assembly trenches. Quiet night.	EBC
	3.5.17		14th Division attacked enemy positions in D21 a + c - 41st Bde on right - 42nd Bde on left - 43rd Bde in reserve at 3.45 am. The Battalion attacked at 3.45 am on right east of the Brigade - 9th R.B. on left & 8 KRRC on right. Strength of the Battalion before attack 550 of all ranks. The attack was carried out with A-C Coys "A" being on the right - Batln. bombers under 2/Lt C.C. HARPER in second wave - B & D Coys in 3rd wave - with "B" on right. At Zero the enemy opened a very heavy M.G. and rifle fire on our troops from St ROHART FACTORY (O15C 51bSW.2) and HILLSIDE WORK (O21b) and an undiscovered trench in D21a. This trench was found to be manned and held in moderate strength and held up the attack temporarily. B & D Coys then reinforced the leading wave and the Battalion managed to force its way into this trench. Here - owing to very heavy casualties - it was obliged to remain. At 11 am the Germans launched a very heavy counter attack on our front driving back the Division on our right went literally thus driving the Bn back to original front line. At 8 pm remnants of the Battalion went back to NIGER TRENCH. Casualties were as follows. KILLED Lts. ASHMAN 2/Lts W.C. HAYNES + L. 4 17 O.R. missing 2/Lt E.C. HARPER - BULMER-RICHARDS + 112 O.R. Wounded Capt GODWYN 2/Lts JACKSON Lt HUTCHISON & 150 O.R. Total 8 off. & 279 O.R.	EBC

Army Form C. 2118.

WAR DIARY
of 3th Bn W3 nchr LI vgty
INTELLIGENCE SUMMARY

(Erase heading not required.) CB3 C

Instructions regarding War Diaries and Intelligence Summaries are contained in F.S. Regs., Part II. and the Staff Manual respectively. Title Pages will be prepared in manuscript.

Place	Date	Hour	Summary of Events and Information	Remarks and references to Appendices
	4.5.17		Shelled with gas shells during day. Relieved by 10th D.L.I at 7 pm and went to HARP	CBC
	5.5.17		Rest. The details left at BASSEUX rejoined. 2/Lt TAYLOR-ROSE rejoined from R.F.C	CBC
	6.5.17		Rest. J.O.C. DUNCAN inected the Battalion	CBC
	7.5.17		Inspections & training of specialists. 2/Lt PARKER rejoined from hospital	CBC
	8.5.17		no work owing to it being a very wet day	CBC
	9.5.17		Training of specialists & rest. Fine day	CBC
	10.5.17		Half the Battalion had baths at NEUVILLE VITASSE. Relieved 5th K.S.L.I in COJEUL SWITCH at 11 am. 180 men on working party at night.	CBC
	11.5.17		Rest. 3 offs & 250 men digging a C.T. across COJEUL VALLEY at night. 2 OR slightly wounded by shell. 2/Lt PALMER admitted to hospital	CBC
	12.5.17		Commanding Officers conference at Brigade HQ 11 am. Lt H.W. SPURGE joined Battalion & takes command of "C" Coy. 2 offs & 300 men working on C.T at night.	CBC
	13.5.17		Rest during day - 3 offs & 300 men working at night	CBC
	14.5.17		Rest. Capt. E.W. MAUDE to ENGLAND for aff't to Indian Army. 2/Lt D.J. BANKS joined and is posted to "B" Coy.	CBC
	15.5.17		Rest. moved back into THE HARP area at 8 pm.	CBC
	16.5.17		Training. N.C.O's class for recently promoted L/Cpls commenced under Right Sgt Major. 2/Lt J. PEEL to BOULOGNE Rest Camp. 2/Lt FITZGERALD rejoined aft Lewis Gun School. Wet day	CBC
	17.5.17		Rest. wet day	CBC
	18.5.17		Training - musketry on improvised ranges. 100 men working 2/Lt's HOLIDAY & GUISE rejoined aft Course duties	CBC
	19.5.17		Training. Following officers rejoined attached from 9th K.R.R.C Lt L.J HETHERINGTON 2/Lt's J WESTALL L.S DAGG - J.S CROWN	CBC

Army Form C. 2118.

WAR DIARY
of 5th Oxf & Bucks Lt Infty

INTELLIGENCE SUMMARY

(Erase heading not required.) CBC

Instructions regarding War Diaries and Intelligence Summaries are contained in F. S. Regs., Part II. and the Staff Manual respectively. Title Pages will be prepared in manuscript.

Place	Date	Hour	Summary of Events and Information	Remarks and references to Appendices
	20.5.17		Church Parade in morning. A working party of 250 OR. at night	CBC
	21.5.17		Reconnoitred trenches in D.30 (51b SW3) 9th/2 Batln bathed at NEUVILLE VITASSE – Musketry	CBe
	22.5.17		Rest – working parties at night	CBC
	23.5.17		Rest. 2/Lt R HALL rejoined from hospital after being wounded 9.3.17	CBC
	24.5.17		Rest. Relieved 7th R.B. as right supporting battalion starting at 11.5pm 5th K.S.L.I. in front line on right – 9th K.R.R.C in front line on left – 9th R.B. left support.	CBC
	25.5.17		3 OR slightly wounded by shells – gas projected at enemy trenches at 3 am. This appeared to blow back & gassed 4 DR. slightly. Shoot at enemy Batln HQ with gas shells at 11 pm.	CBC
	26.5.17		Quiet day. Working parties at night	CBC
	27.5.17		Very fine day. Sudden short burst of enemy shelling on EGRET Trench	CBC
	28.5.17		Fairly quiet day. Working & carrying parties at night.	CBC
	29.5.17		Quiet day. Relieved 5th K.S.L.I. in right sector of front line – 9th R.B. on left – 7th R.W. Kents on right. "A" Coy on right – "B" in centre – "D" on left – "C" in support. Quiet relief. 3 OR killed 4 OR wounded by lucky shot with "woord" bombs during relief. Relief complete 3.15 am on 30th	CBC
	30.5.17		Quiet day. Sudden thunderstorm in afternoon. Support company heavily gas shelled 3 men gassed. 2 OR killed 8 OR wounded.	EBC
	31.5.17		Quiet day. Sudden enemy barrage on front & support lines from 11.30pm to midnight. No casualties	CBC

EB Crawford. Capt & Adjt for Lt Col
Commdg. 5th Oxf & Bucks Lt Infty

Secret

War Diary.

5th Oxf & Bucks L.I.

1 June – 30 June.
1917.

Army Form C. 2118

WAR DIARY
CBC or of 5th Oxf & Bucks Lt. Infty
INTELLIGENCE SUMMARY.
(Erase heading not required.)

Place	Date	Hour	Summary of Events and Information	Remarks and references to Appendices
In the field	1.6.17		Comparitively Quiet day. Foster Avenue with gas and H.E. Shells from 7 pm to 11 pm went 1.O.R. slightly gassed 2. O.R. wounded.	CBC
	2.6.17		Quiet day. The Commanding Officer went on leave, leaving Major Barwell in Command. The enemy recaptured the post from the Division on our right during a relief. 1 O.R. wounded.	CBC
	3.6.17		A large enemy battleplane squadron continually patrolled over trenches from a low altitude from 5 am to 8 am without any interference. were relieved by 6th Duke of Cornwall's Lt. Infty. at 10.15 pm and proceeded to Coteul Switch. The relief was made rather difficult by a counter attack by 18th Division on our right on the post they lost on 2.6.17 1 O.R. seriously wounded.	CB.C.
	4.6.17		Rested in Coteul Switch until 8.16 pm and then moved off to the Rest Camp in Beaurains. Hostile aircraft over at night and dropped bombs on Arras in spite of unclear A.A M.G fire on our part.	CBC
	5.6.17		Training and reorganisation. Games in afternoon	CBC
	6.6.17		The G.O.C. Brigade inspected the camp in the morning. Drill in afternoon	CBC

Army Form C. 2118

WAR DIARY
or of 5th Oxf Bucks. Lt Infty.
INTELLIGENCE SUMMARY.
(Erase heading not required.) CBC

Instructions regarding War Diaries and Intelligence Summaries are contained in F. S. Regs., Part II. and the Staff Manual respectively. Title pages will be prepared in manuscript.

Place	Date	Hour	Summary of Events and Information	Remarks and references to Appendices
	7.6.17		Musketry - arms drill - and bathing in morning. Corps and Divisional Commanders visited lines - they remarked on the excellent turnout of the guard.	CBC
	8.6.17		Reveille 4 am; went for a route march of about 8 miles returning at about 9.30 am. There was a Commanding Officers conference at Bn HQ. at 5 pm.	CBC
	9.6.17		Reveille 3.30 am. Parade 5.20. Marched to MONCHIET — 6½ miles — arriving at 9 am. Went into huts. No one fell out on line of march. 1 O.R. killed by stray shell.	CBC
	10.6.17		Reveille 4.30 am. Parade 6 am. Marched to LAHERLIERE — 4½ miles — and went into billets.	CBC
	11.6.17		Reveille 3.50 am. Parade 5.50 am. Marched to RAINCHEVAL in heavy rain and went into billets	CBC
	12.6.17		Training.	CBC
	13.6.17		Left RAINCHEVAL and marched to LA ROSEL FARM where a recently vacated aerodrome was taken over. 2/Lt Symonds + 70 O.R. joined. C.O. returned off leave	CBC

Army Form C. 2118

WAR DIARY
or of 5th Oxf & Bucks Lt Infty.
INTELLIGENCE SUMMARY. CBC

(Erase heading not required.)

Instructions regarding War Diaries and Intelligence Summaries are contained in F. S. Regs., Part II. and the Staff Manual respectively. Title pages will be prepared in manuscript.

Place	Date	Hour	Summary of Events and Information	Remarks and references to Appendices
	14.6.17		Training. Very hot day Sports etc in evening	CBC
	15.6.17		Musketry – drill etc. Corps Commander visited the Aerodrome	CBC
	16.6.17		Training – musketry – Sgt Majors drill etc.	CBC
	17.6.17		Church Parade at 7. am. Baths. 2/Lt W LINE joined Battalion	CBC
	18.6.17		Reveille 4 am Route march 6 am – 28 men fell out – owing to heat etc	CBC
	19.6.17		Range practice + drill. Transport was inspected by D.C. Brigade at 4 pm	CBC
	20.6.17		Range practice + specialist training. Battalion sports in afternoon	CBC
	21.6.17		Ceremonial parade in the morning. B/gar N.C.O tested helmets in gas	CBC
	22.6.17		Range practice – drill – rapid loading	CBC
	23.6.17		Formation for attack carried out on a drill – Training	CBC
	24.6.17		Church Parade 9.30 am. Rest.	CBC
	25.6.17		Capt B.C. CRAWFORD left for leave 2/Lt J. TAYLOR Rose took over duties as Adjutant. Rest of Bn practice at drill.	JTR
			2/Lt J.A. STACE joined Battalion	JTR
	26.6.17		Divisional Horse Show. No parades on that account 36 other ranks joined Battalion	JTR
	27.6.17		Reveille 3 am Route March 4.30 am. No men fell out. 2/Lts LE DAVIS + E V MULLIS joined	JTR
			Battalion with 150 other Rank too.	

Army Form C. 2118

WAR DIARY of 5th Oxf Y Bucks Lt Infy

INTELLIGENCE SUMMARY. SR.

(Erase heading not required.)

Instructions regarding War Diaries and Intelligence
Summaries are contained in F. S. Regs., Part II.
and the Staff Manual respectively. Title pages
will be prepared in manuscript.

Place	Date	Hour	Summary of Events and Information	Remarks and references to Appendices
	28.6.17		Range practice and training – drill – rapid wiring – bombing.	SR
	29.6.17		Formation for attack carried out as a drill at 6am. Range practice & Coy. Training.	SR
	30.6.17		Inspection by O.C. Brigade of Drill Attack. Breakfast 5.30am. Parade 6.30am – 9am. Company training for Remainder of morning. 2/Lt H.N. PARKER struck off strength of Battalion.	SR

Frank W Cox
2/Lt MADJK
5th Oxf & Bucks Lt Infy

5th Oxf & Bucks Lt Infy

CONFIDENTIAL

War Diary

UNIT. 5th Oxfordshire & Buckinghamshire L. I.

PERIOD. 1st to 31st July 1917.

VOLUME No.

WAR DIARY
INTELLIGENCE SUMMARY

Army Form C. 2118

1st Bn of the 21st (?)

Place	Date	Hour	Summary of Events and Information	Remarks and references to Appendices
VERT GALANT	1-7-17		Church Parade. No Sports won by Batt.	
	2-7-17		Training	
	3-7-17		Capt S. R. Scholar rejoined & resumed duties of Adjutant	
	4-7-17		Training	
	5-7-17		2/Lt SKUCE joined & posted C Coy. Concert by 1st Army T.M. school	
	6-7-17		2/Lt R ENGLAND joined & posted A Coy	
	7-7-17		Sgt detained officers of Batt. rejoined 6th Letter	
	8-7-17		2/Lt A.F. HEARNE joined & posted D Coy. Football final. KSLI 1-11	
	9-7-17		Platoon field firing	
	10-7-17		Training in plan of opr. KSLI. 0-0	
	11-7-17		2/Lt PEEL met brigade vice Lt JACKS. Batt. at 11-20 hrs paraded & march to CANDAS to entrain. Train for marched at 1.15 p.m. Entrained completely 2¾ hrs am. A Coy joined party to arrive entraining site transport at AILLEUL	
MEULE HOUSE	12-7-17		Detrained at AILLEUL marched 2½ hrs to camp. Individually are training grounds	
	13-7-17		Training	
	14-7-17		Battalion with KSLI. 2/Lt HODLE joined. Posted to A Coy	
	15-7-17		Church Parade	

WAR DIARY 5th Bat'n / Bucks of Infy

or

INTELLIGENCE SUMMARY

(Erase heading not required.)

Army Form C. 2118.

Place	Date	Hour	Summary of Events and Information	Remarks and references to Appendices
	16.7.17		Training Specialist	
	17.7.17		Battalion Route march (10 miles) Strength 18 Off. 571 O.R. (11 Counting all Reinforcements) Very hot & dusty. The Commanding Officer, Adjt. & Coy Commanders visit WYTCHAETE.	
	18.7.17		Training (Specialist) Lecture by Officers of R.F.C. in "Contact Patrols"	
	19.7.17		Training (specialist)	
	20.7.17		Training (specialist) Officers visit R.F.C. Squadron at BAILLEUL	
	21.7.17		Training (specialist)	
	22.7.17		Church Parade	
	23.7.17		Attack demonstration in conjunction with R.F.C. connection with Planes, wireless. Fans, Signallers by KSLI at BAILLEUL.	
	24.7.17		Training (specialists)	
	25.7.17		Training (specialist's)	
	26.7.17		Battalion inspected by Army Commander. 2/Lt ENGLAND transferred from C Coy to B Coy	
	27.7.17		Training (specialists)	

Army Form C. 2118.

2/4 Bay of Bucks & Infy

WAR DIARY
or
INTELLIGENCE SUMMARY.
(Erase heading not required.)

Instructions regarding War Diaries and Intelligence Summaries are contained in F. S. Regs., Part II. and the Staff Manual respectively. Title pages will be prepared in manuscript.

Place	Date	Hour	Summary of Events and Information	Remarks and references to Appendices
	22.7.17		Training (specialist)	8/11
	29.7.17		Church Parade cancelled owing to rain	8/11
	30.7.17		Field day cancelled owing to rain. Lecture in Tents. Capt Crawford to hospital.	8/11
	31.7.17		Training Lecture in Tents in absence from NCOs.	
	1.8.17		Lt Cook reported to take over command of C Coy	8/11

M W Kennedy
a/Lt Col

Army Form C. 2118

WAR DIARY
of 5th Oxf. Bucks L.I.
INTELLIGENCE SUMMARY.
(Erase heading not required.)

Instructions regarding War Diaries and Intelligence Summaries are contained in F. S. Regs., Part II. and the Staff Manual respectively. Title pages will be prepared in manuscript.

Place	Date	Hour	Summary of Events and Information	Remarks and references to Appendices
Training (specialist)	1.8.17		Regiment continues training at this centre. Capt. Spring recommended new dress into Staff/Captain L.I. Bde	
	2.8.17		Training Active. Lt. Colonel Lord receives orders to proceed to Englard. Lt. Col. S.R. Sebastian M.C. assumes command of Battalion. Captain Spring assumes duties of Adjutant.	6"C"Coy
	3.8.17		Coy. short route marches by Companies. Lieut. Z. Cresswell proceed for duty posted	
	4.8.17		Coy. Training. Lt. Holiday assumes temporarily duties of Q.M. for F.M. Escorts granted leave FRY. Leave from 5.8.17 – 4.9.17. Lt Mullis detailed for Course at IX Corps school.	
	5.8.17		Church Parade. Orders received than from French area.	
	6.8.17		Battalion return from ST JANS CAPPEL & PRADELLES. Good billets.	
	7.8.17		Battalion parade under CO. for 2 hours normal day of regimental Coy. Commanders	
	8.8.17		Battalion Parade. All morning under CO. Results very good.	
	9.8.17		Battalion Route March 9 mls. no fall out. Major Kerr inspects Physical Training Afternoon by C.O. Palpelson with Lord Airey's Battalion	

WAR DIARY or INTELLIGENCE SUMMARY

Army Form C. 2118

Place	Date	Hour	Summary of Events and Information	Remarks and references to Appendices
in Bayonvillers etc.	10.6.17		Coys at specialist Training. Battalion Drill for 1 hr at 11 A.M. under Commanding Officer. Major General Lawson leaves Brigade to take Command of 56th Division.	
	11.6.17		Coys at Specialist Training. Inoculation in afternoon.	
	12.6.17		Church Parade. Tactical Scheme for Officers & NCOs under Major Parwell. The Brigadier watched the operation two places with the work done. Lts L.R.D. OWEN joined for instruction given by the Officers & NCOs. Lt S EGGINTON joined for duty reported to A Coy. duly reported to A Coy.	
	13.6.17		Battalion Route March (12 miles) 2 Casualties. The men marched well tho' very hot day.	
	14.6.17		Coys at disposal of their Commanders for Specialist Training. Lewis Gun & Bombing Competition in afternoon between Companies. Order received from the side that the BN was organised as a three platoon basis. The idea was that a full strength of good men hands a Battalion the GHQ minimum of 28 could soon be reached who is action.	

Army Form C. 2118.

WAR DIARY
of
INTELLIGENCE SUMMARY.
(Erase heading not required.)

Instructions regarding War Diaries and Intelligence Summaries are contained in F. S. Regs., Part II. and the Staff Manual respectively. Title pages will be prepared in manuscript.

Place	Date	Hour	Summary of Events and Information	Remarks and references to Appendices
	15		Battalion left BORRE Camp at 8.30am. and proceeded to OUDERDOM by lorry where relieved the reserve Brigade of 56th Division. Very heavy rain.	
	16		Rest. Organised for attack. Inspected model trenches in Bde. Corps area. Lecture by Intelligence Officer - 2nd Corps	
	17		Warning order to move forward received at 2am. I am ordered to move by lorry to CAFÉ BELGE on DICKE BUSCH - YPRES Rd. where bivouacked by field. Equipped for attack. Details sent to Transport Camp. 7pm. Battalion moved up to relieve 56th Division in GLENCORSE WOOD also relieving parts of Middlesex Regt. - Q.V.Rifles - Kensingtons - Rangers - Q.W.Rifles. On right "A" on left in JARGON TRENCH and SWITCH. "B" in support near YPRES - MENIN RD. at J.13.a.7.H. "C" in reserve in IGNORANCE TRENCH. Relief was gas shelled at ZILLEBEKE LAKE. Relief complete by 3am. 2/Lts J.T.ROSE and J.W.GUISE were wounded by smalls shell on way to trenches.	
	18		All trenches were found to be bad. At 3pm. and 7pm. JARGON SWITCH and Battn. HQ were heavily shelled - blowing in HQ. dug- out and burying many papers.	
	19		Fairly quiet "D" Coy. established a line of outposts in front of their line.	
	20		Fairly quiet.	

WAR DIARY
INTELLIGENCE SUMMARY.

Army Form C. 2118.

Place	Date	Hour	Summary of Events and Information	Remarks and references to Appendices
	21		Relieved by 5th K.S.L.I. - completed by 2 a.m.	
	22		"B" Coy. reinforced 43rd Infty. Bde.	
	23		Relieved 5th K.S.L.I.	
	24		Heavy Shelling (see attached)	
	25		Relieved by 3rd. R.B. and marched to CAFÉ BELGE	
	26		Moved to ABEELE area	
	27		Refitting	
	28		" and training	
	29		Marched to FLETRE and went into camp	
	30		Training and reorganization	
	31		" "	

15th. August.1917.	Moved in lorries from BORRE to Camp near OUDERDOM where we relieved Reserve Brigade of 56th. Division. Heavy Rain.
16th. August 1917.	Rest. Organisation for attack. Inspected model trenches 2nd. Corps area. Lecture by Intelligence Officer 2nd. Corps.
17th.	2 a.m. Warning order to move forward. 7 a.m. ordered to proceed by lorries to Cafe Belge on DICKIEBUSH - YPRES ROAD. Bivouacked in field. Equipped for attack. Details sent to Transport Camp. 7 p.m. Battalion moved up to relieve 56th. Division on GLENCORSE WOOD sector. We relieved parts of the 7th. Middlesex, Queen Victoria Rifles, Kensington Rangers, and Queens Westminsters. "D" Company on right, "A" on left in JARGON SWITCH and JARGON TRENCH. "B" in support round MENIN ROAD at J.13.a.7.4. "C" Company in reserve in IGNORANCE TRENCH. Relief went off without incident in spite of indifferent guides and some gas shelling by ZILLEBEKE LAKE. Relief complete about 3 a.m.
18th.	The whole area had been the scene of severe fighting and was greatly broken up with shell fire - all shell holes full of water. The trenches were all exceedingly bad, particularly those of "B" Company. At 3 p.m. and 7 p.m. the enemy shelled JARGON SWITCH and MENIN ROAD round Battalion H.Q. which were in the tunnel J.13.a.8.2. very heavily with 7.7's 4.2's and 5.9's. At 7.30 pm about they blew in H.Q. Dugout burying the F.O.O. and Adjutant. The F.O.O. went down sick and the Adjutant remained at duty. Nearly all papers were lost. The H.Q. Dugout was in a tunnel made by the enemy from about CLAPHAM JUNCTION to HOOGE which had been blown in several places. The portion occupied by Battalion H.Q. was full of water to a depth of some 4 inches or more. "C" Company found 2 working parties in JARGON SWITCH which accomplished their work in spite of shelling. At about midnight orders were received for a line of posts to be established from J.8.a.6.2. to J.14.a.9.5. and thence to J.14.a.6.2. "A" Company succeeded in putting out the posts on its front but "D" Company owing to the difficult ground was not able to do so.
19th.	4.30 a.m. A Corps further North attacked and the enemy put up a heavy barrage on our front which did not last very long. Apart from intermittent shelling all round the day was fairly quiet. In the morning the B.G.C. and the Brigade Major came to H.Q. and inquired if it was possible for a line of outposts to be established as ordered and were informed this could be done. During that night the line opposite "D" Company was established more or less. "D" Company was reinforced by a Lewis Gun team from "B" Company and "A" Company was reinforced by a Lewis Gun team from "C" Company.
20th.	The reports received showed that the line was not quite where intended. O.C. "D" Company was s ordered to correct the same that night before relief. During personnel reconnaisance that day Captain Royal-Dawson "D" Company found and had brought in a Sergeant of the Queen Victoria Rifles who had been out 6 days wounded. That night the line was established as ordered and handed over as such.

From midnight 23/4th to 3.30 a.m. 25th.

During the relief the enemy carried out an intermittent bombardment on JARGON SWITCH and the Strong Point J.14.a.3.2.

12.30 a.m. relief complete.

12.30 a.m. to 4 a.m. Bombardment gradually growing in intensity and heavy barrage kept up on MENIN ROAD round the A.D.S. The bombardment of these places did not cease until about 6 p.m.

4 a.m. Bombardment of great intensity, JARGON TRENCH being included. The outpost line was not shelled. During the night the 43rd. Brigade had much the same experience as this Battalion.

4.30 a.m. S.O.S. sent up by 43rd. Brigade. My right Company "D" sent up one S.O.S. light from the support trench to assist although no attack had been launched against him.

4.45 a.m. Heavy enemy bombing attack was launched against D.C.L.I. who were on my right, and my right Company D.C.L.I. fell back to the strong point and my right post conformed.

The enemy appeared to be making particular use of the trench running from J.14.a.1.0. to J.14.a.5.1. This trench was in the D.C.L.I. area the Battalion boundary being J.14.a.6.2.

Directly Captain Royal-Dawson knew what had happened, he himself with the support platoon went forward to restore the line and succeeded in doing so in the face of heavy machine gun fire.

At the same time Lieut. Jacks "B" Company went forward with a party to assist the D.C.L.I. round the Strong Point. Lieut. Jacks was wounded almost immediately and the party taken over by "D" Company. At 7.30 a.m. "D" Company were reinforced by Bombing squads of "A" and "C" Companies who were on the left.

5 a.m. Enemy begun bombing down the outpost line from point J.14.a.5.1. towards my right post and towards the Strong Point. Owing to a shortage of No. 23 Grenades the enemy got within close distance of my right post. Captain Royal-Dawson and 2/Lt. Line having been wounded 2/Lt. Mullis took Command of "D" Company. He formed a defensive flank from my right post towards the Strong Point and there held the enemy.

Soon afterwards Bombs were sent up. A bombing squad was sent to clear our trenche and the D.C.L.I. arranged to clear trench running to the Strong Point. Snipers were put out to catch the enemy if they tried to come over the top.

This bombing squad succeeded in driving the enemy out of the outpost line and the snipers shot many of them as they ran back. This bombing attack having failed the bombing attack towards the Strong Point also fizzled out. The enemy apparently got away down the trench up which they had come. At 9 a.m. I ordered up supports from "C" Company who were in JARGON SWITCH to assist the right and brought forward "C" Company K.S.L.I. to JARGON SWITCH and asked for a further Company of K.S.L.I. for the reserve.

10.15 a.m. Our field guns laid a barrage on my outpost line. The shooting was worst on the extreme right. It improved on the right after about half an hour but it remained on the centre and left all day, although it gradually died down.

2.45 p.m. I sent forward the remainder of "C" Company to reinforce "D" Company.

6 p.m. to midnight fairly quiet. At midnight shelling began again and between 2.30 am. and 4.30 am barrage was laid from JARGON SWITCH to MENIN ROAD and down the ROAD.

5th Bn. Oxf. & Bucks. Lt. Infty.

Casualties for period 17.8.17 to 24.8.17.

DATE.	Killed Offs.	Killed O.R.	Wounded Offs.	Wounded O.R.	Missing Offs.	Missing O.R.	Sick O.R.	Total Offs.	Total O.R.
17.8.17	1	-	1	2	-	-	-	2	2
18.8.17	-	-	-	13	-	-	-	-	13
19.8.17	-	10	-	29	-	-	-	1	39
20.8.17	-	-	-	9	-	-	-	1	9
21.8.17	-	-	-	-	-	-	-	1	-
22.8.17	-	10	2	72	-	2	23	2	107
23.8.17	-	3	3	109	-	3	-	4	115
24.8.17	1	-	-	1	-	-	-	-	1
TOTAL								8.	286.

Capt. O.S. Royal-Dawson Wounded 24.8.17. Died of Wounds 25.8.17.
" H.W. Spurge   "   23.8.17.
Lieut. T. Hutchison   "   23.8.17.
" O.L. Jacks   "   24.8.17.
2/Lt. J.W. Guise   "   17.8.17. Died of Wounds 19.8.17.
" J.J. Taylor-Rose   "
" W. Line   "   24.8.17
" L.E. Davis   "

Vol 29. 42/14 CONFIDENTIAL 28IJ
7 sheet

WAR DIARY

UNIT.   5th Oxf & Bucks L.I.

PERIOD.   1st to 30th September 1917

VOLUME No.

WAR DIARY
or
INTELLIGENCE SUMMARY. 5th Bucks & Bucks L Infy.

Army Form C. 2118.

Place	Date	Hour	Summary of Events and Information	Remarks and references to Appendices
	Sept 1st		Marched to NEUVE EGLISE Area (28 1/40,000 S 18 C & 3) The Commanding Officer, Coy Commanders & Assistant Adjutant went on in advance to reconnoitre the line	WD
	2nd		Marched to Reserve Battalion where relieved 2nd Royal Scots Lothian. Relieved 1/7th Bn Manchester Regt in Right Front Sector, commencing at 8 pm and completing at 1.15 am on 3rd. "B" on right, "C" on left, "D" in Support – "A" in Reserve. 9th K.R.R.C. on our left. 2nd Sherwood Foresters on Right. The relief was completed without any casualties. Heard that Lieut ENGLAND who had gone on to the trenches in advance had been wounded by a bullet on 1st. Commanding Officer went round the line – no wires – had trenches – no work attempted – no communications	WD
	3rd		Quiet day. Concentrated on wiring. Digging new and improving old communication trenches also deepening and the scraping the fire trenches at night.	WD
	4th		Quiet day continued with work commenced on 3rd	WD
	5th		Quiet day continued with work commenced on 4th. Two of "B" Company Posts were approached by the enemy in early morning. They were driven off by bombs and L.G. fire. Suffering casualties. Slight rain.	WD
	6th		Very quiet day. Were relieved by 9th Rifle Bde. Relief complete by 3 am and went into Reserve at BRISTOL CASTLE. Total casualties during tour. 1 officer and 6 OR wounded	WD
	7th		Rest – 130 men of D Coy for work under 62nd Coy R.E. "A" Coy ordered back into reserve owing to the weakness of 9th R.B. – moved off at 8 pm.	WD

Army Form C. 2118.

WAR DIARY
or
INTELLIGENCE SUMMARY.

(Erase heading not required.)

5th Bn Oxf & Bucks Lt Infy

Place	Date	Hour	Summary of Events and Information	Remarks and references to Appendices
	8th Sept		Rest – Training of 2 new L.G. Teams per Company – 140 men working at night. 2/Lieut E. LIDINGTON joined the Battalion – 1 O.R. of "A" Coy wounded. 130 men work at night.	W.D.O.
	9th "		Fine day – slight shelling with 8 inch in afternoon – no damage resulting – 140 men for work at night.	W.D.O.
	10th "		Relieved by 8th K.R.R.C. at 7am and marched to ALDERSHOT CAMP by Platoons at 200× distance. – "A" Coy arrived at 12 midnight.	W.D.O.
	11th "		Fine day – Company and Platoon drill – Lewis Gun Training – 50 O.R. of "B" Coy. for work in evening – 2/Lieut H. VAUGHAN joined the Battalion.	W.D.O.
	12th "		Fine day – Baths and Training – Lewis Gunners on range – 2/Lieut H.D.C. CAMPBELL joined the Battalion and is posted to "C" Coy – 50 men of "C" Coy on working party at night.	W.D.O.
	13th "		The whole Battalion on a working party – digging Practice Trenches for 141st Brigade near NEUVE EGLISE – Lewis Gunners left out for Training. A Court Martial was held in the Camp during afternoon.	W.D.O.
	14th "		Fine day – "A" Coy on Range remainder on Drill etc. 2/Lieut HODLE to Hospital officers relieved Sergeants in afternoon (2 0CC) 2/Lieut BANKS rejoined off leave.	W.D.O.

Army Form C. 2118.

WAR DIARY
or
INTELLIGENCE SUMMARY.
(Erase heading not required.)   5th Oxf & Bucks Lt Infty

Instructions regarding War Diaries and Intelligence Summaries are contained in F.S. Regs., Part II. and the Staff Manual respectively. Title pages will be prepared in manuscript.

Place	Date	Hour	Summary of Events and Information	Remarks and references to Appendices
	15th Sep		Marched to DOULIEU Area and went into very scattered billets 4 men fell out on line of march - 60 men of "A" Coy left for work - reported by motor lorry. Commanding Officer lectured all officers at 5.30 p.m. on Organization etc.	W.D.O
	16th		Very fine day. Church Parade at 9.30am Voluntary firing on the ranges by "B"&"D"Coys. Lieut ANDERSON reported off a course held at ST OMER.	W.D.O
	17th		Fine day. B & D Coys on their ranges the whole day A & C Drill etc. Commanding Officer Conference at Brigade H.Q at DOULIEU at 2.30 p.m. Captain LABOUCHERE and Lieut SYMONDS rode to ARMENTIERES to reconnoitre the trenches (the Brigade is temporarily in Reserve to the 57th Division.) 2/Lieut M.F.FRITZ joined Battalion and posted to "C" Company.	W.D.O
	18th		Marched to BULFORD CAMP (28 T 26 a 5.9) Starting at 1.30pm and arriving at 4.30 pm 5 men fell out. Found the Camp to be most excellent, with small range attached.	W.D.O
	19th		Very hot day. Battalion Parade in the morning also Platoon training. 1 man wounded by a splinter from a shell fired at an observation balloon. 2/Lieut A.E. JARRETT reported off a L.G. Course. Information received that Capt. SPURGE died of wounds on 14th Sept.	W.D.O
	20th		Platoon Training. "B" Coy on the range in the afternoon. Brig General FORSTER and Major PAGET dined at the mess. The Officers played the Officers of the 9th KRRC at football in the afternoon and lost (2-1) by one goal at the expense of 1 casualty. 2/Lieut FITZGERALD strained his ankle)	W.D.O

(A7092). W1. W12859/M1293. 75,000. 1/17. D.D. & L., Ltd. Forms/C2118/14.

Army Form C. 2118.

WAR DIARY
or
INTELLIGENCE SUMMARY.
(Erase heading not required.)   5th Batt. 1 Bucks. [Infantry]

Instructions regarding War Diaries and Intelligence Summaries are contained in F. S. Regs., Part II. and the Staff Manual respectively. Title pages will be prepared in manuscript.

Place	Date	Hour	Summary of Events and Information	Remarks and references to Appendices
	21st Sept		Very fine day. "B" Coy on the range in the morning. Platoon Training by the other Companies. "C" Coy used the range for Lewis Guns during the afternoon. The Brigade Guard (1 Sgt. 1 Bugler 6 O.R.) was supplied by "C" Coy. 2/Lieut FITZGERALD & CAMPBELL to Field Ambulance.	W.D.O
	22nd		Fine day - Platoon Training. Officers servants fired in a competition on the Camp Range. 2/Lieut FORD rejoined off leave. Capt. COOKE'S groom wounded in NEUVE EGLISE.	W.D.O
	23rd		320 men on various working parties - Church Parade at 9.45am. Band played in the afternoon. 2/Lieut G.E.PAYNE and 8 NCO's rejoined off Pioneer Course with 11th Kings Liverpools. 2/Lieut F.LIDINGTON & 8 NCO's went on same course.	W.D.O
	24th		Fine day. Battalion attended Gas Demonstration in the afternoon by Divisional Gas Officer, a very good show and quite interesting. The Assistant Adjutant had his usual unsteady working party on the miniature range.	W.D.O
	25th		Very hot day. "C" Coy found Brigade Guard Company and Platoon Training. Men who did not attend yesterday's Gas Demonstration went with 9th K.R.R.C. at 10 am.	W.D.O
	26th		The Adjutant left at 6.30 am on a month's entirely undeserved leave. We played the Shropshires in the afternoon, and beat them (2-0) against a good game. Four men sent to 42nd M.G.Coy.	W.D.O

Army Form C 2118.

WAR DIARY
or
INTELLIGENCE SUMMARY
(Erase heading not required.)

5th Bn. Oxf. & Bucks. L. Infy.

Instructions regarding War Diaries and Intelligence Summaries are contained in F. S. Regs. Part II. and the Staff Manual respectively. Title pages will be prepared in manuscript.

Place	Date	Hour	Summary of Events and Information	Remarks and references to Appendices
	27th Sept		Fine day. Lewis Gun tests were fired on the range, taking nearly all day. Four new officers arrived Lieut. CHOATE & 2nd Lieuts. "A" Coy ADDINGTON & HORNCASTLE to C and BALDWIN to "D". About 9.45 p.m we were bombed with very unfortunate results. 1 bomb dropping straight on a "C" Coy hut. Six men were killed and 13 wounded.	W.D.O.
	28th		At 7.0 a.m. the Battalion started up to relieve the 6th K.O.Y.L.I at BRISTOL CASTLE. The relief passed off without incident. 2nd Lieut. OWEN was left out of the time, and a class for R.S.M. & 2 N.C.Os Per Company. The day was quiet and we started up to front line to relieve 5th SOMERSET L.T. INFY in the same line as was occupied before.	W.D.O.
	29th		During night there was intermittent shelling of back area, but the front line was quiet. "B" Coy suffered 3 casualties from a rare bomb. Everybody hard at work at night wiring and improving trenches and fitting U frames.	W.D.O.
	30th		From 4.15 to 7.0 a.m. heavy strafe between support and reserve lines causing "C" Coy 8 casualties one of who was C.S.M WILLIAMS. The weather was mostly and the Boche seemed to be afraid of an attack, everything goes to shew he is very windy. Rest of day quiet.	W.D.O.

L.N. D. Owen 2/Lieut.
5th Oxford & Bucks L. Infy.

WAR DIARY
INTELLIGENCE SUMMARY

Army Form C. 2118.

5th Bn Oxford & Bucks L.I.

Place	Date	Hour	Summary of Events and Information	Remarks and references to Appendices
	1.x.17		A day rather troubled by minnies in the early morning. Capt Mullis' H.Q. being blown in, also from start to finish 8.0 am minnies. The day was quiet. Lieut FRITZ who is acting as Intelligence Officer Tried to capture a them along the bank of the DOUVE that was just too late.	A.A.
	2.x.17		A very quiet night and another lovely day to follow. D Coy had two more men killed this morning by a T.M. The men have done a lot of work this tour, wiring and putting in W/T radio; probably we had perfect weather. The 9th R.B. relieved us at night; relief complete being reported at 11.15 p.m. On relief we go back to Bristol Castle once again.	A.A.
	3.x.17		Weather inclined to break; light rain falling at times. The Lewis Gun class is continued and we just manage to make up the required working parties without taking in the class. 7 new Officers joined us from the Transport Camp. 7/Lts. Thorntz and Iranson going to 'A' Company, Battles and Fawcett to 'B', Jourdi and Scott to 'C' and Litchfield to 'D'. 'A' Company had the usual trouble with R.E. guides on the working party.	A.A.
	4.x.17		Much colder this morning and ground getting very dirty. All spare men put on improving trenches and building Elephant shelters. Demand for working parties not so heavy. only 150 instead of 220 as last night. Towards evening the Huns indulged in a little area shelling in our neighborhood; no damage done.	A.A. 29.D stat
	5.x.17		More shelling in the early morning. 'C' Company again suffering. Weather very cold and stormy again. At 6 p.m. orders for relief were suddenly cancelled; move up north exploded; lightly shelled again at night.	A.A.

Army Form C. 2118.

WAR DIARY
or
INTELLIGENCE SUMMARY.
(Erase heading not required.)

Instructions regarding War Diaries and Intelligence Summaries are contained in F. S. Regs., Part II. and the Staff Manual respectively. Title pages will be prepared in manuscript.

Place	Date	Hour	Summary of Events and Information	Remarks and references to Appendices
	6.x.17		A lot of work done on trenches and shelters. No working parties called for and only one carrying party.	
	7.x.17		Cold wet day again. Go up to visit "B" Coy in the Carbo line in the afternoon, if find them pretty happy. Reconnoitring party from 33rd Div. round about tea time.	
	8.x.17		Relieved by 1st Connaughts at 7.0 am. relief complete being reported at 10.45. On relief march back to Bedford Camp. Very wet afternoon and evening. "B" Coy who were left in the Carbo Line on reconno to the R.B.'s arrived in camp about 11.45 pm. thoroughly wet through.	
	9.x.17		A quiet day; spent in cleaning up. 1 hours battalion parade in the afternoon. Orders to move to BERTHEN and omnibus this at night.	
	10.x.17		We leave camp at 10 am. reaching our destination — an old billets near THIEUSHOOK at 2 pm. Rather cramped quarters for the men but everyone soon gets settled in. Nearly misfortune was that the officers mess cart failed to arrive till about 3.30 pm. Orders to move tomorrow up beyond DICKEBUSH came in at 6.	
	11.x.17		A start made for BEDFORD HOUSE at 9.30. Men fell out badly for the first 2 hours but after a drink of tea near LA CLYTTE they pulled themselves together and only one fell out for the rest of the march. We eventually arrived about 5 pm after marching 13 miles. Our accommodation was found to consist of one ruined house and a dirty open field; but everyone settled down pretty soon. The cookers which we luckily brought with us feeding the men with a good meal, the officers mess cart and valise eventually turned up about 9.30 pm.	

(A7092). Wt. W12839/M1293. 75,000. 1/17. D. D. & L., Ltd. Forms/C.2118/14.

Army Form C. 2118.

WAR DIARY
or
INTELLIGENCE SUMMARY.

(Erase heading not required.)

5th Coy 1st Bucks Regt

Instructions regarding War Diaries and Intelligence Summaries are contained in F. S. Regs., Part II. and the Staff Manual respectively. Title pages will be prepared in manuscript.

Place	Date	Hour	Summary of Events and Information	Remarks and references to Appendices
	12.x.17		We came in for a heavy storm of rain in the early morning, and arrival of the men shelters were flooded out; but they soon got down to it after breakfast and made themselves some very decent shelters. We also had the help of 2 R.E. NCOs to put up some temporary huts, and everyone got pretty comfortable by night. Showers of rain fell at intervals all night and all day and the mud became pretty bad round H.Q. before long.	M
	13.x.17		Still the same sort of weather. 'A' Coy went off early on a carrying party for the RE's and lost one man killed just outside Zillebeke. A lot of work put in clearing up the camp area and putting up more huts under R.E. supervision. About 4pm we were ordered to move back to RIDGE WOOD where the rest of the Brigade are, the R.B.'s taking our place here.	M
	14.x.17		Quite a fine morning. B'Coy. [?] made a carrying party as yesterday, and were Intercommunicated. We drove BEDFORD HOUSE soon after noon, having in our 3 days stay made the beginning of quite a good camp there. Our new camp turns out to be rather a miserable affair, no dark having been done on it apparently, but we all squash in at last. HQ settling down very comfortably.	M
	15.x.17		Bright sunny day. Very busy getting ready to go up the line tomorrow. The Corps Commander looked in in the morning, but nothing was said of the status of the camp. E.A's very active in the early evening dropping bombs but we managed to escape all night and HQ mess celebrated its escape with a most successful rum dinner.	M
	16.x.17		We leave RIDGE WOOD at 11am and halted for lunch just off the ZILLEBEKE ROAD. The sector we are to take over appears to be a pretty dusty one in both sense of the word	M

WAR DIARY
INTELLIGENCE SUMMARY

Army Form C. 2118.

5th Bedford & Books [?]

Place	Date	Hour	Summary of Events and Information	Remarks and references to Appendices
	16.X.17 (cont'd)		Our night is to be on the MENIN ROAD and we are left on the SCHERRIABEEK, the right flank apparently being in the air. So far as we know we are only to hold the line till the one coming up for "storm what will happen in the YPRES sector. At 3:30 we move off again and push up our guides again on PLUMERS DRIVE just below TOR TOP. From there onwards we ran into a lot of shelling and when we reached CHAPHAM JUNCTION we found a heavy barrage ready for us. The men are very happy. Later with Capt ELTON says nothing but thanks to some excellent guides they Coys moved up and got through with comparatively few casualties – Casualties about 40 - Considering the intensity of the fire but HUTCHINSON unfortunately was among the wounded and "A" Coy H.Q. suffered severely. One Coy were sent HOOZ INVERNESS COPSE in and one got out of HI charge and from there across the valley was like walking in R.F. during company Pac. 9:30 am really a very fine piece of work.	14
	17.X.17		Enemy artillery and snipers were pretty active all night and casualties kept coming in. The morning turned out bright and calm but quite cold. A pleasant change from yesterday. from 9am = 11:30 the Boche artillery was very active round SPLITIR. H.Q. but our full boo was pretty solid and we didn't worry much. For the rest of the day all was fairly quiet. Even a chance to dry the trenches don't seem so bad, but a very little wet would make them almost untenable. The support Coys. A & D have a full Bac and fair HQ but neither of the front line companies have any accommodation at all.	14
	18.X.17		There was pretty heavy shelling all night most of which missed the front line except for one unlucky hit which wounded Capt Ford and 2/Lt. Clowers.	16

WAR DIARY
INTELLIGENCE SUMMARY.
5th Battn. e Bucks [?]

Army Form C. 2118.

Place	Date	Hour	Summary of Events and Information	Remarks and references to Appendices

18.x.17 (cont'd) — Pte White was also wounded in the support line. Rain fell early in the morning and made the trenches very wet, but fairly dried up a little during the day. About midday we received a message from the Brigade saying what it would entail 2 days longer in the line and then the last Brigade up the next tour; we said yes of course. On the strength of that 'A' and 'D' Coys relieved 'B' and 'C' in the front line; relief was not complete till 3am owing to spasmodic shelling with H.E. and gas. The Boche was apparently using 9cm H.E shells and several of our fellows were caught out by it. From 10 P.M. there was very heavy shelling north of us by the Bosches I think, but it was very hard to tell.

19.x.17 — Yesterday we had 2 Lt. Bobs. to visit us; today we have they Brigadier & B.M's see anything about the ground for a push to be made in this front in about a week from now; following on them we have some Tank Officers & all sorts of other Japan parts admit that at intervals during the day. Shelling intermittent all day; we seem to be keeping up our average of 20 Casualties a day. More rain at midday makes the trenches very wet and the apology for a C.T. leading up to the front line is about 2½ feet in much. About 6 P.M. there was an S.O.S. scare just north of us with the result that the shelling was heavier than usual all night.

20.x.17 — At 11am the Boche put down 15mm annihilating fire from our support line backwards with the result that we had 6 killed and 114 wounded; the stretchers behind us suffered pretty heavily too. I fancy more visitors in the early morning from the 7th D.L.I., all of them seemed very optimistic about their show. Fine dry day; things much quieter. Our heavies put in some indifferent shooting on GHELUVELT CHURCH in the afternoon; altogether they seem rather off colour at present, our front line hardly gets as favourable attention for them.

Army Form C. 2118.

WAR DIARY
or
INTELLIGENCE SUMMARY.
(Erase heading not required)

5th Coy 1st Bucks L.I.

Place	Date	Hour	Summary of Events and Information	Remarks and references to Appendices
	21.x.17		Very fine day. Shoe waters crowded in at intervals in the morning; up to the present in 5 days we have had 21 hostiles. We are relieved by the Rifle Brigade about 6pm, relief being complete at 10.30pm. Guides going out by no means hit thanks to Flt. Hts we got through all night luckily the Boche was pretty quiet and we had few casualties.	[A]
	22.x.17		In taking over the new line we had C, D & B. Coys in the front and A in reserve with 2 platoons south of the MENIN ROAD. 'C' Coy managed to crowd into H free-tences and no did U platoon of A; all the rest were in open trenches which were very little improvement on the ones we had just left except that they were a bit drier. At 5.30am an Army barrage came down, & the Boche retaliated pretty strongly. Our front line was badly shelled B & D suffering severely though there were few casualties there might have been expected. 2/Lt SHERWOOD was unfortunately killed. We crammed in B platoon of D Coy in the free tences round Battln. HQ as soon as things quietened down, which saved a lot of casualties later on. Early in the morning 2/Lt. Lidington of 'B' Coy was hit rather severely and a few more casualties caused in the same Coy. The night was a little quieter.	[A]
	23.x.17		As soon as it got late 'C' Coy relieved 'B' Coy, the relief passing off without incident. We had a lot of trouble over rations in the morning all rations being taken by mistake to the 1st Rifle Brigade and our fellows not having the same to bring up those of the S; however all was fixed up eventually. Every day now we get 2 Army on Boche Barrages but the Boche seems to reply too and each time, which we are not doing for. 2nd Lieuts. of 'A' and Litchfield of 'B' are wounded in the evening. This has been a most unfortunate tour so regards officers casualties.	[A]

Army Form C. 2118.

WAR DIARY
or
INTELLIGENCE SUMMARY.
(Erase heading not required.)

5th Oxf & Bucks Lt Infy

Instructions regarding War Diaries and Intelligence Summaries are contained in F. S. Regs., Part II. and the Staff Manual respectively. Title pages will be prepared in manuscript.

Place	Date	Hour	Summary of Events and Information	Remarks and references to Appendices
	24.x.17		Considerable activity in the air all day; in the afternoon we had about 40 aeroplanes up for about 3 hours. Our relief tonight is to be a pretty complicated affair, 3 battalions relieving us, the 15th Warwicks, 9th Devons and 1st R.W. Kents. The 1st party of relief arrived about 6.15 and after a little trouble all was complete at 10.30 p.m. Most fortunately the Boche was very quiet and we only had about 14 casualties from start to finish. On relief the Batt. went down to SHRAPNEL CORNER where there was hot tea and rum waiting and was taken in lorries straight off to billets in the BERTHEN area. All arrangements worked wonderfully well and everybody was in by 6.30 am. Total of casualties during this tour in the line is 10 Officers killed and 7 wounded 20 O.R. killed 4 missing and 114 wounded & gassed	///
	25.x.17		Most of the day spent in sleeping. Men seem to be fairly comfortable billeted only very few bell tents being in use.	///
	26.x.17		Companies at disposal of Company Commanders. 2/Lt. Brindley and Lieut-Lieut. rejoin the Battn. Lt. Ellis joined up from the M.G.C. while the Battn. was in the line on the 18th.	///
	27.x.17		Fine autumn day. 2/Lt. Haywood left the Battn. for the R.F.C. 2/Lt. Brocwell went to England for a course at HYTHE.	///

Army Form C. 2118

WAR DIARY
or
INTELLIGENCE SUMMARY.

(Erase heading not required.)

5th Oxford & Bucks L. Infy.

Instructions regarding War Diaries and Intelligence Summaries are contained in F. S. Regs., Part II. and the Staff Manual respectively. Title pages will be prepared in manuscript.

Place	Date	Hour	Summary of Events and Information	Remarks and references to Appendices
	28th		Bright sunny day. Church Parade with M.G.C. & T.M.B.	
	29th		Baths allotted the Battn today. The Colonel goes on leave. H.Q. Guard very much better.	
	30th		Training starts at present entirely individual & specialist. A match was arranged with the Shropshires, but unfortunately rain made the ground too wet and it had to be postponed.	
	31st		A. & B. Coys on the range all day firing at 25 yards, unfortunately the firing point is very muddy which rather interferes with good shooting. Inter-Platoon football competition started this afternoon. 3 ties are played off.	

Myard Capt & Adjt
5th Oxf & Bucks L. Infy.

Confidential

War Diary

5th Oxf & Bucks L.I.

1st to 30th November 1917.

Volumn No.

A.C.D 424

42nd Inf Bde

Herewith "War Diary of the Battalion under my command for the month of November 1917.

1/12/17

J.L. Grinnord Capt & Adj for Lt. Col
Commanding 5th Service Bn
Oxford & Bucks. Lt. Infy.

WAR DIARY
INTELLIGENCE SUMMARY.
(Erase heading not required.)

Army Form C. 2118

Instructions regarding War Diaries and Intelligence Summaries are contained in F. S. Regs., Part II. and the Staff Manual respectively. Title pages will be prepared in manuscript.

Place	Date	Hour	Summary of Events and Information	Remarks and references to Appendices
	1.XI.17		'C' and 'D' Coys on the range. Capt. B.K.COOKE leaves the Battn. to go to the Brigade. Lt. PEEL taking his place as Transport Officer.	11/5/nov/17
	2.XI.17		Football match with Brigade H.Q. which we won 3-2. Two hours night work in S.B.R's from 5-30 – 6-30 p.m.	11/5/nov/1
	3.XI.17		Cold nasty day. Had route march round to PRADELLES; no one fell out. Inoculation parade in the afternoon.	11/5/nov/1
	4.XI.17		Very cold church parade service. A scratch rugger match was got up in the afternoon; few of the players had ever played before, but with a little practice we shall get a side together.	11/5/nov/1
	5.XI.17		Bright sunny day. 'A' and 'B' Coys firing on the range at 200 yds. shooting very indifferent owing to bad light. Wishing and cursed comes in that we shall be required for work in forward area in a day or so.	11/5/nov/1
	6.XI.17		Battalion move by bus at midday to a camp 1 kilo. north of YPRES. Everyone accommodated in tents, of which the supply is plentiful; the camp is said to be in a good condition.	11/5/nov/1
	7.XI.17		Working party of 300 found to work on light railway running to ZONNEBEKE from 10-30 to 3 p.m. Regeneration apparently very poor. A party of 15 also found as emergency break-down gang on the line at night.	11/4/nov/1
	8.XI.17		Same work as yesterday. But parties leave camp at 6.10 and return at 3.15 p.m. The R.E's still send work for the parties, and there is considerable murmuring on the track. As it is decided to send the men on in relief, 2 officers at a time, in future. Work in camp goes on steadily, making paths between the tents, and shelter for the cookers etc. The weather luckily is dry, but the ground in camp if moisture no wet as ever.	11/5/nov/1
	9.XI.17		'A' and 'B' Coys leave at 6.10 a.m.; 'C', 'D' and H.Q. at 9.10 for work. We are informed in the afternoon that the method of work is not approved of by the A.D.L.R., so we shall have to return to the original plan. The tents occupied by three cyclist orderlies who unfortunately hit by a bomb just before 7 a.m.; I was killed and 2 wounded; these are the first casualties we have had up here.	11/5/nov/1
	10.XI.17		Miserable wet day. 2/Lt. STACE leaves for 2nd. Army Lewis Course. 2/Lt. FRITZ for 2nd. Army Sniping Course. The Colonel returns from leave.	11/5/nov/1
	11.XI.17		Huns rather more active in shelling the back area today.	11/5/nov/1
	12.XI.17		5 bombs were dropped on the camp this morning about 8 a.m., but luckily no damage was done. Having got	11/5/nov/1

WAR DIARY or INTELLIGENCE SUMMARY

Army Form C. 2118.

Place	Date	Hour	Summary of Events and Information	Remarks and references to Appendices
	12.XI.17 (Contd)		Afternoon from the Dugouts, we return to the method of working the reliefs, not quite to the satisfaction of the Canadian Engineers I think. 'B' Coy. were slightly shelled on the limbers and lost 1 mule killed and 2 slightly injured.	
	13.XI.17		A misty morning, but the sun came out bright before midday. A camp a quarter of a mile from ours was heavily bombed about 9.30 a.m. but little damage was done. 'B' Company had another slight casualty in the afternoon. 3 new Officers arrived. 2/Lts. WILSON, TURNER and THEOBALD.	
	14.XI.17		A heavy mist all day. Artillery on both sides less active.	
	15.XI.17		The work on the Railway is progressing very satisfactorily, and the shelling has been less the last 2 or 3 days. Some Bombs dropped some way from here near the Theosophic Camp about 6 p.m.	
	16.XI.17		'A' and 'B' Companies return early from work in the afternoon owing to heavy shelling. Bivvies made and put up to mark the graves of Capt. HOGAN, 2/Lt. SMITH and 2/Lt. NEWISS and the men of the battalion killed in action in 1916. 2/Lt. WILSON who slightly gassed on the working party and 2 O.R. wounded.	
	17.XI.17		Thick mist all day. Artillery quiet.	
	18.XI.17		Weather still continues dry but misty. 2/Lt. PAYNE leaves for X Corps Gas School for a week's course.	
	19.XI.17		Enemy artillery more than usually active in back areas and YPRES. Work on the railway progressing satisfactorily. 2/Lts. LANE and RICE join.	
	20.XI.17		A wet stormy night.	
	21.XI.17		Work on the railway almost completed.	
	22.XI.17		Working parties considerably troubled by shell fire; luckily there were no casualties.	
	23.XI.17		Bright sunny day. E.A.'s very active.	
	24.XI.17		Strong wind all day. Ground drying up again well.	
	25.XI.17		Very cold wind blowing with occasional storms. One or two of the corrugated iron shelters blown down.	

Army Form C. 2.

WAR DIARY
INTELLIGENCE SUMMARY.
(Erase heading not required.)

Instructions regarding War Diaries and Intelligence Summaries are contained in F. S. Regs., Part II. and the Staff Manual respectively. Title pages will be prepared in manuscript.

Place	Date	Hour	Summary of Events and Information	Remarks and references to Appendices
	26.XI.17		The laying of the rails is finished today and the working parties are now engaged in ballasting and ditching. Very wet night.	1/15 War?
	27.XI.17		Slightly warmer today. We hear we are to be relieved on the 2nd. of next month and move back to BRANDHOEK.	1/15 War?
	28.XI.17		Orders for move cancelled: we are to be relieved by 307th Division tomorrow and move back to WINNEZEELE. Very quiet day	1/15 War?
	29.XI.17		The whole battalion goes up to work in the morning. Bright sunny day; considerable artillery activity on our back areas. We entrain at YPRES at 4.15pm. and reach WINNEZEELE about 8.30. Battalion marches very well from GODESWARDESVELDE. Billets in all cases except for 'A' Company good, but scattered.	1/15 War?
	30.XI.17		'A' Company move to a better and more central billet in the village. Everyone settled in very comfortably.	1/15 War?

War Diary

5th Oxf & Bucks L. I.

December 1917.

Volumn

42nd Inf Bde

Herewith War Diary for the
Month of December 1917 for the
Battalion under my Command. Please

/18.

H. Dumont Capplett, for Lt. Col.
Commanding 5th Service Btn.
Oxford & Bucks. Lt. Infy.

WAR DIARY.

INTELLIGENCE SUMMARY. 5th Bap & Bucks L. Infy

(Erase heading not required.)

Army Form C. 21

Instructions regarding War Diaries and Intelligence Summaries are contained in F. S. Regs., Part II. and the Staff Manual respectively. Title pages will be prepared in manuscript.

Place	Date	Hour	Summary of Events and Information	Remarks and references to Appendices
	1-XII-17		Lewis Gunners on miniature range all morning. Lecture by Commanding Officer to Officers and Sergeants in Lunch standing orders in the evening	1/1
	2-XII-17		Battalion fired Brigade Guard, first turn out. Revolver practice on range for Officers and N.C.O.'s Lewis Gunners.	1/1
	3-XII-17		Cold frosty day. Battn. moved to VLAMERTINGHE, starting at 8.55a.m., and arriving about 2p.m. Everyone accommodated in empty houses; rather crowded	1/1
	4-XII-17		Issuing of greatcoats, inspections etc. 3 new Officers arrived from BUCKS Yeomanry, Capt. C. DEYNS, Lt. THOMAS & 2nd Lt. COOKE.	1/1
	5-XII-17		Several bombs dropped on the Town in the early morning, no damage done.	1/1
	6-XII-17		Bright cold day. 4 Lewis Guns sent up the line to protect 18 pounder Batteries against E.A's. 3 Battalions of the Brigade started for work in forward area, as it looks as if we should not see the line this tour.	1/1
	7-XII-17		Orders received that the Brigade will move into Divisional Support tomorrow. Training in wiring & consolidation of shell-holes carried out.	1/1
	8-XII-17		Battalion entrains at BRANDHOEK at 4.15p.m. Some uncertainty owing to contradictory orders as to location of camp; but everyone was finally settled by 7p.m. A-D & HQ Companies at CALIFORNIA CAMP some 1000 yards EAST of WELTJE, B&C Companies near ST. JEAN. CALIFORNIA CAMP consisted of full-bored and small elephant shelters B&C Companies were much more comfortably settled in Nissen Huts	1/1
	9-XII-17		Carrying parties of 120 found mostly to carry trench boards for the R.E. About 5-30p.m. H.Q. Company moved	1/1

Army Form C. 2118

WAR DIARY
or
INTELLIGENCE SUMMARY. 5th Bn. 1 Bucks L. Infty.

(Erase heading not required.)

Instructions regarding War Diaries and Intelligence Summaries are contained in F. S. Regs., Part II. and the Staff Manual respectively. Title pages will be prepared in manuscript.

Place	Date	Hour	Summary of Events and Information	Remarks and references to Appendices
	9.XII.17 (Contd)		down to the camp occupied by B&C.	1/1
	10.XII.17		B&C Companies on working parties for R.E. on a light railway. A&D. carrying for Hugo Runposts. Cold frosty day.	1/1
	11.XII.17		No working parties found. B&C companies relieve A&D. at CALIFORNIA CAMP. Three of the four Lewis Gun teams sent to R.F.A. H.Q. ago are relieved; casualties 1t killed 1 wounded.	1/1
	12.XII.17		4 Lewis Gun teams lent the Battalion by the 60th to replace those lent to the R.F.A. The Battalion leaves camp for the line about 7-30pm. route via KANSAS X, GRAVENSTAFEL, BELLEVUE, we take over for the 6th D.C.L.I., B.&C.Companies in front, D Company & HQ at METCHELE. What trenches there are arn'nt good & fairly dry.	1/1
	13.XII.17		Relief complete about 1-30am., very few casualties, amongst whom is 2/Lt. TURNER, slightly wounded. The front companies are very much on their own, HQ being too far away to have much control. Dry day, bad visibility.	1/1
	14.XII.17		Fairly quiet day. E.A's active nousual in the early morning. A few casualties in the reserve company.	1/1
	15.XII.17		Bright, cold day. Enemy fairly quiet. Relieved by 6th. D.C.L.I. Apparently trench foot is the great trouble in this line; 1/1 Ot & 143rd. Brigades have suffered heavily with it. So far we have had 2 cases. Relief complete 1-45am.	1/1
	16.XII.17		Several casualties occurred during the relief the Boche apparently having spotted it. 2/Lt. LANE was slightly wounded. Total battle casualties during the tour, 3 Officers wounded, 30 O.R. killed & 18 wounded. The Battalion returns to HASLER CAMP near St. JEAN; everyone pretty comfortably settled in Nissan Huts.	1/1
	17.XII.17		Bright cold day with a lot of frost. The whole Battalion on a working party on a light railway.	1/1

T1134. Wt. W.708—776. 50C.050. 4/15. Sir J. C. & S.

Army Form C. 2118.

WAR DIARY
or
INTELLIGENCE SUMMARY. 3rd Bn Rifle Brigade L Inf By

(Erase heading not required.)

Instructions regarding War Diaries and Intelligence Summaries are contained in F. S. Regs., Part II. and the Staff Manual respectively. Title pages will be prepared in manuscript.

Place	Date	Hour	Summary of Events and Information	Remarks and references to Appendices
	18.XII.17		Working parties out all morning carrying for Engr. Dumps etc. Snows frost again, ground now very hard	
	19.XII.17		The Battalion moves up into the line to the same sector as before, with Companies with the same dispositions. Those men we were very lucky in getting in with only 3 casualties and relief was complete by 10 o'clock.	
	20.XII.17		Frost still holding. Very thick mist all day so that the Commanding Officer was able to get round the line about 10am. 2.3/Lieuts. of D Company who moved forward about 600 yards to a more commanding position on the BELLEVUE Spur. A Company captured one prisoner about 6pm.	
	21.XII.17		Another misty day, but not quite so thick. No yesterday. Capt. BRINDLEY was wounded twice by a sniper in the front line. Strangely enough but otherwise fairly happy; the orders that every man is to wear 2 sandbags on each leg up from off the boot valve.	
	22.XII.17		Bright sunny day; some signs of a thaw. Battalion relieved by 7th KRRC. The enemy apparently discovered the relief, without the 60th had it pretty rough, there coming in and lost a good few casualties. Relief complete by 12.30am. and we managed to get out without losing 2 man inspite of a heavy barrage of H.E. and gas on Le KANSAS CROSS.	
	23.XII.17		HQ, A & C Companies accommodated in CAPRICORN CAMP, B & D in CALIFORNIA. Day of extra resting & cleaning up.	
	24.XII.17		Cold weather continues. Bn on the Canal Bank allotted to the Battalion today. COR. presented with the ribbon of the Military Medal by Sir Aylmer Hunter Weston, the Corps Commander, in the Grand Place YPRES at 3 pm. Capt. dulley & 50 men of D & B Companies form the guard of honour; very great turn out considering they aren't 1 day out of the line by Capt. dulley congratulated.	
	25.XII.17		Frequent snow storms all day. The Battalion moves to the ST OMER area by train, leaving ST. JEAN at 12.40 pm. & arriving WIZERNES 5 pm. From there a march of 14 miles to ST. MARTIN AU LAERT where we find very comfortable billets.	
	26.XII.17		Day spent in cleaning up, and settling into billets, the French people don't seem very eager to house other men or officers owing to having been badly treated previously by English troops.	
	27.XII.17		We have a fine snow-ball fight with 9th R.B. and gain a great victory.	

WAR DIARY

5th Bn. Oxf. & Bucks Lt. Infy.

Place	Date	Hour	Summary of Events and Information.	Remarks & References to Appendices.
	28.12.17		Battalion route march in the morning, roads a bit slippery, but conditions otherwise perfect for marching	1/1
	29.12.17		Training of specialists begun. Revolver Practice for officers in the afternoon on the miniature range. The officers have a very successful Christmas Dinner in the village schule.	1/1
	30.12.17		Slight thaw set in. Christmas Dinner for the men, very nice arranged by all Companies, Roast Pork, 3 kinds of vegetables, Plum Pudding, and a good quantity of Beer, and stout & cigarettes were provided.	1/1
	31.12.17		All the preparators were kated at by the headquarters in the morning In the afternoon there was more Revolver practice for officers. Considerable improvement shown in the shooting	1/1

(signed) Capt & A/C
5th Oxford & Bucks Lt Infy

Vol 33

Dalby 32.D
5 sheet

War Diary

5th Oxf & Bucks L.I.

January 1918.

Volumn -

Army Form C. 2118.

WAR DIARY
INTELLIGENCE SUMMARY.
(Erase heading not required.)

Place	Date	Hour	Summary of Events and Information	Remarks and references to Appendices
	1-1-18		Marched to ST. OMER and entrained for EDGE-HILL (between BUIRE and DERNACOURT, SOMME) Adjutant on leave 2/Lt. CRESWELL took over.	
	2-1-18		Arrived at about 7am. after fairly comfortable journey. Marched to CAPPY to find pretty good billets though a little leaky in places. Various duds left behind rejoined.	
	3-1-18		Training in the morning.	
	4-1-18		Training in the morning.	
	5-1-18		Training in the morning. Classification of Lewis Guns in afternoon gave good results.	
	6-1-18		Church Parade. Sergeants Musketry won by C.S.M. HOLT.	
	7-1-18		Musketry training. Lewis Gun firing in afternoon.	
	8-1-18		Musketry training. Lewis Gun firing in afternoon.	
	9-1-18		Musketry training. Lewis Gun firing in afternoon.	
	10-1-18		Range Practices.	
	11-1-18		Range Practices. Capt. BANKS and 2/Lt. FRITZ returned from leave.	
	12-1-18		Range Practices.	
	13-1-18		Church Parade. Corporals competition. Battalion beaten by K.R.R.C. for Brigade football 1-7. Battalion to BRAY for cinema. Lewis Gun competition. Corporals musketry and privates musketry finished.	

Army Form C. 2118.

WAR DIARY
INTELLIGENCE SUMMARY.

(Erase heading not required.)

Instructions regarding War Diaries and Intelligence Summaries are contained in F. S. Regs., Part II. and the Staff Manual respectively. Title pages will be prepared in manuscript.

Place	Date	Hour	Summary of Events and Information	Remarks and references to Appendices
	14-1-18		Route march through HERBECOURT and DOMPIERRE.	///
	15-1-18		Training. Concert by 9th KRRC.	///
	16-1-18		Training. Half Battalion to BRAY for cinema.	///
	17-1-18		Training. No.2 Platoon won Lewis Gun competition for Brigade shield.	///
	19-1-18		Route March via MARICOURT - LONGUEVAL - MONTAUBAN - CARNOY - MARICOURT. 8.0 miles. Band played at LONGUEVAL. Brass Bands with audience of Burmese Stillmen and American Railway R.E. No.2 Platoon won shooting and was second in Bombing. Lockers won first prize in Brigade transport competition.	///
	20-1-18		The final tie of the Platoon football competition was played, intended in a draw. Divisional Cross country run in the afternoon; our team not having brought their boots were not allowed to run. Race won by some rats.	///
	21-1-18		Replay of football final; won by 'C' Company after a very good game. Score 3-2. No.2 Platoon (Pte. STACE) won Platoon Efficiency Competition; a well deserved win.	///
	22-1-18		Move to LE QUESNEL; arrive 3-16pm. Very good march.	///
	23-1-18		Move to DAVENESCOURT, short march of 6 miles. Battalion accommodated in large French huts. Very comfortable.	///
	24-1-18		Owing to lack of billets at next stage, our stay at DAVENESCOURT. Our band and the R.B's play in plateau ground during afternoon.	///
	25-1-18		Move by lorry to BUCHOIRE, arrive 3-15pm. Billets crowded but quite good.	///

Vol 34

War Diary

5th Oxf & Bucks L.I.

February 1918

Volumn -

WAR DIARY
INTELLIGENCE SUMMARY

(Erase heading not required.)

Army Form C. 2118.

Instructions regarding War Diaries and Intelligence Summaries are contained in F. S. Regs., Part II. and the Staff Manual respectively. Title pages will be prepared in manuscript.

Place	Date	Hour	Summary of Events and Information	Remarks and references to Appendices
	1-2-18		Fine day.	1/1
	2-2-18		Relieved 5th K.S.L.I. in left sector in URVILLERS area. Battalion front approximately 1000 yds. Field & one Company with a second in support; remaining 2 companies at Brigade HQ. Dug out accommodation good; enormous amount of work required on the trenches.	1/1
	3-2-18		Relief complete at 1.30 pm. Very quiet day. All available men wiring at night.	1/1
	4-2-18		The Colonel leaves to take over temporary command of the Brigade; Major Lalouette in command of Battalion. Wire wiring done tonight and improvement of C.T's.	1/1
	5-2-18		Quiet day. Mild weather; trenches becoming very sticky. 1 O.R. wounded on night front platoon.	1/1
	6-2-18		A few gas shells over at intervals during the day.	1/1
	7-2-18		Raining at intervals. C & B Companies relieve A & D in front line and support.	1/1
	8-2-18		Dull wet day. Front line trenches becoming very sticky. 2 Companies in reserve now under orders of the Brigade and not available forward.	1/1
	9-2-18		Work continued in support trench and front line wire. Strong front at Battalion H.Q. commenced.	1/1
	10-2-18		Fine day; observation good.	1/1
	11-2-18		Wiring of old French front line commenced. Officers patrol out, nothing of interest to report. Battalion ordered to parade for inspection by C-in-C on 13th.	1/1

WAR DIARY
INTELLIGENCE SUMMARY.
(Erase heading not required.)

Army Form C. 2118.

Instructions regarding War Diaries and Intelligence Summaries are contained in F. S. Regs., Part II. and the Staff Manual respectively. Title pages will be prepared in manuscript.

Place	Date	Hour	Summary of Events and Information	Remarks and references to Appendices
	12-2-18		Relieved by 9th R.B. Relief complete at 11-30. Returns to same billets at MONTESCOURT. Inspection parade cancelled.	///
	13-2-18		Draft of 200 a.rcos with 7 Officers. Capt. MONEY, Lieuts. STEED, RAMSAY, COOK and 2/Lts. STEWART, HUGHES, BOWEN all from the 6th Bn. Lieut. EDWARDS also joined today from a Labour Company.	///
	14-2-18		Working party of 600 found for night work on Battn Line, all parties returned by midnight.	///
	15-2-18		Large working parties found. Party of 'A' Company working in front CAMBAY WOOD by day shelled out of it on 3 occasions	///
	16-2-18		HAM heavily bombed tonight. Working parties found again.	///
	17-2-18		Bright frosty weather continues. Church parade in morning. Battalion relieves 9th KRRC in right sector; relief complete 10.45. Dispositions; A & D Companies in front line, B & C in support. Line held by posts in some old trench system in front, with a new defence line some 200 yds in rear. Very extended front; trenches in need of repair. 2/Lt. CLARK gwo.	///
	18-2-18		Very quiet. Boche machine guns active on extreme right of sector. Patrol sent out on right; no enemy met with. 2/Lt. FRITZ wounded.	///
	19-2-18		1 Officer & 33 other ranks sent to R.E. to be attached for 1 month, no pioneer Capt. CONWAY leaves for duty with HBd F.A. achered by Capt. IRWIN.	///
	20-2-18		Thaw set in wet night. Patrol out on the left; nothing to report.	///

WAR DIARY
of
INTELLIGENCE SUMMARY.

Army Form

Instructions regarding War Diaries and Intelligence Summaries are contained in F. S. Regs., Part II. and the Staff Manual respectively. Title pages will be prepared in manuscript.

(Erase heading not required.)

Place	Date	Hour	Summary of Events and Information	Remarks and references to Appendices
	21.2.18		Smoke very muchs and falling in everywhere. 3 bombs dropped on Battalion HQ. about 10.30 p.m. apparently by one of our "planes". Patrol out for 3 hours, no enemy seen or met with.	/1/
	22.2.18		Wet Day. "B" and "C" Companies relieve "A" and "D" in front line. Relief complete 10.0 p.m.	/1/
	23.2.18		Considerable work done on communication and new Defence Trenches. Patrol taken out by 2Lt. STACE. 1 man missing. Capt BOARDMAN joins 9th R.B.	/1/
	24.2.18		Sometimes. Three patrols out to look for missing man, but no trace found. Several enemy patrols seen.	/1/
	25.2.18		Wet morning. 2nd Lieuts WELLS and McKECHNIE join from 6th Bn.	/1/
	26.2.18		Work on trenches proceeding well.	/1/
	27.2.18		Rain at intervals. Slight enemy artillery activity on left front and took over MONTESCOURT slightly shelled from 5.30 to 6.15 p.m.	/1/
	28.2.18		Enemy artillery active during afternoon. Relieved by 6th Somersets, of 43rd Brigade. Our brigade sector is now to be held with 1 Battalion only in front, 1 at MONTESCOURT, & 1 at JUSSY. Relief complete 10.30 p.m. Battalion goes out to JUSSY. Billeted in French huts.	/1/

14th Division.
42nd Brigade.

5th BATTALION

OXFORD & BUCKS LIGHT INFANTRY

MARCH 1918

Army Form C. 2118

WAR DIARY
INTELLIGENCE SUMMARY.
(Erase heading not required.)

Place	Date	Hour	Summary of Events and Information	Remarks and references to Appendices
	1-3-18		Baths allotted to half battalion, everyone settled in very comfortably	
	2-3-18		Remainder of battalion at baths. Practice "stand to" ordered.	
	3-3-18		Heavy snow at intervals. Working parties of 300 found to work on rail. Officers' lines starting 8.0am and returning about 3.0pm	
	4-3-18		Working parties as yesterday. 50 men of D. Coy inoculated	
	5-3-18		Snowy day. Working parties start at 9.0am and return about 2.0pm	
	6-3-18		Working parties as yesterday	
	7-3-18		Working parties finish at noon. S.B.R's tested in MONTESCOURT. Officers play N.C.O's & Sergeants soccer. Lost all.	
	8-3-18		Fine weather continues. Working party of 100 only required. 200 men go to cinema at FLAVY, good show.	
	9-3-18		Another 150 men visit cinema. Officers play NCO's again. Same result	
	10-3-18		Working parties as usual. Fine weather continues	
	11-3-18		Relieve 9th R.B. in brigade sector. A & D Coys in front. C in support. B at Brigade HQ	
	12-3-18		Relief complete 12.30am. Trenches in very damp state. Enemy quiet. Lieut RAMSEY leaves for duty with R.F.C.	
	13-3-18		Hd Qd T.M.B. and Lieut STEED following as observer in R.F.C.	
	14-3-18		Work on G.T.S. found forward. Patrol out at night, no enemy seen. Fine weather, enemy very quiet.	

Army Form C. 2118.

WAR DIARY
INTELLIGENCE SUMMARY.
(Erase heading not required.)

Place	Date	Hour	Summary of Events and Information	Remarks and references to Appendices
	15-3-18		Patrol sent as usual; no sign of Boche. E.A's active in early morning.	1/1
	16-3-18		Slight shelling on front trenches during the night. Considerable work being put in on trenches; men working well.	1/1
	17-3-18		Weather still fine. Small party of enemy seen by our night patrol; no identifications obtained.	1/1
	18-3-18		Relieved by 9th KRRC. and return to MONTESCOURT. 'A' Company remaining at Brigade H.Q.	1/1
	19-3-18		Wet day. Baths allotted to Batta.	1/1
	20-3-18		Wet day. Battn. provided working parties at LE FAY FARM. Front exceptionally quiet. Preliminary "action" received at 11-30 p.m.	1/1
	21-3-18		Misty morning. ACTION - 6-5am. Battn. moved up to Battle Zone under command of MAJOR LABOUCHERE. And D companies lose very heavily from shell fire. Enemy reach Battle Zone about 11-30am. Front posts lost, having been obliterated with occupants by shell fire. Second line held in front of Brigade Headquarts along BENAY - ESSIGNY road. Some hand to hand fighting, 8 prisoners taken. Enemy moving in LAMBAY WOOD and ESSIGNY road all afternoon. Line abandoned at night all British troops with-drew behind canal at FLAVY. Casualties. Lt. ANDERSON. 2/Lt. FAWCETT, killed. MAJOR WILLIAMS, 2/Lts. TRAYNOR and BALDWIN wounded. Lt. COOK. 2/Lts. COWINGE and THEOBALD missing. About 150 other ranks casualties.	1/1
	22-3-18		Battn. arrived at PETIT DETROIT about 5-30 am. awaiting orders to move forward. Canal bank.	

Army Form C. 2118.

WAR DIARY
INTELLIGENCE SUMMARY.
(Erase heading not required.)

Instructions regarding War Diaries and Intelligence Summaries are contained in F. S. Regs., Part II. and the Staff Manual respectively. Title pages will be prepared in manuscript.

Place	Date	Hour	Summary of Events and Information	Remarks and references to Appendices
	22.3.18 (Contd.)		killed. All details there under Lt. MONEY and 2/Lt. CRESWELL and COOKE. Col. SEBASTIAN joins Battalion about 10 p.m.	/1/
	23.3.18		Line of Canal lost in enemy morning during thick mist. B Company sent up to reinforce near FLAVY STATION so entirely overwhelmed. Battalion retires before enemy at 11:30 a.m. fighting all the way back to RIEZ DE CUGNY; intense machine gun barrage put down by enemy. Battn. dig in in a strong point. Casualties Lt. Col. SEBASTIAN, 2/Lt. & Capt. NURRIS M.C. wounded, also B Coy. and Staff's missing including Capt. BANKS. Lt. MONEY M.C. (wounded) 2/Lt. CRESWELL, FINLAYSON (killed), HUGHES.	/1/
	24.3.18		Battn. again retires under orders. Heavy enemy machine gun fire causing a few casualties. Battn. collects at GUISCARD and marches via CRISOLLES to SERMAIZE arriving 11 p.m.	/1/
	25.3.18		Men get 3 hours sleep, then take up a position covering the OISE CANAL in positions dug by retreating Battn. During afternoon French troops who had been holding BUSSY in front, retire, and on advance of enemy in large masses, Battn. again retires by orders and marches to THIESCOURT, arriving 10 a.m. Battn. shelled by enemy field guns at close range after leaving SERMAIZE - no casualties.	/1/
	26.3.18		Battn. marches out at 7 a.m. to ECOUVILLON to prepare to take up a position there covering the French. At 11 p.m. march to ÉVRICOURT where men get billets with plenty of straw.	/1/
	27.3.18		Battn. marches to REMY, the young transport. No billets, other sleep in open, officers in school.	/1/

WAR DIARY
INTELLIGENCE SUMMARY.
(Erase heading not required.)

Army Form C. 2118.

Instructions regarding War Diaries and Intelligence Summaries are contained in F. S. Regs., Part II. and the Staff Manual respectively. Title pages will be prepared in manuscript.

Place	Date	Hour	Summary of Events and Information	Remarks and references to Appendices
	28-3-18		Weather broke. Battn moves in afternoon to SARRONS; arriving 11 p.m. everyone wet through. Much trouble in getting billets.	///
	29-3-18		Move at midday to NOGENT, transport following independently, arriving there at 6.30 p.m. Buses expected at 9. 9% no brases. 12% no brases.	///
	30-3-18		Buses at 1 a.m. arrive LOEUILLY 11 a.m. Fairly good billets. Accommodation chiefly occupied by refugees. Rain tumbling down.	///
	31-3-18		Very wet day. 5 Officers and 200 other ranks joined from Gloster & Northumberland Fusiliers 13th Entrenching Battn.	///

42nd Inf.Bde.
14th Div.

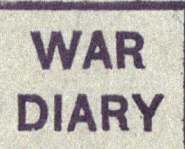

5th BATTN. THE OXFORDSHIRE AND BUCKINGHAMSHIRE
LIGHT INFANTRY.

A P R I L

1 9 1 8

42/14
Army Form C. 2118.
5 Ox & Bucks L.I.
Vol 37

WAR DIARY
or
INTELLIGENCE SUMMARY.
(Erase heading not required.)

Instructions regarding War Diaries and Intelligence Summaries are contained in F.S. Regs., Part II. and the Staff Manual respectively. Title pages will be prepared in manuscript.

Place	Date	Hour	Summary of Events and Information	Remarks and references to Appendices
	1-4-18		Enbused at 3 p.m, taken to ST. NICHOLAS, where we move to small valley behind the BOIS DE GENTELLES in reserve to 151st and 143rd Brigades.	/1/
	2-4-18		Fine day - remain in valley all day. Relieved at night by French. March to BOIS DE BLANGY in pouring rain. Bivouac for night in wood.	/1/
	3-4-18		Remain in wood till afternoon, when we march to HAMELET, Battn. nots here for 3½ hrs to & then move out at 8 p.m. and relieve cavalry holding line just east of HAMEL. All H companies in front line.	/1/
	4-4-18		Heavy bombardment of nine 6.25 a.m. About 8 % Boche attack employing at least 4 waves of troops. Both flanks go. Battn. forced to evacuate position. New line taken up S. of VAIRE. Casualties: Lt. SELMAN killed to CHARLESLEY. 2/Lts. CLIFF, BORMAN, HORNCASTLE, CLARK, wounded; 2/Lieut LABOUCHERE wounded and missing	/1/
	5-4-18		Relieved at 1 a.m. by Australians. March back to AUBIGNY, rest for ½ hour for rum and coffee, then march out and man rear defence line near canal. Capt. SYMONDS in command.	/1/
	6-4-18		Move to new position about 3 m. south of canal. Quiet day. Line put out in front of position. Extraordinary activity overhead in front of RFC.	/1/
	7-4-18		Remain in reserve until evening when Reserve line taken over by Australians. March to ST. FUSCIEN. Pon billets - men very crowded.	/1/
	8-4-18		Wet day, chiefly spent in checking rolls etc.	/1/

Army Form C. 2118.

WAR DIARY
INTELLIGENCE SUMMARY
(Erase heading not required.)

Instructions regarding War Diaries and Intelligence Summaries are contained in F. S. Regs., Part II. and the Staff Manual respectively. Title pages will be prepared in manuscript.

Place	Date	Hour	Summary of Events and Information	Remarks and references to Appendices
	9-4-18		Another wet day. Men drew pay for first time.	///
	10-4-18		March out at 6.0 a. Entrain at SALEUX. Detrain at SAMARCHES and march to BERTHENCOURT S-MER. Good billets. Men get good night's rest.	///
	11-4-18		March to FERRIERES and entrain. Arrive at MARESQUEL at 6 p.m. Long heavy march to HERLY. Men very tired.	///
	12-4-18		Arrive HERLY 3 a.m. Eventually settle in pretty comfortably.	///
	13-4-18		Fine day; spent in cleaning up and reorganising.	///
	14-4-18		March to LAIRES, 14 mile march. Arrive 6.0 p.m. Draft of 11 officers & 323 o.r. from 6th Bn. N.F. amalgamated with battalion.	///
	15-4-18		March to ISBERGUES, arrive 4.0 p.m. Billeted in empty houses near the railway, very slight shelling.	///
	16-4-18		Working parties of 100 found to work on G.H.Q line running through AIRE & LILLERS. Some trouble with men looting.	///
	17-4-18		Working parties of 300 found. Move to MOLINGHEM in the late afternoon. 2 companies billeted in barns and 2 under bivouac sheets in field.	///
	18-4-18		550 Working party.	///
	19-4-18		Same working party as usual. Very cold day.	///
	20-4-18		Work as yesterday. Major N.F. BARNEUL joined from England.	///

Army Form C. 2118.

WAR DIARY
INTELLIGENCE SUMMARY.
(Erase heading not required.)

Instructions regarding War Diaries and Intelligence Summaries are contained in F. S. Regs., Part II. and the Staff Manual respectively. Title pages will be prepared in manuscript.

Place	Date	Hour	Summary of Events and Information	Remarks and references to Appendices
	21-4-18		Work as usual. Preparations made for splitting up the battalion, a small nucleus of 10 Officers & 45 men to be left for instructing American troops.	
	22-4-18		Fine day. Work on same lines progressing slowly; the ground is too wet for trenches to be dug and trenches revetted with soil have to be made.	1/1
	23-4-18		A few shells dropped near the village in the early morning. Work as usual. Band played in the afternoon.	1/1
	24-4-18		Band instruments sent off to 2/4th Transport camp. Orders for battalion to be sent to the base for drafting expected at any moment.	1/1
	25-4-18		Fine day. Work as usual.	1/1
	26-4-18		Same work as yesterday. Farewell dinner of all the officers of the battalion, space rather limited, otherwise very successful.	1/1
	27-4-18		Battalion split up. Officers and men for drafting entrain at BERGUETTE for ETAPLES at 4.30 p.m. The following are left to form a staff for training Americans. Majors BARWELL & COOKE, Capts. WETHERALL, KING, SYMONDS, STACE, 4 ADDINGTON, 2/Lt. McKECHNIE, Capt. PEEL, Lt. & Qmr. TOPLIS & 2/Lt. VAUGHAN also H.Q.R. composed of N.C.O. instructors, C.S.M's & C.Q.M.S's etc. It is hoped that after a lapse of a few months when sufficient drafts have been collected the battalion and also the division will be reformed.	1/1
	28-4-18		March to PREDEFIN, about 14 miles, average billets.	1/1

Army Form C. 2118.

WAR DIARY
INTELLIGENCE SUMMARY.
(Erase heading not required.)

Instructions regarding War Diaries and Intelligence Summaries are contained in F. S. Regs., Part II. and the Staff Manual respectively. Title pages will be prepared in manuscript.

Place	Date	Hour	Summary of Events and Information	Remarks and references to Appendices
	29-4-18		March to CAURON. 16 miles. Battalion now entirely separated from the 6th Sam. L.I. and under the command of	/1/
			MAJOR BARNES. Very comfortable billets	/1/
	30-4-18		Wet day	

WAR DIARY 5 B. OX. & BUCKS. L.I. INFTY.
INTELLIGENCE SUMMARY

Army Form C. 2118.

Vol I

N° 37

Place	Date	Hour	Summary of Events and Information	Remarks and references to Appendices
	1-5-18		Stand by ready to move all morning; order cancelled late in the day.	
	2-5-18		Move to HUMBERT. 2 Officers & 10 O.R. proceed on courses.	
	3-5-18		Fine day. Transport limbers washed.	
	4-5-18		1 Officer & 20 O.R. proceed to base as reinforcements.	
	5-5-18		Church Parade at 10 a.m. at SEMPY, taken by the Rifle Brigade Chaplain.	
	6-5-18		Heavy weather continues. Baths at EMBRY allotted us.	
	7-5-18		Fine day.	
	8-5-18		Baths again allotted us.	
	9-5-18		Weather twice cold.	
	10-5-18		Lecture by the Commanding Officer in the school at 5-30 p.m. 2/Lt. VAUGHAN returns from sniping course. First list of honours gained in recent fighting published; the Battalion is given, 1 D.S.O., 1 Bar to M.C., 3 M.C.'s, 1 D.C.M., & 10 M.M.'s.	
	11-5-18		Officers & O.R.s return from course at First Army School. 2/Lt. T.E. COOKE reports from Base Brose country run in the afternoon.	
	12-5-18		Parade service at SEMPY, under R.B. Chaplain. Wet day. Transport lorries for Base.	
	13-5-18		Rain all day.	

WAR DIARY

OXF. & BUCKS. L.I. INFTY

INTELLIGENCE SUMMARY.

(Erase heading not required.)

Army Form C. 2118.

Place	Date	Hour	Summary of Events and Information	Remarks and references to Appendices
	14-5-18		Baths at EMBRY	///
	15-5-18		Fine day.	///
	16-5-18		Training commenced; Physical training, instruction in map reading, indoor & outdoor tactical exercises and lectures in the evening.	///
	17-5-18		Baths at EMBRY allotted.	///
	18-5-18		Training continued.	///
	19-5-18		Church Parade at SEMPY, at 11:15 am. The Q.M. goes on special leave.	///
	20-5-18		The Commanding Officer leaves for a 3 day course. All available Officers and men on the range at QUILEN from 9.0 am - 1.30 pm. Shooting good, the best in the Brigade.	///
	21-5-18		Range practice put off owing to move tomorrow.	///
	22-5-18		Move by march route to ROYON at 6.0 pm; arrive 8.30. Billets not so comfortable as at HUMBERT	///
	23-5-18		The Commanding Officer returns from his course.	///
	24-5-18		Wet day. No training for the men; indoor schemes for the Officers.	///
	25-5-18		G.O.C. Division comes to see Bn. at training in the morning; everyone out on a company march.	///
	26-5-18		Church Parade at 9.30 at Brigade HQ	///
	27-5-18		Small range made just outside the village.	///

WAR DIARY
INTELLIGENCE SUMMARY.
(Erase heading not required.)

Army Form C. 2

5th B. OXF. & BUCKS. L.T. INFTY.

Place	Date	Hour	Summary of Events and Information	Remarks and references to Appendices
	28.5.18		All day Tactical scheme at SAINS-LES-FRESSINS; all available officers and men take part. 2/Lt. H. WILSON K.O.Y.L.I. joins.	///
	29.5.18		Firing on range during the morning; shooting is fair only. Captains KING & WETHERALL rejoin from 1st. Army Musketry School. Great difficulty in obtaining accommodation for them.	///
	30.5.18		Baths allotted in the afternoon. 2/Lt. H. WILSON proceeds to Base.	///
	31.5.18		Fine weather continues	

Signature
Capt. & ADJT.
5th Service Bn. Oxford & Bucks. L.t. Infy.

42/
14th Division.

5th Div x Buchs L.J.

Vol I 16 – 30.5.15

June 18

Army Form C. 2118.

WAR DIARY
or
INTELLIGENCE SUMMARY.
(Erase heading not required.) 5th Bn Oxford & Bucks L.I.

Instructions regarding War Diaries and Intelligence Summaries are contained in F. S. Regs., Part II. and the Staff Manual respectively. Title pages will be prepared in manuscript.

Place	Date	Hour	Summary of Events and Information	Remarks and references to Appendices
	1-6-18		Move by lorry at noon to CAMPAGNE LEZ BOULONNAIS, route via FRUGES. All 3 battalions of the Brigade comfortably accomodated in same village. We are now attached 49th Brigade, 16th Divn.	111
	2-6-18		Training continues. All NCO's given instruction in the Lewis Gun; officers in reading Aeroplane Photographs; lecture to all ranks every evening by one of the officers, each officer lecturing on his own special subject.	111
	3-6-18		Training as yesterday. Officers & movement officers play the rest at rounders, a very good game just won by the Officers.	111
	4-6-18		The Commanding Officer commenced a series of lectures to Officers on operations; NCO's given instruction in Aeroplane Photographs.	111
	5-6-18		Fine weather continues. Orders received to move tomorrow; this is cancelled later in the evening.	111
	6-6-18		Orders received during the morning to move today to the next village BOURTHES, to make room for an American Divisional H.Q.; American troops for us to train may be expected to arrive in this area very shortly. We move at 5.30 p.m. by march route. Distance 3 miles; the G.S. Waggon having to make 2 journeys with the baggage. Billets at BOURTHES comparatively poor.	111
	7-6-18		Training continues as before. NCO's Class in Physical Training; rest of Lewis Gun, field	36.D 6 sheets

Army Form C. 2118.

WAR DIARY
or
INTELLIGENCE SUMMARY

(Erase heading not required.)

5th Bn. Oxford & Bucks L.I.

Place	Date	Hour	Summary of Events and Information	Remarks and references to Appendices
	7.6.18	(contd)	sketching, and interpretation of aeroplane photographs. Officers also in A.P. & clothing.	/1
	8.6.18		Special leave to England granted to the Officers Corporal. L/Cpl. BATEMAN.	/1
	9.6.18		Wet day; orders received at night that the Americans previously allotted to us for training will not be starved in this area, & that we are to rejoin the 14th Divn in a day or so.	/1
	10.6.18		Lecture in the morning; night operations from 8.30 to midnight; patrols operating against a skeleton outpost company; very successful. The Quartermaster returns from leave.	/1
	11.6.18		Tactical scheme in the afternoon; a small body of cavalry represented by mounted officers of the Bn. & the 9th Rifle Brigade operating against a rear guard.	/1
	12.6.18		Move by march route at 8.15 a.m. back to ROYON, distance 12 miles; route via WICQUINGHEM. & HERLY; spare baggage is taken in a lorry. Halt for dinner for 3 hours at HENOUILLE. Arrive 4.30 p.m; same billets occupied as previously; we come under the 14th Divn. again	/1
	13.6.18		Training continues as before.	/1
	14.6.18		Capt. Peels servant arrives from the base with news that Capt. Peel has been sent to England on June 6th — for six months duty there and that the transport with personnel has gone to the American Army	/1
	16.6.18		The Divisional Commander (Major Gen. L. SKINNER, CMG, DSO) inspected the Battn. today to say farewell	/1

WAR DIARY
INTELLIGENCE SUMMARY.

Army Form 5th Bn Oxford & Bucks L.I.

Place	Date	Hour	Summary of Events and Information	Remarks and references to Appendices
	16.6.18 (cont)		About the same time came orders to the effect that the Bn. would be transferred to the 16th Divn. forthwith and proceed with it to England. On this day also a note of farewell was received from the B.G.C. 42nd Inf. Bde – the Bde. being some 30 miles away – telling us that the 14th Divn. would be split up, and that Bde. Indus were going to England a day or two earlier than those of the 16th Divn. of which formation the Bn. would henceforth belong. The Bde. sent a silk and gold-tasselled flag to commemorate the Bn. winning Platoon in a Bde. competition that some while back.	
	16.6.18		Movement orders received – the boat would not fly the 14th Divn – the boats of the Bn. to march to HESDIN and there entrain (9 p.m.) for BOULOGNE. All remaining transport its personnel would move North to report to O.C. Divnl. Train. We thus lose our chargers, many of whom had come out with the Battn. in 1916 and had become as good "War-horses" as ever we are likely to find. Tonight we dined with the 9th Bn. the Rifle Bde. This Bn. our comrades since Sept 1914 (when the Bn. was formed as a "Light Division" and consisted of men regularly called "The first hundred-thousand" i.e. the first hundred thousand volunteers asked for by F.M. Lord Kitchener) were now under orders to join the 34th Divn. Curiously enough we had asked the Officers of this Bn. to dine with us just before the Bn. left England in the spring of 1915	

WAR DIARY or INTELLIGENCE SUMMARY

5th Bn. Oxfords & Bucks

Army Form C.

Place	Date	Hour	Summary of Events and Information	Remarks and references to Appendices
	17.6.18		The 'Cadre' of the Battalion moved in accordance with orders by march route to HESDIN; leaving ROYON at 9am. The Officers and O.R's of the 9th Rifle Brigade turned out to say goodbye to us; the troops exchanging cheers. A halt of 2 hours at midday was made for dinners and a rest, the march into HESDIN at 3pm and on arriving at the Railway Station found that the 14th Divn. had made no train arrangements for BOULOGNE at all; the Railway Officials had no knowledge of our orders and consequently no authority to arrange us. On the 14th Divn. H.Q. and move left the country we had no chance of obtaining authority except through the 1st Army. Apparently there was done by R.T.O. but the 9pm. train refused to be in Divnl. Orders had not known being too short notice. There entrained the troops reached BOULOGNE at 2.0 am and were in billets by 2.30am. Officers obtained lodgings where they could in the Town.	
	18.6.18		Embarked at 2.0pm in fine weather. The crossing was calm. The troops got tea at FOLKESTONE. The various 'Parties' now gathered under the 16th Divn. left in 2 troop trains for ALDERSHOT, where the Batt. cadre arrived at 10.30pm. Here it was raining and the troops were required to march some five miles to the Rec. Barracks at CROOKHAM and there go into a standing camp. At the Railway Stn. at Aldershot, the Battn. Commander was handed papers from which it appeared that most of the Battalion were to be found were other than those for whom Batties had been sent; and that in our case the 5th Wing O Bucks. L.I.	

WAR DIARY
INTELLIGENCE SUMMARY.

5th B. Reg. C. Bucks.

Army Form C.

(Erase heading not required.)

Place	Date	Hour	Summary of Events and Information	Remarks and references to Appendices
	12.6.18 (cont)		were to form the cadre of a Battalion of the Gloucestershire Regt. (the 18th Bn.)	
	18.6.18		Orders were received for the cadre to proceed to CURTON-ON-SEA (Essex) and there form the New Battalion from drafts, which it was expected would take a week or 10 days to collect. The commanding officer drew up a protest against the change of name which the B.G.C. promised to forward. The commanding officer proceeded independently to London and one private was interviewed at W.O. which the officers of mustering the 5th & Bucks fought hard, were shown down and the reasons for the naming of a new Gloucester Battn. explained.	
	30.6.18		The 18th Battalion was formed & published to first Batt I. and Batt II. Orders. The cadre of the 5th Regt. 4 Bucks. Lt. Infy. was taken on the strength of the Battn. the day.	

J. H. Vernon. Capt. & Adjutant
5th Bn. Bucks. L.Infy.